WINGS
OF FAME™

Aerospace Publishing Ltd
AIRtime Publishing Inc.

Published quarterly by
Aerospace Publishing Ltd
179 Dalling Road
London W6 0ES
UK

Copyright © Aerospace Publishing Ltd
1999

ISSN 1361-2034
Aerospace ISBN 1 86184 037 3
(softback)
1 86184 038 1
(hardback)
AIRtime ISBN   1-880588-23-4

Published under licence in USA and
Canada by AIRtime Publishing Inc.,
10 Bay Street, Westport,
CT 06880, USA

Editorial Offices:
WINGS OF FAME™
Aerospace Publishing Ltd
3A Brackenbury Road
London W6 0BE, UK
E-mail: info@aerospacepbl.co.uk

Publisher: Stan Morse
Managing Editor: David Donald
E-mail: dave@aerospacepbl.co.uk

Editor: John Heathcott
E-mail: john@aerospacepbl.co.uk

Contributing Editors:
David Donald
Dave Willis
Jim Winchester
Sub Editor: Karen Leverington
Proof Reader: Chris Chant
Picture Manager: Nick Stroud
E-mail: nick@aerospacepbl.co.uk

US Correspondent:
Robert F. Dorr
Russia/CIS Correspondent:
Yefim Gordon
Canada Correspondent:
Jeff Rankin-Lowe

Artists: Mike Badrocke
Chris Davey
Malcolm Laird
Perry R. Manley
John Weal
Pete West
Iain Wyllie

Origination by
Chroma Graphics, Singapore
Printed by
Officine Grafiche DeAgostini,
Novara, Italy

The *Wings of Fame* web site,
containing details of every issue of
Wings of Fame, subscription
information and details of other
products, can be found at:

http://www.wingsoffame.com

For their assistance in the preparation of this
volume of *Wings of Fame*, the authors and
publishers gratefully acknowledge the assistance
of the following:

Peter R. Arnold for his invaluable help in
compiling a list of airworthy Griffon-Spitfires

T-33 pilot Horace Linscomb and Dan Hagedorn,
Robert Esposito, David Ostrowski, George
Nowery, Alain Pelletier and Johan van der Wei
for their assistance with the Shooting Star article

Jeff Rankin-Lowe for his help in understanding
the CT-133 and its variants

Former IDF/AF 101 Sqn Six Day War Mirage
pilots Yoram Agmon, Ezra Aharon, Amos Amir,
Yosef Arazi, Giora Epstein, Giora Furman, Ilan
Gonen, David Ivry, Eldad Palter, Guri Palter, Dan
Sever, Daniel Shapira and Avner Slapak for their
help in the preparation of the No. 101 Sqn article

The *Air Combat* article on No. 101 Sqn, IDF/AF
has been reviewed and approved by the Israeli
Censor for publication.

The editors of WINGS OF FAME™ welcome
photographs for possible publication, but cannot
accept any responsibility for loss or damage to
unsolicited material.

Wings of Fame™ is a
registered trademark in the
United States of America of
AIRtime Publishing Inc.

Wings of Fame™ is published
quarterly and is available by
subscription and from many
fine book and hobby stores.

**SUBSCRIPTION AND BACK
NUMBERS:**

**UK and World (except USA
and Canada) write to:**
Aerospace Publishing Ltd
FREEPOST
PO Box 2822
London
W6 0BR
UK
(No stamp required if posted
in the UK)

USA and Canada, write to:
AIRtime Publishing Inc.
Subscription Dept
10 Bay Street
Westport
CT 06880, USA
(203) 838-7979
Toll-free order number in
USA:
1 800 359-3003

Prevailing subscription rates
are as follows:
Softbound edition for 1 year:
$59.95
Softbound edition for 2 years:
$112.00
Softbound back numbers
(subject to availability) are
$16.00 each, plus shipping and
handling. All rates are for
delivery within mainland
USA, Alaska and Hawaii.
Canadian and overseas prices
available upon request.
American Express, Discover
Card, MasterCard and Visa
accepted. When ordering
please include card number,
expiration date and signature.

U.S. Publisher:
Mel Williams
Subscriptions Director:
Linda DeAngelis
**Charter Member Services
Manager:** Janie Munroe
Retail Sales Director:
Jill Brooks
Shipping Manager:
E. Rex Anku

WINGS OF FAME ™

CONTENTS

'Pogo!'
Lockheed XFV-1
& Convair XFY-1

The 'Tail Sitters' or 'Pogosticks', as these two designs were collectively known, did not do a lot of flying – in fact, the XFV never took-off vertically – but flew long enough to probably save the US Navy a large sum of money, earmarked for a concept that was fundamentally flawed and a product of the technological 'euphoria' of the 1950s, when anything seemed possible.

XFY-1 BuNo. 138649 hangs on its massive 16-ft (4.88-m) Curtiss contra-rotating propeller, driven by an equally massive 5,500-shp (4101-kW) Allison XT40 turboprop, in a demonstration of its VTOL ability. Of the two designs only the XFY-1 made the transition between VTO and horizontal (conventional) flight.

The period immediately following World War II was one of radical change in which aircraft designers had to relearn their trade, while also developing a multitude of new ideas. One of these ideas was VTOL (vertical take-off and landing). The sudden emergence of practical gas-turbine, ramjet and rocket engines at last enabled designers to install so much power that it became possible to think of aircraft not only flying at unprecedented speeds but also able to rise vertically off the ground, instead of having to accelerate laboriously to the speed at which a wing provided enough lift.

Why should anyone want to do this? For one thing, the very idea of a vehicle unable to remain airborne except at high speed is obviously inherently dangerous, especially if the ground is covered in dense fog. Air forces began to recognise that in the nuclear age it is nothing short of suicidal to operate from a fixed airfield (today, we seem to have forgotten this). To survive, warplanes had to be hidden in forests and even in villages, and this meant VTOL. Navies also wanted VTOL so that every ship could have a fighter to defend it.

Bachem's Natter

War provides a powerful spur to inventors, and the urge is even stronger when a country faces defeat. In 1944 German designers were ready to try anything. The Bachem Ba 349 Natter (viper), which stood on its tail and was propelled up by rockets, almost became operational. After attacking hostile bombers, the pilot was supposed to bale out, both he and key airframe and engine elements being recovered by parachute! An even stranger idea was the Focke-Wulf Triebflugel (engine wing), which likewise stood on its tail and screwed its way into the sky with the aid of three slender wings mounted like a helicopter rotor on a rotating ring and driven by ramjets on their tips. Unlike a helicopter, this device was to fly horizontally at 621 mph (1000 km/h).

The post-war British government was preoccupied with National Health and the groundnuts scheme, but other countries devoted much

attention to such things as supersonic flight and VTOL. In December 1947 the US Navy Fighter Branch began a formal study of VTOL, with a view to the eventual development of fighters able to operate "from the fantail of a warship or the deck of a fleet oiler or merchant vessel". It was quickly decided that no turbojet then available could be used to power any practical VTOL fighter. Something might be done

with rockets, but the rapid consumption of fuel and oxidant meant that such a VTOL fighter would have to land as soon as it took off.

The only alternative appeared to be to use a turboprop. For a given rate of fuel burn, this engine can develop considerably greater thrust than a turbojet, and, despite the limitation of propellers, it appeared to offer the prospect of creating a VTOL fighter able to fly faster than

Top: XFV-1 BuNo. 138657 is seen here during taxiing trials on its temporary horizontal undercarriage.

Left: The caption to this Lockheed artist's impression reads: "Artist's view shows Lockheed's XFV-1 missile-like, prop-driven, super-power vertical-take-off naval fighter as used by the Air Force for the defence of important industrial plants." Both the USAF and USN had issued VTOL study contracts in 1947, the Navy's desire to take their programme to the hardware stage leading to the construction of the XFV and XFY prototypes.

Right and inset: At NACA's Ames Aeronautical Laboratory extensive 'flight' testing was carried out using a quarter-scale model of the XFV-1. These not only provided answers to stability and control questions thrown up by this new aircraft type, but also allowed engineers to ascertain the design's angle-of-attack and sideslip limits and provided general information of potential value to VTO pilots on the behaviour of such a vehicle. The XFV-1 model was remotely powered and controlled, tests being conducted at wind speeds between 15 and 60 mph (24 and 96 km/h).

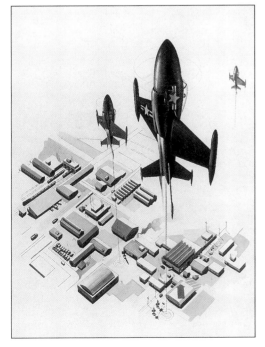

any of the World War II fighters, even the jets. First calculations suggested that speeds around 600 mph (966 km/h) should be possible.

In June 1950 war broke out in Korea, suddenly unlocking the floodgates of funding for all kinds of weapons. Within two months the Navy Bureau of Aeronautics had requested industry to come up with proposals for a "VTOL research airplane capable of development into an operational combat airplane". Six companies submitted eight proposals, from which in March 1951 the Navy picked two somewhat similar designs, one by Convair San Diego and the other by Lockheed Burbank. Three examples were ordered of the Convair, designated XFY-1: BuNos 138648 for static tests and 138649/50 for flight. Two flight

examples of the Lockheed were ordered, designated initially XFO-1 and then XFV-1: BuNos 138657/8. Later, the Convair was to be dubbed the Pogo, from the then-popular pogo stick, and the Lockheed the Salmon, after its chief test pilot.

The basis of each was the Allison YT40. This comprised two T38 power sections driving reduction gears transmitting the power to a specially developed Curtiss Turbolectric contra-rotating propeller (most T40 propellers, fitted to the XA2D Skyshark, XA2J Savage and XP5Y and R3Y Tradewind, were by Aeroproducts). It had a diameter of 16 ft (4.88 m), and comprised two units each with three blades welded from thin steel sheet.

Each T38 power section was of the fixed-

shaft type. The four-stage turbine drove the 17-stage axial compressor and then the coupling gearbox, which at a drive ratio of 0.0635:1 drove the propellers. Thus, though there were spring-loaded over-running clutches so that each power section could be started independently by an AiResearch air-turbine motor drawing compressed air from a starter truck, the whole massive assembly formed one unit.

Thus, unlike the British Double Mamba, each of the T40's two power sections was permanently geared to both propellers. There was no point in trying to get 'twin-engine safety'; if either power section were to fail in hovering flight, the aircraft would fall like a brick. The pilot had direct control over propeller pitch. Another unusual feature was the sheer size of the spinner and hub, with a diameter similar to that of the aircraft's fuselage. This was partly because it was intended that a future interceptor version should have the radar antenna inside the front spinner. Without a redesign of the gearbox, the antenna dish would have had to rotate with the front propeller.

The powerplant was almost the only feature common to the two aircraft. Though both were of what was to be called the 'pogo' type, standing on their tails pointing skywards, the Convair was a tailless delta while the Lockheed had a much smaller wing and a huge tail of cruciform (like a cross) type. Of course, both were of all-metal stressed-skin construction, with a smooth flush-riveted outer surface. Both also had a tiny fuselage only just long enough to house the 14-ft (4.27-m) powerplant, above which was the cockpit with a primitive ejection seat (this was before the US Navy's association with Martin-Baker).

Delta wing experience

Convair had been the principal pioneer of the delta wing. Not surprisingly, the XFY-1 had a wing of broad delta shape, with a leading-edge angle of 52°. This edge was fixed, and at its inboard end merged into the engine air inlets which led to ducts passing under the wing. The trailing edge, which was slightly swept, was fitted with full-span one-piece elevons, driven by electro-hydraulic power units. Under the engine was a compact ducted oil radiator, and the jetpipes of the two power sections were led back to the extreme tail. Somehow, the Convair designers at Lindbergh Field, led by R. C. 'Dick' Sebold, Director (later Vice-President) of Engineering, managed to find room in the tall but narrow body for 580 US gal (483 Imp gal; 2196 litres) of fuel.

To enable the device to stand upright on the ground, it was fitted with grotesquely large upper and lower fins and rudders. They were almost mirror images, the rudder drive being on the left in the upper surface and thus on the right in the lower. The complete ventral fin could be jettisoned so that, in theory, it would be possible in emergency to make a conventional landing, at least on water, with the propeller feathered. The only landing gears were four shock struts, each carrying a tiny castoring wheel, near the tips of the fins and on the streamlined pods on the

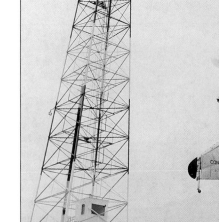

Left: Unlike the XFV-1, which could take-off conventionally with the aid of its temporary undercarriage, the XFY-1 had to take-off vertically if it was to fly at all. The so-called 'vertical taxi trials' that began in the airship hangar at Moffett NAS were transferred to this outdoor rig. Safety cables attached to the propeller hub would have taken the aircraft's weight had its engine failed.

Above: 'Skeets' Coleman straps into the XFY-1's ejection seat. Note its angle at which it is pitched, to permit safe ejection in the VTO regime.

Far left: Convair's James F. 'Skeets' Coleman talks to the press after the XFY-1's first flight on 1 August 1954. Coleman won the Harmon Trophy in 1954, as the first pilot to make a vertical take-off, transition to conventional flight and make a vertical landing.

Left: Lockheed's chief engineering test pilot, Herman 'Fish' Salmon, after whom the aircraft was eventually named, is seen here in the XFV.

broad wingtips. These wingtip fairings, which had a vertical-elliptical cross-section, were intended in a derived interceptor version to house the armament. This was to comprise either two (according to some accounts, four) 20-mm cannon or 48 Mighty Mouse folding-fin rockets.

Lockheed's approach

The Lockheed XFV-1 naturally came under V-P Engineering Hall L. Hibbard, but it was of even greater interest to C. L. 'Kelly' Johnson, who in 1952 became Chief Engineer and later formed and directed the unique Skunk Works. He was not particularly thrilled by the idea of a VTOL turboprop, and largely left it to the project engineer Art Flock. Lockheed preferred straight (unswept) wings of low thickness/chord ratio, and was about to embark on the amazingly small wing of the F-104. The XFV-1 wing was appreciably larger than that, but still much smaller than that of the Convair rival.

It was sharply tapered on both edges. It appeared to have flaps, because painted lines indicated the 'no step' area, but really had no movable surfaces. Stability and control were left to the tail, which again was relatively enormous

Right: Each design utilised a transporter/elevator to facilitate its movement during maintenance and the like. The XFY-1's transporter was a compact design, able to be towed by a Jeep, incorporating a tilting cradle in which the aircraft sat. In the background of this view may be seen several examples of Convair's P5Y naval patrol flying-boat, another design whose development was hampered by the failings of the Allison XT40.

Below and below right: Some 2 ft 6 in (0.762 m) longer than the Convair aircraft, the XFV-1 required a correspondingly larger transporter, which also allowed the aircraft to be lowered onto its temporary undercarriage, if necessary.

and of cruciform shape in order to provide a stable base on which to mount the four small castoring wheels. They were carried on shock struts in small fairings on the tips of the fins, which were slightly swept. All four surfaces were identical, each fin having a tabbed rudder.

The engine drove a propeller similar to that of the XFY. The air inlets were wrapped tightly

on each side immediately behind the spinner, leading to short ducts inside the fuselage. Of course, both types of aircraft needed a radiator to take away the considerable amount of heat from the lubricating oil circulating through the engine and gearbox, but the ducted radiator of the Lockheed was significantly more prominent. The two jetpipes, which were much shorter than those of the Convair, discharged through the aft end of the duct where the energetic jets were expected to assist in drawing air through the radiator in hovering flight. Downstream, the fuselage underskin was steel.

The pods on the wingtips were larger than those of the XFY, and were in fact fixed fuel tanks of circular cross-section, with a small horizontal 'tailplane' on the outboard side. Despite this, the total fuel capacity was less than

that of the Convair rival, at 508 US gal (423 Imp gal; 1923 litres). Again, in an operational version the tip pods would have housed armament of two or four cannon or 48 FFARs (folding-fin aircraft rockets).

Ground breaking

Though these were quite small aircraft, they broke new ground in several respects. To support their test programmes they needed a large number of test rigs and other devices, some of which were needed just to move them about and hoist them upright. Lockheed created a ground vehicle able to do both tasks. Convair also erected an enormous gantry in which an XFY-1 could hover while tethered from above. It also constructed a 'vertical maintenance hangar' of two halves, each fitted with multiple platforms and staircases. These halves could be closed around the upright aircraft, in a manner repeated by the even bigger maintenance structures later needed for ICBMs and spacecraft launchers. Lockheed did not build such a structure, but its trolley-mounted tapering ladder which reached up 22 ft (6.7 m) to the cockpit was still in use at Burbank many years later. At Indianapolis, Allison had to conduct extensive testing of YT40 engines at all angles to 90°. There were a number of potentially dangerous failures, which fortunately never happened to engines used for VTOL flying.

Another new feature was that no aircraft of such a size had ever housed anything like so much horsepower. As originally built, both were fitted with the YT40-A-6, with a take-off power of 5,100 shp (3803 kW) plus 830 lb (3.69 kN) of jet thrust (in practice, not much of this thrust could be used effectively), giving a total eshp (equivalent shaft horsepower) of 5,500 (4101 kW). It was the intention at an early stage to replace the Dash 6 engines with the YT40-A-14, rated at 7,100 eshp (5294 kW). The planned production interceptors, to be called the FV-2 and FY-2, were expected to be powered by the significantly better Allison

Right and far right: Gaining access to the cockpit of both types necessitated the use of an elaborate ladder system. Once at cockpit level, the pilot clambered into his ejection seat, angled 20° forward/up.

T54 engine. This would have been based on two T56 power sections, as used in such famous aircraft as the C-130, P-3 and E-2, and would have started life at 7,500 eshp (5592 kW).

Another way in which these aircraft thrust into the unknown is that, after vertical take-off, they entered a realm of flight never before explored. For example, they had wings, but in hovering flight these performed no function and only added weight. All they had were enormous rear control surfaces which were in a hurricane slipstream from the propellers. To assist the manufacturers, the National Advisory Committee for Aeronautics (NACA, predecessor of NASA) undertook major research programmes using various models. Convair and Lockheed could do conventional tunnel testing, but the NACA could do more complex investigations into stability and control in the VTOL and hovering modes.

NASA model testing

The chief models were very large, about one-quarter full size, and they had accurately scaled propellers driven by electric motors. The Convair was tested at Langley Laboratory in Virginia, while the Lockheed was tested at Ames, California. The models were 'flown' by an operator outside the tunnel. One problem

Right: Photographs of the XFV-1 Salmon in flight are comparatively rare and colour views more so. Here the aircraft is seen at altitude on a flight from Edwards AFB, in company with a USAF T-33 chase aircraft.

Below right: The aircraft's first free flight took place from Lockheed's Burbank, California facility, on 23 December 1953. Here it is seen on a later flight, having risen about 6 ft (1.83 m) off the runway at Edwards AFB.

was determining how difficult it would be to use the control surfaces to move the aircraft laterally to get it over the correct spot, especially in a wind; too much lateral movement could make the hovering aircraft swing like a pendulum. Eventually, it was agreed that both designs were flyable, but nothing could be done about the most fundamental problem.

With a conventional aircraft, fore/aft movement of the stick or yoke gives an immediate response. Hovering while hanging from the propeller leaves the pilot with no control over rate of descent except via the power lever (throttle). This is a second-order control. To illustrate, suppose you are trying to land one of these aircraft. As you near the ground you try to slow the rate of descent by applying more power, but initially this has no effect. As the engine spools up – and with a massive single-shaft assembly like the YT40, this process was sluggish – it gradually puts more power into the propeller, slowing the descent. It is extremely difficult to judge how far to move the lever, though; you find you are now climbing again, so you close the throttle. The aircraft continues to climb while the rpm drop off, whereupon the aircraft begins to drop like a stone. In a panic, you slam the throttle open to avoid hitting the ground, and start again.

In the days before FADEC

Today it would be possible to use a FADEC (full-authority digital engine control) linked with a precise radar altimeter so that each landing went like clockwork. Such things did not exist in the early 1950s, and these VTOLs presented the pilot with a severe and indeed dangerous challenge.

Of course, a significant problem for that unfortunate pilot was that he had to climb up to a cockpit almost as high as a house, and then settle into a seat with his body almost upside down. The best that could be done was to mount the seat on pivots so that in the vertical attitude it could be tilted forward through 45°. The Germans had toyed with such seats in their tail-standing aircraft, but any pilot will at once

recognise the limitations. Not least of the pilot's difficulties was that when hovering or landing he had to keep looking back and down over his shoulder. Some later VTOL aircraft test programmes, such as the Ryan X-13 jet delta, assisted the pilot by providing the operating pad with a tall pole marked off in black and white to give a height indication, and the Navy considered that operating a turboprop VTOL from, say, a fleet oiler could have been made less hazardous by painting a scale of feet on the ship's mast nearest to the operating platform.

Lockheed (perhaps wisely) decided that with the A-6 engine it was never going to achieve VTO at all, and started off with the first XFV-1 modified for conventional take-offs. A lofty fixed landing gear was designed and attached under the forward fuselage, and the four castoring tail-standing wheels were replaced by two conventional tailwheels attached to the lower fins. It was then trucked to Edwards

AFB, where chief engineering test pilot Herman 'Fish' Salmon began taxi testing.

On 23 December 1953, without the spinner fairing over the aft propeller, he exceeded

The XFV flew more than the XFY but accomplished less. Though it made a number of successful transitions to hovering flight from a conventional take-off, the XFV-1 never completed a vertical take-off or landing. Thirty-two flights were made in all, totalling 23 hours, before the Lockheed project was finally cancelled in June 1955. BuNo. 138657 was displayed at Lockheed's Burbank facility for a number of years, before being donated, in 1981, to the Naval Air Museum at Pensacola, Florida.

Specifications

	CONVAIR XFY-1	LOCKHEED XFV-1
Powerplant	one 5,500-eshp (4101-ekW) Allison XT40-A-6 turboprop	
Propeller	one 16-ft (4.88-m) Curtiss six-bladed contra-prop	
Span	27 ft 7¾ in (8.43 m)	27 ft 4¾ in (8.35 m)
Length	34 ft 11¾ in (10.66 m)	37 ft 6 in (11.43 m)‡
Wing area	355 sq ft (32.98 m²)	246 sq ft (22.85 m²)
Empty weight	11,742 lb (5326 kg)	11,599 lb (5261 kg)
Gross weight	16,250 lb (7371 kg)	16,221 lb (7358 kg)
Fuel capacity	580 US gal (2182 litres)	508 US gal (1923 litres)
Maximum speed	474 mph (763 km/h) at sea level	not recorded
Estimated max. speed	610 mph (982 km/h) at 15,000 ft (4572 m)	580 mph (933 km/h)§
Climb rate	2 min 42 sec to 20,000 ft (6096 m)	5 min to 30,000 ft (9144 m)*
Estimated range	500 miles (805 km)	450 miles (724 km)

§ with YT40-A-14 powerplant
* estimated
‡ in VTOL configuration; 36 ft 10¼ in (11.23 m) in CTOL configuration

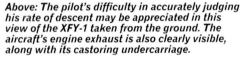

Above: The pilot's difficulty in accurately judging his rate of descent may be appreciated in this view of the XFY-1 taken from the ground. The aircraft's engine exhaust is also clearly visible, along with its castoring undercarriage.

Above right: The caption to this Convair photograph reads, "X marks more than the spot – A space even smaller than the black cross (arrow, beneath propellers) on the 8,100-foot runway at Lindbergh Field, San Diego, is all the Convair XFY-1 'Pogo' needs for take-off and landing".

Below: This sequence, showing the XFY-1 landing vertically, was apparently photographed at Brown Naval Auxiliary Air Station on 4 November 1954, the day before the type's public debut. Note the clouds of dust produced by the wash from the aircraft's contra-prop.

lift-off speed and for a few seconds actually flew. The YT40-A-6 had not been cleared for flight, and when photographs of both aircraft were released in March 1954 neither had flown. Salmon at last began CTOL flying on 16 June 1954. By this time the Navy had recognised that tail-standing turboprops were unlikely to win in combat against, for example, MiG-15s.

Meanwhile, Convair's test pilot James F. 'Skeets' Coleman kept plugging away in the VTOL mode. Although its aircraft was fractionally heavier than the Lockheed rival, Convair never doubted that it could get off the ground with the Dash 6 engine, and on 4 June 1954 Coleman got daylight under the wheels. To eliminate the problem of wind he was inside the airship hangar at Moffett Naval Air Station. From the centreline of the roof, 195 ft (59.5 m) from the floor, a cable ran down to a lug on a

ball race on the front propeller shaft, the front spinner being removed. After prolonged 'vertical taxi trials' he gained some confidence in judging how to work the power lever.

After, according to Convair, a total of 280 'flights' in the airship hangar, on 1 August Coleman made a historic pioneer VTOL from the apron outside the hangar. He went to 40 ft (12 m) and backed down. Then he went to 150 ft (45.7 m) and backed down. In October he at last made a full transition to wing-supported flight and returned to a VL. After doing this 70 times, on 2 November 1954 he did it all very convincingly in public, at Brown Naval Auxiliary Air Station. Soon, Convair sent up a photo aircraft which formated with the Pogo high over San Diego.

According to most US sources, the XFY-1 was "the first VTOL aircraft to fly in the history

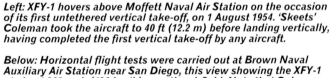

Left: XFY-1 hovers above Moffett Naval Air Station on the occasion of its first untethered vertical take-off, on 1 August 1954. 'Skeets' Coleman took the aircraft to 40 ft (12.2 m) before landing vertically, having completed the first vertical take-off by any aircraft.

Below: Horizontal flight tests were carried out at Brown Naval Auxiliary Air Station near San Diego, this view showing the XFY-1 at about 265 mph (426 km/h) over the airfield. Note that Coleman flew with the cockpit open and his seat in the VTO position.

of aviation". Of course, the term is meant to exclude helicopters and direct-lift autogyros. Other possible claimants begin with an Allison J33 turbojet in a tethered rig which lifted off on 31 May 1951, though this was hardly an aircraft. On 3 July 1953 Squadron Leader Ron Harvey began testing the Rolls-Royce Flying Bedstead. He carried out the entire test programme, on many occasions without autostabilisation, knowing that if he returned to the ground with a lateral speed as high as 2 mph (3 km/h) the rig would overturn and kill him because, despite his recommendation, it had no crash pylon. After Harvey had fully explored this VTOL, it was fitted with a crash pylon and handed to the manufacturer, whose chief test pilot Captain R. T. Shepherd received all the credit.

The Bedstead was a 'flat riser', which overcame the basic problems of tail-standing devices. On 16 November 1954 the first flat riser to look like an aircraft, the Bell VTO, lifted off with two swivelling Fairchild J44 engines.

The XFY-1 flew for about 40 hours, making numerous full transitions, and to that extent the programme must be considered to have been a success. Meanwhile, 'Fish' Salmon had also made a complete transition, in spring 1955. Unfortunately, it was the reverse of what had been intended. The XFV-1 took off by racing down the Edwards runway, transitioned into hovering flight, transitioned back into forward flight and then returned to terra firma in a fast landing. He never did succeed in making a VTO, let alone a VL. Total flight time on the XFV-1 was about 23 hours, in 32 flights.

Cancellation

The Navy finally cancelled both programmes in June 1955, and only one example of each type ever flew. It was said that a contributory factor was the lack of a zero-zero ejection seat. Bearing in mind the immaturity of the engine power sections, gearbox and propeller, the rudimentary nature of both the engine/propeller and flight control systems and the underlying total absence of any prior experience of this form of VTOL and hummingbird-like hovering flight, the whole effort must be considered a remarkable success. Allison had severe problems testing the T38 and T40 engines, and the Turbolectric propellers also suffered dangerous malfunctions, even on large commercial transports. The fact that neither of these VTOL aircraft crashed, and that Coleman and Salmon survived the whole programme, must to some degree have been a matter of pure luck.

Largely thanks to the Korean War, both Convair and Lockheed were prosperous giants,

and termination of these programmes went almost unnoticed. Neither bothered to publicise its turboprop VTOL, and each aircraft rated only one brief mention in the annual *Jane's All the World's Aircraft*. Both the flight articles still exist, the XFY-1 in the San Diego Aerospace and the Lockheed aircraft at the National Air & Space Museum's Garber Facility in Maryland.

Bill Gunston

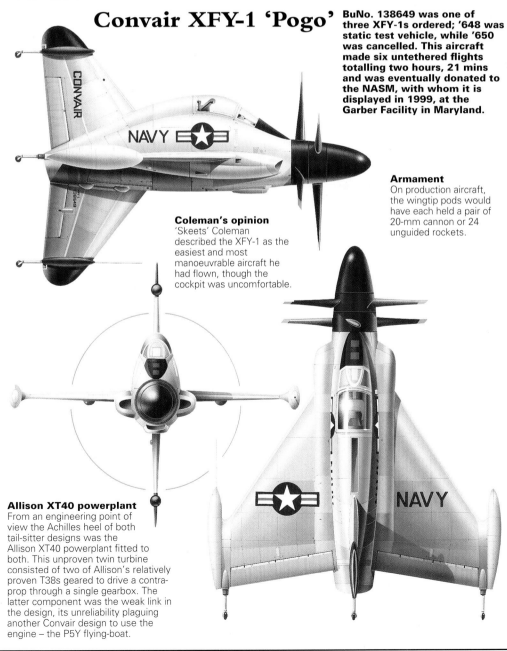

Convair XFY-1 'Pogo'

BuNo. 138649 was one of three XFY-1s ordered; '648 was static test vehicle, while '650 was cancelled. This aircraft made six untethered flights totalling two hours, 21 mins and was eventually donated to the NASM, with whom it is displayed in 1999, at the Garber Facility in Maryland.

Armament
On production aircraft, the wingtip pods would have each held a pair of 20-mm cannon or 24 unguided rockets.

Coleman's opinion
'Skeets' Coleman described the XFY-1 as the easiest and most manoeuvrable aircraft he had flown, though the cockpit was uncomfortable.

Allison XT40 powerplant
From an engineering point of view the Achilles heel of both tail-sitter designs was the Allison XT40 powerplant fitted to both. This unproven twin turbine consisted of two of Allison's relatively proven T38s geared to drive a contra-prop through a single gearbox. The latter component was the weak link in the design, its unreliability plaguing another Convair design to use the engine – the P5Y flying-boat.

11

Superfortress in Korea

Boeing's B-29 at war in the Far East

Strategic bombers of World War II became 'medium' bombers in the new conflict that began in June 1950 on the Korean peninsula. Soon all of the enemy's strategic targets were rubble, but the now-weary B-29 flew on until the end, adapting to roles far from that for which it had been designed a decade before.

Boeing's B-29 Superfortress was one of the most famous aircraft to emerge from World War II. If any single aircraft type could ever be credited with bringing that war to an early end, it would have been the B-29. As the Cold War developed rapidly in the late 1940s, the B-29 became the backbone of the new USAF's Strategic Air Command (SAC). The aircraft's new tasking was to prevent another war, and no one ever suspected that it

would soon be flying in a major regional war that involved the United Nations against the spread of Communism. By this time, the giant B-36 had begun to enter SAC's inventory and the B-29 officially had its classification reduced to that of a medium bomber.

Official USAF records state that as of 31 May 1950, the Far East inventory for the big Boeing bomber was 22 B-29s, six RB-29s, 24 WB-29s and four SB-29s. These numbers were far

below the standard for entering a war, especially compared to the 365 F-80s in-theatre. Fewer than four weeks after these figures were published, the call went out for help in Korea. The closest Bomb Group (the 19th) was based on Guam, as was the 31st Strategic Reconnaissance Squadron with its RB-29s.

On 28 June, 20th Air Force received orders to move all of its Guam-based bombers to Okinawa's Kadena AB. The response was immediate. That afternoon, four of the 19th's bombers flew combat missions against the invading North Koreans: two ran the roads between Seoul and Kapyong and the other two covered a similar area between Seoul and Uijongbu. They were looking for enemy troops and tanks. The results were poor, for this was not the most effective way to use the B-29. However, they had been sent over for a purpose; a show of force to an enemy that did not expect any opposition.

The invasion of South Korea began during very bad weather, preventing 5th AF from getting a clear picture of what was taking place and how large the scale was.

This strike photo shows just how effective the B-29s could be. Note that the entire enemy supply complex has been covered with 500-lb GP bombs. This strike was flown by the 22nd Bomb Group on 20 September 1950, less than a week after the Inchon landing.

M.P.I. *stood for both* **Mighty Pretty Injun** *(Indian) and 'Mean Point of Impact'. It flew with the 98th Bomb Group on numerous missions into North Korea. Korea was probably the last conflict in which bomber nose-art would be so widespread and unrestrained.*

The first Superfortress to cross into hostile airspace was not from a bomb squadron but was a WB-29 from the 512th Reconnaissance Squadron (Weather). It flew this first 'Buzzard Special' mission on 26 June, only one day after the enemy crossed the 38th Parallel. In the months of July, August and September the squadron's aircraft were over the Korean Peninsula every day. By the end of September, the 512th was putting two aircraft up every day to run the full length and width of Korea. The vital data was transmitted to the 8th Fighter Bomber Wing, which used the information to form their daily F-80 missions. The callsigns for these two aircraft were BUZZARD KING (over North Korea) and BUZZARD DOG (other areas).

Interdiction weapon

Early in the morning of 29 June, the 19th sent nine aircraft with 500-lb GP bombs from Kadena to destroy buildings and certain facilities around Kimpo, and the main rail station at Seoul. Their bomb runs were as low as 3,000 ft (915 m). This event marked the first gross misuse of the B-29 as an interdiction weapon. When the aircraft were a few minutes from their set targets, a frantic call went out for them to change course and hit the rail bridge over the Han River. Thousands of enemy troops were bunched up on the north bank, but there was not enough time to turn the bombers and the call went unheeded.

With the war almost five days old, the 5th AF began to get an overall picture. The sheer numbers of North Korean troops and the overwhelming quantity of equipment and supplies rolling south were hard to believe, and had to be confirmed before an organised plan could be developed. The requests for the B-29s suddenly far exceeded their capacity. On the afternoon of 29 June, 20th AF requested that the 19th Bomb Group send a large number of Superfortresses against the big enemy airfield complex at Wonsan. The only bombers in a position to respond had been loaded with 260-lb fragmentation bombs, which would have been useless against anything other than troops, so the Wonsan request was put aside and, instead, the 19th sent its aircraft to bomb the heavy troop concentrations bottled up at most of the big bridges. This same mission was repeated the next day.

By 1 July, the situation had become critical. Friendly ground forces were being swept to the south by the NKPA and, even though the efforts by the limited number of aircraft available to 5th AF had been great, the invaders were not being stopped or showing a hint of slowing down. On 3 July, General Stratemeyer

The two B-29 groups in-theatre in the early days of the war set about destroying North Korea's five main industrial centres, specifically chemical, explosive and metal production plants, oil refineries and rail yards. By October 1950 these targets had been neutralised and the two pioneer groups (the 22nd and the 98th – seen here) were rotated home. The Communists, however, had other ideas.

sent out an urgent request for 23 more B-29s to back up the 19th Bomb Group. Through the efforts of General Hoyt Vandenberg, approval was secured to move both the 22nd and 92nd Bomb Groups from SAC's command to FEAF. Remarkably, this move happened on the same day the request went out. There was no doubt that pulling these two units would hurt but, given the number of top-priority industrial targets in North Korea, the orders stood.

Both groups were used to packing up and moving on a moment's notice. The 22nd flew to Okinawa from its base at March AFB, California and the 92nd began its journey to

Yokota AB, Japan from Spokane AFB, Washington. With their 8,000-mile (12875-km) moves accomplished, they wasted no time before getting busy. On 13 July, nine days after getting orders to move, the groups were flying their first combat missions deep into North Korea. Their first target was Wonsan, which they hit heavily.

This ability to move from the US to a hostile area with little delay was an early indicator of just how professional SAC had become in a short period of time.

On 10 July, immediately before the 22nd and 92nd arrived in theatre, the 19th was still

Above: A head-on view of a 92nd Bomb Group B-29 parked at Yokota AB, Japan. The 92nd and 22nd Bomb Groups responded to the call for help at the same time. The 92nd's recognition symbol was a 'W' within a circle, and the 22nd's was an 'I' in a triangle.

concentrations in some of the small villages. Such targets had to be removed slightly from the front lines, reducing the risk of accidentally hitting friendly forces.

Close support vs interdiction

With the war less than three weeks old, a 'tug-of-war' was developing between General MacArthur and FEAF Vice-Commander for Operations, Major General Otto Weyland. Simply put, MacArthur wanted all FEAF aircraft to be committed to working an area in close proximity to the front lines, directly supporting his ground troops. Weyland knew this was a complete waste of his B-29s and insisted on using the medium bombers in an interdiction role to go after industrial targets deep in North Korea. With three bomb groups in-theatre by then, a compromise was reached to use two groups in interdiction tasking while the remaining one (temporarily) gave support to the front lines. Two groups worked the interdiction role because high command did not want to see the current nine NKPA divisions swell to 12, which would have

carrying the brunt of the medium bomber workload. It sent out 10 aircraft, in single-ship configuration, to seek out targets of opportunity such as tanks, trucks, etc. Each bomber found several targets and was able to make three to 10 bomb drops before returning to Kadena. The results were considered excellent, especially against fixed targets such as bridges and supply dumps. Moving targets were extremely hard for the bombers to hit, but one of the B-29s did catch a slow-moving 20-car train and scored direct hits, putting it out of business. The following day, the 19th went after enemy troop

92nd Bomb Group
325th, 326th & 327th BSs

1950 – Strategic campaign

28 June After an overnight move from its base on Guam to Kadena AB on Okinawa, the 19th Bomb Group bombed any and all targets such as bridges, tanks, troop columns and trucks.

8 July Bomber Command officially established.

13 July The first FEAF Bomber Command strike was carried out. Fifty B-29s from the 19th, 92nd and 22nd Bomb Groups participated, hitting the Wonsan oil refinery, dock areas and marshalling yards with 500 tons of bombs. Damage to targets was significant.

16 August Ninety-eight B-29s dropped 859 tons of bombs in a (3 x 7-mile/5 x 11-km) area northwest of Waegwan. This was the first instance of saturation bombing of the war and caught 40,000 North Korean troops within the area. It was also a massive effort to lend close air support.

15 September All 18 strategic targets in North Korea were neutralised. Some 30,000 tons of bombs were dropped in approximately 4,000 sorties during this brief period. Included in these key targets were Hungnam's chemical-industrial complex, which was hit by more than 1,200 tons of bombs in three successive attacks carried out between 30 July and 3

August. Most of the major targets in the greater Pyongyang area were destroyed. Four B-29s were lost during this phase.

22 October Due to the lack of important targets left to bomb in North Korea, General Stratemeyer cut back the number of sorties by B-29s and, at the same time, released the 22nd and 92nd Bomb Groups from their combat commitment. They returned to their stateside bases and the control of SAC.

8 November One of the heaviest attacks of the war involved 79 B-29s. This was a daylight mission against the Sinuiju supply and communications complex.

Jumped by MiGs

"On 12 April 1951, our group was called out to bomb some bridges over the Yalu. Our arrival time over the target was set as 10 a.m., so we had to launch from Kadena at 5 a.m. The weather was clear and the sun high, about 4 o'clock high. After hitting the IP and turning on the bomb run, I saw many shiny little 'arrowheads' dropping down on the fight flight behind us. Those shiny MiGs made me think of arrowheads and their polished aluminium finish really made them glint in the sun.

"Our escort this day was F-80s and they were weaving above us. When the MiGs jumped us, the F-80s had their hands full. The next thing I remember was a big tracer from six o'clock just missing our rudder and passing right by my blister. They were coming at us from several angles. During this time, I saw one of our B-29s (28th Squadron) take a hit in the wing. Fuel was streaming out of a large hole and the aircraft started sliding out of formation to the right, and going down.

"During this same time, our lead bomber – *Dragon Lady* – took a cannon shell through one of the front window panels, killing the bombardier and hitting the aircraft commander in the throat. Minutes later, he bled to death after turning over the controls to the co-pilot. They stayed in formation and the bomb drop was made by the radar operator who had taken over for the dead bombardier. The drop was made by radar.

"Moments later, our tail gunner called out that a MiG was coming in fast and breaking towards the 8 o'clock. I was ready and picked him up just as he came out from behind our vertical fin. He was very close and I put the centre dot of my sight right on his cockpit. I fired off about 20 rounds from both top turrets. My tracers appeared to be hitting exactly where I wanted them to. What happened after that was spectacular. The MiG started tumbling tail over nose.

"I looked back at our 5 o'clock position and saw another of our B-29s starting down. Three of the four in that flight did not make it to the bomb release point! The fourth bomber in the flight – *No Sweat* – was badly damaged and limped back to Taegu, and crash-landed. I understand that one of the blister gunners in *No Sweat* was credited with two MiG-15s that day. Upon returning to Kadena, I found that I had fired almost 1,000 rounds per gun. It was so intense that I don't remember firing that much, but our radar operator later told me that the vibrations from the aft turret made it hard for him to keep his pencils on his table! If our escort that day had been the F-86s, maybe the MiGs would not have done so much damage."

Sgt Lyle Patterson, gunner, 30th Bomb Squadron, 19th Bomb Group

Above: **Sgt Ercel Dye, a tail gunner in the 371st Bomb Squadron, climbs into the waist section of his Superfortress prior to a mission. He has all of his survival gear on, and his combat missions are tallied on his special cap. He duelled with a MiG-15 on 12 April 1951 and came out on the winning end.**

Above left: **Dragon Lady** *limps through its bomb run after taking devastating hits from MiG-15s. Note the clear panel of the cockpit that has been shot out. The cannon rounds came in at an angle, killing the bombardier instantly and hitting the pilot in the neck. The pilot bled to dead a short time later. The co-pilot flew the aircraft out and the radar operator made the bomb drop.*

happened if the flow of supplies and troops had not been stopped.

As the US Navy carriers took up positions off the coast of North Korea, some early confusion existed regarding which targets belonged to which service. Bomber Command had cut orders for the 19th Group to hit the airfields around Pyongyang on 4 July; the day before, Task Force 77 had been given the green light to attack the same targets and had slated the strikes to continue for two days. To have had two separate groups of aircraft over the same target at the same time would have invited disaster, so permission was given for the 19th to stand down for 4 July, with their aircraft fully loaded and ready.

FAC control

By mid-July, orders were coming down from FEAF to help General Dean's battered 24th Division. The B-29s that had been bombing bridges and buildings north of the bomb line now concentrated on enemy troops, vehicles and tanks. Flying singly, they worked with forward air controllers. This met with limited success because, on many occasions, they could not make radio contact with the FACs. The first attempt was made on 10 July by the 19th Bomb Group, with unknown results. On the following day, the 19th returned and this time

their communications were perfect and they reported excellent results against specific targets in the towns of Wonju, Chinchon and Pyongtaek. This was not the way to use the bombers, however, and 5th AF commander General Partridge ordered this practice to cease immediately. The 19th resumed the task of searching out larger targets far north of the bomb line.

On 14 July, the 92nd BG was selected to send 10 of its B-29s to attack targets along the front lines, as directed by 5th AF controllers. They worked this mission in single ships, taking off at nine-minute intervals from Yokota AB, Japan. Eight bombers successfully contacted ground control along the zones where the

ground troops were fighting; three were pulled off this assignment while en route and diverted to the Kimpo area, where it had been reported that several NKAF aircraft were parked; the remaining six bombers successfully attacked their targets in and around Chongju. They also did considerable damage to rail tunnels and bridges in the same area. As they pulled off to head back to base, they saved some ordnance to hit the marshalling yards at Wonju. These areas had been set up as major supply depots for the enemy troops fighting on the front lines.

The spaced interval of nine minutes meant the bombers arrived in the FAC's area too close together and the controllers had trouble using

Seven crew members of B-29 **Mighty Pretty Injun** *of the 98th BG pose in their winter gear during the cold weather in late 1951. This picture was taken at Yokota AB prior to a mission.*

"Bombs fall on Communist hordes in North Korea as mighty bombers of the US Far East Air Forces Bomber Command unleash another of their concentrated attacks on the enemy's supply centers" according to the caption to this USAF photograph of 98th Bomb Group B-29s.

98th Bomb Group
343rd, 344th & 345th BSs

them to the best advantage, so, on the next day, the same mission was repeated at 30-minute intervals. This time there were 11 B-29s in the strike package and they were much more effective. The results were considered satisfactory, but questions still arose about why the bombers were being used in this fashion.

The decision makers in FEAF Bomber Command knew that committing one full bomb group to a tactical mission, like this one, was a total waste of a proven strategic asset. It was next to impossible to bomb effectively an obscure target from 10,000 ft (3048 m). This

was called, again, to General MacArthur's attention, and this time he agreed. He relaxed his stance and stated that he would like to have one group work the area between the 38th Parallel and the front lines, reasoning that it might help dry up the supplies being delivered to the enemy and, in turn, weaken their ability to mount any effective offensive. This was a welcomed decision, but the 92nd BG continued to work with ground control between 15 and 18 July.

It was no secret that the North Koreans were using the big rail complex at Seoul to bring in

and distribute their supplies to the front lines, using trucks to move it from there to the Pusan area. Even with the efforts of the fighter-bombers, there was still a glut of rolling stock arriving safely in the Seoul area. On 5 August, Bomber Command ordered the 22nd and 92nd Groups to hammer the marshalling yards. The 19th had attacked the same area the day before, with positive results, but it required two groups to put the complex out of business. The results were excellent. With this success under their belt, two days later (7 August) both groups were sent to Pyongyang to disable its large rail complex. The mission did heavy damage, but it remained partially operational.

Neutralising airfields

According to Bomber Command's organiser and initial leader, Major General Emmett 'Rosy' O'Donnell, the primary mission for his B-29s was to neutralise enemy airfields, thus eliminating the NKAF as a factor in the war. It was also determined that the three medium bomb groups working in-theatre were not

The capital of North Korea, Pyongyang, absorbed more bomb tonnage than any other target during the war. Bomber Command commander General 'Rosie' O'Donnell stated that it would take at least 100 B-29s to take all the targets in and around Pyongyang. This B-29 seen unloading over North Korea was from the 93rd Bomb Squadron, 19th Bomb Group.

Below: One of the high-time B-29s to fly combat in the Korean War rests between missions. Although its serial is not discernible, this aircraft is probably Dragon Lady of the 19th Bomb Group.

Evil-Eye Fleegle from the 93rd Bomb Squadron, 19th Bomb Group flies a high-altitude bombing mission against retreating Chinese Army forces. At this time, June 1951, the enemy forces were being pushed out of South Korea. These missions were relatively safe, as there was no triple-A or MiG activity this far south.

enough to take out all the major targets in North Korea. On 29 July, the Joint Chiefs proposed to send the 307th Group and its sister unit the 98th Group, and on 1 August these units received their movement orders. The 307th was under control of 2nd AF and the 98th was part of 15th AF.

The 307th flew its first mission, from Kadena, on 8 August, exactly one week after lifting off from its home base at MacDill AFB, Florida. The assignment was to bomb the marshalling yards at Pyongyang, where most of the rolling stock was destroyed. The accumulation of stock caught there had been caused by the effective strikes on rail lines, bridges and Seoul's complex. This left North Korean logisticians wondering how to move the goods south of their capital.

The 98th Bomb Group set up its base of operations at Yokota AB, Japan, having been based at Spokane AFB before the move. Its first mission was flown on 7 August, only five days after departing the US.

By the middle of August 1950, FEAF Bomber Command knew exactly what had to be done to bring the war to a successful conclusion, at least from their view. The war was going very badly for the ground troops, who were bottled up in a small pocket on the southern tip of the peninsula. The original estimates of the strength of NKAF had been set at about 132 aircraft, all vintage World War II aircraft and no jets. Nevertheless, Bomber Command gave top priority to destroying enemy airfields and checking any reports of hostile aircraft parked or

Above: A big formation of 19th Bomb Group Superforts approaches the North Korean coast. After the first four months of the war, relatively few 'maximum efforts' of 20 or more bombers were mounted. Tactics evolved into raids by formations of four or five aircraft after most of the North's major strategic targets were destroyed.

Although B-29s are associated with strategic attack from high level, in Korea they were sometimes used at low level, even working with forward air controllers. This remarkable picture was taken by an RB-29 of the 91st SRS from its perch above a 98th Bomb Group B-29 making a low level bombing pass over a North Korean airfield. During the critical days in July 1950, the 19th BG in particular worked numerous low-level missions in single ships. These tactical missions were a gross misuse of the Superfortress.

A gaggle of 93rd Bomb Squadron bombers flies loose formation en route to North Korea. The location was between Okinawa and North Korea, and the date, late 1951.

River. As the 'flare-fortress' approached the target area, eight heavily armed B-26s were waiting. The flares lit the entire area and revealed, to their dismay, that the pontoon bridge had not been used that night. If it had been, the damage done by the Douglas Invaders would have been significant.

Flare ships

General Stratemeyer recognised the potential for B-29 flare ships working with the B-26s at night. On 11 September, he told 5th AF and FEAF Bomber Command to begin experimental missions related to developing this concept. They would start by targeting moving targets such as trucks and trains, for which the specified B-29s were loaded with 100 M-36 parachute flares. One problem showed up quickly: these were old flares and over 65 per cent did not work, so newer British-made flares were used.

Each flare ship orbited an area known to have heavy traffic, and periodically would drop a flare, which ignited at 6,000 ft (1828 m) and slowly drifted to the ground, illuminating the entire area. The B-26s, armed with bombs and 0.50-in rounds, would pounce on anything that moved. The biggest score came on the night of 22 September. One B-29 hung out a long series of flares along a stretch of tracks, and caught a munitions train moving south of Suwon towards Kumchon. The B-26 Invaders swarmed in and hit every section of the train, triggering secondary explosions for over 30 minutes. This had to have crippled the North Koreans, as they had just begun their retreat to the north. Each night, four B-29s were assigned to this task. With the acute shortage of B-26s in-theatre, General Stratemeyer ordered his flare ships to illuminate and bomb their own targets. On many occasions, they carried delayed-action fused bombs and dropped them along the well-travelled roads, right before dark, the intent being to harass vehicular movement.

As the Pusan break-out was in its early stages, 12 B-29s were assigned to work the roads, non-stop, all night long. When the sun came up, the fighter-bombers took over. At the first signs of a panic retreat by North Korean troops, 13 B-29s were loaded with surrender leaflets and continually dropped them right ahead of the northbound enemy. In several incidents, over 100 soldiers surrendered with the leaflets in their pockets. Bomber Command continued to protest over the misuse of its bombers, but the leaflets proved to be an effective weapon.

With the arrival of the 98th and 307th Bomb Groups, the B-29 had reached its inventory peak for the entire war. Five bomb groups now operated in the Far East, three based at Okinawa and two at Yokota AB, Japan. With a force of this size, the key targets located in the extreme northern sectors of North Korea were definitely in harm's way. The month of

Left: 4 July 1951 was celebrated on Okinawa with another large raid over North Korea. Morale was high at Yokota where the 307th BG had joined the established 19th, but hopes that the war would be over quickly faded soon after the 22nd and 92nd BGs were sent home in October 1950.

operating from bases in North Korea. Command also determined that all industrial targets north of the 38th Parallel could be taken out by massive incendiary raids, as was the case in Japan in 1945. General Stratemeyer stated that he could knock out all military targets in and around Pyongyang with 100 B-29s.

With Chinese logistics personnel assisting, the North Koreans were trying to move as many supplies and replacement troops southward as they could. It was a 'do or die' situation for them, for they needed to crush the UN forces in the perimeter. This translated into an enormous amount of truck traffic every night. The 3rd Bomb Wing's B-26s were pressed to their limits to stop this nocturnal movement. On the night of 30 August, a specially rigged B-29 was sent out to drop flares in an attempt to illuminate the pontoon bridges that had been hastily put up over the Han

A large number of Bomber Command's conferences were held at Itazuke AB, Japan. The squadron commanders would come in from Kadena and Yokota to attend. This 98th Group B-29 is shown departing Itazuke after one such get-together sometime in 1951.

The Indian warrior's head design that appeared on 19th Bomb Group aircraft can be seen clearly in this view of a 93rd Bomb Squadron aircraft. Red trim denoted the 93rd, the 28th Bomb Squadron had green trim, and the 30th had blue. In the background are B-29s from the 307th Bomb Wing, which in common with the other groups used a letter and geometric symbol.

In Alis Vincimus

19th Bomb Group
28th, 30th & 93rd BSs

September brought the destruction of North Korea's armed forces, rail capacity, bridges and industry. With the Inchon invasion and the break-out of the Pusan perimeter, there was very little need for the B-29s to be pulled into an ineffective interdiction role, as they had in prior weeks. From now, they would do what they did best: strategic bombing.

Rain of destruction

The month-long rain of destruction began on 2 September, when the 307th sent 25 bombers to hit known Communist supply build-ups in and around the towns of Kumchon, Kochong and Chinju. In minutes, they dropped 865 500-lb GP bombs to bracket all three targets. Large secondary explosions were observed. Another devastating blow to the Communist efforts came two weeks later, when 8th Army asked that two bomb groups be used to saturate two targets. The areas to be hit each measured approximately 500 x 5,000 yd (457 x 4572 m), on either side of the spot where the old rail and road bridges crossed the Naktong River at Waegwan. To accomplish this mission,

42 B-29s were sent in carrying 1,600 GP bombs. There had been little time to plan the mission – one of the first examples of 'carpet bombing' in Korea – but 8th Army said the results had been excellent. This was the first major medium bomber assignment carried out after the Inchon landing.

From 10 days prior to Inchon, the B-29s had been pounding all the rail complexes and marshalling yards from Seoul northward, for which they used the more destructive 1,000-lb GP bomb. This also included the complete destruction of all bridges within a 25-mile (40-km) radius of the landing area, the goal being to completely isolate the Seoul/Inchon area from any outside help. The next step was for all five bomb groups to become involved in

Above: The 19th Bomb Group had at least one very talented artist in its ranks. Lemon Drop Kid *shows a caricature of Bob Hope and carries the name of his then-current movie. This picture was taken at Kadena AB, Okinawa, the 19th's home base.*

carpet bombing everything immediately in front of the UN troops who were breaking out of the perimeter. As news of the Inchon landing hit the North Koreans on the front lines, there was mass confusion, and as their leaders realised that they could easily be cut off, panic set in. When UN troops punched through, the retreating NKPA and their equipment were caught in a devastating attack from the B-29s.

Beginning in early September, all five bomb

The Koza Kid *of the 30th Bomb Squadron, 19th Bomb Group was named for a village on Okinawa and the artwork (lifted from an early* MAD *magazine) was said to resemble the local inhabitants. It was soon removed. The bomber's crew chief, Sgt James Stark, is in the picture.*

1951: MiG menace

12 April Thirty-two bombers, using 300 tons of high explosives, hit the massive railroad bridge linking Sinuiju and Antung, Manchuria. The damage done to the bridge was extensive, but the MiGs swarmed all over the formations. B-29 gunners damaged at least 22 MiGs; two B-29s were shot down and several were damaged.
Early May A special type of bombing technique was perfected in which the B-29s used 500-lb fragmentation air-burst bombs, proximity-fused to explode over the heads of enemy troop concentrations. This tactic was known to have stopped at least three potential offensives in certain areas.
26 June Nearly 9,000 effective sorties had been

flown by the medium bombers by this date, the first anniversary of the war's beginning.
14 August Sixty-eight B-29s struck the Pyongyang supply centre in a daylight raid. The 19th and 307th Bomb Groups were heavily involved in this mission.
25 August The east coast rail centre at Rashin was hit by 35 B-29s in the most successful raid of the year. More than 7,000 ft of rail yards, an 18-track storage area, repair shops, engine houses and warehouses were destroyed by 350 tons of explosives. This was the 'kick-off' mission for Operation Strangle, the interdiction campaign to cut off supplies to the Chinese front-line troops.
September Communications, rail and highway bridges, supply centres and two major enemy airfields were prime objectives for the B-29s in 21 major bombing missions. Other night-flying Superfortresses

radar-aimed almost 2,500 500-lb bombs on Chinese troops and material/supplies along the front lines.
October MiG-15 activity tripled when the bombers were in their area. As many as 200 opposed the medium bomber formations in a single battle. Three B-29s were lost on 24 October while bombing Namsi. Battle damage to a large number of bombers was significant.
27 October B-29 gunners shot down six MiGs with no loss to the bombers.
29 October Decision was made to switch to all-night operations exclusively. The results proved to be equally effective and the MiG threat was diminished considerably.
25 December Sixteen B-29s dropped their 10-ton loads on bridges and airfields near Hwanju. Very little AA opposed them.

One half of a 307th Bomb Group formation is shown here on approach to its target; the inhospitable mountainous terrain of North Korea is visible far below. The blue trim colour on the vertical stabiliser indicates these aircraft were assigned to the 372nd Bomb Squadron.

307th Bomb Group
370th, 371st & 372nd BSs

groups began working as a team each night with the intention of removing the NKPA from the designated 'hot spot', a large triangle stretching from Seoul to Wonsan to Pyongyang. On 9 September, one group hit the marshalling yards in and around Seoul. The other units ran a systematic rail cut campaign in areas where there were no villages and where repairs would be the most difficult. Normally, the large enemy work forces who undertook repairs each night were housed during the day in neighbouring villages. The flights responsible for the rail cuts usually comprised eight aircraft, from each group; as many as 60 Superfortresses were involved in the project. In total, they made 46 major rail cuts using 1,000-lb GP bombs.

The surge by UN forces to break out were met with fanatical resistance, for the North Koreans had a manpower reserve for just such an offensive. On 16 September FEAF Bomber Command sent 82 B-29s to prevent these reserves from entering combat, but heavy cloud cover made effective bomb drops impossible. With UN forces in such close proximity to the target area, all of the B-29s were diverted to North Korea to hit targets of opportunity. Had the weather been clear, one can only guess how much death and destruction that many bombers would have caused.

Wonsan locomotive works

During October, the medium bombers gradually targeted every important target in North Korea. Their effectiveness was so great over Pyongyang that it was estimated that more than 40,000 factory workers had been put out of a job. A early as January 1949, the capital city had sprouted a myriad of small arms and munitions factories. The same thing happened with the Wonsan Locomotive Works, the largest such facility in all of Korea: it was flattened and over 2,000 workers were displaced.

Now it was time for the B-29s to take on the toughest targets, and the only ones left: those on the Yalu River. The most dangerous of these were the bridges, which had been built in the late 1930s and early 1940s by the Japanese, using forced labour and POWs. They contained a significant amount of steel and concrete and would prove very difficult to bring down.

Above left: A FEAF B-29 climbs into the twilight en route to another North Korean target. The growing MiG threat forced the switch to night raids exclusively in October 1951.

Far left: Never Hoppen, a 19th Bomb Group Superfortress, was part of Bomber Command's early 1951 blitz that put as many as 24 bombers over a single target on the same mission. This was done every day for a period of time. The 19th rotated this commitment with its sister 307th Bomb Group.

Over-Exposed was a suitable name for one of the RB-29s of the 91st SRS. This photograph was taken at Yokota AB, Japan in 1951. When the Korean War began in June 1950, there were only six RB-29s in the Far East Theatre.

In this post-war photo, Colonel James V. Edmundson emerges from a B-36 after a mass flight, non-stop training mission from the US to Japan. He had been the 22nd Bomb Wing commander in Korea.

Bridge Busting in the B-29

"In all, the 22nd Bomb Group flew 195 individual sorties against bridges, destroying 78 and severely damaging 24 more. This score was computed from photographs. A bridge could not be considered destroyed unless at least one span was knocked into the water. And we had pictures to prove it. A bridge was declared damaged when the photo interpreter determined that it was no longer usable except for foot travel.

"These bridge-busting missions were usually flown by individual aircraft at an average altitude of 10,000 ft. The procedure was to drop from one to four bombs on each run, making several runs and taking pictures after each drop, until the bridge was out. Then we would move on to another bridge. This type of work demanded pinpoint accuracy on the part of the bombardier. This developed into some real competition between our aircrews!

"In running a mission, we would dispatch as many as 15 B-29s, each against an individual bridge. We usually had a few spare bridges left to assign to other bombers as secondary targets. Either one of my squadron commanders or myself would go along in

one of the aircraft, as an airborne commander, with a scoreboard listing all of that mission's bridges. Each bomber would report in, by radio, when he had knocked out his bridge or when he was forced to leave it without knocking it out. New assignments would be made as targets were crossed off or released for reassignment.

"On the days when the boys were really hot, getting their bridges on the first bomb, we would begin to run short of targets and there would really be a race to get to the last few targets towards the end of the mission! On those days, we would begin to have a real traffic problem in the air over the remaining bridges! One of our crews destroyed four bridges in one day, while another crew lost one engine en route to the target. They continued on with three engines. They were able to knock out two bridges before returning to Kadena. On 31 August 1950, the 22nd received a letter of commendation from General Stratemeyer, Commanding General of FEAF, for having destroyed 18 bridges, including the extremely vital Sinanju bridge, during a three-day period from 27 through 29 August.

"The tail markings on some of the B-29 units were

The weapon of choice to take out the large, Japanese-constructed bridges in North Korea was the 1,000-lb bomb. Note the pinpoint precision displayed by the strike on the mid-point of this bridge over the Yalu River. This attack, on 30 August 1950, was one in a series of daylight bombing attacks against targets on the Yalu, at a time when the UN forces were hard-pressed to stop the North Korean advance.

confusing. When we left for Korea, the tails of the 22nd aircraft had the 'Triangle I'. I'm not sure why, but that was the way we brought them over. While we were on Okinawa, SAC changed all tail markings. The 15th AF units were all in circles, the 2nd AF were in triangles and 8th AF had the squares. The letters for each group were usually taken from the commander's names. My 22nd Group was 'Circle E'. Colonel Dave Wade commanded the 92nd at the time and their marking was the 'Circle W'. So we went into Korea with the 'Triangle I' and returned with the 'Circle E'."

Colonel James V. Edmundson,
Commanding Officer, 22nd Bomb Wing

By the middle of October, Bomber Command had taken out all the key targets in North Korea and the UN forces were pressing toward the Yalu. There was very little to keep five bomb groups busy and the total sortie rate had been reduced to 15 per day. On 22 October, General Stratemeyer released the 22nd and 92nd Bomb Groups to return to their SAC bases stateside. They began their departures on 27 October, just days before the Chinese entered the war. As they departed for home, no one would have believed that the war that was 'all but over' would last another 32 months! During the first week of November, when the Chinese overpowered the UN ground forces, there was some thought of bringing the two groups back, but authorities were confident that three groups would be adequate.

The days ahead for the 19th, 98th and 307th Bomb Wings were a mix of easy ones and pure hell. Throughout the war, the most lucrative targets were in the extreme northwest corner of

This picture was taken seconds before bomb release on a high-altitude drop over North Korea in the spring of 1951. Note the bomb bays loaded with 500-lb GP bombs. The B-29 was part of the 307th Bomb Group

Korea; however, the triple-A continued to get more sophisticated, especially that coming from the north side of the Yalu, and the deadliest threat of all was about to be introduced – the MiG-15. On 12 November, the 98th sent several B-29s to attack the town of Manpojin, on the south bank of the river. Hostile fire coming from the north bank damaged several bombers, one being shot up so badly that it limped back to the nearest base, which was Taegu. Severe icing conditions at the optimum 8,000 ft (2438 m) forced the aircraft to drop lower, leading to more problems. Overall, it was not an effective mission and, unfortunately, there would be more like it.

The first six months of 1951 brought an end to most of the major military movement in and around the front lines. The initial Chinese

The red trim on the vertical stabiliser of this B-29 indicated assignment to the 93rd Bomb Squadron on Okinawa. When this photo was taken in the spring of 1951, the 19th Group had already been involved in the war for over nine months. They were still in-theatre when the ceasefire was ordered in July 1953.

offensive in November 1950 pushed the UN forces below the 38th Parallel. In the spring of 1951, the lines were stabilised and the Communists were slowly pushed back almost to where they had been when the war started. At this time, the war became a serious game of chess between the Chinese logistics command and FEAF. It was also a contest of packing tens of thousands of workers into small areas to repair major bomb damage. Very little of this was played out during the day, being instead a

Since all of their missions were flown over water, each B-29 crewmember had the responsibility of making sure all of their survival equipment was in working order and accounted for before each mission. This 19th BG crew is double checking survival gear prior to flying a long mission from Okinawa to North Korea and back.

The epic battles of 23 October 1951 saw three B-29s lost and many damaged by MiGs. Below right, two of Command Decision's gunners study the damage to their bomber after the mission. This hole was probably caused by a hit from the MiG's 37-mm cannon. Left to right are S/Sgt Robert Spenard and Cpl Harry Ruch. Ruch was credited with one of the three MiGs claimed by B-29s this day. Below, three MiGs bore in on Command Decision during the battle.

Above: The crew of Command Decision poses for the press cameras after its fifth MiG kill. The mission flown on 27 October 1951 netted the aircraft four MiG kills, and one later kill made Command Decision the war's only 'ace' B-29.

1952: Interdiction

March Some 460 combat sorties were flown in this month by the medium bombers of FEAF Bomber Command's interdiction campaign aimed at reducing the supplies moving into the front-line areas. Major hits on bridges and neutralisation of two enemy airfields. Close support accounted for 16 per cent of the missions flown.
25 March Forty-six Superfortresses hit twin bypass bridges at Pyongyang with 1,000-lb GP bombs.

28 March Bomber Command's 100,000th ton of explosives of the war fell squarely on the rail bridge at Chongju. Also on this night, 47 medium bombers attacked the rail bridges at Sinanju.
April Bomber Command's mission to keep two main railroad lines and 18 airfields unserviceable continued. Bridges were considered secondary targets for the month. Approximately 3,000 tons of bombs were dropped in 383 sorties, for no losses. Weather was terrible for most of the month.
May Bomber Command took responsibility for keeping two major rail lines unserviceable. Some 66

spans were destroyed on the 10 bridges targeted. Some 400 sorties were flown with a total of 3,489 tons of bombs dropped. All were night missions, and close support missions continued at about the same ratio as previous months.
June Bomber Command concentrated on bridges on the same two rail lines, against which an average of 11 B-29s went every night. In 390 sorties during that month, 3,432 tons of bombs were dropped. Twenty-nine bridge spans were dropped into the water. Most missions were flown in adverse weather.
11 July Fifty-four medium bombers demolished 590

98th Bomb Group 'Superforts' form up for a rare daylight mission over North Korea. Most of their missions were flown at night, especially during the final two years of the war. They were protected from the night-flying MiG-15s by F-94s and Marine F3Ds. The latter was the most effective because it had the capability to mingle in the bomber stream, making it difficult for the Communist ground controllers to distinguish them from the B-29s.

war waged at night.

The weather over North Korea was not conducive to visual bombing, so FEAF Bomber Command had to find additional ways to make its B-29s more effective. The combination of bad weather, radar-ranging anti-aircraft weapons and the MiGs made that difficult. The B-26s from the 3rd Bomb Wing had good results with SHORAN (short-range navigational radar) missions; if successfully applied to the medium bombers, it would make them effective after dark, removing them from the threat of Communist fighters and reducing the importance of bad weather. On 7 May 1951, the 98th Bomb Group sent one aircraft (44-62253) to the rear maintenance facility to be equipped with the necessary SHORAN equipment. On 1 June, this bomber flew its first experimental SHORAN bombing mission.

APN-3 SHORAN adopted

It was successful, and orders were issued for each of the three bomb groups to equip two bombers with the APN-3 transceivers. These aircraft could then lead the bomber streams and all could drop their ordnance off the lead ship.

For the year 1951, Bomber Command posted the following statistics on what its B-29 Operations had accomplished. The target list showed the following final totals; troops and supply dumps were attacked 108 times. Marshalling yards were the objective of its bombers on 217 different missions. Airfields were hit 132 times, bridges accounted for another 150 missions and six missions were against specific, unidentified industrial complexes. The bottom line results for these missions were listed as 3,678 buildings destroyed, 213 major rail cuts, 1,007 rail cars destroyed, 37 bridges damaged and 76 airfield runways damaged and out of commission for at least a week. These results were contributed by all three Bomb Groups that remained in theatre.

After the war ended, FEAF Bomber Command also released the figures for 1952. They included the following data: troop

22nd Bomb Group
2nd, 19th, 33rd, 408th BS

One of the most colourful B-29s in the 22nd Bomb Group, Mule Train was piloted by Major George Ham. Called into combat in early July 1950, the 22nd was released from control of FEAF Bomber Command and returned to SAC just before the Chinese entered the war.

buildings and damaged another 135 in an attack on supply-building complexes, factories, vehicle parking and storage areas in the northwest sector of Pyongyang. In all, 65 bombers were sent to hit various targets on this night.
30/31 July A new Korean War record was set when 63 Superfortresses hit a single target, the Oriental Light Metals Company at Yangsi on the Yalu River. In all operations for the night, 68 bombers hit several targets, also a new one-night record.
14 August Twenty-five medium bombers from the 307th Wing attacked an enemy supply centre at Anak,

west of Sariwon.
12 September Suiho Hydro electric plant on the Yalu River was hit during the night by 35 Superfortresses, and rendered completely unserviceable. The target was 34 miles (55 km) from Sinuiju and was the largest such plant in Asia. Fifteen bombers were assigned to various other targets, giving Bomber Command a total of 50 sorties for the night.
19 September First daylight raid in nearly one year, in which 33 B-29s from Kadena overflew the width of North Korea and hit targets on the east coast.
22 September The 19th Bomb Wing flew its 500th

mission of the war, attacking a variety of targets in Pyongyang.
30 September Forty-eight B-29s hit Namsam-ni Chemical Plant on the Yalu River. Much of its capacity was destroyed.
14 December Superfortresses of the FEAF Bomber Command flew their 1,000th mission of the war.

Above: This unidentified B-29 had to land at Kimpo AB after it was jumped by MiG-15s. The ever-increasing number of MiGs forced Bomber Command to end all daylight bombing missions in the extreme northern areas of North Korea from early 1951.

Above left: No, this B-29 was not under attack by a MiG-15. With no enemy aircraft activity in the area, an F-86 Sabre plays in and out of the bomber stream. In the face of the MiG's ability to climb up through the bomber formations at high speed, the F-86s were positioned below, above and on the flanks of the B-29s.

With bomb bay doors open, this 98th Group aircraft has come all the way up the west coast of Korea and is approaching its target located in the extreme northwest corner of the peninsula. It has been over water since it left Japan.

Guided bombs in Korea

VB-3 'Razon'

It was quickly realised that all the major bridges in North Korea could not be brought down by the standard 500-lb GP bombs. The most successful weapon, initially, was the 1,000-lb GP bomb. In the early autumn of 1950, the 19th Bomb Group's aircraft had been through a modification which enabled them to carry the larger bombs. The first speciality weapon utilised was the 1,000-lb 'Razon' bomb, which had remotely controlled fins that could alter the bomb's course by radio signals sent by the bombardier, allowing guidance of the bomb after it had left the aircraft. The range and azimuth corrections could be transmitted and the course was altered to enhance a direct hit on the target. The 'Razon' name for the VB-3 bomb stemmed from the earlier VB-1 'Azon', which was a contraction of 'AZimuth ONly'.

When the bombs were first used by the 19th, problems arose with the guidance system. Of a total of 489 'Razon' bombs used in the Korean War, 331

A 'Tarzon' falls towards the aiming circle on a US test range. Real targets, however, did not have an approach route marked on the landscape, and combat results were poorer than expected.

responded and were directed into a suitable strike, a success rate of some 67 per cent. Improvements were made to the last groups of bombs delivered to Kadena, and, of the final 150 bombs used, 96 per cent responded to the signals and made devastating hits. In the very few months during which they were used, the bombs took out 15 major bridges. One bomb was not enough for the tougher bridges, so on average four were used. The 19th Bomb Group phased out the use of the 'Razon' in December 1950.

VB-13 'Tarzon'

This weapon, which began arriving on Okinawa in December 1950, was the most destructive used during the war in Korea. The 12,000-lb (5443-kg) monster, designated VB-13, had a similar guidance system to the 'Razon' but its destructive capability was many times greater. The 19th Group dropped 10 such bombs during the latter part of December and had only one direct hit, due to inexperience with 'Tarzon' operations. Over the next few months, the bombs were in short supply, but the 19th ordnance personnel and the bombardiers constantly improved their skills.

The big hit came on 13 January 1951, when a 'Tarzon' was dropped from 15,000 ft and made a direct hit on one of the larger bridges. It chopped two spans off neatly and the entire structure tumbled into the water; after three more drops, the bridge splintered into a mass of twisted steel.

In the last week of March 1951, three 19th medium bombers took off for a mission against the toughest bridge in North Korea – Sinuiju – loaded with the 'Tarzon'. One developed mechanical problems and turned back. The second aircraft made it over the target but missed the bridge. The third bomber, piloted by Colonel Payne Jennings, the 19th Group commander, was lost at sea. It was later discovered that if the 'Tarzon' was jettisoned at low level, over water, the tail assembly would break off, arming the bomb, resulting in an instant detonation. The conclusion was drawn that this had probably happened to Colonel Jennings, as they would have let go the bomb right before they ditched their B-29.

From that point on, the use of the 'Tarzon' was

curtailed for safety reasons. Finally, on 13 August, the programme was discontinued completely. A total of 30 'Tarzon' bombs was dropped. Six completely destroyed the bridges at which they were aimed, one bridge was damaged, three bombs were duds and 19 missed their targets.

B-29 gunner S/Sgt Royal Veatch shows off the two MiG-15 kills credited to his B-29. This aircraft was one of the high timers during the early days and had a major role in the use of the big 'Tarzon' bombs as noted by the oversized symbols, which show the annular wing around the bomb's midriff.

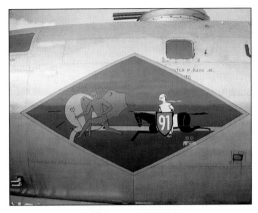

91st SRS

The 91st Strategic Reconnaissance Squadron played a vital role in the war. Its aircraft flew all over North Korea, unescorted, taking pictures of potential targets, post strike photos and dropping propaganda leaflets. When the MiG-15s entered the war in November 1950, the RBs backed off from 'MiG Alley' unless they had fighter protection. The squadron's aircraft had a distinctive 'Circle-X' on their vertical stabilisers.

Superfortress nose-art

As well as being a terrible pun, the **My Assam Dragon III** nose-art dates back to 1944 in China, when the 51st Fighter Group first used it. In 1951, it was adopted by the 19th Bomb Group.

The crew of **Sit 'N Git** of the 19th BG obviously had a poor opinion of their elderly B-29. The B-29 was one of the few aircraft of the war not loved much by its crews, being mechanically troublesome, with poor speed and altitude performance and no longer being state-of-the-art.

Howard Hughes' **The Outlaw** (1943) was one of the most talked-about movies made up to that time. Its star, Jane Russell, seemed a suitable subject for nose-art to one 28th BS, 98th BG crew. This aircraft was destroyed in a non-fatal crash at Kadena on 8 October 1951.

Haulin Ass was piloted by Lt Joe Robertson of the 98th Bomb Group.

*Left: Lt James Alexander's **Ace in the Hole** of the 98th BG absorbed heavy battle damage over the target area and managed to make it back to Kimpo. Kimpo, Suwon and Taegu air bases were safe havens for disabled 'Superforts', as Iwo Jima had been in World War II.*

*Above: The only B-29s from the 19th Bomb Group that did not have professional nose-art were the newly arrived replacement aircraft. They did not remain bare for long. **Margie's Mad Greek! III** was probably a replacement, and is seen here in late 1951 or early 1952 at Kadena.*

Combat photographer

Contrary to what one might think, a large percentage of the bombing missions did not go exactly as planned. Between mechanical problems, adverse weather, anti-aircraft fire and the MiG-15s, sometimes it seemed that the odds were against them. S/Sgt Richard Oakley was a non-flying PIO photographer for the 19th. He had never flown in any type of aircraft, before he talked the group CO into letting him fly on a mission to get some good pictures of the 19th's aircraft. This mission was a classic example of 'Murphy's Law'.

"I had talked the CO into letting me ride on a mission, in hopes of getting pictures of our aircraft in formation and also to snap a rare shot of the MiG-15, if any appeared. This mission was in early November 1950 and the MiGs were just beginning to work south of the Yalu River. After attending an early briefing, we went out to the aircraft and climbed in. Our aircraft was *The Outlaw*, 42-65306. My position was in the waist section amidst all the equipment and gear –

radar, etc. After a long flight over water, we crossed land and the rest of our squadron aircraft joined up. In a short while, I noticed little puffs of black smoke with orange centres. This was the first I knew of flak.

"While we were in formation, I snapped several shots of our aircraft. As I was doing this, I could hear the 'pings' of shrapnel hitting the bottom of our aircraft. We reached our target, opened the bomb bay doors and made the drop. Rather uneventful, so far. We made the turn to the west for the long flight back to Okinawa. Before we had taken off, we were informed that a typhoon was approaching Okinawa and they would monitor its progress. Well, we got the call that it had got bad and we were diverted down to Yokota, Japan. This would give us a little time in Tokyo and we were all excited. After we landed, we were informed that we had to be back on the line early the next morning to load our own bombs.

"We loaded up and took off for our target, which was one of the major industrial targets in North Korea – Rashin (Najin). It was up in the northeastern corner, close to Manchuria and Russia. As we approached the target at 24,000 ft, I was told that the temperature outside the aircraft was minus 50° F. We were in the number four slot, which meant our bombardier was just watching the lead ship for the drop signal. We lined up and came over the target, and nothing happened. We made a wide circle out over the ocean for a second run – nothing happened. Finally, on the third time, we dropped and headed back.

"However, there was a problem. Our bomb bay doors would not close and the added drag was making it very difficult to stay in formation. We sure didn't want to be a lone ship in this area! We managed to stay close until we crossed the bomb line and were over friendly territory. The drag had cost us valuable fuel and the navigator informed us that, at best, we would only have one hour's fuel left when we reached Okinawa. This was very close, but our 28th Squadron CO was on board and he stated that we were going back to Kadena, regardless. We all made sure our parachutes and dinghies were close by. A short while later, the navigator gets on the radio and tells us that due to increased headwinds, we would only have about 30 minutes of fuel left when we arrived.

One of Richard Oakley's photographs shows maintenance crews preparing a 19th BG aircraft for another night mission.

"At that time, the aircraft commander gets on the radio and states that since it was his aircraft and crew, we were going to Itazuke, Japan for fuel. As we were making our approach, the problems still were not behind us – it is not recommended to make a landing in a B-29 with the bay doors open, as there is very little clearance! Our pilot brought it in smooth as could be and that was not a problem after all. We got more fuel and the problem with the bay doors was solved. There was water in the hydraulic lines and they had frozen, which prevented the doors from closing. We took off and as we approached Okinawa, the tail end of the typhoon was still in the area and visibility was zero- zero. Ground control talked the pilot in for a perfect landing. As I attended the debriefing, I wondered if all missions were like this one!"

S/Sgt Richard R. Oakley, PIO Photographer, 19th Bomb Group

KB-29 'Superfort' tankers

The Korean War saw the first combat deployments of fighters aided by air-to-air refuelling. Here a KB-29P of the 91st Air Refueling Squadron tops up F-84Gs of the 27th Fighter-Escort Wing en route to Misawa, Japan in October 1952.

Below: In Korea itself, a few tankers were operated by Detachment 4 of the 98th Bomb Wing out of Yokota AB, Japan. Their first combat mission (with F-80s) was flown in July 1951 and further trials were carried out with F-84s of the 9th FBS, but the practice was not widely adopted before war's end.

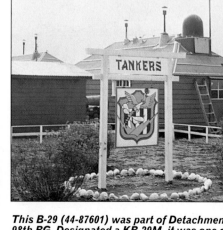

This B-29 (44-87601) was part of Detachment 4, 98th BG. Designated a KB-29M, it was one of the first aerial tankers in existence and featured a drogue refuelling hose that connected with probe-equipped wing tanks on F-80s and F-84s.

B-29 weapons

The B-29 could carry ordnance ranging from small incendiaries to atom bombs. Thankfully, the latter were not used in Korea, and initially, neither were incendiary bombs, but in November 1950 MacArthur approved their use against urban targets, and many cities and towns were laid waste in an effort to cut supply lines and deny Communist troops shelter. Thousand-pound bombs were used effectively against bridge abutments and other hard targets, but the main weapon of choice was the World War II-vintage 500-lb demolition bomb.

Below: These 19th BG crew members are unloading ammo after a mobility exercise on Kadena during the final weeks of the war. About 10,000 rounds of 0.50-in calibre were needed for the B-29's 10 machine-guns.

Above: This large bomb, capacity unknown, needed its own miniature railway to reach Sic 'Em of the 98th BG at Yokota. The significance of the figure on the bomb (presumably a record bomb tonnage) is not clear.

Top: Armourers set the fusing on 500-lb bombs that will soon be loaded aboard 92nd BG B-29s.

Below: Purple Shaft of the 19th BG is prepared for another mission. A full bomb-load for a B-29 was 40 500-lb GP bombs.

1953: To the end

17 March Forty B-29s hit the North Koreans at their northern and southern limits, with 27 aircraft striking a large supply area on the Yalu River and the remainder handling the southern extremities on the front lines.
July Twelve bombers from the 307th Bomb Wing hit front-line positions where several Chinese divisions had massed for a large-scale attack. Some 120 tons of explosives were dropped along the 50-mile (80-km) front.
15 July Fifteen Superfortresses from the 19th Bomb Wing unleashed 150 tons of high explosives against massed Communist troops along the east/central front-line positions. They were called in on short notice and the bomb drop broke up a potential assault by the Chinese.

16 July Twenty-three bombers from the 98th Bomb Wing hit Communist front-line positions with 230 tons of bombs, to counter continued Chinese troop build-ups.
17 July The efforts by the Chinese to mount offensives and gain ground before the war ended had not let up. Twenty-three bombers from the 307th Bomb Wing at Kadena AB hit the front lines again.
18 July For the fifth consecutive night, the B-29s hit front-line positions. The force of 24 medium bombers from the 19th Bomb Wing marked the largest single B-29 unit strike since August 1952. Twenty bombers dropped 16,000 20-lb anti-personnel bombs into massed Chinese troops in the Kumhwa and Iron Triangle areas, while four other bombers put 4,000-lb high-explosive bombs into troop and gun

emplacements. This strike brought a five consecutive night total of bomb tonnage to 970.
26 July FEAF Bomber Command B-29s mounted their last scheduled bombing effort of the three-year war by attacking two Communist airfields in the extreme northwest corner of North Korea. Ten B-29s from the 307th Bomb Wing hit these airfields while three other bombers concentrated on enemy positions at the front. Also, two 98th Bomb Wing bombers and two RB-29s from the 91st SRS dropped millions of leaflets over numerous areas behind enemy lines.
27 July Phasing out of Korea at 15.06, seven hours prior to the deadline, a lone RB-29 from the 91st SRS completed the last photo-reconnaissance mission. It was the final FEAF Bomber Command combat sortie flown prior to the ceasefire.

Left: One of the 307th Bomb Group's aircraft taxis out to the main runway at Kadena. It was part of a flight of four that was taking off in late afternoon for a night mission, 1952. This unusual view was taken from the control tower.

Below: At Kadena, and the other B-29 bases, each individual bomber was surrounded by a myriad of maintenance equipment, bombs and support personnel. When they were not flying a mission, they were constantly under the watchful eye of the maintenance and ordnance crews. The parking area shown was used by the 307th Bomb Group on Okinawa.

concentrations and supply dumps were hit 156 times, marshalling yards 77 times, airfields 15 times, bridges 142 times, and industrial targets 46 times. The number of buildings that had been destroyed was set at 9,159; rail cuts had escalated to 302 and rail cars destroyed was set at 217; the number of bridges damaged rose to 99 and airfields put out of commission (temporarily) numbered 11. The figures indicate that the Communists were doing everything possible to rebuild or replace most of their bombed assets. It was also becoming obvious that they were abandoning the attempt to build and repair airfields to sustain a viable air force on North Korean soil; the overwhelming strength of UN air forces meant they did not have the firepower to protect their airfields south of the Yalu River.

Tactics perfected

By January 1953, Bomber Command had perfected its tactics: the average number of bombers on any given mission was five. The average time between first and last aircraft across the target was less than one minute, 20 seconds. This was a vast improvement over the final three months of 1952. This made it easier for the protective night fighters to stay with the formation and also cut down on the total time that the bomber stream was exposed to anti-aircraft fire.

As 1953 began, the end of the war was still

not in sight, and conditions at the front were a stalemate. When spring arrived, the armistice talks heated up and attention shifted to gaining as much ground as possible before papers were signed. The pace of interdiction for all fighter-

Below: A 98th BG Superfortress pulls up over North Korea. B-29 units in the Korean war were identified within their groups by coloured trim. In this case, the green fin tip denotes the 344th BS. Squadron colours were usually red, blue or green and were often applied to the lower nose, as well.

bomber types rose sharply, and in the seven months before the war ended the B-29s destroyed 16,077 buildings. Efforts were stepped up heavily in June/July due to the Communists' all-out efforts to rebuild airfields and have aircraft in place south of the river before the war ended. The final report revealed that the bombers had caught 21 aircraft on the ground and destroyed them on a single night's mission.

The myth has grown that B-29s were shot down at an alarming rate. However, statistics released in late 1953 indicate just how successful the Superfortress was and how effective it had been in eliminating the Communist war machine on North Korean soil. Only 16 medium bombers were lost to enemy aircraft, four to anti-aircraft fire and 14 to various operational causes. There is no doubt that more bombers would have been lost to hostile MiG-15s had it not been for the efforts of the F-94Bs of the 319th All Weather Squadron and the F3Ds of Marine Night Fighter Squadron VMF(N)513. The night-hunting MiGs were perfecting the art of interception using their ground control, and both these US night-fighters effectively kept them away from the bomber streams.

More impressive statistics have surfaced concerning the B-29s. Their gunners shot down a total of 33 enemy fighters (16 of these

B-29 versus tank

"On one mission, I had a running gun battle with a Soviet-built T-34 tank. We were at a relatively low altitude when we hit the coast. I was sitting up in my bombardier's station with a clear frontal view. The coastal highway was right ahead and on it was a single tank, and he had already spotted us. Its turret was turning in our direction and its gun was being elevated. Regulations specified that the lower forward guns only be fired in self-defence – shell casings flying backward might damage the radome or, worse, the radar antennas. I asked my pilot to fly one wing low while I engaged the tank. He did so, and thus commenced a historical air/ground battle between a B-29 and enemy armour. Slightly below 12,000 ft [3658 m], my bullets probably fell harmlessly on him; in turn, his ordnance barely reached our altitude. The battle was over in a couple of minutes and it was a draw – I felt it had been a one-on-one duel between the tank driver and me.

"Another mission stands out in my memory, a 100-bomber mission flown in front-line support of our troops. Our group was loaded with 100-lb GP bombs specially mounted to fit five on a release station. This meant each B-29 carried 100 of these bombs. On rest leave shortly after the mission, we ran into some grateful infantry officers who had been on the ground

Bombardier 1st Lt Harry Wolfe relaxes at his station after the bomb drop. His 98th Group Superfortress flew its missions out of Yokota AB, Japan. During the early weeks of 1953, the 98th was heavily involved in dropping surrender leaflets over North Korea. These were known as 'paper routes'.

at the time of the bomb drop. They really appreciated the effort. I don't think we got as many enemy troops as we had hoped for, but it sure cut up a lot of the countryside!"

1st Lt Harry B. Wolfe, bombardier, 98th Bomb Gp

kills were MiG-15s) and were credited with 17 probables (all MiGs) and 11 damaged (all MiGs). The Korean War lasted over 1,100 days, of which the Superfortresses flew all but 26, equating to 21,000 individual sorties delivering

167,000 tons of bombs. For an ageing, out-dated World War II-vintage aircraft, the B-29 posted some of the most impressive statistics witnessed in any war.

Warren E. Thompson

In the summer of 1953, many of the high time B-29s were ferried back to the US by aircrews that had finished their obligations. This 19th Bomb Group B-29 (pilot: Captain Louis Branch) is on its way back to CONUS as 'Branch's Bunch' line up their survival gear for inspection in front of their bomber, which now sports numerous unofficial inscriptions.

Right: Wearing rather inaccurate 92nd BG markings, B-29 45-21739 is displayed at the Korean War Museum on Yoi-do airfield in Seoul. This Superfortress was one of those recovered from the weapons range at China Lake, California in the early 1970s, and did not participate in the war.

When it entered service in 1942, the Seafire Mk IB, the first variant of this naval derivative of the Spitfire, was the fastest naval fighter in the world. Developed to urgently fill a requirement for a Sea Hurricane replacement, it was far from suitable for the carrierborne role, but nonetheless went on to give a good account of itself in combat, particularly in the Mediterranean and Far East. Meanwhile, as the Seafire was about to make its debut, the Spitfire was undergoing its own transformation. Reworked to take a new, more powerful engine, the Rolls-Royce Griffon, the Spitfire was able to maintain its position as one of the Allies' most potent interceptors – a position held by the type until the dawn of the jet age.

Supermarine SPITFIRE (Griffon-engined variants) and SEAFIRE

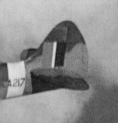

Inset: Seafire Mk IICs of No. 880 Sqn are seen aboard HMS Indomitable in mid-1943. No. 880 Sqn was one of the first FAA units to re-equip with Seafires in late 1942, operating Mk IIs and IIIs in both hemispheres for the duration of the war.

Main picture: Spitfire development was coming to an end when this formation was photographed by Charles E. Brown in 1945/46. Flanking the Spitfire Mk 22 prototype, PK312, are Mk 21s LA217 and LA232.

Spitfires at sea

Deck suitability trials with Spitfire Mk VB BL676 began during Christmas week 1941 aboard HMS *Illustrious* in the Clyde. The urgency of the trials programme was such that the carrier was pressed into service despite sustaining damage some 10 days before in a collision in the mid-Atlantic. A sizeable part of its flight deck was unusable as a result. In early 1942 the somewhat clumsy 'Sea Spitfire' name first proposed for the new type was abandoned and the compressed Seafire name officially adopted.

Left and below: Vokes filter-equipped Spitfire Mk VB BL676 Bondowoso was the first of the so-called 'hooked' Spitfires. Converted for deck landing acceptance trials it was followed by 166 further conversions to Seafire Mk IB standard. New serials were issued; BL676 became MB328.

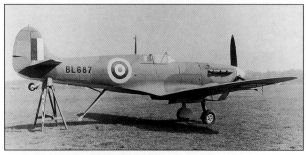

Right: The A-frame arrester hook fitted to 'hooked' Spitfires and early Seafires (up to Mk XV) is here seen in the deployed position. BL687 was the first 'production' conversion from Spitfire Mk VB standard carried out by Air Service Training Ltd at Hamble, becoming Seafire Mk IB MB329.

'Hooked' Spitfire Mk IIB P8537 lifts its tail as it roars down the deck of a carrier during trials.

Below: Seen aboard HMS Furious, the first carrier to take the Seafire into action, is a Mk IB of No. 801 Sqn (note the winged trident emblem beneath the cockpit). The lack of catapult spools on the Mk I was of little consequence as Furious, in which the squadron was embarked from October 1942, had no catapult.

Throughout the early years of World War II the Royal Navy had suffered from the lack of a high-performance carrier-based fighter. Following successful deck operating trials with Hurricanes during 1941, it was only to be expected that the Spitfire would also be considered for the role. A key to the Spitfire's success as a fighter was the mating of the most powerful engine available and a cleverly designed lightweight airframe; this made for an excellent land-based fighter, but not one that would be robust enough to withstand the rough-and-tumble of carrier operations. The entire service career of the navalised version of the fighter, the Seafire, was dogged by that fundamental problem.

The initial trials to test the suitability of the Spitfire for deck operations took place in December 1941. Commander H. Bramwell DSC RN, Commanding Officer of the RN Fighter School, made a series of landings on HMS *Illustrious* in a Spitfire Mk V fitted with an A-frame hook mounted under the fuselage. The carrier was available for only a short time and the trials were in no way comprehensive. However, they did show that the idea of adapting the Spitfire to operate from aircraft-carriers was worth pursuing. As a result, the Royal Navy initiated a programme to modify a batch of Mk V Spitfires for this purpose.

Seafire F.Mk IB and F.Mk IIC

The initial navalised variant of the Spitfire, the Seafire Mk IB, was an existing Mk VB aircraft modified for the task. The B referred to the type of wing and the armament of two 20-mm cannon and four 0.303-in (7.7-mm) machine-guns; there was no Seafire Mk IA. In addition to the arrester hook, the navalised variant was fitted with slinging points for hoisting it on and off decks. It also carried specialised naval radio equipment in the shape of a high frequency R/T set, a homing beacon receiver and naval IFF equipment. For training purposes another batch of Spitfire Mk VBs was modified to a lower standard, with the arrester hook, navy R/T set and IFF equipment but without the slinging points or beacon receiver. To differentiate these aircraft from those fully equipped for carrier operations, the latter were known as 'hooked Spitfires'.

Meanwhile, work advanced rapidly on a batch of new-build Seafires, Mk IICs. This variant was based on the Spitfire Mk VC, which had a redesigned and more robust wing

Into service, 1942

23 June 1942 saw the first Seafire Mk IICs reach an operational FAA squadron, No. 807 at Lee-on-Solent. Four other squadrons followed suit in the second half of 1942, all receiving Mk IICs, except No. 801 Sqn, which acquired Mk IBs and was to be the only front-line unit to be equipped with a full complement of the early Seafire variant. The next front-line unit to receive the Mk I (for operational use, rather than training) did not do so until the summer of 1943, when torpedo-bomber/reconnaissance squadron, No. 842, acquired six examples with which to form a fighter flight. With most of the FAA's Seafire Mk IIs earmarked for use during the Salerno landings, Operation Avalanche, No. 842 Sqn was provided with Mk IBs withdrawn from training units in July, undertaking trade protection duties during the occupation of the Azores. No. 894 continued to operate Mk IBs until March 1944.

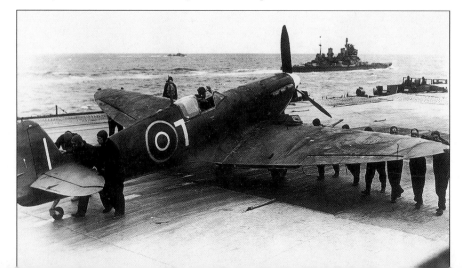

New build Mk IIs

As derivatives of the Spitfire Mk V, both the Seafire Mk I and II were powered by a Merlin 45 or 46, though in naval service their superchargers were modified to produce +14 lb boost at low level, instead of the standard +12 lb. Later, as it was found that Seafires had difficulty in overtaking fleet shadowers at low level, further modifications were made to allow +16-lb boost. Both Seafire Mk Is and IIs were modified, but in terms of outright performance the F.Mk IIC was inferior to the Mk IB. In the latter, airframe strengthening increased empty weight by six per cent, while catapult spools and the revised shape of the 'C' wing increased drag. Altogether, these changes took 15 mph (24 km/h) off the aircraft's top speed at all altitudes. Ultimately, the need to improve the Mk II's low-level performance led to a major re-engining programme, a large number of F.Mk IICs being fitted with a new Merlin 32 engine, of the type being installed in FAA's Fairey Barracuda Mk IIs and already in use by the RAF in their Spitfire Mk XIII low-level PR variant. L.Mk IICs, as these aircraft were designated, could be distinguished by their four-bladed propellers and entered service in May 1943, remaining in use until late 1944. Finally, from the L.Mk IIC was derived a camera-equipped variant – the LR.Mk IIC – effectively a naval equivalent to the Spitfire Mk XIII. Around 30 were converted and served with No. 4 Fighter Wing from late 1943.

Above: A Mk IIC, newly converted from Spitfire Mk VC standard, is readied for its first flight after weighing and CofG determination at Vickers-Supermarine's Worthy Down airfield.

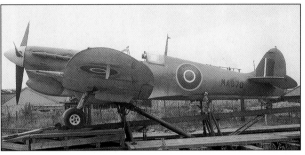

Left: The first production Mk IIC, MA970, made its maiden flight on 28 May 1942 and served as a trials aircraft until a take-off collision with a Westland Welkin at Farnborough in 1944 brought about its destruction. Here it stands on a catapult rig at Farnborough in June 1942.

Below left: By September 1942 MA970 had been fitted with a four-bladed propeller of the type that would equip the Merlin 32-powered L.Mk IIC.

Below: Mk IIC MB293 was converted to L.Mk IIC standard shortly after completion in November 1942. Here it is seen during trials in 1944 of the Mk III light universal carrier with small bombs and reconnaissance flares.

structure. As well as the naval modifications applied to the Seafire Mk IB, it had catapult spools and some strengthening of the fuselage to accommodate the stresses of deck landing. Again, the C referred to the type of wing fitted, and there was no Seafire Mk IIA or Mk IIB.

At the start of the naval fighter programme, Supermarine engineers began design work on a wing-folding mechanism for the Seafire. While this was highly desirable for carrier operations, it was not indispensable, and to hasten the entry of the Seafire into front-line service, both the initial variants lacked wing folding.

The first Seafire Mk IBs and Mk IICs were taken on Royal Navy charge in June 1942. In the weeks to follow, five fighter squadrons re-equipped with the Seafires and began working up. No. 801 Squadron received Mk IBs, while Nos 807, 880, 884 and 885 Squadrons received Mk IICs.

In action during Torch

A total of 54 Seafires in five squadrons was embarked on carriers taking part in Operation Torch, the invasion of Morocco and Algeria. Nos 801 and 807 Squadrons embarked in HMS *Furious*, No. 880 in *Argus*, No. 884 in *Victorious*, and No. 885 Squadron in *Formidable*. For this operation the Seafires, like other Royal Navy aircraft involved, wore US national markings: since the Royal Navy attack on the French fleet at Oran in 1940, the latter service was known to be hostile to the Royal Navy and it was believed the French defenders would be less likely to fire at aircraft bearing US markings.

The Seafire first went into action on 27 October 1942, when Lieutenant S. Hall of No. 800 Squadron claimed hits on a Junkers Ju 88 that had been shadowing *Furious*.

On 8 November 1942, the first day of the landings, all Seafire units flew in support of British troops going ashore

Many Seafire L.Mk IICs operated with clipped wings to improve roll rate at low level. LR691 is a No. 808 Sqn aircraft precariously positioned on the port catwalk after a landing mishap aboard escort carrier HMS Hunter *early in 1944, during exercises prior to the D-Day landings.*

Training with the Seafire

Operating from an aircraft-carrier, the Seafire novice needed to get to grips with an aircraft that had a long nose, finely balanced controls and an approach speed that was little more than its stall speed – all features inconducive to safe operation at sea! The bulk of Seafire Mk I production was allocated to training units, in particular Nos 1 and 2 Naval Fighter Schools, at Yeovilton and Henstridge respectively, and the School of Naval Air Warfare at St Merryn.

Below: Seafire Mk IB NX890 'AC-C' formates with a pair of similar aircraft from No. 736 Sqn, the School of Air Combat. Established in May 1943, the unit took over from the RAF Fighter Leaders' School the task of training naval fighter leaders, and operated Seafires and Spitfires until late 1944.

Top: This photograph by Charles E. Brown shows a formation of No. 760 Sqn aircraft (including Seafire Mk IICs MB217 and MB264) in November 1942, when the unit formed part of the Fleet Fighter School.

Above: Student pilots familiarise themselves with a No. 760 Sqn Mk IIC at Yeovilton, November 1942.

Below: A Seafire Mk IB of No. 760 Sqn makes a successful landing aboard Ravager, *an escort carrier employed for deck landing training from 1943.*

in Algeria. In addition to the 54 Seafires, the Royal Navy fighter force in the area comprised some 80 Sea Hurricanes and Martlets. The main Vichy French air threat to the landings in Algeria comprised 75 Dewoitine D.520 fighters and 54 LeO 451 and Douglas DB-7 bombers. In addition, there was a potentially dangerous torpedo bomber unit equipped with 13 Latécoère 298s.

The Seafire Mk IICs of No. 807 Squadron, operating from *Furious*, were particularly active. Early that morning the unit sent 10 aircraft to strafe the airfield at Tafaraoui, causing the destruction of four LeO 451 bombers. On their way back to their carrier they passed La Senia airfield, then under attack from Albacores and Sea Hurricanes. French D.520s then appeared on the scene and, after a brief fight, Sub-Lieutenant G. Baldwin shot down one, to gain the Seafire's first confirmed aerial victory.

After the first day, French resistance in the air came to a virtual end. As invading troops seized airfields ashore and

land-based fighter units flew in from Gibraltar, the dependence on the aircraft-carriers to provide fighter cover waned. At dusk on 9 November *Furious* and two escort carriers were withdrawn. The last of the Seafires departed from the area in *Victorious* and *Formidable* on 13 November.

During Torch the Seafires flew about 180 combat sorties. They destroyed three enemy aircraft and damaged three more in the air, and destroyed four on the ground in strafing attacks. During the operation 21 Seafires were destroyed, more than one-third of the force engaged. Three fell to enemy action, while nine more were wrecked in deck landing accidents. Of the rest, most ditched or made forced landings ashore after running out of fuel. Several pilots became lost in the haze, which was particularly severe on the first day. Two pilots were killed during the operation.

It would be misleading to judge the Seafire's performance during Torch solely on its kill-to-loss ratio. The Vichy French combat units in the area possessed enough modern aircraft to cause serious damage and disruption to the troops coming ashore. The only fighters able to prevent this, during the initial phase of the invasion, had been those operating from the carriers. In flying conditions that were far from ideal, the Royal Navy pilots ensured that the landings went ahead without any serious interference from the air.

Once the invaders were established ashore, the Seafires and other Royal Navy aircraft reverted to British national markings.

In action during Avalanche

The next major action involving the Seafire was Operation Avalanche, the landings at Salerno near Naples, Italy in September 1943. This time the beachhead was some 230 miles (370 km) from the newly captured airfields in Sicily, close to the maximum effective radius of action of the available Allied land-based fighter types. Spitfires could spend only 20 minutes on patrol at such a distance, while the twin-engined P-38 Lightning could spend 40 minutes over the landing area. However, if enemy aircraft approached the beachhead in force, there could be no rapid reinforcement of the beachhead patrols from land-based fighters. Until the invaders were able to capture an airfield ashore and bring it into use, the main source of fighter cover for the landings would be provided by carrier-based fighters. The Seafires operating from carriers close to the beachhead would be able to spend 60 minutes on patrol.

Right: '7-B' is MB240, an early production, Supermarine-built F.Mk IIC, with two Hispano 20-mm cannon and four Browning 0.303-in machine-guns fitted. The FAA had hoped to take advantage of the capacity of the 'C' wing to carry four cannon, but the weight penalty and its effect on take-off performance were too great. As service experience was gained in the Mediterranean, a number of Mk IIC aircraft were fitted with the ungainly Vokes air filters carried by Spitfires in the theatre. However, their use was short-lived as the extra drag and weight reduced climb rate to less than that of the Grumman Martlet Mk IV.

Moreover, reinforcements were readily available should a large enemy force be detected arriving.

The Royal Navy Force assigned Force V, with the small carrier *Unicorn* and the smaller escort carriers *Attacker*, *Battler*, *Hunter* and *Stalker*, to provide air cover for the Avalanche beachhead area. The five ships carried a total of 106 Seafire L.Mk IICs. From dawn on the first day of the landings, 8 September, until dawn on 14 September, the Seafires flew a total of 713 combat sorties from carriers and 56 more from airstrips established ashore. German bombers and fighter-bombers made several attempts to hit targets ashore, but most of their attacks were broken up or otherwise disrupted. The raiders inflicted no serious damage on the troops moving ashore. Seafires shot down two enemy aircraft and claimed to have inflicted damage on four others, for none lost to enemy action.

On the negative side, no fewer than 83 of these Seafires were wrecked or damaged beyond immediate repair in a succession of landing accidents during the operation. On average, one deck landing in nine resulted in the loss of, or serious damage to, a Seafire. Seven pilots were killed and three injured. Thirty-two Seafires were wrecked in catastrophic deck landing accidents, an average of one in every 22 sorties. The primary cause of the crashes was the light winds present in the area throughout much of the

Hook down, a Seafire F.Mk IIC prepares to touch-down aboard Indomitable *during mid-1943.*

Operation Torch

Operation Torch, the Allied landings in North Africa, was the first such invasion by an amphibious force to benefit from large-scale carrierborne co-operation. The FAA contributed seven carriers from Force 'H' to the operation, four of which were equipped with Seafires from five squadrons. No. 880 Sqn, in HMS *Argus*, had 18 Seafire Mk IICs, No. 885 Sqn aboard *Formidable* had six Mk IICs, while Nos 801 and 807 Sqns (12 aircraft each) joined *Furious*, the former with a handful of Seafire Mk IBs. Finally, No. 884 Sqn joined the second fleet carrier, HMS *Victorious*, also with six Mk IIs. It proved to be an auspicious start to the Seafire's combat career; three enemy aircraft were shot down and another seven damaged, three of these in the air. In all, 160 sorties were launched, many in the Tac/R role, during which 21 Seafires (40 per cent of those available on 8 November) were lost; only three of these were due to enemy action; most of the result of very poor visibility off the coast.

Deck crewmen hold down a Seafire as it is run up before a sortie from HMS Formidable. *MB156/'Ø-6G', an F.Mk IIC of No. 885 Sqn, was flown by Sub-Lt J. D. Buchanan during one of the type's first combats of Operation Torch on 8 November 1942. In this aircraft, Buchanan shared, with another of No. 885's pilots, in the destruction of a Vichy French bomber (sources differ as to the exact type) thus claiming one of the first Seafire kills of the war.*

In North African skies

MB113/'6H-B'
Though it does not carry a known unit code, official records show that this Seafire Mk IIC was on strength with No. 885 Sqn (HMS *Formidable*) at the time of Operation Torch. As information regarding the codes used by aircraft of No. 884 Sqn during the action has not survived, it is possible that MB113 was in fact with the latter squadron aboard HMS *Victorious*. Of note are the 'U. S. NAVY' legend, painted over the fuselage band, and stars.

Such was the fragility of the Seafire and the inexperience of many FAA pilots, that many sorties ended like this, with the hapless aircraft damaged, often seriously. This is a No. 807 Sqn L.Mk IIC aboard HMS Battler during the Italian landings in 1943.

operation. When they landed on the slow escort carriers, the Seafires approached the deck at a relative speed somewhat higher than normal, compounded by many pilots having only limited deck landing experience in Seafires. In the resultant heavy landings, many Seafires suffered damage to the undercarriage or wrinkling of the skin of the rear fuselage, or both. Either fault was enough to keep a fighter out of action until it could be brought to a shore base for overhaul.

As in the case of Torch, the Seafire operations during Avalanche need to be viewed in a wider context than simply the victory-to-loss ratio they achieved. Working with Allied land-based fighters flying from Sicily, the

Seafires established a high degree of air superiority over the landing area. A few warships off the coast suffered serious bomb damage and had to withdraw, but the unloading operation went ahead with relatively little interference. In the grim arithmetic of combat attrition, the loss of seven pilots and the write-off of 30 or so relatively cheap Seafires – for whatever reason – was a small price to pay for safeguarding a major landing operation involving 200,000 men and 35,000 vehicles.

Despite that overall success, Avalanche established an unfortunate reputation for the Seafire that remained with it for the rest of its service career. The converted landplane had a fine turn of speed and was a match for any likely opponent in combat. Against this, it was obviously too fragile to survive long in the rough-and-tumble of prolonged deck operations. For repeated safe landings the Seafire required a reasonably good wind speed over the deck, which meant either a fast carrier or a strong wind, or preferably both. Most important of all, it required a pilot familiar with the Seafire's traits during a deck landing. The purpose-built American F4U Corsair and the F6F Hellcat were stronger, faster and altogether better aircraft for naval operations than the Seafire. The Royal Navy had placed large orders for both types but, until they arrived in quantity, the Seafire, for

Husky and Avalanche

Operation Husky, the invasion of Sicily, again involved elements of Force 'H', including HMS *Indomitable* (with 28 Mk IICs of Nos 880 and 899 Sqns, and 12 L.Mk IICs of No. 807 Sqn) and *Formidable*, with five No. 885 Sqn Mk IICs in addition to 28 Martlet Mk IVs. The operation began on 10 July 1943, aircraft of Force 'H' flying daytime defensive patrols over its own ships and others passing through the area until the 15th. Sicily fell quickly and by 21 August Force 'H' was ready for its next task – the invasion of the Italian mainland, codenamed Avalanche. During this action *Formidable* and *Illustrious* (which had replaced the damaged *Indomitable*, and had No. 894 Sqn aboard, with 10 Seafire Mk IICs) were to provide protection for an inshore carrier force made up of *Unicorn* and four escort carriers (*Attacker, Battler, Hunter* and *Stalker*), all with Seafire L.Mk IICs aboard. D-Day was 9 September.

Below: Long-range escort HMS Venomous changes course astern of HMS Formidable. Most of No. 885's aircraft at this time appear to have been converted from Spitfire Mk Vs fitted with the much-maligned Vokes filter.

Right: Weatherbeaten No. 885 Sqn F.Mk IICs are seen aboard HMS Formidable in the Ionian Sea immediately prior to Operation Husky. In the background are other vessels of Force 'H', including the battleships Rodney and Nelson. The carrier to the right is almost certainly Formidable's sister ship, Indomitable.

Far left: HMS **Hunter** *was one of the four US-built 'Attacker'-class escort carriers (supplied under Lend-Lease) in Force 'V' during Operation Avalanche. All were equipped with between 17 and 20 Seafire L.Mk IICs.*

Left: This sequence of photographs, taken aboard **Hunter** *during Avalanche, shows the serious damage that could be done to a Seafire in a landing mishap – an all too common occurance during the Salerno landings. This Seafire L.Mk IIC has nosed over, damaging the engine in its mountings and shattering its propeller. The damage is so severe, in fact, that the decision is made to salvage the engine and cut the airframe into managable pieces before shoving these over the side.*

all its limitations, would have to hold the line.

The next variant of the Seafire to appear, the Mk III, entered service with No. 894 Squadron in November 1943. This, the first Seafire to have folding wings, was powered by a Merlin 55 engine. The wing-folding operation was performed manually and each wing had two folds, the first immediately outboard of the main undercarriage legs, where the wing was hinged upwards past the vertical position. The second fold, necessary for the fighter to fit within the 16-ft (4.9-m) ceiling limit of British carriers' hangars, was achieved by folding the wingtip outwards and downwards. Thus, viewed from the front, the folded starboard wing looked like a letter 'Z' and the port wing looked like a reversed 'Z'. A jury strut on each side locked the folded wing in position. With the necessary locks, hinges and the additional strengthening of the wing, the folding mechanism imposed a weight penalty of 125 lb (57 kg). The modification reduced the wing's torsional rigidity by about 10 per cent.

Operation Dragoon and on to the Pacific

The final Allied invasion operation in the Mediterranean was Operation Dragoon, the landings on the south coast of France which began on 15 August 1944. Seven Royal Navy escort carriers supported the operation, HMS *Emperor*, *Pursuer*, *Searcher*, *Attacker*, *Khedive*, *Hunter* and *Stalker*. In addition to 75 Hellcat and Wildcat fighters, the carriers bore 97 Seafires L.Mk IICs, LR.Mk IICs and L.Mk IIIs.

On the first day the Seafires were employed principally on defensive patrols over the landing area. It quickly became clear that the Luftwaffe was in no position to mount any sort of strong reaction against the landings. As a result, from the second day, the Seafire and other units reverted to flying armed reconnaissance missions ahead of the advancing Allied troops. Targets of opportunity, mainly road and rail traffic, were bombed and strafed. By 19 August the first airstrips were completed ashore, enabling land-based fighters to take over the air defence task.

Despite low winds and occasional spells of poor visibility, the Seafire units suffered a relatively low accident rate during Dragoon.

The F.Mk III and the L.Mk III equipped several squadrons which deployed to the Far East with the British Pacific Fleet in the spring of 1945. During operations from escort carriers, the fighter continued to suffer serious losses in deck landing accidents. Only during the final two months of the war against Japan, when experienced pilots operated the fighter from the large fleet carriers, was the Seafire at last able to demonstrate its real worth. Nos 887 and 894 Squadrons in *Indefatigable*, and Nos 801 and 880 Squadrons in *Implacable*, performed particularly successfully during this period.

The most successful action in the Seafire's entire service career took place on 15 August 1945, the very day when hostilities ended in the Pacific. Eight aircraft from Nos 887 and 894 Squadrons escorted six Avengers to attack a coastal target in Japan. Between 12 and 14 A6M5 'Zeke' fighters

Seafire Mk III

The Seafire F.Mk III, with its folding wings, Merlin 55 engine (with automatic boost control and a barometric governor), four-bladed propeller and 'cleaned up' wing enjoyed a speed advantage of some 20 mph (32 km/h) at all altitudes over the Mk IIC and had a corresponding improvement in climb rate. However, its low-level performance was still inferior to that of the L.Mk IIC and after 103 F.Mk IIIs had been completed, production switched to the L.Mk III, with a Merlin 55M powerplant and a redesigned exhaust system. The first of these entered service five months after the F.Mk III, in February 1944 mainly in the low-level short-range defence role, the FAA by then being able to deploy Lend-Lease Corsairs and Hellcats at medium and high levels. The L.Mk III was followed later in the year by a small number of FR.Mk IIIs equipped with cameras and intended to replace the LR.Mk IIC. This variant was confined to service in the Far East and Pacific.

Above: Once again we see MA970, the first production Seafire Mk IIC, now reworked as the Mk III prototype.

Right: LR765 was the first production Seafire Mk III and, along with the 25 aircraft that followed it off the production line, lacked folding wings. In fact, this aircraft was later redesignated a Mk IIC, as it also had a non-standard Merlin 50 engine and a three-bladed propeller. Most of these early production aircraft were later brought up to full Mk III specification.

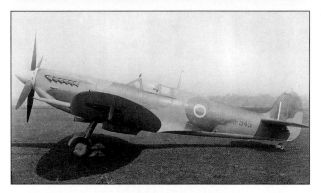

Right: The L.Mk III, distinguished by its Merlin 55M (with a cropped supercharger impeller for peak power at low altitude), was produced in larger numbers than any of the Merlin-engined Seafires. NF545 was completed by Westland in March 1944 and, after a spell at A&AEE Boscombe Down, joined No. 899 Sqn.

Below: A Seafire Mk III of No. 887 Sqn lands on HMS Indefatigable, in the Far East in 1945/46. Having caught No. 5 wire it is brought to a halt and is soon surrounded by a deck party. As the hook is disengaged, other men work to fold the wings, before the aircraft is struck below.

(8.08 Imp gal), one-third greater than that of the Merlin. Based on the design of the Rolls-Royce 'R' that had powered the Schneider Trophy racing seaplanes, the new engine was named the Griffon. The initial production version, the Griffon IIB, was fitted with a single-stage supercharger and developed 1,735 hp (1294 kW) for take-off. By cleverly positioning the components, the designers kept the length of the new engine within 3 in (7.6 cm) and its weight within 600 lb (272 kg) of the equivalent figures for the Merlin. Moreover, since the Griffon's frontal area was little greater than that of its predecessor, it was an obvious candidate to power a high-performance variant of the Spitfire.

The designations given to Spitfire variants were anything but logical. Nowhere was this more noticeable than with the first Griffon-powered aircraft, DP845. Essentially, the aircraft was a Mk III airframe, with revised and strengthened bearers to hold the larger engine. This aircraft initially had been designated the Mk IV. Soon after its maiden flight, in November 1941, the Ministry of Aircraft Production issued a directive to rationalise the growing profusion of Spitfire mark numbers. As a result, and with no significant changes, DP845 was redesignated as the Mk XX. Finally, in April 1942, still with no significant change to the aircraft, there was a further change of mark numbers and the Griffon-powered prototype became the Mk XII.

Powered by a 1,735-hp Griffon II engine fitted with a single-stage two-speed supercharger, DP845 had a maximum speed of 372 mph (599 km/h) at 5,700 ft (1737 m), increasing to 397 mph (639 km/h) at 18,000 ft (5487 m). The prototype was remembered with particular affection by Jeffrey Quill, chief test pilot at the Supermarine company: "DP845 was my favourite Spitfire. It had a wonderful performance at low altitude; it had a low full throttle height and a lot of power on the deck."

Early in 1942 the Luftwaffe introduced a new phase in its bombardment of the United Kingdom, with fighter-bomber attacks on coastal targets. The Messerschmitt Bf 109s and Focke-Wulf Fw 190s approached their targets at low altitude and high speed. There was little or no radar warning and by the time defending fighters reached the target the raiders were usually well clear.

The new threat led the RAF to issue a requirement for an interceptor optimised to counter these low-altitude high-speed raiders. In the summer of 1942 it was decided to run a comparative speed trial at low altitude, pitting the newest British fighter types against a captured Fw 190 fighter.

ran in to intercept the force and a dogfight developed. In the ensuing action the Seafires claimed eight enemy fighters destroyed, one probably destroyed and two damaged. One Seafire was shot down and another suffered damage. For their part, the Avengers delivered their attack and withdrew without loss.

Griffon-engined Spitfires

Meanwhile, as the Seafire entered service, the RAF was preparing to receive the first examples of a new Spitfire variant powered by a new and considerably more powerful engine than the Merlin.

In 1939 Rolls-Royce began development of a new combat aircraft engine with a cubic capacity of 36.75 litres

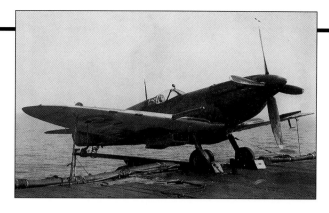

The event took take place at Farnborough, watched by a VIP audience. The Hawker Typhoon was considered to have the best performance at low altitude against the German fighter, but the Supermarine company was asked to send a Spitfire – any Spitfire – to make up the numbers. Jeffrey Quill decided to take DP845; the famous pilot described what happened next.

"On 20 July we all took off from Farnborough and flew to a point near Odiham, where we moved into line abreast formation. On the command 'Go!' we all opened our throttles and accelerated towards Farnborough, where an assortment of dignitaries had assembled to see which aircraft was the fastest. It was generally expected that the Fw 190 would come in first, the Typhoon second, and the poor old Spitfire would come limping in some way behind the other two. Well, I won the race easily in DP845, the Typhoon

East of Suez

East of Suez, the Seafire's lack of range was to prove an even greater handicap. Many fighter units re-equipped with American-built aircraft, but as insufficient numbers were available, the Seafire continued to serve. A small number of Seafires (Mk IICs equipping a flight of No. 834 Sqn aboard HMS *Battler*) were on trade protection duty in the Indian Ocean from October 1943 and towards the end of the year another squadron was added (No. 889 Sqn in *Atheling* with Mk IIIs). However, it was not until the beginning of 1945 that the FAA's striking power was concentrated in the Far East, with the Seafire Mk III eventually equipping eight squadrons east of Suez, aboard the escort carriers of the 21st Aircraft Carrier Squadron and the fleet carriers *Implacable* and *Indefatigable*. Notable actions for which the Seafires provided fighter cover included the attacks on Japanese oil refineries in Sumatra in January and the occupation of Rangoon and Penang in May and August. In the Pacific during March/April, meanwhile, British Pacific Fleet Seafires (Nos 887 and 894 Sqns in *Indefatigable*) were in action over the Sakishima Islands. It was during this action that Seafires made their first combat claims in the Pacific and Sub-Lt Richard Reynolds of No. 894 Sqn became the FAA's first (and only) Seafire ace, downing three 'Zeros' to add to two BV 138s claimed off Norway. With the arrival of HMS *Implacable* (No. 38 Wing – Nos 801 and 880 Sqns), operations over Truk in the Caroline Islands in June saw Seafires in action once again and by August Seafires were flying over the Japanese mainland.

Below: Taken using the oblique camera in Seafire FR.Mk III NN612 on the last day of operations over Japan, this photograph shows a No. 880 Sqn Mk III sporting one of the non-standard drop tanks used by the squadron. Unhappy with the unreliability of the Seafire's standard 45- and 90-Imp gal (205- and 410-litre) slipper tanks, No. 880 Sqn modified 60 surplus 90-Imp gal (410-litre) tear-drop tanks, originally intended for use on RAAF P-40s and obtained via USAAF personnel from a base in New Guinea. No. 880 Sqn supplied two crates of whiskey in payment!

Operations in 1944

Seafire deployments during 1944 were diverse, encompassing land-based as well as carrier operations. Seafire units provided part of the escort for anti-shipping strikes off the Norwegian coast, in particular the well-known attacks on the German battleship *Tirpitz* mid-year, while in June a detachment from No. 879 Sqn with Seafire Mk IIIs had provided shore-based tactical reconnaissance for the Desert Air Force in Italy. Prior to the Normandy landings (Operation Overlord) Seafire Mk IIIs of Nos 887 and 894 Sqns based at Culmhead provided a fighter escort for RAF Typhoons on cross-Channel fighter-bomber sorties and during the landings in June four FAA units, with shore-based Seafires and Spitfires, carried out gunnery spotting for naval guns offshore. During Operation Dragoon, the invasion of southern France in August, of nine American and British carriers taking part, four of the latter had Seafire units aboard. As well as combat air patrols, Seafires also made tactical reconnaissance and bombing sorties over the beachhead. The latter were performed by aircraft of No. 4 Fighter Wing, this being the first major use of the Seafire in the fighter-bomber role.

Below: No. 899 Sqn was designated a Seafire Operational Training Unit, converting RAAF pilots to form the nucleus of a planned Australian FAA. Two courses were held, the first aboard HMS Indomitable, in Australia at the time. Here a No. 899 Sqn Seafire Mk II comes to grief with a RANVR pilot aboard. Note the mixture of Pacific Fleet markings on the aircraft's fuselage and Type 'C' roundels on the upper wings.

Top left: One of No. 807 Sqn's L.Mk IIIs rests, firmly tied down on an outrigger, aboard HMS Hunter in the Aegean Sea, October 1944.

Left: With a 500-lb bomb under its fuselage, a Seafire L.Mk III of No. 899 Sqn, No. 4 Fighter Wing, gets airborne from HMS Khedive during Operation Dragoon in August 1944. With a bomb on board, a Seafire could not be catapulted. Thus, only two Seafire wings flew bombing missions – No. 4 Wing from American-built assault carriers (whose catapults were incompatible with the Seafire anyway), and No. 38 Fighter Wing in the fleet carrier Implacable. The latter had a sufficiently long deck to allow a fully laden Seafire to get airborne without the use of a catapult.

Below: A No. 801 Sqn Seafire Mk III loses a propeller blade in a typical example of 'pecking', as 'N/147' noses over slightly after catching the wire on landing aboard Implacable around the the time of VJ-Day.

A Seafire Mk III lands after a strike on the Sumatran oil refineries in early 1945. The aircraft, of No. 894 Sqn, has ploughed into the barrier, its starboard undercarriage leg forced backwards and into the radiator, and its propeller blades disintegrating.

Far right and far right bottom: Here the results of the landing accident suffered by PP479 'D-5X' of No. 889 Sqn (the subject of the artwork opposite) are seen, the aircraft having lost all three undercarriage legs after missing the arrester wire and been caught in the barrier.

Below: Though frequent, and often spectacular, deck landing accidents cost comparatively few lives. However, this horrific example not only proved fatal, but indirectly led to the disbandment of the squadron. On 29 June 1944, aboard HMS Atheling in the Indian Ocean, this No. 889 Sqn Seafire missed the arrester wire on landing, crashed over the barrier and ploughed into an aircraft parked ahead of it. Two pilots and three members of the deck party were killed. The carrier had arrived in the Bay of Bengal in May, but after several accidents that cost the lives of a number of its pilots, including the CO, No. 889 Sqn was disbanded on 11 July.

came second and the Focke-Wulf was third, which was absolutely the wrong result!"

Following this trial the Spitfire XII was selected as the RAF's new low-altitude fighter. Production began in the summer of 1942, against an order for 100, and the first was delivered that November. Production Mk XIIs had wings clipped to 32 ft 8 in (9.96 m), to increase speed at low altitude and improve their rate of roll. Compared with the Mk IX, the main production variant of the Spitfire at this time, the Mk XII was 14 mph (22 km/h) faster at sea level and 8 mph (13 km/h) faster at 10,000 ft (3050 m); at altitudes above 20,000 ft (6100 m), however, the performance of the Mk XII fell away rapidly and it was slower than the Mk IX.

The report on the aircraft, written by the Air Fighting Development Unit at Duxford in December 1942, stated: "In the air the handling of both EN223 and another production Spitfire Mk XII which was made available by Supermarine for one day, were felt to be far superior to the normal Spitfire Mk IX or Mk VB, being exceptionally good in the lateral control which is crisper and light due to the clipped wings. The longitudinal stability is much better than that of the Spitfire Mk V, and in the dive it was particularly noticed that when trimmed for cruising flight, it stays in easily at 400 mph [644 km/h] IAS and does not recover fiercely. In turns the stick load is always positive and the control very comfortable. The rudder, however, is most sensitive to changes in engine settings and needs retrimming for most alterations of flight as it is too heavy to be held by the feet for long periods. The Spitfire Mk XII has the usual Spitfire stall characteristics. The engine runs noticeably more roughly than a Merlin."

In order to provide increased rudder authority to counter the greater engine torque of the Griffon engine, early in its career the Mk XII was fitted with a broad-chord rudder with a pointed tip.

Mk XII in service

In February 1943 No. 41 Squadron moved to High Ercall in Shropshire to re-equip with the Mk XII. In April the only other unit to receive the new variant, No. 91 Squadron, began its conversion. Both squadrons had previously operated the Spitfire Mk VB. As far as pilots were concerned, the main difference between the Mk XII and the previous version of the Spitfire was that the Griffon

Seafire versus 'Zeke'

Testing of a captured Mitsubishi A6M6 Model 52 yielded the following results in comparison with a Seafire L.Mk IIC.

Peak speeds: Seafire L.Mk IIC: 338 mph (544 km/h) at 5,500 ft (1677 m); Zeke 52: 335 mph (539 km/h) at 18,000 ft (5488 m) The comparative speeds in miles per hour are:

Height	Seafire L.Mk IIC	Zeke 52
sea level	316 mph (508 km/h)	292 mph (470 km/h)
5,000 ft (1525 m)	337 mph (542 km/h)	313 mph (504 km/h)
10,000 ft (3050 m)	337 mph (542 km/h)	319 mph (513 km/h)
15,000 ft (4575 m)	335 mph (539 km/h)	327 mph (526 km/h)
20,000 ft (6100 m)	328 mph (528 km/h)	333 mph (536 km/h)
25,000 ft (7625 m)	317 mph (510 km/h)	327 mph (526 km/h)
30,000 ft (9150 m)		317 mph (510 km/h)

Climb: The 'Zeke 52' climbs at a very steep angle and gives the impression of a very high rate of climb. The Seafire L.Mk IIC, however, has a much better initial climb and remains slightly superior up to 25,000 ft (7625 m). The climb of the Seafire is at a higher speed, but at a more shallow angle. The best indicated climbing speeds of the 'Zeke' and the Seafire are 120 and 160 mph (193 and 257 km/h) respectively.

Manoeuvrability, turning plane: The 'Zeke 52' can turn inside the Seafire L.Mk IIC at all heights. The 'Zeke 52' turns tighter to the left than to the right.

Manoeuvrability, rolling plane: The rate of roll of the two aircraft is similar at speeds below 180 mph IAS (290 km/h), but above that the aileron stick forces of the 'Zeke' increase tremendously, and the Seafire becomes progressively superior.

Dive: The Seafire is superior in the dive although initial acceleration is similar. The 'Zeke' is a most unpleasant aircraft in a dive, due to heavy stick forces and excessive vibration.

Tactics: Never dogfight with the 'Zeke 52' – it is too manoeuvrable. At low altitudes where the Seafire is at its best, it should make use of its superior rate of climb and speed to obtain a height advantage before attacking. If jumped, the Seafire should evade by using its superior rate of roll. The 'Zeke' cannot follow high speed rolls and aileron turns.

Conclusions: The Seafire L.Mk IIC is 24 mph (38 km/h) faster at sea level, this difference decreasing to parity between 15,000 and 20,000 ft (4575 m and 6100 m). The 'Zeke 52' is 10 mph (16 km/h) faster at 25,000 ft (7625 m). The 'Zeke' is very manoeuvrable and can turn inside the Seafire at all altitudes. The 'Zeke' fights best between 115 and 180 mph IAS (185 and 290 km/h). The rate of roll of the Seafire is better than that of the 'Zeke' above 180 mph IAS (290 km/h).

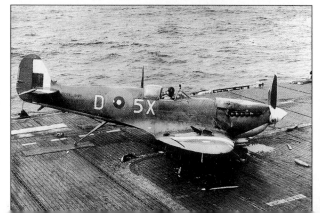

Written off
Piloted by Sub-Lt F. Logie, this aircraft met its end after a landing accident in June 1945. In light winds, the aircraft floated over arrester wires, snagging the barrier and losing all three undercarriage legs. Beyond repair aboard the carrier, it was dismantled and stowed below decks until *Hunter* next reached Trincomalee, Ceylon where it was off-loaded, pronounced 'beyond repair' and scrapped.

Folding wings
The main improvement introduced in the Seafire Mk III was the folding wing, allowing the armoured carriers *Illustrious*, *Formidable* and *Victorious* to at last stow their Seafires below decks. Each wing folded in two places, just inboard of the inboard cannon bay, and between mainplane and wingtip. Power-assisted folding was rejected as imposing too great a weight penalty.

Supermarine Seafire F.Mk III No. 807 Sqn, 4th Fighter Wing HMS *Hunter* June 1945

With No. 807 Sqn aboard, 'Attacker'-class escort carrier HMS *Hunter* participated in Operation Dragoon in August 1944, and after a short short spell in the Aegean underwent a refit at Alexandria before departing for the Eastern Fleet. During April and May 1945, No. 807 Sqn provided fighter support for the re-occupation of Rangoon and by June was covering anti-shipping strikes in the Andaman Sea. PP479 was delivered to the FAA in late September 1944, issued to No. 807 Sqn and subsequently written off in mid-1945.

Improved performance
The Seafire Mk III gained a 20 mph (32 km/h) advantage over the Mk II at all heights thanks to its new engine (with multi-stack exhausts) and four-bladed propeller and other measures, including the removal of redundant cannon stubs and the fitting of smaller cannon belt feed fairings on the top surface of the wing. The Mk III remained inferior at low level, though this was of little importance given its role as medium- to high-level fighter.

Propeller 'pecking'
The greatest cause of Seafire unserviceability due to deck landing damage was propeller 'pecking', the result of failing to make a 'three point' touch-down at the instant the arrester hook took the weight of the aircraft. If the landing was less than perfect the aircraft tended to rotate forward, thanks to the positioning of the A-frame hook so close to the aircraft's CofG, with the result that the propeller blade tips struck the deck. Generally damage was confined to the blades (which were then simply sawn off), though damage to the engine and bearers by shock-loading could result. Often more serious damage was done as the aircraft fell back on its tailwheel.

Finish
Slate Grey and Extra Dark Sea Grey formed the basis for the finish applied to FAA fighters in the British Pacific and Far Eastern Fleets. The undersides of the aircraft were Sky Type 'S', the propeller spinner Sky Type 'S' or Light Grey. This aircraft also sports white SEAC bands and small Roundel Blue/White roundels.

Merlin powerplants
The standard Seafire F.Mk III was powered by a Merlin 55, of the type fitted to some Spitfire Mk Vs. This produced the same output as the Seafire Mk II's Merlin 45 or 46 – 1,470 hp (1096 kW) at 9,250 ft (2819 m) – but benefited from an automatic supercharger boost control, with barometric governing of 'full throttle height'. A four-bladed propeller, as introduced on the L.Mk IIC, was standard. Produced in greater numbers than any of the Merlin-engined Seafires, the L.Mk III had a Merlin 55M installed, capable of producing 1,585 hp (1182 kW) at 2,750 ft (838 m).

Tailhook
All Merlin-engined Seafires were equipped with an A-frame hook, as fitted to the so-called 'hooked Spitfires' during the earliest deck landing experiments. From the Mk XV, a 'stinger'-type hook was fitted, hinged at the foot of the rudder post.

Below: Seafire Mk IIIs, with a mixture of Pacific Fleet and temperate markings, are seen leaving Brisbane harbour in August 1945.

Bottom: In the US towards the end of the war, trials were flown to compare the relative merits of the Seafire Mk III, Grumman F6F Hellcat and Mitsubishi J2M2 Raiden (Allied code name 'Jack') in combat. The programme was conducted by the US Navy from its Patuxent River airfield.

engine rotated in the opposite direction to the earlier Merlin, so instead of a mild tendency to swing to the left on take off, the new version tried to swing more strongly to the right. If the pilot was aware of the difference and applied sufficient rudder trim to compensate for the swing before it developed, he could cope with the change, but those who failed to do so were in for an exciting ride. There are authenticated cases of pilots making their first flight in a Griffon-powered Spitfire, and giving a firm push on the throttle on take-off without sufficient rudder trim or none at all. The fighter would swing viciously to the right, sometimes leaving the runway and careering across the grass. In extreme cases, where the rudder trim was set to the left (as on Merlin-powered Spitfires), the aircraft finally got airborne heading in a direction almost 90° to the intended direction of take-off. Provided the pilot was aware

of the difference and applied sufficient rudder trim to counteract for the swing before it developed, however, the take-off in the Mk XII was simple enough. Squadron Leader Tom Neil, commander of No. 41 Squadron when the first of the new fighters arrived, later commented:

"As the Mk XII was reputedly faster than the Typhoon low down it was regarded as something of a 'hot ship' and there was a painful air of smugness abroad at dispersal. Our collective ego, however, was knocked sideways when the first XII was delivered by a pretty, pink-cheeked young thing in ATA [Air Transport Auxiliary] uniform, who taxied in with a flourish and stepped out as though she had been flying nothing more vicious than a Tiger Moth."

First Mk XII victory

In April 1943, No. 41 Squadron was declared operational and the unit moved to Hawkinge near Folkestone. From there it flew standing patrols in an attempt to catch enemy fighter-bombers making tip-and-run attacks on coastal targets. Initially, these operations had little success. The Spitfire Mk XII fired its guns in anger for the first time on 17 April, when Flying Officer C. Birbeck strafed an enemy patrol boat. Later that day, Flight Lieutenant R. Hogarth encountered a Junkers Ju 88 near Calais and shot it down.

Although the Mk XIIs had few encounters with enemy aircraft at this time, their sorties were not devoid of excitement, as Tom Neil explained:

"One of our early problems was to convince the Typhoons at Lympne and Manston that we were on their side. Our clipped wings gave us the appearance of 109s and there were several ugly encounters between the Typhoons and ourselves, with us on the receiving end. Fortunately, we could just out-distance a Typhoon provided we saw it in time, otherwise blood would have been spilled."

No. 91 Squadron joined its sister unit at Hawkinge in May 1943 and it, too, began operations, demonstrating its effectiveness with the Mk XII on the evening of 25 May. A small force of Fw 190s fighter-bombers from Schnellkampfgeschwader 10 was detected on radar running in at low altitude to attack Folkestone. The two Spitfires at readiness were scrambled, as were two more that had just landed after a patrol. These Spitfires engaged the Focke-Wulfs before the latter reached their target, forcing several to jettison their bombs into the sea. Only one bomb fell on the town, and that caused minor damage. Meanwhile, four other Mk XIIs had scrambled. In the ensuing chase across the channel the fighters claimed the destruction of six enemy aircraft, two of which were credited to the unit's commander, Squadron Leader Raymond Harries.

Just over a week later, on the morning of 4 June, No. 41 Squadron broke up another attack on Eastbourne by enemy fighter-bombers. Again, most of the Germans were forced to jettison their bombs. Flying Officer Solack was credited with the destruction of one Focke-Wulf, and ground gunners claimed three others. Soon afterwards, the daylight tip-and-run fighter-bomber attacks came to an end, as Schnellkampfgeschwader 10 shifted to night raids.

With the lifting of the requirement to counter the fighter-bomber attacks, the two Mk XII units shifted to

Mks IV, XX & XII

On 27 November 1941, Jeffrey Quill took the first Spitfire Mk IV prototype into the air from Worthy Down. Powered by a Rolls-Royce Griffon IIB, the Mk IV was essentially a re-engined derivative of the stillborn Mk III, and represented a considerable improvement over the Mk V in terms of performance. When, soon after its maiden flight, the Ministry of Aircraft Production rationalised Spitfire designations, the Mk IV became the Mk XX, this appellation applying to the second Griffon-powered aircraft, DP851 (flown in August 1942) from the outset. Meanwhile, by mid-1942 concern regarding the threat posed by Focke-Wulf Fw 190 making fighter-bomber raid across the Channel forced a rethink. Orders placed with Supermarine as far back as August 1941, for the construction of 750 Mk IVs (to be built at the Castle Bromwich Aircraft Factory) were cancelled and DP845 was reworked as the prototype of a low-altitude fighter, the Mk XII.

Above: The large Rotol propeller spinner and revised cowling contours were the only clue that an engine considerably larger than the Merlin was installed in DP845. Note that by this time the aircraft was close to production Mk XII standard, with clipped wingtips and a 'C' wing/armament fit.

Left: By spring/summer 1942, DP845 was known as a Mk XII and had gained a broad-chord rudder and Mk VC wing, with two cannon and four machine-guns installed.

Far left: DP845 is seen here in its original configuration as the first Spitfire Mk IV, mocked-up with six Hispano 20-mm cannon and still equipped with a narrow-chord rudder. Note the retractable tailwheel.

fighter sweeps and escort missions over enemy territory.

The Spitfire Mk XII's performance at low or medium altitude was unmatched by any opposing fighter type, and, during offensive patrols over France, pilots found it difficult to lure enemy fighters into turning fights low down. The German fighters' usual tactic, when they encountered Spitfires or other Allied fighters below them, was to make a diving attack from above and then zoom back to altitude and position themselves for a re-attack if necessary. From previous hard-won experience, they knew it was unwise to enter a turning fight with any variant of the Spitfire lower down.

Throughout the rest of the year the two squadrons flew sweeps and escort missions over enemy territory. The most successful action involving Mk XIIs took place on 20 October 1943, during the fighter sweep Operation Rodeo 263. Both squadrons took part in the sweep, flying as a wing under the command of Group Captain Grisham. As the force crossed the French coast it came under fire from accurate flak; one Spitfire suffered damage, and another was detached to escort it home. The rest of the force continued inland, climbing to 18,000 ft (5484 m) and heading for the Tricqueville-Bernay-Beaumont area. Near Rouen a pack of about 25 Bf 109s and Fw 190s dived on the Spitfires from the sun. The Mk XIIs turned to port and climbed, to face their attackers head on. The action developed into a fierce dogfight, and for once the German pilots did not dive away. That proved an unwise move, and during the ensuing mêlée the two Spitfire squadrons claimed the destruction of nine

enemy fighters without loss to themselves.

During the months that followed the pattern of operations continued, though never again did the Mk XIIs encounter an enemy force as aggressive as that on 20 October.

The last Mk XII in the batch of 100 had left the production line at Eastleigh in September 1943, and no further order was placed for the variant. Early in 1944, No. 91 Squadron was withdrawn from operations to become the first unit to re-equip with the Spitfire Mk XIV. No. 41 Squadron soldiered on with the Mk XII for a few more months before it also received the new variant at the end of the summer.

Spitfire Mk XIV

An obvious next step for the Griffon Spitfire was for it to be fitted with an engine that had a two-stage supercharger to give improved performance at high altitude. The new engine, the Griffon 61, appeared in the spring of 1943 and developed an impressive 1,540 hp (1148 kW) for take-off and 2,035 hp (1517 kW) at 7,000 ft (2134 m). Six Spitfire Mk VIIIs were modified to take the new engine, to become prototypes for the Spitfire Mk XIV. To absorb the additional engine power, the new variant featured a five-bladed propeller, and to cancel out the greater torque from larger engine and propeller, it had a larger fin and rudder. The Mk XIV had small additional fuel tanks fitted in each wing leading edge close to the fuselage, holding a total of 25 Imp gal (116 litres). This helped compensate for the higher rate of consumption of the more-powerful Griffon engine.

Flight tests with the initial Mk XIV conversions revealed this variant to be an extremely effective fighter. Its performance was a huge improvement over the Mk IX and

Below left: In this view of an early Mk XII, the resemblance of the aircraft's underside to that of the Mk V, from which the production Mk XII was derived, is clearly evident.

Below: EN221, the first production Mk XII, was extensively test flown by the manufacturer, initially with standard wingtips and a fixed tailwheel.

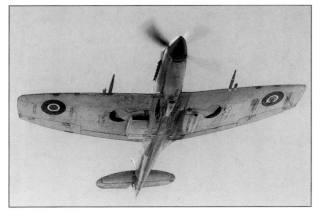

Mk XII in service

The first production Mk XII, EN221, appeared in October 1942 and in December the third aircraft was despatched to the Air Fighting Development Unit at Duxford. Such was the urgency of the requirement for a low-level interceptor that No. 41 Squadron received its first aircraft in February, at High Ercall. Production ceased in September, with 100 completed. The type's success against the low-level raiders making 'tip and run' attacks on English coastal targets was limited, given the lack of adequate radar warning of fast, low-level targets. Towards the end of their short service careers, the Mk XIIs joined the fight against the V-1 flying bomb menace launched against London from June 1944. Large numbers of 'Divers' were shot down before the Mk XII left the front-line RAF in September.

Above right: MB882, the last Mk XII built, is seen here in its element, at low level.

Right: MB858 first flew in July 1943, and was delivered to No. 41 Sqn in September. No. 91 Sqn was the only other Mk XII unit.

Below: MB882, coded 'EB-B', was flown by Flt Lt Don Smith in April 1944. An Australian, Smith first saw action in mid-1942, claiming three kills while flying Spitfire Mk Vs on Malta. Posted to No. 41 Sqn in 1943, he added another victory in a Mk XII, before becoming CO of No. 453 Sqn (Spitfire Mk IXBs) in 1944 and scoring a final victory.

the Mk XII. Jeffrey Quill said that in his view the Mk XIV had the best fighting ability of any of the Spitfire variants. That did not mean it was an easy machine to fly, however.

"… the Mk XIV, with its tremendous power, increased propeller solidity and increased all-up weight and moments of inertia, was a good deal more of a handful for the pilot and so required more attention to 'flying' than its predecessors. Directional stability was a problem and the aircraft was apt to shear about a lot with coarse use of the throttle; large changes in speed required prompt attention to rudder trim. We at Supermarine tried all manner of expedients to improve the directional characteristics of the Mk XIV. The only real answer was to fit a much larger fin and rudder, but it was a major design change and the Spitfire 22 was the first production version to be fitted with it.

"So far as the Mk XIV was concerned, I took the view that performance was paramount; and if the pilots had to work a bit harder and concentrate a bit more on their flying, that was better than sending them to war in an aircraft of inferior performance."

Comparative air fighting trials against a captured Fw 190A and a Bf 109G confirmed Quill's view: the Spitfire Mk XIV showed itself to be superior to the German fighters in almost every respect.

The new variant went into production in the autumn of 1943 and by the following spring Nos 91, 322 and 610 Squadrons had converted to the Mk XIV. All three units were fully operational in June 1944, when the Luftwaffe commenced its attack on London with the first of its 'secret weapons'.

Griffon-Spitfires versus V-1 flying bombs

Early on the morning darkness of 13 June 1944, the Luftwaffe opened a new phase in the bombardment on London, employing the V-1 flying bomb. In Britain the new weapons was immediately nicknamed the 'Doodlebug'. By the end of the month German ground launching sites had fired just under 2,500 of these weapons at the capital; roughly one-third reached the Greater London area, causing just under 2,500 deaths and more than 7,000 cases of serious injury. The remaining missiles missed the city, or were brought down by fighters, guns or barrage balloons before reaching it.

The defenders quickly took the measure of the new German weapon. The V-1s were not manufactured to normal aircraft tolerances, so there were large variations in their performance. The majority flew at speeds around 350 mph (563 km/h), though the fastest were tracked at 420 mph (676 km/h) and the slowest came in at around 230 mph (370 km/h). There were similar variations in altitude; most crossed the coast at between 3,000 and 4,000 ft (915 and 1220 m), but the highest was recorded coming in at 8,000 ft (2440 m) and the lowest flew at tree-top height,

Hawkinge-based Mk XII

EN237/'EB-V'
Sqn Ldr Thomas Neil flew EN237 while OC of No. 41 Sqn at Hawkinge, spring 1943. Neil was a Battle of Britain veteran who scored all of his 12 victories during 1940/41. Mk XIIs generally flew in standard Fighter Command day fighter camouflage (Ocean Grey/Dark Green over Medium Sea Grey); EN237 was one of the first delivered to the squadron.

Another stop-gap: Mk XIV

The Spitfire Mk XII had been optimised for low-altitude operations. Further evolution resulted in the Mk XIV, a development of the Mk VIII fitted with a two-stage Griffon and intended as a high-altitude interceptor. Six Mk VIIIs were converted as prototypes. They were JF316 (fitted with a Griffon III of the type installed in late production Spitfire Mk XIIs, with single-stage supercharging), JF317 (the first to fly; fitted with a two-stage Griffon 61), JF318 (Griffon 61), JF319 (Griffon 65), JF320 (Griffon 61) and JF321 (Griffon 61). The last named went to Rotol at Staverton, where it was employed as a contra-rotating propeller trials airframe. The Mk XIV was to be the most numerous Griffon-engined Spitfire variant to see wartime RAF service, production ending in late 1945 after 957 had been completed.

which usually led to their early demise. The missile's time in the air, from the launching site to London, was about 25 minutes.

After some changes, the defenders put together a reasonably effective system to counter the flying bombs. Four belts of defences protected the capital. The first belt, running from mid-Channel to about 10 miles (16 km) short of the coast, was the Outer Fighter Patrol Area where fighters could be vectored in to engage the flying bombs. At the coast was the Gun Belt, with about 800 heavy AA

Far left: JF321 is seen here with a contra-prop fitted and an enlarged tailfin, with a straight leading-edge, of an interim design.

Above: JF318, the third Mk XIV, is seen here in its original configuration, with a Mk VIII tailfin and 'C' wing.

Left: Production FR.Mk XIV TZ138 was sent to Manitoba, Canada for cold weather trials in the winter of 1946/47. Adapted from a design intended for the de Havilland Tiger Moth, the skis fitted to this aircraft assisted only during taxying and take-off and were designed to fall away from the aircraft as it left the ground.

AFDU trials, Duxford 1944

Early in 1944 the Air Fighting Development Unit at Duxford flew a Spitfire Mk XIV in a comparative trial against captured examples of the Fw 190A and Bf 109G-6. Excerpts from the official trials reports are given below:

SPITFIRE XIV versus Fw 190A
Maximum Speeds: From 0-5,000 ft (0-1525 m) and 15,000-20,000 ft (4573-6100 m) the Spitfire XIV is only 20 mph (32 km/h) faster; at all other heights it is up to 60 mph (97 km/h) faster than the Fw 190A.
Maximum Climb: The Spitfire XIV has a considerably greater rate of climb than the Fw 190A at all altitudes.
Dive: After the initial part of the dive, during which the Fw 190 gains slightly, the Spitfire XIV has a slight advantage.
Turning Circle: The Spitfire XIV can easily turn inside the Fw 190. Though in the case of a right-hand turn, this difference is not quite so pronounced.
Rate of Roll: The Fw 190 is very much better.
Conclusions: In defence, the Spitfire XIV should use its remarkable maximum climb and turning circle against any enemy aircraft. In the attack it can afford to 'mix it' but should beware of the quick roll and dive. If this manoeuvre is used by an Fw 190 and the Spitfire XIV follows, it will probably not be able to close the range until the Fw 190 has pulled out of its dive.

SPITFIRE XIV versus Bf 109G
Maximum Speed: The Spitfire XIV is 40 mph (64 km/h) faster at all heights except near 16,000 ft (4878 m), where it is only 10 mph (16 km/h) faster.
Maximum Climb: The same result: at 16,000 ft the two aircraft are identical, otherwise the Spitfire XIV out-climbs the Bf 109G. The zoom climb is practically identical when the climb is made without opening the throttle. Climbing at full throttle, the Spitfire XIV draws away from the Bf 109G quite easily.
Dive: During the initial part of the dive, the Bf 109G pulls away slightly, but when a speed of 380 mph (611 km/h) is reached, the Spitfire XIV begins to gain on the Bf 109G.
Turning Circle: The Spitfire XIV easily out-turns the Bf 109G in either direction.
Rate of Roll: The Spitfire XIV rolls much more quickly.
Conclusion: The Spitfire XIV is superior to the Bf 109G in every respect.

guns and 1,800 lighter weapons positioned between Beachy Head and Dover; fighters had strict orders to keep out of this zone, thus allowing the gunners freedom to engage any airborne target that came within range without having to worry about identification. The belt from 10 miles inland to 10 miles short of London was the Inner Fighter Patrol Area, where more fighters could engage the V-1s. The fourth belt ran from the edge of the Greater London to 10 miles in front of it. There, about 1,000 barrage balloons were deployed to ensnare as many as possible of the missiles which had passed through the other defensive belts.

Left and below: From autumn 1944, Mk XIVs were completed to FR.Mk XIVE standard, with a bubble canopy and cut-down rear fuselage (containing an extra 33-Imp gal/150-litre fuel tank), camera ports and the 'E' wing. MV247 (left), is an early example, seen here with a 90-Imp gal (409-litre) external fuel tank.

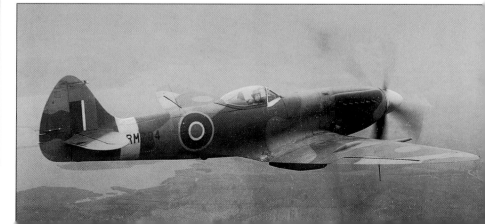

Above: Resting on the PSP, possibly on an airfield in Belgium in early 1945, RN119, a mid-production F.Mk XIVC carries the 'AE' codes of No. 402 Sqn, RCAF, a 2nd TAF unit engaged in fighter-bomber, bomber escort and defensive duties in the final months before VE-Day.

ADGB and 2nd TAF

Air Defence of Great Britain squadrons were the first recipients of the Mk XIV, Nos 610, 91 and 322 (Dutch) Sqns re-equipping in early 1944. All were operational by June, when the V-1 flying bomb offensive began, becoming the most successful Spitfire units engaged in anti-'Diver' operations. Some aircraft were modified to run on 150-octane fuel and at +25 lb boost in order to wring an extra 30 mph (48 km/h) out of the aircraft at low level. This gave a modified aircraft a top speed of 400 mph (644 km/h) at 2,000 ft (609 m). When the main V-1 bombardment ended in September (as the Allied armies overran their launch sites in France), Mk XIV squadrons, of which there were seven by the end of the month, were transferred to the 2nd Tactical Air Force. From then until the end of the war in Europe, the Mk XIV was 2nd TAF's main air superiority type. By the end of the year, camera-equipped FR.Mk XIVs were in service and equipped four squadrons, including two tactical reconnaissance units – Nos II (AC) and 430 Sqns.

Initially, the Spitfires engaging the V-1s belonged to No. 150 Wing based at Lympne, comprising Nos 1 and 165 Squadrons with Mk IXs and No. 41 Squadron with Mk XIIs. Neither version had enough speed at low altitude to engage the faster V-1s, so, to alleviate this deficiency, Nos 91, 322 and 610 Squadrons – the first three units with the Mk XIVs – were ordered to assist in the defence of the capital. For these operations some Spitfire Mk XIVs had their engines modified to run on 150 octane petrol allowing

Right: 2nd TAF fighter-reconnaissance units Nos II (AC) and 268 Sqns operated camera-equipped FR.Mk XIVEs. This aircraft, based at Twente in the Netherlands in the final weeks of the war, is a No. 268 Sqn aircraft, notable for its lack of unit code letters.

CFE Mk XIV/Vampire trials

The F.Mk XIV was one of the fastest Spitfire variants. For a piston-engined aircraft it was certainly no slouch, and at the end of World War II it was acknowledged as one of the most effective air superiority fighters in service, yet it was outclassed in almost every significant aspect of air combat by the de Havilland Vampire Mk I. The comparative trial took place at the Central Fighter Establishment at West Raynham in the summer of 1946. The report on that trial, excerpts of which are reproduced below, puts figures to the superiority achieved by the first-generation jet fighter. In making a comparison, the properties of their different types of engines needs to be appreciated. The piston engine maintained power throughout the speed range, whereas the jet engine produced maximum power only at the top end of the speed range, which gave the Spitfire an advantage over a jet aircraft at low speeds. The Spitfire XIV used in the trial was a fully operational aircraft fitted with a Griffon 65 engine giving 2,015 hp (1503 kW) at 7,500 ft (2286 m).

Maximum Level Speeds: The Vampire (Goblin II engine) greatly superior in speed to the Spitfire XIV at all heights as shown below:

Approximate speed advantage over Spitfire XIVE:

Altitude	Speed
sea level	140 (225 km/h)
5,000 ft (1525 m)	120 mph (193 km/h)
10,000 ft (3050 m)	110 mph (177 km/h)
15,000 ft (4575 m)	110 mph (177 km/h)
20,000 ft (6100 m)	105 mph (169 km/h)
25,000 ft (7625 m)	85 mph (136 km/h)
30,000 ft (9150 m)	70 mph (112 km/h)
35,000 ft (10675 m)	70 mph (112 km/h)
40,000 ft (12200 m)	90 mph (145 km/h)

Acceleration and Deceleration: With both aircraft in line-abreast formation at a speed of 200 A.S.I. (322 km/h), on the word 'Go' both engines were opened up to a maximum power simultaneously. The Spitfire initially drew ahead, but after a period of approximately 25 seconds the Vampire gradually caught up and quickly accelerated past the Spitfire.
The rate of deceleration for the Spitfire is faster than the Vampire even when the Vampire uses its dive brakes. Once again this shows that the Vampire's dive brakes are not as effective as they should be.
Dive: The two aircraft were put into a 40° dive in line-abreast formation with set throttles at a speed of 250 mph (402 km/h) IAS. The Vampire rapidly drew ahead and kept gaining on the Spitfire.
Zoom Climb: The Vampire and Spitfire XIV in line-abreast formation were put into a 45° dive. When a speed of 400 IAS (644 km/h) had been reached, a zoom climb at fixed throttle settings was carried out at approximately 50°. The Vampire showed itself vastly superior and reached a height 1,000 ft (300 m) in excess of the altitude of the Spitfire in a few seconds, and quickly increased its lead as the zoom climb continued. The same procedure was carried out at full throttle settings and the Vampire's advantage was outstandingly marked.
Climb: The Spitfire XIV climbs approximately 1,000 ft (300 m) per minute faster than the Vampire up to 20,000 ft (6100 m).
Turning Circles: The Vampire is superior to the Spitfire XIV at all heights. The two aircraft were flown in line-astern formation. The Spitfire was positioned on the Vampire's tail. Both aircraft tightened up to the minimum turning circle with maximum power. It became apparent that the Vampire was just able to keep inside the Spitfire's turning circles. After four or five turns the Vampire was able to position itself on the Spitfire's tail so that a deflection shot was possible. The wing loading of the Vampire is 33.1 lb per sq ft (1.3 kg/m²). compared with the Spitfire XIV's 35.1 lb per sq ft (1.47 kg/m²).
Rates of Roll: The Spitfire XIV has a faster rate of roll at all speeds. The higher the speed the faster the Spitfire rolls in comparison with the Vampire. As previously mentioned, at speeds of 500 IAS (805 km/h) there is a feeling of overbalance and aileron snatch when attempting to roll the Vampire.
Combat Manoeuvrability: The Vampire will out-manoeuvre the Spitfire type of aircraft at all heights, except for initial acceleration at low speeds and in rolling. Due to the Vampire's much higher speed and superior zoom climb, the Spitfire can gain no advantage by using its superior rate of climb in combat.

Left: The well-known F.Mk XIVCs of No. 610 'County of Chester' Sqn formate for an official photographer shortly after the unit re-equipped with the type in January 1944. Based at Exeter and then Culmhead, No. 610 moved to West Malling in June to help combat the V-1 offensive. Fifty V-1 kills were claimed by the squadron.

SEAC service

As the war in Europe came to an end, Spitfire Mk XIVs were made available to squadrons in the Far East. In June 1945 No. 11 Sqn, stationed in India, was the first unit outside Europe to receive examples of the variant, but the war ended before they became operational. Nos 17 and 132 Sqns followed suit shortly afterwards, and in late 1945/early 1946 further units in the region were re-equipped, namely Nos 20, 28, 136 (renumbered No. 152 Sqn in May) and 273 Sqns. After the Japanese surrender, the British Commonwealth Air Forces of Occupation (Japan) was established and included Spitfire units Nos 11 and 17 Sqns between April 1946 and 1948 (the former also operating Mk XVIIIs).

a maximum of +25 lb boost to be used; this increased the fighter's speed by about 30 mph (48 km/h) at low altitude, to about 400 mph (644 km/h) at 2,000 ft (610 m).

About 90 per cent of the V-1s shot down by fighters fell out of control and detonated upon hitting the ground; the rest detonated in mid-air. Provided the fighter was more than 150 yd (137 m) from the explosion, there was little risk of serious damage. Sometimes fighters suffered minor damage if they flew through a cloud of burning petrol from the missile's fuel tank, after the detonation, or were hit by small pieces of wreckage hurled great distances by the force of the explosion. It could be hazardous if fighter pilots engaged flying bombs from within 150 yd, however. On 3 August Captain Jean Marie Maridor, a French pilot flying Spitfire Mk XIVs with No. 91 Squadron, was in hot pursuit of a flying bomb heading towards the military hospital at Benenden. Maridor closed to short range to ensure the destruction of the missile, but when he opened fire the warhead detonated. The Spitfire was wrecked and its pilot was killed. In total, Maridor was credited with the destruction of 11 flying bombs, but the last of them took him with it.

Dicing with 'Divers'

The V-1 was controlled by elevators and a rudder, having no ailerons. As a result, the missile was particularly vulnerable to any interference in the rolling plane. Fighter pilots developed the technique of flying alongside the missile, placing a wingtip under that of the flying bomb and then banking steeply to flip the missile out of control. On 20 August Flight Sergeant Paul Leva, a Belgian with No. 350 Squadron based at Hawkinge, was operating in the inner Fighter Patrol Area. Flying one of his unit's recently acquired Spitfire Mk XIVs, he employed this technique to bring down a V-1. Later, he wrote:

"… the bomb went unscathed through the two first

Griffon-engined Spitfire deployment, May 1945

When the war in Europe came to an end, two squadrons of Air Defence of Great Britain were operational with the Spitfire Mk 21. Four squadrons in No. 83 Group in Germany operated the F.Mk XIV and two more operated the FR.Mk XIV. One squadron in No. 84 Group in Holland operated the FR.Mk XIV. In Ceylon one squadron was in the process of equipping with F.Mk XIVs, and several other units in that theatre were scheduled to re-equip with this variant.

ROYAL AIR FORCE
Fighter Command
No. 11 Group

No. 91 Sqn	F.Mk 21	Ludham
No. 1 Sqn	F.Mk 21	Ludham

2nd Tactical Air Force
No. 83 Group (Germany)

Nos 414, 430 Sqns	FR.Mk XIV	Schneverdingen
Nos 41, 130, 350 Sqns	F.Mk XIV	Celle
No. 402 Sqn	F.Mk XIV	Wunstorf

No. 84 Group (Holland)

No. 2 Sqn	FR.Mk XIV	Twente

No. 222 Group (Ceylon)

No. 132 Sqn	F.Mk XIV	Vavuniya

A Spitfire Mk IX-equipped fighter-bomber unit within 2nd TAF during 1944, No. 132 Sqn was transferred to the Far East in early 1945, re-equipping with Mk VIIIs in Ceylon. Preparations for the expected Allied invasion of Malaya coincided with the receipt of Mk XIVs in May, the squadron embarking in HMS Smiter. However, with the Japanese surrender No. 132 was transferred to Hong Kong, sailing into Hong Kong harbour in September (above). The squadron was based at Kai Tak (left) for seven months, engaged in air defence and anti-piracy patrols before disbandment in April 1946.

Far left: No. 136 Sqn moved to India in November 1941, equipped with Hurricanes. From December 1943 the unit operated Spitfire Mk Vs, Mk VIIIs from 1944 and finally Mk XIVs from February 1946. This Mk XIV was probably photographed in Kuala Lumpur.

Below left: Spitfire FR.Mk XIVEs of No. 11 Sqn, RAF are seen at Miho, Japan in about 1946, as part of the Commonwealth occupation force.

Below: No. 273's Sqn's FR.Mk XIVEs were based in Thailand and Indo-China in 1945/46.

Mk XIVs at home and abroad

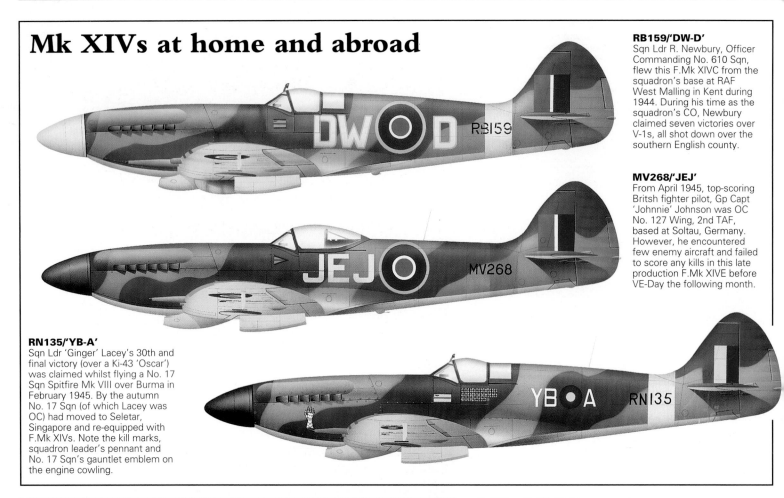

RB159/'DW-D'
Sqn Ldr R. Newbury, Officer Commanding No. 610 Sqn, flew this F.Mk XIVC from the squadron's base at RAF West Malling in Kent during 1944. During his time as the squadron's CO, Newbury claimed seven victories over V-1s, all shot down over the southern English county.

MV268/'JEJ'
From April 1945, top-scoring Britsh fighter pilot, Gp Capt 'Johnnie' Johnson was OC No. 127 Wing, 2nd TAF, based at Soltau, Germany. However, he encountered few enemy aircraft and failed to score any kills in this late production F.Mk XIVE before VE-Day the following month.

RN135/'YB-A'
Sqn Ldr 'Ginger' Lacey's 30th and final victory (over a Ki-43 'Oscar') was claimed whilst flying a No. 17 Sqn Spitfire Mk VIII over Burma in February 1945. By the autumn No. 17 Sqn (of which Lacey was OC) had moved to Seletar, Singapore and re-equipped with F.Mk XIVs. Note the kill marks, squadron leader's pennant and No. 17 Sqn's gauntlet emblem on the engine cowling.

Mk XVIII

Virtually indistinguishable from a late-production FR.Mk XIV, with its 'E' wing and bubble canopy, the Spitfire Mk XVIII differed primarily from the former in having a strengthened wing structure and undercarriage. Performance was very similar to that of the Mk XIV, power coming from the same Griffon 65 engine. The first prototype, NH872, flew in June 1945, too late for the variant to see wartime service. However, six RAF squadrons would eventually fly the type, all of them stationed overseas. The first to re-equip was No. 60 Sqn in Singapore, in January 1947, followed by Nos 11, 28 and 81 Sqns, also in the Far East, and Nos 32 and 208 Sqns in the Middle East. The Mk XVIII production run (mainly to FR.Mk XVIII standard) was comparatively short, 300 being completed before production ended in early 1946.

Above: SM843 was the Mk XVIII production prototype and, although ordered as an F.Mk XVIII, was completed to 'FR' standard, with vertical and oblique camera fittings. '843 became a trials airframe and was sold for scrap in 1953.

Right: A No. 32 Sqn FR.Mk XVIIIE, flown by Flt Lt F. E. Dymond, commander of 'A' Flight, taxis at its dusty base in Palestine during October 1947.

defence lines and, directed by the controller, I duly spotted the ugly little brute with the glowing tail below me. I banked to enter a steep dive, gathering speed and getting nearer and nearer to my target.

"Alas, though, I was not near enough. Soon, with my speed dropping after levelling off, I could see that the

distance separating us did not diminish any more and even began to increase.

"Utterly disappointed, I nevertheless opened fire, aiming high to compensate for the distance. I had the happy surprise to see some impacts and bits flying off the wings. I fired burst after burst, damaging the bomb still more.

FEAF and MEAF actions

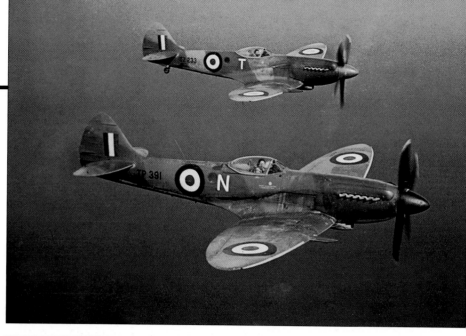

Operating in an environment where there was no effective opposition to air power, the post-war FEAF was required to fly obsolete types like the Spitfire, while the RAF in Europe was equipped with modern machines. Thus, it was in the Far East that the last operational Spitfire sorties took place. Spitfire Mk 14s and 18s of No. 28 Sqn and Mk 18s of Nos 60 and 81 Sqns took part in the opening actions of Operation Firedog, the British campaign against Communist guerrillas on the Malay Peninsula. Spitfires flew ground attack and fighter-reconnaissance sorties in the region until 1951, when No. 60 Sqn became the last RAF unit to use the 'Spit' in an offensive capacity, when it launched a strike against terrorists in the Kota Tinggi area of Johore on 1 January 1951. In the Middle East, Nos 32 and 208 Sqns, equipped with Spitfire Mk Vs and IXs, were deployed to police Palestine in the transition from UN mandate to the State of Israel. Both units re-equipped with Mk 18s, in 1947 and 1946 respectively, their main role being the provision of air support for army units. With the creation of Israel, in May 1948, came attacks by neighbouring Arab states. On 22 May, Ramat David airfield was bombed by Egyptian Spitfire Mk 9s, two of No. 208's Mk 18s being destroyed. A further attack later that day was met with swift resistance, four REAF Spitfires being downed – two by No. 208 Sqn and two by RAF Regiment AA fire. As related elsewhere, No. 208 Squadron also became embroiled in a skirmish with Israeli Spitfires in January 1949, losing four aircraft to IAF pilots.

Although no vital part was hit, its speed diminished and it entered a shallow dive.

"My hopes went soaring again, I was now approaching my target so fast that I had to throttle back. Ready for the kill, I positioned myself at what I estimated was the right distance. I depressed the trigger, but instead of the staccato of firing bullets I heard only the whistling sound of escaping compressed air.

"The voice of the controller came on again: 'Any luck?'

"'No,' I said forlornly. 'I damaged it, but have no ammunition left. It's very slow now and losing height. I am practically flying in formation with it.'

"'Tough luck,' said the controller. 'Time to turn back now – you are getting very near the balloon barrage.'

"It was then that suddenly, spurred no doubt by my frustration, I remembered the briefing of the intelligence officer [who earlier had spoken of sending V-1s out of control by tipping up one wing].

"'Wait,' I said. 'I think I can try something.' Adjusting the throttle I eased myself forward until I came abreast the bomb. What a sight it was at close range! The wings were so ragged with the impact of the bullets that I wondered how it could still fly almost straight and level.

"Positioning myself slightly underneath, I placed my starboard wingtip under the port wing of the bomb. I came up slowly, made contact with it as softly as I could, and then moved the stick violently back and to the left.

"This made me enter a steep climbing turn and I lost

sight of the bomb. I continued turning fast through 360°. Then I saw it – well below me, going down steeply, hitting the ground and exploding with a blinding flash."

The wingtip of the Spitfire made a poor battering ram. When Leva landed at Hawkinge he found that his fighter's wingtip was badly bent where it had come into contact with the V-1. The wing tip had to be replaced.

Above: No. 208 Sqn's Mk 18s saw considerable action in the Middle East, with the mixed fortunes of victory over REAF Spitfires, and somewhat humiliating overwhelming defeat at the hands of IDF Spitfires.

Left: Spitfire FR.Mk 18 TZ240 taxis past a guard post sandbagged against terrorist attack at Ein Shemar airfield, Palestine in 1948. When No. 208 Sqn repainted its aircraft with Type 'D' roundels and fin flashes, the squadron's 'RG' code letters were abandoned. Single aircraft letters were retained.

Above: No. 60 Sqn's Mk 18s were equipped as fighter-bombers, their cameras replaced with extra internal fuel capacity. This line-up, including TP197 nearest the camera, was photographed at Kuala Lumpur in 1950.

Left: During the Korean War, Spitfire Mk 18s of No. 28 Sqn, FEAF carried recognition stripes, though the unit was not involved in the conflict. This aircraft was photographed at Kai Tak in late 1950.

Above: No. 681 Sqn, formed in 1943 from No. 3 PRU at Dum Dum, near Calcutta, operated PR.Mk XIXs from July 1945, these aircraft supplementing and eventually replacing Spitfire Mk XIs. By then based at Palam, the unit was renumbered No. 34 Sqn on 1 August 1946, and survived another 12 months before disbanding. Here five of the squadron's aircraft, including PM545/'A', are seen at Palam in 1946/47.

Long-serving Mk XIX

Built to replace the PR.Mk XI as the RAF's primary single-engined reconnaissance type, the Spitfire Mk XIX entered service with No. 542 Sqn in May 1944. Equipping seven PR squadrons by war's end, the bulk of Mk XIXs was flown in the European theatre, though a number also served in the Middle and Far East.

Above left: The seventh production Mk XIX, RM632 was built without a pressure cabin. Delivered to RAF Benson on 6 May 1945, it had reached No. 542 Sqn by 4 June. RM632 failed to return from a PR sortie on 6 January 1945 – one of the RAF's last Spitfire losses of the war.

Top and above: Though completed in early 1945, PS858 did not reach an operational unit until the following year, having been flown by A&AEE Boscombe Down during trials of 90- and 170-Imp gal (409- and 773-litre) drop tanks. The latter is depicted in these views of the aircraft. Visible below the aircraft's exhausts is the air intake for the Griffon 66 engine's cabin pressurisation blower.

Later, pilots developed a more elegant method of disposing of V-1s if they could move into a position alongside it. The fighter's wing was placed over the top of that of the V-1, thus destroying the lift on that side of the flying bomb and forcing the V-1 into a steep bank from which it was unable to recover. The great advantage of this method was that there was no physical contact between the two aircraft, so the fighter suffered no damage.

'Wing tipping'

The 'wing tipping' tactic could be used only against V-1s flying relatively slowly, which explains why the method accounted for only a very small proportion of the missiles brought down. The great majority of V-1s destroyed by fighters fell to cannon fire. Three days after Leva sent his V-1 down out of control, Flight Lieutenant T. Spencer of No. 41 Squadron achieved the rare feat of destroying two missiles in a single sortie. The facts that he was flying the Spitfire Mk XII – which was slower than the Mk XIV – and the weather conditions were far from perfect, made his accomplishment all the more remarkable. The report on the action stated:

"Red Section [2 aircraft] airborne 0805 to 0915 from Lympne, under Kingsley 11 Control on Ashford [area] Patrol, was informed that flying bomb was approaching East of Folkestone. Seeing AA fire F/Lt T. Spencer dived from 9000' to 2000' and saw Diver [codename for V-1] at 10 o'clock 1000' above, over a point some 2 miles south of Mersham in hazy visibility. The Diver at 3000' on course

Below: PM655 carries the '6C' code of the Photo-Reconnaissance Development Unit at RAF Benson around 1950.

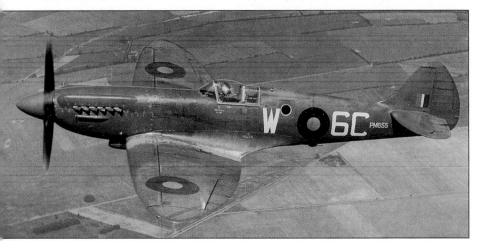

310° was travelling at 240 mph.

"Climbing, F/Lt Spencer opened fire with one- and two- second bursts. Closing from 250 yards to 80 yards from astern and slightly below, seeing strikes on the jet. He overshot the Diver and saw it go down near railway line at approximately R 5056 at 0820 hours.

"On the same patrol and under Kingsley 11 Control from Ashford F/Lt Spencer was informed that Diver would pass 4 miles due W of Ashford. Seeing flares [fired from Observer Corps posts on the ground to indicate the passage of a V-1 overhead] he dived from 10,000' and saw Diver at 2 o'clock. Closed and saw no strikes from 4-second burst. A second burst of 2 seconds obtained strikes on port side of fuselage and port wing root. The petrol tank exploded with black smoke and Diver flicked to port and went in north of railway line near Harrietsham R 3171 at 0907 hours. Diver was at 2500' on 340° doing 360 mph. Weather hazy."

In total, Spencer shot down six flying bombs, all while flying the Spitfire Mk XII. The top-scoring Spitfire pilots against the V-1s all flew Mk XIVs, however. Flying Officer R. Burgwal of No. 322 Squadron, a Dutchman, was credited with 21 of the missiles destroyed. Squadron Leader N. Kynaston and Flight Lieutenant R. Nash, both of No. 91 Squadron, were credited with 17 and 16 flying bombs, respectively.

The first phase of the V-1 bombardment on London came to an end in September 1944. Following the end of that commitment, in October the first three Spitfire Mk XIV squadrons redeployed to airfields in France and Belgium. In following weeks, four more squadrons

Mk XI/XIV hybrid

The Spitfire Mk 19 effectively combined the wing tankage and camera installation of the Merlin-engined Mk XI with the Griffon power of the Mk XIV. With the range of the former and the performance of the latter, the Mk 19 was an outstanding reconnaissance aircraft that was destined to serve the RAF for 10 years in the absence of a jet-powered replacement with sufficient range.

Supermarine Spitfire PR.Mk 19 No. 81 Squadron, RAF Seletar March 1954

Delivered to No. 6 Maintenance Unit on 30 March 1945, PS888 moved to RAF Benson in April before being issued to No. 542 Sqn (the first unit to operate the type) on 17 June. Two days before Christmas 1950 the aircraft was shipped to the Far East where, on 1 April 1954, '888 (suitably named *The Last!*) had the distinction of flying the last sortie by an operational RAF Spitfire.

Performance

The Mk 19 had a top speed close to that of the Mk XIV fighter, though with a full fuel load its climb performance was rather worse. Cruising speeds of 370 mph (595 km/h) at 40,000 ft (12192 m) were generally sufficient to keep it out of reach of German wartime jets. During exercises after the war, Mk 19s were regularly flown at heights of 49,000 ft (14935 m) during PR sorties; not until the introduction of swept-wing jet fighters was the Spitfire Mk 19 seriously threatened.

Fuel capacity

The first 25 production Mk 19s had larger leading-edge fuel tanks than later aircraft, with a capacity of 86 Imp gal (391 litres) each. Total internal fuel capacity was increased to 256 gal (1164 litres), some 3½ times greater than that of the Spitfire prototype. Mk 19s frequently flew with external fuel, carried in a 90-Imp gal (409-litre) centreline slipper tank.

Colours and markings

During wartime service, Spitfire Mk 19s were finished, like most of the RAF's high-altitude PR assets, in PRU Blue, with low-visibility Type 'B' roundels and a standard three-colour fin flash. Post-war aircraft differed in having Type 'D' roundels applied over a modified PRU Blue paint scheme, with grey upper fuselage surfaces.

Griffon 65/66

The first 25 Mk 19s were completed without cabin pressurisation and therefore without the need for a cabin blower drive. The addition of this feature to the Griffon 65 (which powered these early aircraft) resulted in the Griffon 66, this variant powering the other 200 examples completed.

Last sortie

On 9 July 1957, PS853 brought 19 years of continuous RAF service by the Spitfire to a close when, in the hands of Flight Lieutenant J. Formby, it made the last operational flight by an RAF Spitfire. The meteorological sortie began at RAF Woodvale, Lancashire, base of the Temperature and Humidity Flight, and concluded at the same station at 1118 hours that day.

'Super Spitfire'

In order to fully exploit the power of the Griffon 60-series engine, Supermarine knew that a new Spitfire variant, with a considerably stiffer wing, would be needed. Spitfire Mk 21 was the designation given to the project, though consideration was allocating an entirely new name to the aircraft – Victor. The first aircraft modified was Mk XX DP851. This 'interim Mk 21' aircraft was fitted with a Griffon 61 and modified wings with a revised internal structure, thicker gauge skinning and pointed tips. A broad-chord rudder and redesigned cockpit windscreen and curved canopy were other features and, although it initially flew with a four-bladed propeller, a five-bladed example was soon substituted. Flight tests were promising, but the aircraft was written-off in a landing accident in May 1943. The true 'F.Mk 21 Victor' prototype (as it was briefly known), was PP139. This aircraft flew in July and differed from DP851 in a number of respects. It had bigger ailerons which gave the wing a straighter leading edge – the first change to basic outline of the Spitfire's wing since the Mk I. It also had pointed wingtips (later removed), increased wing tankage, four 20-mm cannon (no machine-guns) and redesigned undercarriage to improve ground handling and increase clearance for its 11-ft (3.35-m) propeller. The first production Mk 21 (LA187) flew in March 1944, though the solution of handling problems postponed the issue of aircraft to No. 91 Sqn until January 1945.

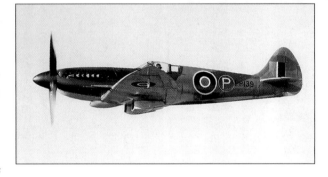

The second Griffon-engined Spitfire (the Mk XX), DP851, is seen here (top right) in original 'Victor' guise, re-engined with a Griffon 61 driving a four-bladed propeller. The latter was later replaced with a five-bladed unit (middle right).

Right: In this view of PP139 its revised windscreen, cockpit canopy, pointed wingtips and four-cannon armament are readily discernible.

Far right: LA235 was one of a number of Mk 21s tested with a Griffon 85 engine and contra-prop. Though popular with pilots at the CFE and AFDU, its unreliability, extra weight and expense counted against it.

Below: No. 91 Sqn's Spitfire Mk 21s, based at RAF Ludham in Norfolk, carried 'DL' unit codes.

equipped with the new variant joined them: Nos 41, 130, 350 and 403 Squadrons.

For the remainder of the war, the Spitfire Mk XIV was the RAF's primary high-altitude air superiority fighter type operating over northern Europe. During their initial operations over Europe, the Mk XIV units were constrained by bad weather and the poor condition of the newly captured airfields. The units spent most their time on armed reconnaissance missions, strafing vehicles and railway rolling stock when they could be found. There were few encounters with enemy aircraft, especially the sought-after jet types. Mk XIV pilots had fleeting encounters with the latter, before Flight Lieutenant Fredrick Gaze of No. 610 Squadron shot down a Messerschmitt Me 262 fighter-bomber near Munster on 14 February. On 12 April Gaze had another success, when he was credited with a half share of the destruction of an Arado Ar 234. On 19 April Pilot Officer 'Blackie' MacConnell of No. 402 (Canadian) Squadron caught an Arado Ar 234 jet bomber on the landing approach for Lübeck/Blankensee airfield and shot it down.

During the final weeks of the war, as the Allied forces

Mk 21s at war – briefly

Though over 3,000 Mk 21s were ordered (almost all to be built by CBAF), mass cancellations meant that only 120 were completed. No. 91 Sqn's modified aircraft were finally operational by April 1945, and by VE-Day in May, No. 1 Sqn was working-up on the type. The only other front-line RAF units to fly the Mk 21 were Nos 122 and 41 Sqns, from February and April 1946, respectively.

No. 41 Sqn F.Mk 21s bask in the summer sun at Lübeck, Germany, shortly after VE-Day.

First with Mk 21s

LA224/'DL-V'
Delivered to No. 91 Squadron on 9 March 1945, LA224 was the 38th production Mk 21 and among the unit's operational aircraft based at Ludham at the end of the war. The variant's front-line career was to be rather short, No. 91 Sqn re-equipping with Meteor F.Mk 3s in October 1946. LA224 was finally struck off charge on 22 August 1947.

advanced deeper into Germany, the Spitfire Mk XIV units had more opportunities to engage. Typical of the hectic days was 20 April, when Nos 41, 130, 350 and 402 Squadrons all saw action. The units' total claims were 14 Fw 190s, two Bf 109s and an Me 262. The period of heavy fighting continued until the first week in May, then it petered out. On the morning of 5 May, No. 130 Squadron sent a pair of Mk XIVs to patrol the Hamburg area. Flight Lieutenant Gibbins and W/O Seymore sighted a Siebel Si 204 light transport and shot it down, the final victory claimed by the Royal Air Force over Europe during World War II.

Production of the Mk XIV came to an end late in 1945, with a total 957 fighter and fighter reconnaissance versions (reconnaissance variants of the Spitfire were described in detail in *Wings of Fame* Volume 5).

Throughout the Mk XIV's production run, the variant underwent continual changes, as a result of which the final aircraft off the line were considerably more effective fighting machines than those which had appeared early in 1944. The first improvement was the introduction of the Mk II Gyro gunsight. This device calculated automatically the deflection angle, that is to say, the distance ahead of the target that a pilot needed to aim to hit an enemy aircraft. The system worked on the principal that if a pilot followed an enemy aircraft into the turn and held his gunsight on the aircraft, the rate of turn was proportional to the deflection angle required to hit the enemy. A gyroscope measured the rate of turn, and tilted a mirror which moved the position of the sighting graticule to show the required deflection angle. The deflection angle increased with range, however, so the gunsight incorporated a simple optical system for measuring range. Before the engagement the pilot set on the sight the approximate wingspan of the enemy aircraft. As he closed on the enemy aircraft, he operated a control mounted on the throttle arm to adjust the diameter of the sighting graticule so that it appeared the same size as the

enemy plane's wingspan. Since the wingspan of the target aircraft had been set on the sight, the adjustment of the graticule 'told' the gunsight the range of the target. An analog computer in the gunsight worked out the correct point ahead of the target at which the pilot should aim in order to score hits. Once fighter pilots got used to the new sight, the general accuracy of air-to-air deflection shooting improved dramatically.

Early production Mk XIV aircraft were fitted with the 'C' type wing, with the standard armament of two 20-mm Hispano cannon with 120 rounds of ammunition each, and four 0.303-in machine-guns, with 350 rounds each. Later production aircraft featured the 'E' type wing, with two Browning 0.5-in machine-guns with 250 rounds each, instead of the four 0.303-in weapons. The 0.5-in machine-gun delivered a heavier penetrative punch than the smaller weapon it replaced, and was far more effective against air-to-air and air-to-ground targets. Aircraft fitted with the 'E' type wing were readily identifiable because the 20-mm

The first Griffon-Spitfire operator, No. 41 Sqn, was also an early recipient of the F.Mk 21. These photographs were taken at Lübeck shortly after the end of the war. LA226 (above) was one of the few Mk 21 airframes still extant in 1999. It was stored at the RAF Museum Restoration & Storage Centre at RAF Cardington. Other known survivors are LA198, under restoration in Scotland for eventual display in Glasgow, and LA255, owned by the No. 1 Sqn Association and stored at RAF Wittering.

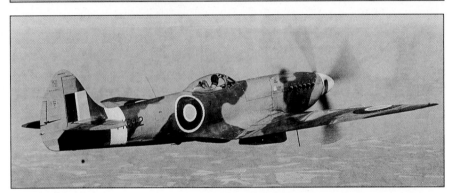

Top: This colour view of a Mk 22 shows well the revised planform of the Mk 20-series Spitfires, with a straighter leading edge.

Above: Mk 22 prototype PK312 is seen here in its original configuration, with its Mk 21-type tailfin. Its performance was on a par with that of the Mk 21.

Above right: Towards the end of 1945, PK312 was fitted with an enlarged tailfin and tailplane of the type first flown on the 3rd Spiteful prototype in June 1945. Note also the outer set of undercarriage doors, introduced on the Mk 21.

The same, but different

The only differences between the Mk 21 and its successor, the Mk 22, were the latter's cut-down rear fuselage and bubble canopy, changes that in the past had not resulted in the issue of a new mark number. The first example, PK312, was delivered in March 1945. Handling problems that plagued the new Spitfire designs were finally addressed towards the end of 1945, when enlarged tail surfaces, to the same design as those fitted to the Supermarine Spiteful, were incorporated in the Mk 22. Production totalled 278, though only one regular RAF squadron flew this variant – No. 73 Sqn – which converted to the type from Spitfire Mk XIs while based on Malta in 1947. Within a year, however, they had been replaced by de Havilland Vampires; the bulk of Mk 22 production was delivered to the RAuxAF, equipping 12 squadrons.

bubble-type canopies. The change brought an enormous improvement in rear view compared with the earlier canopy. With this modification, the pilot could see around the fin and past it as far as the tip of the tailplane on the opposite side. By banking the aircraft slightly during weaving action, the view into the danger area behind and below the fighter was also much improved. Production aircraft fitted with bubble canopies began reaching the operational squadrons early in 1945 and they immediately became popular with pilots.

The Mk 18

The Spitfire Mk XIV had been a hasty improvisation, combining the airframe of the Mk VIII with the Griffon 61 engine. The fighter proved a success, despite pilots having to be careful not to overstress the aircraft in combat. The 'definitive' Spitfire variant, the Mk 21 (described below), had a redesigned wing built to cope with much higher stress factors, but there would be delays in bringing it into front-line service. As an interim measure, the Spitfire Mk 18 was produced. Externally, this variant resembled the late production Mk XIV fitted with the 'E' type wing and armament, bubble canopy and additional fuel tanks in the rear fuselage. The Mk 18 featured a strengthened wing, which restored the fighter's strength factors, and incorporated a strengthened undercarriage to cope with greater take-off weights. The Mk 18 made its maiden flight in June 1945, too late to play any part in World War II; however, it later played an important part in the Royal Air Force's post-war overseas deployment.

Had the war continued into 1946, this definitive fighter variant of the Spitfire was set to become the RAF's main air superiority type. Powered by the Griffon 65 engine, it featured a completely redesigned wing with a much-strengthened internal structure. The new variant carried the four 20-mm cannon armament as standard. The first production prototype of the Mk 21, PP139, made its maiden flight in July 1943.

The new variant differed from its predecessors in several respects. To improve rolling performance, the ailerons were 5 per cent larger in area than those of early Spitfires. Instead of the Frise balance type used earlier, the ailerons were attached with piano-type hinges pivoting on the upper surface. As another innovation, balance was achieved using balance tabs. To improve ground handling, the track of the main undercarriage was widened by 7¾ in (19.7 cm). The five-bladed propeller was 11 ft (3.34 m) in diameter, 7 in (17.8 cm) larger than that of the Mk XIV. To provide the necessary ground clearance, the length of the main wheel oleo legs was increased by 4½ in (11.4 cm). Initially, PP139 was fitted with a revised, curved windscreen, and a fin with a straight leading edge; later, however, the shapes of these

cannon were moved from the inboard to the outboard cannon positions, about 12 in (30 cm) further out. On each side, the 0.5-in machine-gun occupied the vacant inboard cannon position.

To improve the view in the all-important rear sector, towards the end of 1944 Mk XIVs began coming off the production line fitted with cut-back rear fuselages and

Like the Mk 21 before it, the Mk 22 was tested with a Griffon 85 and contra-prop. Prototype PK312 was so-equipped from September 1946, while late-production example and ex-No. 615 Sqn, RAuxAF aircraft PK664 (left) followed suit after its sale to Vickers in 1954. This aircraft was stored at RAF Museum Restoration & Storage Centre at RAF Cardington in 1999.

Post-war RAuxAF ops

Large numbers of Spitfires served with Royal Auxiliary Air Force fighter units between 1946 and 1951. As well as Merlin-engined Mk IXs and XVIs, Griffon-engined Mk 14s, 21s and 22s were operated by 12 RAuxAF squadrons at different times.

features reverted to those of the Mk XIV.

The first production Mk 21, LA187, made its maiden flight in March 1944. It featured the new wing, with extended-span pointed tips, and Mk XIV-type fin and rudder. In November 1944 the prototype Mk 21 underwent a brief trial at Boscombe Down, where service pilots were unanimous in condemning the fighter's unpleasant handling characteristics:

"The rudder trimmer tab was very sensitive and required a very delicate touch to trim the aircraft for flight without yawing. This latter characteristic was accentuated by the large change of directional trim with speed, power and applied acceleration, rendering it necessary for the pilot to retrim the aircraft frequently during manoeuvres in order to avoid what appeared to be dangerous angles of sideslip.

"The directional qualities of the aircraft deteriorated markedly with altitude and also noticeably with aft movement of the cg. The bad directional qualities, linked with their effect on the longitudinal control, gave rise to very peculiar corkscrew behaviour of the aircraft, particularly at high Mach numbers, and at none of the loadings tested did the pilot feel comfortable when carrying out combat manoeuvres in the region of the aircraft's optimum performance altitude [25,000 ft/7620 m]."

For a fighter aircraft, these were serious shortcomings. Good directional handling qualities over a wide range of speeds and altitudes are an important attribute for an air superiority fighter, since during operations its success depended on its stability as a gun platform.

While the Boscombe Down trials were in progress, pilots at the Air Fighting Development Unit conducted tests to assess the Mk 21's value as a fighting aircraft. Their comments on the fighter's handling were even more scathing than those stated above:

"Whilst this aircraft is not unstable in pitch, above

25,000 ft the instability in yaw makes it behave as if it were unstable about all three axes. Because of its higher wing loading the high-speed stall comes in earlier than with other marks of Spitfire and in a steep turn the general feeling of instability, combined with its critical trimming qualities, is unpleasant. The control characteristics are such that this aircraft is most difficult to fly accurately and compares most unfavourably with other modern fighters."

The AFDU report concluded with a list of recommendations that could not have been more damning

Above and below: No. 600 'City of London' Sqn reformed at Biggin Hill on 10 May 1946, as a Royal Auxiliary Air Force unit. Initial equipment consisted of Spitfire Mk XIVEs (one of eight RAuxAF squadrons so-equipped), to which were added Mk 21s in March 1947.

Left: No. 602 'City of Glasgow' Sqn had the longest association with Spitfires of any RAF squadron, stretching as it did over 12 almost continuous years. The squadron first re-equipped with Spitfire Mk Is in May 1939 and later flew aircraft of Marks II, V, VI, IX, XVI, XIV, 21 (seen here) and 22. The unit's last Mk 22 was retired in early 1951.

Top: RAuxAF squadrons were allocated codes in the 'RAx' range, 'RAT' being that of No. 613 'City of Manchester'. This unit reformed as an auxiliary unit at Ringway in 1946, initially with Spitfire Mk 14s. They were replaced with Mk 22s in late 1948. Note that the aircraft retain the wartime ADGB camouflage applied before they left the factory.

Above: Eventually RAuxAF aircraft lost their camouflage, gained Type 'D' roundels and, in some cases, unit bars either side of the fuselage roundel, in the style of some regular squadrons. PK570/'F' is a Mk 22 of No. 603 'City of Edinburgh' Sqn.

to this latest Spitfire variant:

"It is recommended that the Spitfire Mk 21 be withdrawn from operations until the instability in the yawing plane has been removed and that it be replaced by the Spitfire XIV or Tempest until this can be done. If this is not possible then it must be emphasised that, although the Spitfire Mk 21 is not a dangerous aircraft to fly, pilots must be warned of its handling qualities and in its present state it is not likely to prove a satisfactory fighter.

"No further attempts should be made to perpetuate the Spitfire family."

The highly critical comments could not have come at a more embarrassing stage in the production programme. The Ministry of Aircraft Production had issued contracts for nearly 3,000 Spitfire Mk 21s. At the huge Castle Bromwich complex outside Birmingham, work was in full swing to retool the works to begin mass production of the new variant. Moreover, with each day that passed, more aircraft from the initial batch were coming off the line – all with the same poor handling characteristics as their predecessors.

Commenting on this unpleasant situation from his viewpoint as Supermarine's chief test pilot, Jeffrey Quill said:

"From the time I first flew the Spitfire 21 it was clear that we had a hot potato. There was too much power for the aeroplane and what was needed were much larger tail surfaces, both horizontal and vertical. The work to design and build these was already in hand, but would take several months to complete. In the meantime the great production 'sausage machine' was already rolling. So the immediate problem was to make the handling of the Mk 21 in the air reasonably tolerable, so that the aeroplane would be operationally viable pending the happy day when the much larger tail did become available … The AFDU were quite right to criticise the handling of the Mk 21, although in my opinion their report overdid it a bit. Where they went terribly wrong was to recommend that all further development of the Spitfire family should cease. They were quite unqualified to make such a judgement, and later events would prove them totally wrong."

The root cause of the fighter's problem was over-control, and in each case modifications to the controls provided a cure. Supermarine experimented with several expedients: different types of tabs, anti-balance tabs, changes to the horn-balanced area, etc. In the end, the over-control in the rudder sense was cured by removing the balance action of the rudder trim tab. The over-control in the elevator sense was cured by reducing the gearing to the elevator trim tab by half, and by fitting metal-covered elevators with rounded horn balances of reduced area.

It took three months to select and develop the various changes and incorporate them in a Mk 21, LA215. In March 1945 pilots at the AFDU flew the modified Spitfire, and commented on its suitability as a sighting platform:

"There has been considerable improvement in the qualities of the aircraft as a sighting platform and it is considered that the average pilot should be able to hold his sight on the target throughout all combat manoeuvres. The rudder was noticeably heavier than on the production aircraft and this reduced the amount of unintentional side-slip, except at speeds in excess of 400 mph [644 km/h] Indicated when the pilot is liable to over-correct."

Their report on the modified Mk 21 concluded by giving the variant a clean bill of health:

"The critical trimming characteristics reported on the production Spitfire 21 have been largely eliminated by the modifications carried out on this aircraft. Its handling qualities have benefited to a corresponding extent and it is now considered suitable both for instrument flying and low flying.

"It is considered that the modifications carried out on the Spitfire 21 make it a satisfactory combat aircraft for the average pilot."

The modifications to the controls were rapidly incorporated into aircraft on the production line. By then, No. 91 Squadron based at Manston had already begun to re-equip with unmodified Spitfire 21s; as modified aircraft became available, they were delivered to the unit and the unmodified machines were sent away for modification. By

One of a number of Spitfire Mk 22s known to have participated in air races during the late 1940s/early 1950s, this No. 607 'County of Durham' Sqn aircraft displays a prominent race number on the occasion of 1948 Cooper Trophy air race.

Mk 23 – a Valiant attempt

The Valiant, as it was to have been named, was a Spitfire Mk 21 derivative with which engineers attempted to make use of the latest research into wing aerodynamics, research that ultimately led to the laminar flow wing and its adoption for the Supermarine Type 371 Spiteful. In the interim, Supermarine proposed the 'Type 372 Spitfire F.Mk 23', which used a normal Mk 21 wing raised by 2 in (5.08 cm) at the leading-edge in order to improve the pilot's view and increase speed without increasing drag or pitching movement appreciably. The new wing was tested on Spitfire Mk VIII JG204, but results were disappointing. Mk 21 PP139 was then modified as an 'F.Mk 23', incorporating the revised wing and a new tailfin with a straight leading edge (right). Testing began in 1944, a contract for 438 'laminar flow wing LF.Mk VIII (F.Mk 23)' aircraft having been placed. However, by this time the F.1/43 (Spiteful) prototype had flown, leaving the Valiant dead in the water. PP139 reverted to Mk 21 standard and was eventually scrapped at Eastleigh.

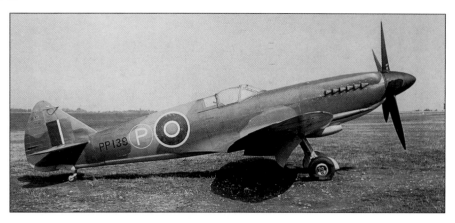

the early part of April 1945, the squadron had received its full complement of 18 modified aircraft. On 8 April the unit was declared operational, and it moved to Ludham in Norfolk.

On the morning of 10 April the new variant flew its first combat sorties, when two aircraft carried out an uneventful armed reconnaissance of The Hague in Holland looking for V–2 launching activity. That afternoon the Mk 21 fired its guns in anger for the first time, when a flight of four aircraft strafed shipping off the Dutch coast. In the ensuing firefight two of the new Spitfires were shot down, but in each case the pilot was rescued.

Following this inauspicious start to the career of the Mk 21, the squadron settled into its operational routine. The main fare was armed reconnaissance missions over Holland, combined with patrols off the coast looking for German midget submarines operating in that area. These missions bore fruit on the morning 26 April, when Flight Lieutenants W. Marshall and J. Draper caught a Biber-type one-man submarine on the surface off The Hook. Each Spitfire carried out two strafing runs on the boat with

cannon. Following the last attack run, the submarine was seen to be sinking and stationary; as it disappeared, it left a large patch of oil and wreckage on the surface.

During its four weeks of operations before the war came to an end, No. 91 Squadron flew a total of 154 operational sorties with the Mk 21. Combat losses amounted to two of the new fighters, both of them on the first day.

The Seafire F.Mk XV and F.Mk 17

The Seafire Mk XV was essentially a navalised version of the Spitfire Mk XII, but without the latter's clipped wings The new naval fighter was powered by the same Griffon IV engine with single-stage supercharger, developing 1,735 hp (1294 kW). The Mk XV had a maximum speed 383 mph (616 km/h) at 13,500 ft (4115 m), giving a useful improvement in performance over the earlier marks. The variant went into production in the winter of 1944, but it entered service too late to see action.

Production Mk XV and later Seafire variants were fitted with a 'sting'-type arrester hook, which extended from the

Post-war 'Spits'

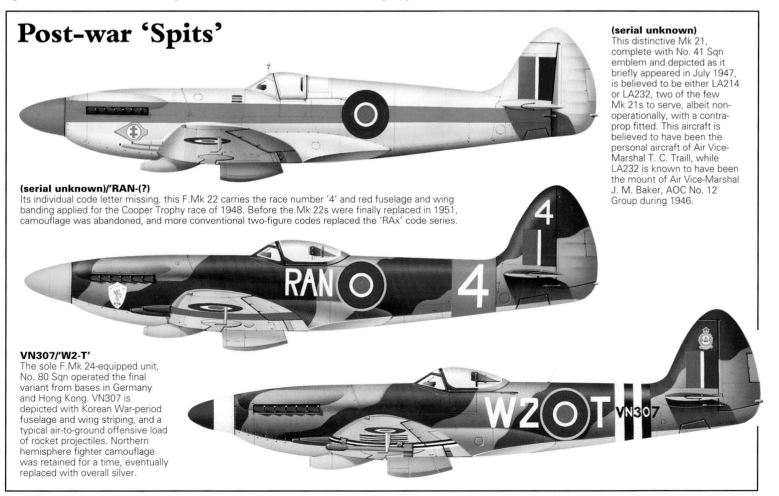

(serial unknown)/'RAN-(?)
Its individual code letter missing, this F.Mk 22 carries the race number '4' and red fuselage and wing banding applied for the Cooper Trophy race of 1948. Before the Mk 22s were finally replaced in 1951, camouflage was abandoned, and more conventional two-figure codes replaced the 'RAx' code series.

VN307/'W2-T'
The sole F.Mk 24-equipped unit, No. 80 Sqn operated the final variant from bases in Germany and Hong Kong. VN307 is depicted with Korean War-period fuselage and wing striping, and a typical air-to-ground offensive load of rocket projectiles. Northern hemisphere fighter camouflage was retained for a time, eventually replaced with overall silver.

(serial unknown)
This distinctive Mk 21, complete with No. 41 Sqn emblem and depicted as it briefly appeared in July 1947, is believed to be either LA214 or LA232, two of the few Mk 21s to serve, albeit non-operationally, with a contra-prop fitted. This aircraft is believed to have been the personal aircraft of Air Vice-Marshal T. C. Traill, while LA232 is known to have been the mount of Air Vice-Marshal J. M. Baker, AOC No. 12 Group during 1946.

Mk 24 – the last word

Not only the last word in piston-engined fighter design, but one of the last such aircraft to enter service as the jet age dawned, the Mk 24 brought the development of the land-based variants of Reginald Mitchell's interceptor to a close. Though recognisable as a Spitfire, the Mk 24 was far removed from and bore little relation to the Mk I of 1938. Its engine (a Griffon 61) produced over twice the power of the Merlin 'C', the airframe was considerably larger and weighed in at just over 10,000 lb (4536 kg) all up – a loaded Mk I topped 5,800 lb (2631 kg) – and its 20-mm cannon armament packed considerably more punch than the Mk I's eight 0.303-in machine-guns. In fact, the Mk 24 differed little from the Mk 22. The main differences were the addition of two small fuselage fuel tanks and fittings for the carriage of underwing rocket projectiles. Late production examples had Hispano Mk V cannon, with shorter barrels than those fitted to the earlier example. Supermarine built 54 Mk 24s to which were added a further 27, converted from Mk 22s.

Above: Completed in February 1946 as the 14th production F.Mk 24, PK713 saw no service use and was eventually scrapped in 1956.

extreme tail of the aircraft and gave it a better chance of picking up one of the arrester wires. A few late production Seafire Mk XVs, and all F.Mk 17s, featured a cut-back rear fuselage and bubble canopy. The F.Mk 17 featured several detailed improvements over its predecessor, including the fitting of extended-stroke oleo legs to the undercarriage to give useful additional clearance for the propeller during deck landings. The Mk 17 also had provision to carry more fuel in underwing tanks stressed for combat.

The Seafire F.Mk XV equipped nine first-line units. The F.Mk 17 replaced it in three units, and equipped two others, before it passed out of first-line service in 1949.

The Seafire 45 was a navalised version of the Spitfire F.Mk 21. The prototype appeared in October 1944, fitted with a sting-type arrester hook, naval radio equipment and

slinging points. Flight tests revealed that the modified Mk 21 was unsuitable for deck operations, however. The powerful Griffon 61 engine, driving a five-bladed propeller, produced an uncomfortable twisting moment when the aircraft flew at high power settings at low airspeeds. This manifested itself in a marked tendency for the fighter to 'crab' during take-off or when it climbed away after a missed approach. Moreover, the revised wing fitted to the F.Mk 45 had to undergo a lengthy redesign if it was to fold. As a result, the 50 F.Mk 45s built were all confined to trials and second-line tasks.

The Seafire F.Mk 46, the penultimate step on the Seafire's evolutionary ladder, featured the cut-back rear fuselage, bubble canopy and broad-chord fin and rudder fitted to production Spitfire F.Mk 22s. Also, and more importantly for the Seafire's continued life as a naval fighter, the Griffon 87 engine drove a Rotol six-bladed contra-rotating propeller. The latter gave torque-free

Hong Kong's Mk 24s

Just one RAF unit operated Spitfire Mk 24s – No. 80 Sqn – based at Gütersloh, Germany. The first examples reached the squadron in January 1948, but in July 1949 the squadron moved to Kai Tak, Hong Kong to reinforce the colony in the face of the Communist threat from mainland China. In Hong Kong its complement of aircraft was eventually to include VN496, the last production Spitfire of all, completed at the South Marston factory in February 1948. No. 80 Sqn operated its Spitfires until January 1952, when they were replaced with de Havilland Hornets, bringing the front-line service of the Spitfire fighter in the RAF to an end.

Right: Upon arrival in Hong Kong harbour, No. 80 Sqn Spitfire VN314 is craned from the carrier HMS Ocean on to a lighter for transfer ashore.

Below and below right: Kai Tak airfield and the mountainous terrain around the colony were home to No. 80 Sqn's 'W2'-coded F.Mk 24s for 2½ years, the squadron eventually operating at least 40 of the 54 production examples.

power at all speeds, bringing about a vast improvement in deck handling characteristics compared with those of its predecessor. The F.Mk 46 still lacked wing-folding, however, so this variant was also unsuitable for first-line embarked operations. Only 24 examples were built.

The definitive Seafire

Externally, the F.Mk 47, the definitive Seafire variant, looked little different from the F.Mk 46. The most significant change was the installation of a completely new type of folding wing, with only one fold on each side. To keep within the 16-ft (4.9-m) hangar ceiling limit, the hinge line was moved farther outboard from the main wheel legs than it had been with the earlier system. Production versions of the Seafire 47 were fitted with a hydraulically-powered wing-folding system operated from the cockpit. This innovation greatly reduced the demands on the overworked deck handling teams. Other changes to the Mk 47 included an extension of the carburettor air intake to a position under the extreme nose, 20 per cent greater flap area, and long-stroke oleo legs to absorb the shock of landing at higher weights than previously. Production aircraft were built as FR.Mk 47s, able to carry one vertical and one oblique camera in the rear fuselage. The variant also had a fighter-bomber capability, with provision to carry a load of up to 1,500 lb (680 kg) of bombs or eight rockets.

The Royal Navy placed an order for 90 Seafire FR.Mk 47s, but following the end of World War II the urgency went out of the production programme. The aircraft were built at a rate of only about three per month, with the result that it took until January 1948 to amass enough fighters to form the first operational unit. No. 804 Squadron exchanged its F.Mk XVs for FR.Mk 47s, and later that year it took its new aircraft to sea aboard the light fleet carrier *Ocean*.

In April 1949 No. 800 Squadron became the second

Exported aircraft

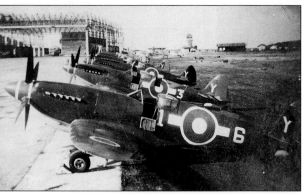

Mk XV – the first 'Griffon-Seafire'

Above and right: Had the war in the Far East continued, Seafire Mk XVs would have replaced Mk IIIs. No. 806 Sqn reformed in August 1945, sailing for the region in April 1946, joining HMS Glory in September with F.Mk XVs. After a tour of Australia, the squadron returned home and disbanded. These examples of No. 806 Sqn aircraft (in wartime camouflage and sporting Glory's 'Y' deck code) were photographed around this time.

Potential difficulties in the adaptation of the Spitfire Mk VIII and IX for naval use centred around the need to strengthen its airframe for carrierborne use to such an extent that an unacceptable weight penalty would have resulted. Impressed with the potential of the Griffon/Spitfire marriage, the FAA therefore ordered that development of the next Seafire variant be based on the Spitfire Mk XII. In fact, the resulting Seafire Mk XV was, like the Spitfire Mk XII, a Mk V derivative, with the folding wings from the Seafire Mk III and the enlarged tail and retractable tailwheel of the Spitfire Mk VIII plus, of course, the engine installation of the Mk XII. Production began in the winter of 1944, but was not until September 1945 that the first squadron (No. 801 Sqn, in Australia) was able to re-equip with the variant. By the middle of 1946, the Mk III had been completely replaced. The Mk XV's Griffon VI engine, a derivative of the Griffon IIB fitted to the Spitfire Mk XII, gave the new Seafire an excellent low-level performance, but was to be the source of considerable problems during the first months of operation. The engine's M-ratio supercharger clutch was prone to slipping at high rpm settings, resulting in a power loss at crucial times, like take-off. Giving the potential dangers that this presented, embarked flying was prohibited from August 1946 – at a time when the Seafire Mk XV was the FAA's only front-line shipboard fighter. It was not until early 1947 that a modified clutch was developed. Mk XV production totalled 434, all by Westland and Cunliffe-Owen, the variant equipping nine front-line squadrons.

(and last) front-line unit to re-equip with the Seafire FR.Mk 47. Lieutenant 'Tommy' Handley joined the unit as senior pilot (deputy commander) when it was based at Royal Naval Air Station Sembawang, Singapore. He had flown several variants of the Seafire, and found the FR.Mk 47 the nicest of them all.

"The Seafire 47 was a superb aeroplane in the air. It was a better fighter than previous marks, could carry a greater weapon load and had a better range and endurance. The Rolls-Royce Griffon fitted with the injector pump was a most reliable engine, and the squadron experienced no engine failures of any kind. The contra-rotating propellers were a big advance, and even at full throttle on take-off there was no tendency to swing. Also, there was no change of rudder trim in a dive, which helped considerably when operating in the ground attack role."

In February 1950 Handley's squadron, together with No. 827 operating Fireflies, embarked in HMS *Triumph* for a tour of the Far East. At each British naval base along the route, the carrier's air group flew ashore and continued its training programme from there. With the Seafire's earlier reputation in mind, those in authority sought to keep the FR.Mk 47's deck operations to a minimum.

Handley remembered: "Seafires were not easy to deck land. The Mk 47 was a much heavier aircraft than the previous marks, and heavy landings often resulted in damaged oleo legs. Also, the fuselage aft of the cockpit was not sufficiently strengthened to withstand anything but a near-perfect deck landing. The long sting hook made catching a wire reasonably easy, but if the landing was much off-centre or made with any skid or slip on, then the wire would shake the aircraft rather like a terrier shakes a rat. The result could be a wrinkling of the after fuselage section."

During April, May and June 1950 Handley made only 26 deck landings, an average of about two per week. Most of his take-offs were unassisted runs off the deck, but he also made some catapult launches. The catapult was used in light winds, or when a large number of aircraft were on deck and those at the front had insufficient room to make a full take-off run.

Triumph's enjoyable jaunt round the west Pacific came to a sudden and unexpected end on the morning of 25 June 1950, when North Korean troops stormed south and began

Right: The second Mk XV prototype, NS490, was photographed during flight trials carried out during 1944 by the manufacturers, A&AEE and RAE Farnborough.

Lower right: SR449 is a standard production Mk XV completed in October 1944. Note the bulged trim tab on the rudder, a feature of the first 384 Mk XVs introduced to compensate for the increased torque produced by the Griffon engine. When the 'stinger' hook was introduced, the entire rudder was redesigned.

Below and below right: No. 804 Sqn Mk XVs are seen during operations from HMS Theseus in early 1947.

Seafire Mk XV operations aboard HMS Warrior (on loan to the Royal Canadian Navy) off Nova Scotia in March 1946, are seen here. Note that PR504/'B' (lower left) is a late-production aircraft with a 'stinger' hook and has underwing pylons fitted. The Mk XV was able to carry the same air-to-ground load as a Mk III, namely a single 500-lb bomb on the centreline, or four R/Ps.

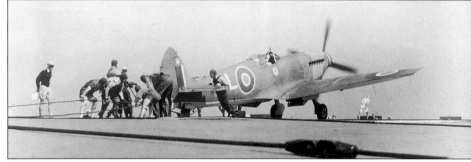

Above: Another of No. 803 Sqn's aircraft is disengaged from an arrester wire on Warrior. Note the unit badge below the cockpit, maple leaf on the fin and camouflaged engine cowlings, presumably 'borrowed' from another aircraft.

advancing into South Korea. On the next day the US Navy was ordered to provide support for South Korean forces. On 27 June the Royal Navy placed its forces in Japanese waters under the operational control of the US Navy, for the same purpose. Escorted by a cruiser and two destroyers, *Triumph* left Japan and arrived off the west coast of Korea on 2 July. There it joined US Navy Task Force 77 which included the carrier *Valley Forge*.

First strike by Mk 47s

On the following morning the two carriers launched a joint strike against airfields in the Pyongyang area. It was the Seafire Mk 47's first operational mission from a carrier and, as Handley explained, some of these fighters needed to use RATOG (rocket-assisted take-off gear) to get airborne.

"For the strike we had a big range of aircraft on deck. On a small carrier like *Triumph* that meant the aircraft at the head of the range did not get a full take-off run, so the four Seafires at the front were fitted with RATOG. RATOG was not popular – carrier operations were hazardous enough, without having to rely on cordite and more electric circuitry. The technique was to fire the rockets late in the take-off run, as the aircraft passed a mark on the deck. Firing the rockets gave quite a push, though not as much as going off the catapult. Once airborne, the pilot would jettison the rocket packs. With free take-offs or

using RATOG we could launch at 15-second intervals (catapulting was a much slower business, with about one launch per minute)."

The raiders found no enemy aircraft on the airfield, so they attacked the hangars with rockets and cannon fire. There was some return fire and one Seafire was hit by a machine-gun round. Another suffered minor radiator damage after it flew through debris thrown up by the explosions of its rocket projectiles.

On the next day, 4 July, *Triumph* launched seven Seafires and 12 Fireflies to attack rail targets. Following these initial strikes Task Force 77 withdrew from the combat zone.

When the carriers returned to the area, on 18 July, it was agreed that *Triumph*'s aircraft would fly combat air patrols (CAPs) and anti-submarine patrols to cover the Task Force, leaving the more-capable US Navy aircraft free to strike at targets ashore. Handley described the defensive operations:

"Usually we carried a 50-gal [Imperial] 'torpedo' tank under the fuselage. In addition we could carry a 22-gal combat tank under each wing. The combat tanks were stressed for combat manoeuvres, but we did not like them because they reduced our maximum speed by about 20 kt. They could be jettisoned, but as there were few spares we were ordered not to drop them except in a dire emergency. Shortage of range was never a problem for the Seafire 47s during the Korean conflict. All my flights were two hours or thereabouts and we always returned to the carrier with stacks of fuel."

The problem of wrinkling of the Seafire Mk 47's rear fuselage, which earlier would have prevented these fighters from flying, was solved by simply ignoring it.

Aéronavale Mk XV

SR520/'54.S-26'
Escadrille 54S was one of seven Escadrilles de Servitude to operate Seafire Mk XVs alongside 1 Flottille and 12 Flottille until 1951. Note the retention of the FAA colour scheme and serial number, to which was added Aéronavale roundels, codes and 'tricouleur' rudder striping.

54.S-26   SR520

Mk 17 – last of the first

The last of the 'first-generation' Seafires, the FR.Mk 17 first entered service in 1946. Generally similar to the Mk XV, the new variant differed primarily from the latter in having a bubble canopy and enlarged rudder, as fitted to the last 30 Mk XVs. The other useful change was the fitting of strengthened undercarriage with longer-travel oleos to reduce the risk of propeller 'pecking'. While the Mk XV had been unable to carry cameras, the Mk 17 had provision for a pair of F.24 cameras, or a small fuel tank in the lower fuselage behind the cockpit. The Mk 17's strengthened wings were also plumbed to allow the carriage of two small slipper-type 'combat tanks' of 22½-Imp gal (102-litre) each, or two 250-lb (114-kg) bombs. With the end of the war, production was cut back considerably to 233 and the variant spent less than two years in front-line service.

Above: NS493 was the third Seafire Mk XV prototype and was fitted with a bubble canopy during 1945. In the event, the last 30 Mk XVs were completed with the new canopy design.

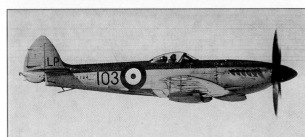

Right: This profile of SX194 shows well the revised lines of the FR.Mk 17. '194 was a No. 781 Sqn aircraft based at RNAS Lee-on-Solent, as indicated by the 'LP' tailcode.

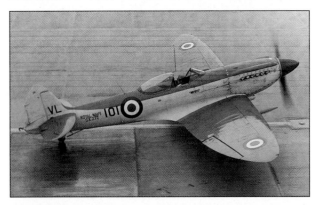

Right: Seafire Mk 17s remained in service until the final days of FAA Seafire operation. No. 764 Sqn, a fighter training unit equipped with Mk 17s at RNAS Yeovilton, was the last unit to fly Seafires of any variant, finally disbanding in late 1954.

Above: With his cockpit canopy open to facilitate his escape in the event of a ditching a No. 800 Sqn pilot is catapulted from HMS Triumph. The aircraft carries a 50-Imp gal (227-litre) 'torpedo' drop tank as introduced on the Mk XV, which proved more reliable than the 'slipper' tanks used on earlier Seafires.

Right: The busy deck of HMS Triumph plays host to No. 800 Sqn Seafires and No. 827 Sqn Firefly Mk 1s. The Seafires each carry four R/P launchers and are finished in the overall Extra Dark Sea Grey that was standard before 1948.

"Soon after we began operations nearly all the Seafires had wrinkled rear fuselages. The wrinkling was not really visible to the human eye, but if you ran a hand over the skin you could detect the trouble spots. The worry was that the structure was less strong than it should have been. The engineer officer said they were outside the limits for peace-time flying – but he let them fly on operational sorties!

"We found that we had far fewer deck landing accidents once we started flying more. Flying on operations nearly every day, we became better at deck landings and aircraft were damaged less frequently."

Throughout this period no enemy aircraft were encountered, and the CAP missions became a matter of routine. The only spell of excitement was on 28 July, when a pair of Seafires intercepted a B-29. Commissioned Pilot White was closing on the bomber when the latter's nervous gunners opened up at the unfamiliar fighter approaching them; an accurate burst struck the Seafire, which caught fire. White baled out and was picked up from the sea by a US destroyer. Suffering from burns, he was returned to *Triumph*.

Following this brief spell of operations, *Triumph* put into Kure dockyard for maintenance. On 11 August the carrier rejoined the blockade of the west coast of Korea, and the Seafires resumed operations. On 29 August No. 800 Squadron lost its commander, Lieutenant Commander Ian MacLachlan, in a tragic accident aboard *Triumph*. A Firefly ran into the crash barrier, shattering its wooden propeller and, in a million-to-one chance, a piece of blade flew through an open scuttle and struck him on the head, inflicting fatal injuries. Handley was promoted to lieutenant commander and assumed command of the Squadron.

Throughout most of September the Seafires flew operations against rail targets, and on 20 September Handley led an armed reconnaissance of the Chinnampo

The FAA's Spitfire 21 – Seafire 45

Never intended for squadron service, the Seafire Mk 45 represented the first step on the road to a second generation Griffon-Seafire. A Seafire Mk 21 airframe was fitted with a 'stinger' hook, slinging points and a naval radio set, while its undercarriage wheel fairings were cut back to increase clearance over arrester wires (the outer wheel bay doors being correspondingly enlarged). Serialled TM379, the aircraft flew in August 1944, but flight testing showed it displayed considerable instability (as had the Spitfire Mk 21) and proved to be somewhat maintenance heavy. Fifty Mk 45s were built, the last in late 1945. The variant saw limited second-line service, having been judged unsuitable for operational flying.

Above: TM379 is seen in its original form, effectively a Spitfire Mk 21 with essential naval equipment installed.

Top left: TM379 was later fitted with a Griffon 87 and contra-prop and an enlarged tailfin and rudder, the latter to correct the type's instability problems.

Left: This view of the second production Mk 45 (LA429) clearly shows the cut back undercarriage fairings introduced on this variant.

area. That uneventful mission turned out to be the last one flown by Seafires in Royal Navy service. On the following day the carrier put in to Sasebo, Japan, and a few days later set sail for the United Kingdom.

No. 800 Squadron had started the conflict with 12 Seafires, and during its course the unit received 14 replacements for aircraft lost or damaged. The squadron flew 360 operational sorties, of which 115 were against shipping or ground targets. The Seafires encountered no hostile aircraft and suffered no losses to enemy action. As mentioned, one Seafire was shot down by a 'friendly' B-29, and another was lost when its hook refused to lower and the pilot had to bale out.

When *Triumph* left the operational area the unit possessed nine flyable FR.Mk 47s, but with the pressure of war removed, peacetime rules came into play. The unit's

Stage two – the Mk 46

TM383, originally intended to be the second Mk 45 prototype, was actually completed as the first Mk 46. It boasted several important changes over the earlier mark, namely a contra-rotating propeller (and associated Griffon 87 engine) and a Spiteful-type empennage. These features transformed the aircraft's performance to that of "a delightful pilot's aeroplane". Plumbing for wing 'combat tanks' was included; the total fuel capacity of the Mk 46 was some 228 Imp gal (1036 litres), almost double that of the Mk IB – 115 Imp gal (523 litres). Only 24 were built before production switched to the Mk 47.

Left: A handful of second-line units flew Mk 46s. This No. 778 Sqn aircraft was based at RNAS Ford sometime between 1946 and 1948. At this time No. 778 was a Service and Carrier Trials Unit.

Below: LA542, the second of just 24 Mk 46s, flew in December 1945. A few served with No. 1832 Sqn, RNVR.

The Royal Naval Volunteer Reserve was established in 1947, in parallel to the long-established RNVR for seamen, to provide an economical reserve of air and ground crews that could be called upon in an emergency. The RNVR squadrons soon became major Seafire operators, in the same way that Royal Auxiliary Air Force units operated a large number of Spitfires. Aircraft of Mks XV, 17, 46 and 47 equipped four different squadrons until 1954.

Above: This No. 1833 Sqn, RNVR Seafire Mk 17 came to grief while operating from HMS Triumph during annual training exercises in the English Channel in June 1952.

Right: SX311 '167/BR' prepares to leave Triumph. The aircraft's 'BR' tailcode indicates that its shore base was Bramcote.

Right centre: Seafire Mk 17 SX165 '115/JA' of No. 1831 Sqn, RNVR is caught by the barrier aboard HMS Illustrious on 22 September 1949. Note the two propeller blades that have become separated after striking the deck.

Right bottom: No. 1833 Sqn, RNVR was the only reserve unit to receive Mk 47s, flying the variant for just under two years from 1952 to 1954.

Below: No. 1832 Sqn, RNVR was the only unit, regular or reserve, to fly Seafire FR.Mk 46s. Based at Culham, the aircraft arrived in August 1947 and were retired in January 1950.

engineer officer immediately declared six of the survivors to be unserviceable due to wrinkling of the rear fuselages. At the end of 11 weeks of operations, of 26 Seafires originally on strength or received as replacements, No. 800 Squadron was reduced to three flyable aircraft. Upon its return to the United Kingdom, the unit disbanded; it would reform in the following year with Attacker jet fighters. So the Seafire ended its first-line career in the Royal Navy.

Seafire in retrospect

From start to finish the Seafire was an improvisation, an attempt to modify a successful land-based fighter into one that could operate from a carrier. Aircraft design is a matter of compromise, and any improvement made in one area is usually at the expense of capability in others. To wring the highest possible performance from his fighter design, Reginald Mitchell had kept its structural weight as low as possible; he had not designed the aircraft to take the shock of repeated heavy landings on heaving carrier decks. Despite the addition of some local strengthening, the Seafire's airframe was simply not robust enough to accept such treatment. This was reflected in the rate at which Seafires were wrecked or seriously damaged in deck operations, whenever they flew in conditions that were anything less than perfect.

Yet, in the absence of any serious competitor, the Seafire was by far the most effective British-built carrier fighter of the World War II period. It played a major role in establishing air superiority over the beachhead during the initial stages of the Torch and Avalanche landings, contributing materially to the success of those important operations. For that alone, the effort and expense of modifying the Spitfire into a naval fighter and bringing it into service were fully justified.

After the war there was a rapid rundown of the Spitfire force as the RAF reduced its strength and many units converted to jet fighters. During the early post-war period the Spitfire Mk 18 became the main type equipping fighter and fighter reconnaissance units in the Middle East and the

Far East. Production ran to some 300 aircraft and the variant equipped five first-line squadrons.

The Mk 18 saw some action with Nos 32 and 208 Squadrons based in the Suez Canal zone, when these units inadvertently became involved in clashes during the Arab-Israeli conflict at the time of the establishment of the Israeli state. It also saw action with Nos 28 and 60 Squadrons, both based at Sembawang on Singapore Island, which carried out attacks against Communist guerrillas in Malaya. Flying Officer John Nicholls of No. 28 Squadron described his unit's first combat mission against guerrillas on 2 July 1948:

"I went off with my squadron commander, Squadron Leader Bob Yule, to a target just across the causeway from Singapore, in South Johore. We took off at first light so that we could get in our dive attacks before the usual mid-morning layer of cumulus cloud developed. When we reached the target area we cruised round for more than half an hour, looking for something resembling our briefed objective, before eventually we did attack. Diving from 12,000 ft we dropped our 500 pounders, two from each aircraft, then we carried out a series of strafing runs with cannon and machine-guns. There was nobody firing back; it was really like being on the range – except that the target was far less distinct.

Top and above: These two views of Mk 47 prototype PS944 illustrate the wing-fold incorporated in the final Seafire variant. The first 14 aircraft had manually folding wings; the remaining 76 were fitted with hydraulic jacks and locks.

Last of the line – Mk 47

Few production piston-engined fighters were as fast or could climb as quickly as a Seafire Mk 47. RN trials between a Mk 47 and three of its contemporaries – the Sea Fury, Sea Hornet and Sea Vampire – showed that while each had its own area of superiority, the Seafire had the highest dive speed and climb rate at altitudes above 25,000 ft (7620 m). Though outwardly similar to the Mk 46, the Mk 47 differed from it in important respects. It had folding wings, which finally allowed the new-generation Seafire to be deployed aboard RN carriers. The wings were also strengthened to carry a 500-lb bomb each and electrical gun-firing was also fitted. Early production aircraft had the Griffon 87 engine, but most were fitted with the Griffon 88, which benefitted from a petrol injection system to ensure steady fuel flow under all *g* conditions. In all, just 90 were built, the last in March 1949.

Above: PS947, the fourth Mk 47, is seen landing during carrier trials, possibly aboard HMS Illustrious. Note that this aircraft has a production standard chin supercharger intake.

Below: This fully loaded Mk 47 carries a pair of 500-lb bombs and 135 Imp gal (614 litres) of external fuel, the latter in a pair of 22½-Imp gal (102-litre) underwing 'combat tanks' and a centreline 90-Imp gal (409-litre) drop tank. With external tankage the Mk 47 had a genuine range of 1,000 miles (1609 km).

"During the months that followed we flew several similar strikes. Most of the targets were in deep jungle, and sometimes half a dozen of us would circle for up to an hour looking for the hut or whatever it was we were supposed to hit. Then the first pilot who reckoned he had found it would bomb, and the rest of us would follow and aim at his bursts; after that we would strafe the area until we had used up our ammunition. At that time our intelligence on the whereabouts of the enemy was poor. Moreover, only rarely could our troops go in and find out what the air strikes had achieved. Sometimes a week or so after the attack we might hear a report that the target basha hut had been hit by cannon shells, but by the time the ground forces reached it there was rarely any sign of the actual terrorists.

"In the beginning it was a rather hit and miss affair, with one far more likely to miss than to hit."

The Spitfire attacks against supposed guerrilla positions in the jungle was one of the few roles in which the famous fighter failed to perform well.

Although the Mk 21 had been intended as the definitive fighter variant of the Spitfire, production ended after just 120 aircraft had been built. They formed the equipment of only four regular first-line squadrons. The rest of the production order, which at its peak stood at nearly 3,000 aircraft, was either cancelled or transferred to other variants of the Spitfire.

Seafires abroad

The navies of both Canada and France obtained ex-RN aircraft-carriers in the years immediately after World War II, acquiring Seafire Mk IIIs as interim fighter equipment. These were later replaced by Mk XVs, the Griffon-engined variant also serving in the Burmese air force, though strictly as a land-based aircraft. The Irish Air Corps was the fourth foreign Seafire operator, using land-based Mk IIIs.

These Aéronavale Seafire Mk IIIs of 1 Flottille and Escadrille 54S are aboard Arromanches. The Escadrille 54S aircraft in the foreground is interesting as it appears to be a recent delivery, retaining its FAA colour scheme, roundels and codes, with Aéronavale overpainted.

The next major production fighter variant, the Spitfire Mk 22, was essentially a Mk 21 with a bubble canopy and the new broad-chord tail assembly. The latter gave greatly improved control authority, and cured most of the Mk 21's remaining unfortunate traits. The majority of Mk 22s went to Royal Auxiliary Air Force squadrons, reserve units manned by the so-called 'weekend pilots'. During 1948 12 of the 20 Auxiliary squadrons received Spitfire Mk 22s.

One of No. 800 Sqn's Mk 47s makes a low pass with 'everything down' over HMS Triumph, after a missed approach. Fixed 22½-Imp gal (102-litre) 'combat' fuel tanks under each wing were a common fit during operations in Korean waters, given the distances involved when on offensive sorties.

Griffon-engined Spitfire and Seafire deployment, January 1950

Although the Spitfire had been replaced by jet fighters in many home defence squadrons and the re-equipment of others was proceeding apace, even at this late date the Spitfire still made up a substantial part of the service's order of battle. Squadrons in the 500 and the 600 series were Royal Auxiliary Air Force units, manned by part-time volunteers. In the Royal Navy the Seafire had largely been replaced by the Sea Fury and only No. 800 Squadron, with Seafire FR.Mk 47s, continued to operate the type.

ROYAL AIR FORCE
No. 11 Group

No. 600 Sqn	F.Mks 21, 22	Biggin Hill
No. 614 Sqn	F.Mk 22	Llandow
No. 615 Sqn	F.Mks 21,22	Biggin Hill

No. 12 Group

No. 502 Sqn	F.Mk 22	Aldergrove
No. 504 Sqn	F.Mk 22	Wymeswold
No. 602 Sqn	F.Mk 22	Abbotsinch
No. 603 Sqn	F.Mk 22	Turnhouse
No. 607 Sqn	F.Mk 22	Ouston
No. 608 Sqn	F.Mk 22	Thornaby
No. 610 Sqn	F.Mk 22	Hooton Park
No. 611 Sqn	F.Mk 22	Woodvale
No. 612 Sqn	F.Mk XIV	Dyce
No. 613 Sqn	F.Mk 22	Ringway

British Air Force of Occupation (Germany)

No. II Sqn	FR.Mk XIV	Wunstorf

Middle East Air Force
No. 205 Group (Egypt)

No. 208 Sqn	FR.Mk 18	Fayid

Far East Air Force
Air Headquarters Hong Kong

No. 28 Sqn	FR.Mk 18	Kai Tak
No. 80 Sqn	F.Mk 24	Kai Tak

Air Headquarters Malaya

No. 60 Sqn	FR.Mk 18	Kuala Lumpur

ROYAL NAVY
13th Carrier Air Group

No. 800 Sqn	Seafire FR.Mk 47	HMS Triumph

Above: The lack of recognition stripes on these 800 NAS Seafires and 827 NAS Firefly FR.Mk 1s aboard Triumph, suggests that the photograph was taken early on in Korean operations. Having joined ships of the US 7th Fleet in Task Force 77 off the Korean coast, the 13th CAG initially flew offensive sorties using both aircraft types. However, the Firefly's limited endurance led to increased use of No. 800 Sqn's Seafires in an offensive role, often armed with R/Ps.

Left: Its wings folded, this No. 800 Sqn Mk 47 has been struck below and is seen being pushed off one of Triumph's two lifts and into the hangar. The Mk 47's wings folded through 90° just outboard of the cannon bays, reducing its folded span to just over 19 ft (5.79 m). Overall height was 16 ft (4.88 m), just within the limit imposed by RN carrier design. By the time Triumph had been withdrawn from operations off Korea, in September 1950 (after eight operational patrols over 35 days), the squadron had just four serviceable Seafires, only one of which was fit for combat.

Below: FR.Mk 47 '180/P' lifts its tail wheel moments before getting airborne from Triumph in Korean waters, July 1950. Note the use of rocket-assisted take-off gear (RATOG), a necessity with a full load and light winds.

Far Eastern swansong

By July 1949, the FAA had just one operational Seafire squadron remaining. The first of the two Mk 47 units, No. 804 Sqn in HMS Ocean, had converted to the Sea Fury in Malta, passing the best of its Seafires to No. 800 Sqn aboard Triumph. In early August Triumph sailed for the Far East and by the beginning of October had reached Singapore, where the 13th CAG was put ashore and began operations from Sembawang, in co-operation with RAF aircraft, against Communist terrorists in Malaya. These continued until re-embarkation in February 1950. Exercises off the Philippines, a refit in Singapore and a cruise to Australia and Japan followed and on 24 June, Triumph sailed for Hong Kong. The following day, North Korean troops crossed the 38th parallel and the British Far East Fleet was put at the immediate disposal of the United Nations. Seafire operations in Korea ran from 1 July until 20 September, the carrier then returning to UK, where No. 800 Sqn disbanded on 10 November, bringing FAA Seafire operations to a close.

Supermarine Seafire FR.Mk 47 No. 800 Sqn, FAA HMS *Triumph* 1951

VP461 ('178/P') was delivered to the FAA in April 1948 and was among No. 800 Sqn's aircraft serving with the 13th CAG aboard HMS *Triumph* during offensive operations with the US 7th Fleet over North Korea. Seafire operations in the Korean theatre began on 1 July 1950 and continued until 20 September.

Wing folding
The Mk 47 was the first Seafire built with power-operated wing-folding (a system of hydraulic jacks and locks), though it was omitted from the first 14 aircraft.

Markings
VP461 sports the standard FAA colour scheme for carrier-based aircraft of the day – Extra Dark Sea Grey over Sky. Serials and codes are in black, and '182', plus *Triumph's* deck letter, 'P'. Black and white stripes were applied to FAA aircraft in Korea as a recognition aid for American forces, unfamiliar with RN aircraft. The problem had come to a head on 28 July 1950, when a USAF B-29 fired on a No. 800 Sqn Seafire, the latter's pilot having to abandon the aircraft after it caught fire.

Air-to-ground role
This aircraft is equipped for the air-to-ground role given to No. 800 Sqn while in Korean waters. A 500-lb bomb and 22½-Imp gal (102-litre) 'combat' fuel tank are carried under each mainplane, while on the centreline is a 50-Imp gal (227-litre).

Powerplant
Griffon 80-series engines were equipped with the geared drive necessary to turn a contra-rotating propeller. In early production Seafire Mk 47s the Griffon 87 was installed; from the 15th aircraft the Griffon 88 was substituted. This had a fuel injection pump fitted in place of the 87's carburettor.

RATOG
Tested on Seafire Mk IIIs but never used operationally during World War II, the ability to use rocket-assisted take-off gear (RATOG) became standard on all Seafires from Mk XV, and was something of a necessity with a full load in light winds.

Keith Fretwell

Spitfire Colours

Great Britain

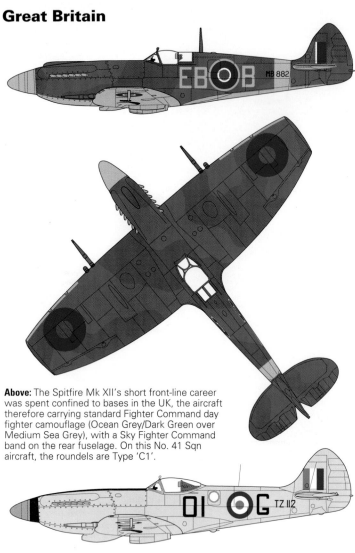

Above: The Spitfire Mk XII's short front-line career was spent confined to bases in the UK, the aircraft therefore carrying standard Fighter Command day fighter camouflage (Ocean Grey/Dark Green over Medium Sea Grey), with a Sky Fighter Command band on the rear fuselage. On this No. 41 Sqn aircraft, the roundels are Type 'C1'.

Above: Post-war, camouflage was often removed, the aircraft finished in all-over silver and serial numbers applied on the lower surface of the wing. After 1947 Type 'D' roundels and a new fin flash were applied. This is a No. II (AC) Sqn, FR.Mk XIVE.

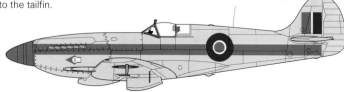

Above: No. 600 Sqn, RAuxAF received Spitfire Mk 21s in 1947, initially operating the aircraft in wartime camouflage and markings. RAuxAF aircraft wore three-letter 'RAx' codes from 1946.

Above: Squadron markings made a reappearance in the peacetime RAF, from 1948. On some aircraft they replaced unit codes (as on this No. 603 Sqn, RAuxAF Spitfire Mk 22), the aircraft code moving to the tailfin.

Above: This distinctive one-off, silver and red colour scheme, with No. 41 Sqn badge, was applied to a Mk 21 at the behest of an air vice marshal in the late 1940s.

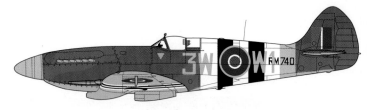

Above: No. 322 (Dutch) Sqn flew Spitfire Mk XIVs briefly during 1944. This aircraft carries 'invasion stripes' (as worn during Operation Overlord) and a Dutch orange triangle marking.

Above: In the Far East, Dark Earth/Dark Green camouflage was applied to Spitfire Mk XIVs initially. 'SEAC bands' and codes/serials were white; the 15-in (38.1-cm) roundels and fin flashes, roundel and light blue.

Above: Towards the end of the war, Dark Grey replaced Dark Earth in SEAC colour schemes and 'SEAC bands' gave way to a white band on the rear fuselage. This is a No. 132 Sqn aircraft based in India in August 1945.

Above: No. 60 Sqn, the last RAF Spitfire fighter unit to see active service, flew FR.Mk 18s in Malaya during the 'emergency'. Its aircraft were Dark Green/Dark Sea Grey over Medium Sea Grey, with a distinctive yellow/black nose marking.

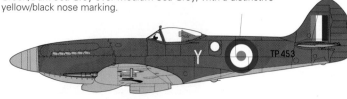

Above: In the Middle East, the camouflage applied to No. 208 Sqn's Mk 18s followed the FEAF pattern with white unit/aircraft codes and Type 'D' roundels.

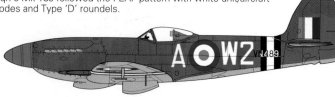

Above: Based at Kai Tak, Hong Kong No. 80 Sqn's Spitfire F.Mk 24s carried recognition markings in the Korean War, though they were not actively engaged. Otherwise standard FEAF markings were applied.

Above: PM655 displays standard wartime overall PRU Blue colours, with toned down national markings. In post-war PRDU service, codes were added.

Above: In the Far East during the 1950s, PR.Mk 19s mostly flew in PRU Blue (seen here on PS888, with grey fuselage upper surfaces) or in natural metal finish, with Type 'D' roundels.

Sweden

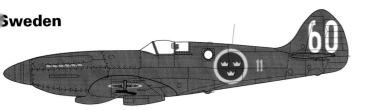

Above: Sweden operated its 50 Spitfire Mk 19s (S.31s) in PRU Blue, with a two-digit code on the fin. The '11' marking on the fuselage refers to the aircraft's unit – Flottilj 11.

Hong Kong AAF

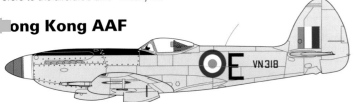

Above and right: Upon taking over No. 80 Sqn, RAF's Mk 24s, the HKAAF removed all camouflage, adopted an overall silver finish but otherwise retained standard RAF markings. A single-letter aircraft code was added.

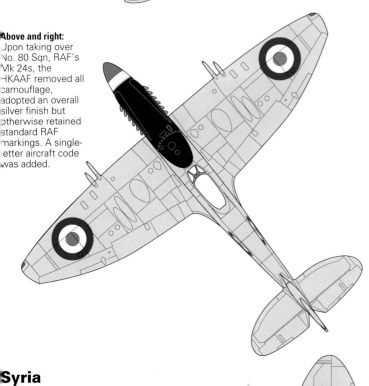

Syria

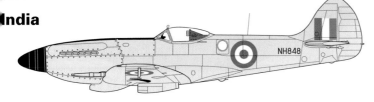

Above: Little is known of Syria's Mk 22s. When delivered they were finished in overall silver, with a black anti-glare panel, national markings and a serial or code number in Arabic on the fin.

India

Above: Initially flown in RAF SEAC camouflage and markings, many of the IAF's large fleet of Spitfire Mk XIVs later flew in natural metal with Indian national markings. RAF serials were retained.

Turkey

Above: Turkey's small batch of PR.Mk 19s are believed to have been camouflaged, with national markings and a three-figure serial. The '133' figure shown here would appear to be an aircraft code; the Mk 19s were serialled 6551-6554.

Belgium

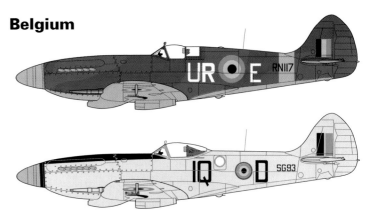

Above: Belgium's first Mk XIVs were delivered in standard RAF camouflage, over which were applied Belgian national marks and new unit codes. Later, camouflage was stripped off, an anti-glare panel painted forward of the cockpit and modified markings, with new serial numbers, applied.

Southern Rhodesia

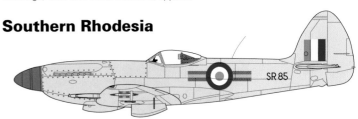

Above: This No. 1 Sqn, SRAF F.Mk 22 is finished in overall gloss light grey with a red spinner. Standard RAF Type 'D' roundels are carried in six locations, all flanked by green/yellow bars.

Egypt

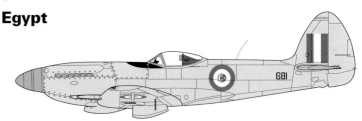

Above: Like similar aircraft operated by Syria, little is known of Egypt's Mk 22s. On delivery they were similarly finished in overall silver, with national markings and new serial numbers applied.

Thailand

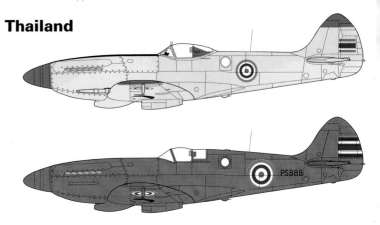

Above: Thailand's Spitfire Mk XIVs were flown in overall silver, with minimal markings other than national insignia. Their PR.Mk 19s included ex-FEAF aircraft, which were simply given Thai markings and retained their PRU Blue colours.

Canadian civil racer

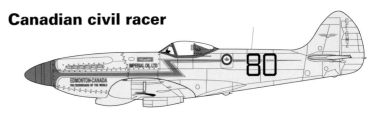

Above: CF-GMZ was formerly FR.Mk XIVE TZ138, shipped to Canada in late 1945 for cold weather testing. Struck off charge in March 1949, the aircraft was sold and is depicted here as it was when participating in the 1949 Cleveland Air Races. Placed third in the Tinnerman Trophy Race, the aircraft was clocked at 359.565 mph (578.662 km/h). Then owned by Imperial Oil Ltd. of Edmonton, the aircraft had a polished natural metal finish, with red striping.

Seafire Colours

Great Britain

Above: Despite its US Navy markings, this Seafire Mk IIC is a Fleet Air Arm machine (possibly of No. 807 Sqn aboard HMS *Furious*) shown as it was marked for Operation Torch, the invasion of North Africa, November 1942.

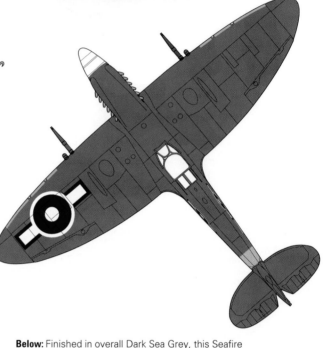

Above: As a recognition aid for American forces, black and white striping was applied over the Extra Dark Sea Grey/Sky scheme on Seafire FR.Mk 47s in action over Korea in 1951. This a No. 800 Sqn aircraft, carrying the deck letter of its ship, HMS *Triumph*.

Below: Seafire Mk XVs were due to be delivered to FAA units in the Pacific as World War II drew to a close. These deployments eventually took place in 1946/47, the aircraft involved being finished in the, by then, standard Extra Dark Sea Grey/Slate Grey camouflage, with Sky undersurfaces. '141-7/T' is a No. 804 Sqn aircraft based aboard HMS *Theseus* in late 1946.

Below: Finished in overall Dark Sea Grey, this Seafire F.Mk 46 was on strength with No. 1832 Sqn, RNVR in 1947. Note the Type 'C1' roundel, three-digit aircraft code and 'CH' station code (for Culham).

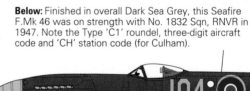

Burma

Above: Burma's Seafire Mk XVs flew in 'natural metal', with an anti-glare panel over the nose and national markings on the fuselage tail and under the wings. Some aircraft are known to have carried single letter codes; this machine is depicted with British civil Class-B marks for delivery purposes.

France

Above: Shortly after delivery, the Aéronavale's Seafire Mk IIIs flew in standard FAA colours, with French roundels, unit marks (in this case, for 1.Flotille) and aircraft identity ('22') applied over the existing British markings.

Ireland

Below: Ireland's Seafire Mk IIIs were finished, like its T.Mk 9s, in overall green, with a two-colour Celtic Boss and three-colour wing stripes.

Canada

Below: RCN Seafire MK XVs were eventually finished in standard FAA Extra Dark Sea Grey over Sky colours, but with Canadian 'maple leaf' roundels. The 'TG' code on this aircraft referred to Training Air Group Number 1, the last operators of the type in 1948/49. This machine was the Commander Air's aircraft at HMCS *Shearwater* in 1946.

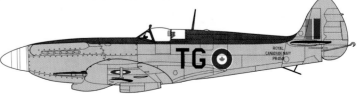

Spitfire/Seafire details

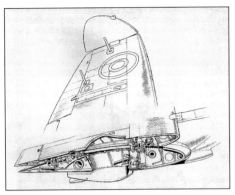

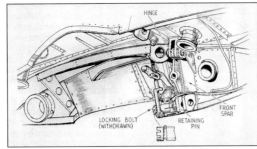

Left and above: The wing-folding mechanism employed in the Seafire Mk III is shown here, the main 'break' being just inboard of the cannon bays.

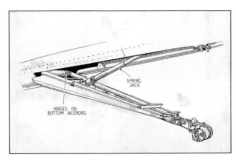

Seafire Mk Is, IIs, IIIs and some Mk XVs employed an arrester hook hinged below the lower fuselage.

Seafire FR.Mk 17 cutaway drawing

1 Starboard wingtip
2 Navigation light
3 Starboard aileron
4 Browning 0.303-in (7.7-mm) machine-guns
5 Machine-gun ports (patched)
6 Ammunition boxes (350 rounds per gun)
7 Aileron control rod
8 Bellcrank control hinge
9 Starboard wing folded position
10 Jury strut
11 Aileron cables

21 Propeller hub mechanism
22 Spinner backplate
23 Coolant system header tank
24 Coolant filler cap
25 Rolls-Royce Griffon VI engine
26 Exhaust stubs
27 Front engine mounting
28 Engine bottom cowling
29 Radio suppressor
30 Engine bearer
31 Coolant pipes
32 Carburettor air intake
33 Engine bearer lower strut
34 Main spar stub attachment

46 Bottom main fuel tank (48-Imp gal/218-litre capacity)
47 Rudder pedal bar
48 Sloping fuel tank bulkhead
49 Fuel cock control

50 Control column hand grip
51 Engine throttle and propeller controls
52 Radio controller
53 Bullet proof windscreen
54 Gyro gunsight
55 Windscreen side panels
56 Port wing folded position
57 Folding wing tips
58 Pitot tube
59 Spent cartridge case ejector chute
60 Sliding bubble-type canopy
61 Headrest
62 Head armour plate
63 Pilot's seat

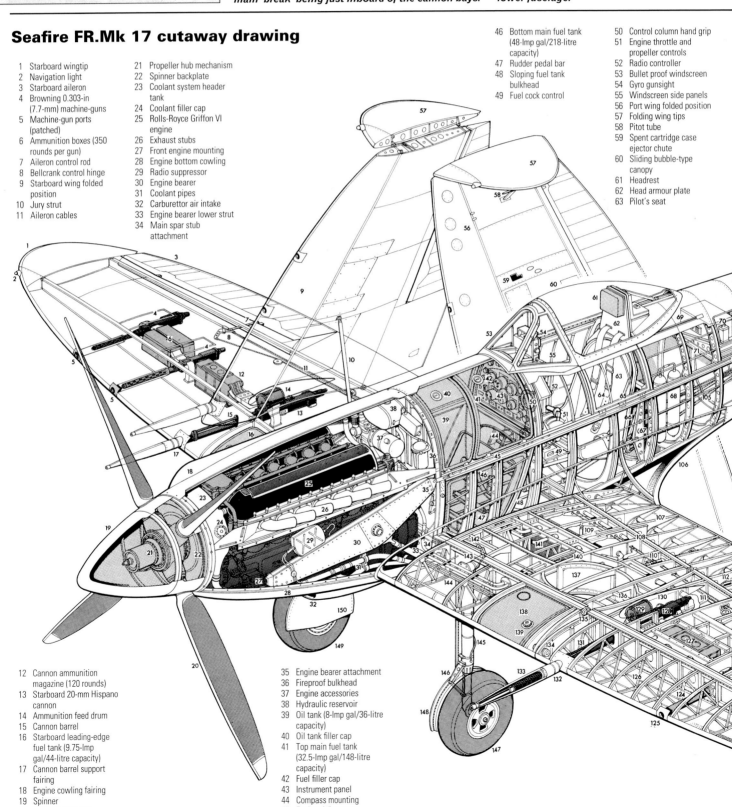

12 Cannon ammunition magazine (120 rounds)
13 Starboard 20-mm Hispano cannon
14 Ammunition feed drum
15 Cannon barrel
16 Starboard leading-edge fuel tank (9.75-Imp gal/44-litre capacity)
17 Cannon barrel support fairing
18 Engine cowling fairing
19 Spinner
20 Rotol four-bladed constant-speed propeller

35 Engine bearer attachment
36 Fireproof bulkhead
37 Engine accessories
38 Hydraulic reservoir
39 Oil tank (8-Imp gal/36-litre capacity)
40 Oil tank filler cap
41 Top main fuel tank (32.5-Imp gal/148-litre capacity)
42 Fuel filler cap
43 Instrument panel
44 Compass mounting
45 Fuel tank/longeron attachment fittings

Rolls-Royce's Griffon 60 series powerplants, with two-stage, two-speed supercharging, transformed the altitude performance of second generation Griffon-powered Spitfires and Seafires. The Griffon 65 (left) powered Spitfire Mks XIV, XVIII and XIX (early examples), while the Griffon 61 equipped Seafire Mk 45s. The Griffon 80 series was derived from the 60 series and was equipped to drive a contra-prop (right); Spitfire Mk 46 had a Griffon 85, while the Mk 47 employed a Griffon 87 or, in later aircraft, Griffon 88, the latter with fuel injection. Three-speed Griffon 100 series engines, intended for the Spiteful and Seafang, were test flown in late-mark Spitfires.

Below: The much improved 'sting' arrester hook, hinged at the foot of the rudder post, was introduced on the Seafire Mk XV and is seen here in the deployed position.

64 Safety harness
65 Side entry hatch
66 Back armour
67 Seat support frame
68 Air bottles
69 Sliding canopy rails
70 T.R.5043 radio transmitter/receiver
71 Radio rack
72 Fuselage main longeron
73 Radio access hatch

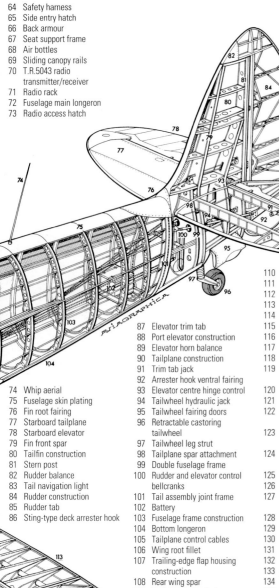

74 Whip aerial
75 Fuselage skin plating
76 Fin root fairing
77 Starboard tailplane
78 Starboard elevator
79 Fin front spar
80 Tailfin construction
81 Stern post
82 Rudder balance
83 Tail navigation light
84 Rudder construction
85 Rudder tab
86 Sting-type deck arrester hook

87 Elevator trim tab
88 Port elevator construction
89 Elevator horn balance
90 Tailplane construction
91 Trim tab jack
92 Arrester hook ventral fairing
93 Elevator centre hinge control
94 Tailwheel hydraulic jack
95 Tailwheel fairing doors
96 Retractable castoring tailwheel
97 Tailwheel leg strut
98 Tailplane spar attachment
99 Double fuselage frame
100 Rudder and elevator control bellcranks
101 Tail assembly joint frame
102 Battery
103 Fuselage frame construction
104 Bottom longeron
105 Tailplane control cables
106 Wing root fillet
107 Trailing-edge flap housing construction
108 Rear wing spar
109 Radiator shutter jack

110 Flap jack
111 Gun heater duct
112 Flap synchronising jack
113 Split trailing-edge flap
114 Aileron control bellcrank
115 Aileron hinge
116 Port aileron construction
117 Wing tip construction
118 Port navigation light
119 Folding wing tip latching handle
120 Wing rib construction
121 Front spar
122 Browning 0.303-in (7.7-mm) machine-guns
123 Ammunition boxes (350 rounds per gun)
124 Machine-gun muzzle blast tubes
125 Machine-gun ports
126 Leading-edge nose ribs
127 Cannon ammunition magazine (120 rounds)
128 Port Hispano 20-mm cannon
129 Ammunition feed drum
130 Cannon wing fairing
131 Cannon barrel
132 Barrel support fairing
133 Recoil spring
134 Leading-edge joint spigot
135 Wing fold spar hinge
136 Wing fold joint rib
137 Mainwheel well
138 Leading-edge fuel tank (9.75-Imp gal/44-litre capacity)
139 Fuel tank filler cap
140 Oil radiator
141 Coolant radiator
142 Main undercarriage hydraulic jack
143 Retraction link
144 Oil and fuel pipe runs
145 Mainwheel leg shock absorber
146 Undercarriage torque links
147 Port mainwheel
148 Mainwheel fairing door
149 Starboard mainwheel
150 Starboard wheel fairing door

Left: In this view of the tailfin of a Seafire Mk 47, the stinger tailhook may be seen in the stowed position. Use of the 'hold back' is shown, while ahead of the retractable tailwheel, a arrester wire guard is fitted to prevent damage to the former as a result of snagging.

Rocket-assisted take-off gear (RATOG) was tested on Seafire Mk IICs MB141 (above) and MB307 but rejected as unsafe. Early problems included damage to both the aircraft's fabric work and the ship's deck caused by the ferocity of the flame produced by the four rockets.

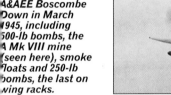

Seafire weapons

Given the limited bomb load-carrying capability of the Merlin-engined Seafire, the rocket projectile (R/P) was a far more suitable weapon. It could be aimed with the aircraft's existing gunsight and afforded the pilot a higher degree of immunity against light flak, as R/Ps were usually fired out of their range. As early as October 1943, theoretical tactics for the use of R/Ps were formulated, but as the heavy Universal launcher proved incompatible with the Seafire, R/P use was delayed until the lightweight zero-length Mk VIII launcher (seen on Seafire Mk III PP921, below left) was developed. When HMS Implacable sailed for the Far East in May 1945 it had sets of launchers aboard, but clearance for operational use was not given until after hostilities had ceased. Four launchers for 110-lb R/Ps (each with a 60-lb HE head) would have been the standard fit, though there was a considerable drag penalty. Unsurprisingly, though tandem R/Ps were trialled (below), they were not proceeded with.

Above: The standard load for a Seafire fighter-bomber was a 500-lb bomb (Medium Capacity or Semi-Armour Piercing), seen here suspended beneath a Mk III taking-off from HMS Khedive during Operation Dragoon, or a 250-lb GP bomb. With the weight and drag penalty imposed by the former, the Seafire Mk III's range was reduced to less than 100 miles (161 km). Given the aircraft's lack of air brakes, a glide-bombing technique was used and dive angle limited to 40° so as to avoid overstressing the aircraft's airframe.

Above: A number of alternative loads were trialled at A&AEE Boscombe Down in March 1945, including 500-lb bombs, the A Mk VIII mine (seen here), smoke floats and 250-lb bombs, the last on wing racks.

Production

Production Seafire Mk IIIs were built by Westland and Cunliffe-Owen. These two scenes, from Westland's Yeovil factory in January 1944, show Mk III production in full swing. Note the Welkin high-altitude fighters in the background (below). Seafire NF482 (below, left foreground) eventually served with the Aéronavale.

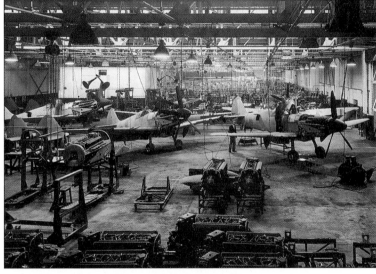

Above: With a 'sea' of Griffon engines in the foreground, Spitfire Mk 21s undergo final assembly at Supermarine's South Marston plant in 1945.

Below: Staff temporarily 'down tools' as the photographer records the final assembly of Mk XVIIIs at High Post in 1946.

The RAF's last Spitfires

Such was their usefulness, and in the absence of a PR version of the Meteor, Spitfire PR.Mk 19s were not only the last Spitfires in the operational RAF, but were destined to be the last active RAF Spitfires of all. No. 81 Sqn, operating from Seletar, flew the last Spitfire sortie on 1 April 1954. Back in the UK, Mk 19s remained on secondary duties until 1957, while a single example was flown again briefly, by the Central Fighter Establishment, in 1963. Two remain 'on the books' 40 years later, though purely as show aircraft, with the Battle of Britain Memorial Flight at RAF Coningsby.

Right: At the height of Operation Firedog, Spitfire PR.Mk 19 PS888 taxis as it begins the last sortie by an operational Spitfire on 1 April 1954. This routine flight, of a type soon to be taken over by Meteor PR.Mk 10s like the example in the background, was tasked with photographing suspected Communist guerrilla positions in the Malayan jungle.

Far right: Operated under contract by Short Brothers and Harland Ltd, the Temperature and Humidity (THUM) Flight at Woodvale retired its three Mk 19s in 1957. One was reactivated by the CFE at Binbrook in 1963, to assist in the training of Lightning pilots, pending deployment to Indonesia where fighter opposition was expected to include P-51s!

Above: One of No. 81 Sqn's Mk 19s dashes across Malayan jungle, on a PR sortie during the Malayan 'emergency'.

The final Spitfire variant, the Mk 24, looked little different from the Mk 22. The main changes were two additional fuel tanks fitted in the rear fuselage, and wing fittings to carry six 60-lb rockets. Supermarine built 54 Mk 24s, and converted 27 Mk 22s still on the production line to this configuration. The final Mk 24, the last of more than 20,000 Spitfires built, left the factory at South Marston near Swindon in February 1948.

Only one first-line Spitfire unit received the Mk 24 – No. 80 Squadron in January 1948, then based in Germany. In July 1949 the unit moved to Hong Kong to provide limited air defence for that colony. The last RAF unit to operate the Spitfire in the fighter role, No. 80 Squadron re-equipped with Hornets in January 1952.

Griffon-powered Spitfires in retrospect

Considering that the cubic capacity of the Rolls-Royce Griffon was one-third greater than that of the Merlin it replaced, the relative ease with which the larger engine fitted into the Spitfire was remarkable. The first Griffon-powered variant, the Mk XII, was optimised for the low-altitude air superiority role. It had only limited utility and did not remain long in first-line service. The Mk XIV that replaced it was a much more formidable fighter, with considerably enhanced high-altitude performance. That variant ensured that the RAF possessed a piston-engined fighter as good as any in existence at the end of the war. Had the Griffon not been available, the Spitfire's tenure in first-line service might well have ended some time around 1947. With the Griffon, the fighter's useful life continued for five more years.

Following the end of the war, the RAF's regular home defence fighter units rapidly re-equipped with jet aircraft. The early jets did not take kindly to having to operate from short airfields in hot and dusty areas, however; as a result, the Spitfire FR.Mk 18 and later the F.Mk 24 continued to perform usefully in the Middle East and the Far East until the last of them was replaced in 1952. In the Auxiliary Air Force the Spitfire F.Mk 22 equipped several units during the immediate post-war period, until the last of them re-equipped with jet fighters in 1951.

Dr Alfred Price

Above: This scene at RAF Lyneham in the immediate post-war period, showing withdrawn Spitfires awaiting disposal, was typical of a number of RAF stations.

Right: Partially broken up Spitfire Mk 24s await their final appointment with the cutting torch, which came in June 1956, when most of these airframes were sold to Enfield Rolling Mills. Very few Mk 24s survived the wholesale scrapping of late-mark aircraft that accompanied the arrival of jets in large numbers. Aircraft stationed overseas at the time of their withdrawal were usually scrapped locally; of the Hong Kong-based Mk 24s, VN485 was fortunately spared. As the HKAAF's last operational Mk 24, '485 was displayed in Hong Kong for some years before being repatriated to the UK in 1989 and placed in the care of the Imperial War Museum.

Griffon-powered Spitfire warbirds

Of the 49 Spitfires in airworthy condition in mid-1999, 10 (pictured here) were Griffon-powered aircraft of Mks XIV, XVIII and XIX, reflecting the fact that these marks were the late-production Spitfires built in the greatest numbers and were among the large numbers of Spitfires exported as they became surplus to RAF requirements; five of the airworthy warbirds are former Indian Air Force aircraft. Five of these aircraft were based in the UK, with four registered in the US and a single example in France. One machine, PM631 of the Battle of Britain Memorial Flight (BBMF) has been in continuous service with the RAF since 1945.

Compiled with the assistance of Peter R. Arnold

MV293 (G-SPIT)

Above: Owned by The Fighter Collection, Duxford, this FR.Mk XIVE originally served with the IAF. Its first post-restoration flight was in 1992.

NH749 (NX749DP)

Above: David Price operates this FR.Mk XIVE (another ex-IAF aircraft, flown in 1983) from the Museum of Flying at Santa Monica, Calif.

NH904 (N114BP)

Above: This FR.Mk XIVC is owned by Bob Pond of Palm Springs, Calif. and served with the RAF and Belgian air force. Restoration came in 1981.

PM631

Above: Completed after the end of World War II, this Mk XIX was among the last Spitfires in RAF service in 1957 and continues to fly with the BBMF.

PS853 (G-RRGN)

Above: Purchased by Rolls-Royce plc in 1996, this ex-BBMF Mk XIX entered RAF service in early 1945 and is a veteran of the THUM Flight.

PS915

Above: This Mk XIX joined the BBMF briefly in 1957, but was grounded soon afterwards. Restored to fly in 1986, it has rejoined the BBMF.

SM832 (F-AZSJ)

Above: Another airframe recovered from India, this F.Mk XIVE flew in 1995 after restoration and was owned by Christophe Jacquard of Dijon in 1999.

SM969 (G-BRAF)

Above: Owned by the late Doug Arnold's Warbirds of GB, this ex-IAF FR.Mk XVIIIE last flew in 1992, but has since been stored at Bournemouth.

Soon to fly?

TP280 (N280TP)

Above: Flown after restoration in 1992, this FR.Mk XVIIIE flew with the IAF as HS654 and was owned by Rudy Frasca of Urbana, Illinois in 1999.

TZ138 (N5505A)

Above: This FR.Mk XIVE (the former Imperial Oil racer, CF-GMZ) was restored by Pete Regina of Van Nuys, Calif and flown in 1999.

Above: Of a number of Griffon-engined Spitfires in the throes of restoration, one of the closest to completion in 1999 was FR.Mk XVIIIE SM845 (G-BUOS), formerly HS687 of the IAF.

Below: One of the more interesting Spitfire restoration projects of recent years must be that of former No. 81 Sqn, RAF and RThaiAF Mk XIX PS890, photographed at the Planes of Fame Museum, Chino, California in June 1999. As may be seen, the aircraft has been fitted with the Griffon 50-series engine and contra-prop from an Avro Shackleton. It is believed that the aircraft, which was expected to fly in the latter half of 1999, would be used in a series of attempts to break time-to-height records for piston-engined aircraft.

Seafires

Seafire L.Mk IIIC PP972, a veteran of Aéronavale operations, spent many years as an instructional airframe before being rescued from a scrapyard and restored for static exhibition in France in the early 1980s. Purchased by Precious Metals Ltd of Bournemouth in 1992 and registered G-BUAR, the aircraft was nearing the end of a restoration to flying standard in 1999. Its first flight was expected in 2000/01.

While there were, in 1999, no airworthy Seafires in existence, a number of long-term restoration projects were in various stages of completion. Of these, PP972 was perhaps the closest to its first flight when photographed in January 1999.

Griffon-Spitfire Operators

With large numbers of surplus Spitfires available after the end of World War II, a brisk trade in ex-RAF aircraft was done. Most of those exported were Merlin-engined Mk IXs and XVIs, though a handful of countries picked up Griffon-powered aircraft, otherwise, mainly of Mks 14 and 22. Belgium and India amassed the largest fleets. Such was their usefulness, photo-reconnaissance Mk 19s were also a popular choice and were among the last Spitfires to see service anywhere.

Dr Alfred Price, with additional material by John Heathcott

United Kingdom
Royal Air Force

Continuous RAF front-line use of Griffon-engined Spitfires spanned 14 years from early 1943 (when the first Mk XIIs were delivered to No. 41 Sqn), to 1957, when the THUM Flight retired its last PR.Mk XIX.

Wartime units

The following front-line RAF squadrons (fighter units unless noted otherwise), operated Griffon-engined Spitfires from 1943 until the end of World War II:

Mk XII: Nos 41, 91, 595 (anti-aircraft co-operation)
F./FR.Mk XIV: Nos II (fighter-reconnaissance), 11, 41, 91, 130, 268 (fighter-reconnaissance), 322, 350, 402, 430, 610
PR.Mk XIX: (photo-reconnaissance units, except where noted) Nos II (fighter-reconnaissance), 16, 541, 542, 681, 682, 683, 684
F.Mk 21: No. 91

Post-war units

The following units became operational with 'Griffon-Spitfires' (in a few cases, for a second time) after the end of World War II. No. 541 Sqn, a wartime PR unit that operated Mk XIXs at the time of disbandment in 1945, reformed in 1947 within Bomber Command, with Mk 19s. Again, all are fighter units unless stated:

F./FR.Mk XIV: Nos 16 (fighter-reconnaissance), 17, 20, 26, 28, 132, 136, 152, 268 (fighter-reconnaissance), 273,
FR.Mk XVIII: Nos 11, 28, 32, 60, 81 (reconnaissance), 208 (reconnaissance)
PR.Mk XIX: (photo-reconnaissance units, except where noted) Nos 16 (fighter-reconnaissance), 34, 60, 81, 82, 268, 541
F.Mk 21: No. 1, 41, 122
F.Mk 22: No. 73
F.Mk 24: No. 80

RAuxAF units

The Auxiliary Air Force was re-established in June 1946 (becoming 'Royal' in December the following year and finally disbanding in March 1957) as a territorial force made up of part-time volunteer pilots and a nucleus of ground personnel from the regular air force. Of the 20 squadrons formed, a dozen were equipped with Griffon-engined Spitfires at some point before the last Mk 22s were replaced by Meteors in July 1951.

F./FR.Mk XIV: Nos 600, 602, 607, 610, 611, 612, 613, 615
F.Mk 21: Nos 600, 602, 615
F.Mk 22: Nos 502, 504, 600, 602, 603, 607, 608, 610, 611, 613, 614, 615

Numerous second-line units operated Spitfires, including Griffon-engined aircraft. These included the various Operational Coversion and Training Units, tactical trials establishments (like the Central Fighter Establishment and Photographic Reconnaissance Development Unit), Civilian Anti-Aircraft Co-operation Units (especially Nos 2 and 4 CAACUs – both notable operators of the Spitfire Mk 21) and, as related elsewhere, the Temperature and Humidity Flight at Woodvale.

In 1999, the RAF's Battle of Britain Memorial Flight operated, among other types, two PR.Mk XIXs (PM631 and PS915).

No. 208 Sqn was first equipped with Spitfires in December 1943, when Mk VCs were acquired for service in the Western Desert. Mk IXs and Mk VIIIs followed, the unit acquiring FR.Mk XVIIIs post-war. Wartime codes 'RG' (above) were soon abandoned and by 1948, Type 'D' roundels had been applied, as seen on TZ233 (left), up on trestles for gun repairs and harmonisation at Fayid, Egypt.

Right: No. 32 Sqn flew Spitfire Mk 18s for just under two years between 1947 and 1949. TP373 is seen at Ein Shemar, Palestine in 1948.

Below: RAF's last three PR.Mk 19s (from the front, PS386, '888 and '890 of No. 81 Sqn) are seen at Seletar in early 1954, the RAF's operational Spitfires' last year of service.

Above: Carrying recognition stripes at the time of the Korean War, a No. 28 Sqn Spitfire FR.Mk 18E lands at Kai Tak, Hong Kong in about 1950.

Below: PR.Mk XIX PS925 carries the '6C' code of the Photo-Reconnaissance Development Unit at RAF Benson in the late 1940s/early 1950s.

Photographed in 1990, when it was still in RAF service as one of three Mk XIXs with the battle of Britain Memorial Flight, PS853 formates with a No. 229 OCU Tornado F.Mk 3. The Spitfire has since been sold to fund the rebuilding of BBMF Hurricane LF363 and was owned by Rolls-Royce plc in 1999, registered G-RRGN.

Right: FR.Mk XIV NH803 was among a number of examples of this mark to serve in the Far East. Pictured post-war, the aircraft has been stripped of its wartime camouflage and has Type 'C1' fuselage roundels of a smaller-than-standard pattern not uncommon post-war.

Hong Kong Auxiliary Air Force

No. 80 Sqn, RAF began re-equipping with de Havilland Hornets in December 1951, passing eight of its Spitfire F.Mk 24s (PK687, PK719, PK720, VN308, VN313, VN318, VN482 and VN485) to the Hong Kong Auxiliary Air Force. These were operated until 1955, Flt Lt Adrian Rowe-Evans taking part in the Queen's Birthday Flypast on 21 April, the type's last day of operation. By then the HKAAF had just four Spitfires – two Mk 24s (VN318 and VN485) and two PR.Mk 19s, both ex-No. 81 Sqn aircraft (PS852 and PS854).

VN485 was put on display at Kai Tak the following July and remained there until 1989, when it was obtained by the Imperial War Museum. It is displayed at the Museum's Duxford site.

HKAAF F.Mk 24 VN482/'N', clearly no longer in airworthy condition, is seen at Kai Tak after its withdrawal from use.

Belgium
Force Aérienne Belge/Belgische Luchtmacht

In 1947 the Royal Belgian Air Force purchased 134 F/FR.Mk XIVs. Of these, 132 were delivered and equipped the 1st Fighter Wing (Nos 349 and 350 Sqns) at Beauvechain and the 2nd Fighter Wing (Nos 1, 2 and 3 Sqns) at Florennes. Later, some of these aircraft went to the 10th Wing at Chièvres (Nos 23, 27, 31 Sqns) which was designated a fighter-bomber unit in 1952. The Mk XIV remained in first-line service until December 1952, when several of the surviving aircraft were transferred to the Fighter School at Coxijde. The type finally passed out of service in 1954.

'Clipped-wing' F.Mk XIVE 'UR-S' carries the 'shooting star' emblem of No. 2 Sqn, 2nd Fighter Wing. Belgian Mk XIVs were serialled SG1-SG132, the prefix standing for 'Spitfire-Griffon'. Similarly, the serials of FAB Mk IXs were prefixed 'SM' – 'Spitfire-Merlin'.

Egypt
(Royal) Egyptian Air Force

In 1949 the Egyptian government placed an order for 20 Spitfire F.Mk 22s, an agreement being signed between Vickers and the Egyptian Government on 1 May 1950 for their supply. All were ex-RAF aircraft, bought and refurbished by Vickers for a total cost of £239,000. Nineteen were delivered, the last in late 1950. Little is known of the subsequent use of these aircraft; all served with No. 2 Sqn at Helwan until about 1953. Their serial numbers were possibly 680-699.

Above: An REAF Spitfire Mk 22, complete with national markings and a new serial number, is run up at the beginning of its delivery flight.

Spitfire FR.Mk XIVs of No. 4 Sqn, Royal Indian Air Force are seen at Iwakuni, Japan soon after their arrival to join the British Commonwealth Occupation Force. Nineteen aircraft were ferried to Japan aboard the RN carrier HMS Vengeance. After a week these machines moved to Miho where they remained for just over a year, flying surveillance patrols over the coastal areas of Shimane and Tottori prefectures, in conjunction with 268 Indian Brigade, to prevent illegal immigration. Note the retention of SEAC markings and, on at least one aircraft, a wartime camouflage scheme.

India
(Royal) Indian Air Force

The wartime Indian Air Force became the Royal Indian Air Force in March 1945, and by the end of the war totalled nine squadrons, equipped with Spitfires and Hurricanes of various marks. In August 1947, the RIAF disbanded and the force split between India and the newly formed Pakistan, the 'new' RIAF becoming the IAF once more in 1950.

During the two-year transition period, the following RIAF units operated Spitfire Mk XIVs: No.1 Sqn (March-August 1947), No. 4 Sqn (October 1945-mid-1947), No. 6 Sqn (November 1945-May 1947), No. 7 Sqn (December 1945-July 1947), No. 8 Sqn (December 1945-May 1947), No. 9 Sqn (January-June 1946) and No. 14 Sqn (1950-1951).

By mid-1946, all RIAF fighter units were equipped with Spitfires (including Mk VIIIs), No. 4 Sqn taking 19 Mk XIVs to Japan in April as part of the British Commonwealth Occupation Force.

The exact number of Mk XIVs operated by the RIAF is unclear, though it is known that a batch 20 was delivered in 1947, along with 58 Mk 18s. The latter equipped Nos 2, 9 and 14 Sqns. A further 42 Mk 18s and 13 PR.Mk 19s followed in 1949, the Mk 19s equipping No. 101 PR Flight (No. 101 PR Sqn from 1950) at Ambala and Palam until 1956.

After the partition of India, two years of fighting on the North-West Frontier and in Kashmir saw Spitfire Mk XIVs and 18s (based at Cawnpore, Poona and Srinagar) join the RIAF's Tempest Mk II force in attacking ground targets. No. 101 Flight's PR.Mk 19s were also employed.

By the mid-1950s the Spitfire had all but disappeared from IAF service, No. 14 Sqn dispensing with its last Mk 18s in 1957.

A handful of Mk XIVs and 18s also equipped the Central Flying School (at Jodhpur) and the Advanced Flying School (at Ambala) in the early 1950s.

Below: A No. 4 Sqn, RIAF, F.Mk XIV is craned aboard RN carrier HMS Vengeance for the trip to Japan as part of the BCOF. On the lighter below are two FR.Mk XIVEs, one of which carries a serial number in the MV2xx range. Note the way in which lifting gear was attached at a point near the engine bearers and that this necessitated removal of the engine's upper cowl.

Southern Rhodesia
Southern Rhodesian Air Force

In March 1951, 11 Spitfire F.Mk 22s, serialled SR58-68 were delivered to the SRAF. A second batch of 11 followed in December, two of which (SR79 and SR89) crashed during, or shortly after, delivery. The remaining nine machines were serialled SR80-88. SR84 was written-off in December 1953. The Mk 22s equipped Nos 1 and 2 Squadrons until the early 1954.

In 1955, the SRAF having received de Havilland Vampire FB.Mk 9s , 10 of the remaining Spitfires were sold on to Syria.

Spitfire F.Mk 22 SR65 of No. 1 Sqn rests in the east African in the sun at New Sarum airfield, Salisbury in June 1953.

Sweden
Flygvapnet

Sweden received 50 ex-RAF Spitfire PR.Mk XIXs in 1948, these equipping Divisions 1, 2, 3 and 5 of reconnaissance unit Flottilj 11 at Nyköping until August 1955. In Flygvapnet service the aircraft were designated S.31 and serialled 31001-31050.

Though initially earmarked for transfer to the Indian air force, PS935 was refurbished as 31001 – the first Mk XIX for the Flygvapnet. Here the aircraft poses for the camera prior to delivery in October 1948.

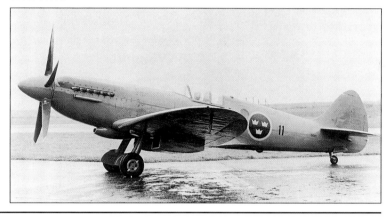

Syria
Syrian Air Force

In 1953 the Syrian government placed an order for 20 Spitfire F.Mk 22s, and deliveries began in the following year. Though it is known that the aircraft were serialled 501-520, little is known of their subsequent use.

This rather sorry-looking aircraft was among the Mk 22s operated by the Syrian air force and was one of four photographed near Damascus prior to the Six Day War in 1967.

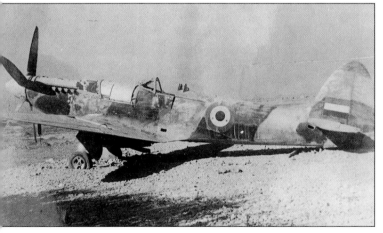

Thailand
Royal Thai Air Force

In 1950 the Thai government purchased 30 reconditioned Spitfire F/FR.Mk XIVs for the Royal Thai Air Force. These carried the serials U14-1/93 to U14-30/93 and equipped No. 1 Sqn of No. 1 Wing and No. 1 Sqn of No. 4 Wing between 1951 and 1954. A handful were then passed to No. 12 Sqn and flown for about a year.

Three PR.Mk 19s are also known to have been sold to the Thai air force in mid-1954.

All were ex-FEAF aircraft and were PS888, the RAF's last operational Spitfire, PM630 and PS836, the latter becoming U14-27/97 in Thai service.

An RTAF FR.Mk XIV with clipped wings and six zero-length rocket rails fitted , is seen in pre-delivery guise with an overall silver finish.

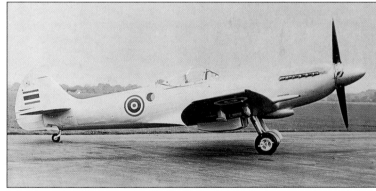

Right: PS888, the aircraft which flew the last operatonal RAF Spitfire sortie in 1954, was then sold to the RTAF and is seen here in service. Note the retention of its RAF serial number.

Turkey
Türk Hava Kuvvetleri

Among the 207 Spitfires received by the THK after World War II were four Spitfire PR.Mk 19s from ex-RAF stocks – PM548, '654, '656, and '657. After reconditioning in the UK the aircraft were delivered in 1947/48 and serialled 6551-6554 (not necessarily in that order), and were operated until at least 1954 by three reconnaissance units at different times, including 3 Bölük (Company), 10 Kesif Alay (Regiment). Bases included Afyon, in western Turkey, and Merzifon to the north.

Seafire Operators

Foreign use of the Seafire was naturally less than that of the Spitfire, given that the latter were more plentiful and there was little call for a carrier-capable aircraft outside the major powers. That said, both Canada and France operated the type from ex-RN carriers, as stop-gaps until more suitable aircraft became available. Burma and Ireland purchased 'denavalised' Seafires for land-based operations.

Dr Alfred Price, with additional material by John Heathcott

HMS Indefatigable, with No. 887 Sqn Mk IIIs aboard, made a goodwill visit to New Zealand in November 1945 before returning to the UK. Here the ship is seen in Wellington harbour.

United Kingdom
Fleet Air Arm
Wartime units

While Seafire Mk Is and IIs were the sole equipment in some FAA fighter units, only No. 801 Sqn was equipped completely with Seafire Mk Is; in other front-line units these early Seafires generally operated alongside Seafire Mk IIs. Units with Seafire Mk IIs and IIIs were either fighter units equipped exclusively with Seafires, or attack squadrons (e.g. torpedo-bomber/reconnaissance units with Swordfish) with a fighter flight of Seafires. The following units operated Merlin-engined Seafires during World War II and in the early post-war years.

Mk IB: Nos 801, 807, 809, 816, 842, 879, 885, 887, 894, 897 Sqns
F./L./LR.Mk IIC: Nos 801, 807, 808, 809, 816, 833, 834, 842, 879, 880, 884, 885, 886, 887, 889, 894, 895, 897, 899 Sqns
F./L.Mk III: Nos 802, 803, 805, 806, 807, 808, 809, 879, 880, 883, 885, 886, 887, 889, 894, 899 Sqns

Post-war units

When No. 801 Sqn disbanded in mid-1946, the front-line career of the Merlin-engined Seafire came to an end. This squadron had already received the first operational Griffon-engined Mk XVs, this variant going on to serve with nine front-line units. The following units operated Griffon-engined Seafires post-war.

F.Mk XV: Nos 800, 801, 802, 803, 804, 805, 806, 809, 883 Sqns
FR.Mk 17: Nos 800, 805, 807, 809, 879 Sqns
FR.Mk 47: Nos 800, 804 Sqns

RNVR units

The first Royal Naval Volunteer Reserve squadrons were established in 1947, four of them operating Seafires at different times. No. 1833 Sqn operated both generations of 'Griffon-Seafire', though not the Mk 46.

F.Mk XV: Nos 1831, 1832, 1833 Sqns
FR.Mk 17: Nos 1830, 1831, 1832, 1833 Sqns
FR.Mk 46: No. 1832 Sqn
FR.Mk 47: No. 1833 Sqn

Non-operational units

These comprised a myriad of different squadrons and flights, often operating a variety of types concurrently. Those employing Seafires, during wartime and post-war, were engaged in a variety of tasks, including training, trials and evaluation and communications.

Secondline squadrons that, at one time or other, are known to have operated Seafire(s) were: Nos 700, 703, 706, 708, 709, 715, 718, 719, 721, 727, 728, 731, 733, 736, 736B, 737, 738, 740, 744, 746, 748, 751, 757, 759, 760, 761, 764, 766, 767, 768, 770, 771, 772, 773, 775, 776, 777, 778, 779, 780, 781, 782, 787, 787Y, 790, 791 794, 798, 799 Sqns

Right: A Seafire Mk 17 of No. 1833 Sqn, RNVR prepares to land at a shore base. The Mk 17 saw less than two years of frontline service, but went on to equip four Reserve squadrons.

Below: No. 801 Sqn L.Mk IIIs are seen ashore, possibly at Skeabrae, in late 1944/early 1945, prior to sailing into action in the Far East.

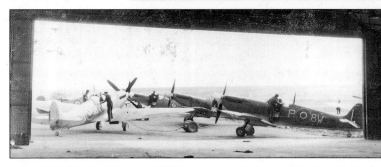

Below: The Station Flight at RNAS Lossiemouth operated Seafire Mk 46 LA546 '900/LM' during early 1948. It was the personal mount of Capt. (later Admiral Sir) Caspar John.

Above: Seafire F.Mk IIIs of No. 880 Sqn visited Australia after VJ-Day. Here they are seen at Hobart on the Australian island state of Tasmania. Note the Seafires' P-40-type centreline drop tanks, unique to this squadron.

Burma
Union of Burma Air Force

Burma's Seafires were interesting hybrids, essentially 'denavalised' Mk XVs fitted with Spitfire Mk XVIII wings. Refurbished by Airwork Ltd, the 20 aircraft were delivered in 1951 to serve alongside Spitfire Mk XVIIIs in the counter-insurgency role.

Serialled UB401-420, these aircraft served with No. 1 Squadron for at least three years (at least one source suggests as long as 10 years), flying sorties against Burmese separatists, but were finally replaced by Sea Furies, possibly as early as 1954, bringing the Seafire's front-line service to an end.

Below: UB415 has had a single letter 'O' code applied, presumably while serving with No. 1 Sqn.

Seen shortly after delivery, Burma's Mk XVs were equipped with centreline drop tanks and underwing bomb racks.

Canada
Royal Canadian Navy

No. 803 Sqn, FAA equipped with Sea Hurricanes and Fulmars and after operations in and around the Indian Ocean, disbanded in August 1943. Upon its reformation in June 1945, it received 25 Seafire L.Mk IIIs and was to join the 19th CAG for service aboard an 'Implacable'-class carrier. However, VJ-Day brought a change of plan, the unit re-equipping with 12 Spitfire Mk XVs in August.

Within six months No. 803 Sqn had been transferred, with 35 Seafires, to the RCN to equip the 19th CAG aboard HMCS *Warrior*, on loan to the Canadian government. Based at Dartmouth, Nova Scotia when not embarked (and while problems with the Seafires' supercharger clutches were rectified), No. 803 returned, with *Warrior* to the UK in mid-1947, re-equipping with Hawker Sea Furies for service aboard HMCS *Magnificent*. The Seafire Mk XVs were passed to No. 883 Sqn.

This unit, like No. 803 Sqn, had been allocated to the RCN, reforming at Arbroath in September 1945 with Seafire Mk IIIs. The intention had been that this unit would join the British Pacific Fleet as part of the new 10th CAG but, again, VJ-Day made this

unnecessary. No. 883 moved instead to Nutts Corner in November, picking up No. 803's Mk XVs as it did so. Manning difficulties had meanwhile prevented its transfer to the RCN, and it disbanded at Machrihanish the following February.

Reformed in May 1947, No. 883 Sqn was again earmarked for transfer to the RCN, initially flying Seafire Mk XVs from Dartmouth and HMCS *Warrior* with the 18th CAG. In September 1948 it relinquished its Seafires for Sea Fury FB.Mk 11s and was renumbered No. 871 Sqn (later VF-871).

The Seafires were then relegated to second-line use, with Training Air Group Number 1. Their swansong came in 1949, when a flight of 10 Seafires was formed for a display at the Canadian National Exhibition. Though two of its pilots, including the flight's CO, Lt-Cmdr (P) C. G. Watson, were killed in a training accident, the display by 'Watson's Circus' went ahead to considerable acclaim.

Above: Though it carries the 'AA' codes of No. 883 Sqn, this Mk XV landing at an RCAF base at River, Manitoba in September 1948 had, by then, been handed over to Training Air Group No. 1.

Right: Mk XV PR434 'AA-J' is seen on its shore base at Dartmouth, Nova Scotia in 1947/48.

France
Aéronautique Navale

From March 1946, the French navy was supplied with 48 refurbished late-production Seafire L.Mk IIIs for use by 1 Flottille (1F) at its Hyères base. After working up 1F embarked in the light fleet carrier *Arromanches* (ex-HMS *Colossus*), then on loan from the RN, for carrier training.

Between January and June 1948, an additional 65 Mk IIIs were delivered, these consisting of 30 flyable aircraft and 35 for component recovery. This allowed the

formation of a second Seafire squadron – 12 Flottille – by splitting 1F in August 1948.

Meanwhile, with the activities of Communist insurgents in Indo-China reaching serious levels, *Arromanches* sailed for the region, to relieve *Dixmude* (ex-HMS *Biter*), on 30 October 1948, with 24 of 1F's Seafires and 12 SBD-5 Dauntlesses of 4F aboard. Arriving off Saigon on 29 November, the carrier disembarked most of its aircraft to Bien Hoa from where they immediately

began operational missions (mainly Tac/R and strafing) under the direction of the Armée de l'Air. Both squadrons rejoined *Arromanches* on 10 December and began operations against targets further north from the Gulf of Tonkin. By mid-January 1949, a lack of spares and losses due to light winds had reduced the strengths of both units to such an extent that their continued presence off Indo-China was pointless.

Arromanches returned to the northern hemisphere, 1F and 12F re-equipping with 15 Seafire ex-FAA Mk XVs, delivered in

June 1949. However, with an attrition rate similar to that of the RN, the Aéronavale had insufficient serviceable aircraft with which to maintain a squadron aboard *Arromanches* in the Mediterranean, and in 1950 F6F-5 Hellcats arrived to replace the remaining Seafires.

Training and communications units based ashore also flew both Seafire marks until about 1949. These were Escadrilles de Servitude 1S, 2S, 3S, 4S, 10S, 11S and 54S. The last named of these operated Mk IIIs and XVs until 1951.

Above and right: Seafire L.Mk IIIs (including '1.F-22') of 1F are seen during operations from Arromanches in about 1948. Apart from a short spell off Indo-China, deployments were confined to the Mediterranean and Atlantic.

Ireland
Aer Chor nah-Eireann/Irish Air Corps

The Irish Air Corps took delivery of 12 'denavalised' Seafire L.Mk IIIs in February 1947 to re-equip No. 1 (Fighter) Squadron at Gormanston, then flying Hurricane Mk IIs. The aircraft had been refurbished by Supermarine at Long Marston and were finished in an overall grey/green scheme, with red spinners.

The unit operated these aircraft for two years, though the last of the aircraft - 155 (ex-PR237) – was not finally withdrawn until June 1954. It was thus the last Merlin-engined Seafire in service anywhere.

Seven of the IAC's dozen Seafire L.Mk IIIs are seen here together, sometime shortly after their delivery. Note the black panther badge of No. 1 Sqn, painted on the nose of 149. Though the Seafires were withdrawn in 1954, the IAC's two-seat Spitfire T.Mk 9s lasted another seven years.

United States
US Navy

During and after World War II, the USN received 12 Seafire Mk IBs, 49 Mk IICs, and single examples of Mks XV and 47. All flew with second-line units or test establishments.

The Mk I and Mk II aircraft are believed to have received the USN designation FS-1 (Fighter, Supermarine, first variant), though some sources suggest that this designation was reserved for a batch of ex-RAF Spitfire Mk Vs that, in the event, were not delivered.

A handful of Seafire L.Mk IICs were transferred to the USN in August 1944 and allocated to the Liberator Wing based at Dunkeswell, Devon. Fitted with American VHF radios, these aircraft provided air combat training for the Liberator crews, in order to familiarise them with the tactics employed by fighter pilots in the skies over Europe.

Senta A Pua!

1st Brazilian Fighter Group

Among the many units of many nations that fought for the Allied cause in World War II, the small group of Brazilian Thunderbolt pilots of 1º Grupo de Aviação de Caça had one of the proudest records, and have maintained their 'go for it' spirit to the present day.

The night of 15 August 1942 was a quiet one off the northeastern coast of Brazil and the 4,800-ton liner *Baependy* steamed over calm waters some 20 nm (23 miles; 37 km) off the coast of Sergipe. Fully lit, the ship was alive with music. The passengers had just left the dining room and an orchestra played in honour of the ship's executive officer, whose birthday was being celebrated on the main deck. At 7.12 pm a loud explosion jolted the ship. All lights went out and general panic ensued. Those passengers who were not at the dance were resting in their cabins. In two minutes the *Baependy* had gone under: of 306 passengers onboard, 270 went down with the ship; 142 Brazilian Army personnel who were

being ferried to bases in Recife perished with the liner.

In the distance, Korvettenkapitän Harro Schacht, commander of *U-507*, watched the explosion of the Brazilian steamer. The *Baependy* was the first victim of a five-day killing spree undertaken by that particular German submarine. After the carnage, 607 passengers on Brazilian ships were dead, and public opinion was aflame. Brazil had severed diplomatic ties with Germany and Italy in January 1942, but the sinking of five ships in quick succession took the Rio de Janeiro crowds to the streets. War with the Axis was inevitable.

In 1942, the Brazilian air force was a fledgling

institution. A mere year had passed since the aviation branches of the Brazilian Army and Navy had been combined to form the Força Aérea Brasileira, or FAB. The initially motley bunch of obsolete aircraft – including Boeing 256s, Vought V-65B Corsairs, Vultee V11 GB-2s and North American NA-46s, among others – soon began to grow into modern flights of Lend-Lease B-25 Mitchells, Curtiss P-40Es and P-40Ks. North American T-6 Texans, Lockheed Venturas and Hudsons, Consolidated Vultee PBY-5 Catalinas and other aircraft allowed young Brazilian air force officers to scan the seas in search of enemy submarines. From bases lining the 8000-km (5,000-mile) long coastline, Brazilian and American crews began a relentless hunt for the roving wolfpacks that hunted in the warm waters. For over a year, the Brazilian air force honed its combat skills flying endless hours over the Atlantic in search of enemy submarines.

Soon, however, pursuing the enemy off the territorial waters was not enough. A Brazilian Expeditionary Force was organised for combat in Europe. Not to be outdone by the Army, the air force decided to send its own contingent to fight alongside the American ally. On 7 December 1943 a C-87 transport took off from Natal Air Base for Africa. Onboard was a committee formed

Top: Pilots of 1º GAvCa gather around P-47D-28-RE 44-19666 of Esquadrilha Amarela (Yellow Flight). Each flight was identifed by a letter. The others were: A – Vermelha (Red), C – Azul (blue) and D – Verde (green).

Left: At war's end, the surviving Thunderbolts of the 'Jambocks' returned to Brazil. Joined by other P-47s acquired in the early 1950s, these aircraft formed the backbone of the FAB for many years.

Jet equipment, in the form of Gloster Meteor F.Mk 8s, arrived in May 1953 and were known as F-8s in Brazilian service (two-seat T.Mk 7s were TF-7s). Here a 'Jambock' Meteor scores a direct hit with napalm on the enemy's washing during a demonstration at Santa Cruz.

by high-ranking Brazilian army and air force officers whose mission was to liaise with the US forces then struggling for a foothold in North Africa. After 11 hours over the Atlantic and stops at Dakar, Tindouf and Casablanca, the Liberator finally landed at Algiers. For the next few weeks, the four air force officers involved in the mission learned first-hand what awaited the units being formed at home. Despite the limitation in numbers of experienced pilots, the Brazilian government decided to send two units to the same theatre of operations the as that to which the Brazilian Expeditionary Force would be assigned.

Establishment

On 18 December 1943 the 1st Brazilian Fighter Group was created by government decree number 6.123. An Observation and Liaison Flight was also created and sent to the combat zone. On 27 December, 34-year-old Major Nero Moura, from the town of Cachoeira do Sul in Brazil's southernmost state of Rio Grande do Sul, was picked as its commander; he immediately chose 16 officers and 16 NCOs from the extensive lists of volunteers that had flooded the Air Ministry since October. These men would be the flight leaders, the ground staff commander and officers in charge of operations, intelligence, engineering, supplies, logistics, ordnance, and communications, as well as the sergeants in charge of the flight line and maintenance, among others. A Brazilian air force group was equivalent to a USAAF squadron. The unit was formed into four flights and the initial cadre of handpicked flight leaders in turn chose their men from country-wide volunteers. Once the group was complete, Major Nero Moura's 32 key men left for Orlando, Florida, where they undertook initial training at the USAAF School of Applied Tactics. After 10 days of lectures, which included briefings by USAAF aces just back from Europe and the Pacific, the group transferred to Alachua Army Airfield near Gainesville, Florida, where they began flight

practice on the Curtiss P-40N Warhawks of the 1166th School Squadron. The Brazilian pilots sent to Florida were experienced flyers, most with over 1,500 flight hours' experience; however, Brazil had been at peace for a long time and the most basic rudiments of air combat had to be quickly learned. During the next 50 days, these men were exposed to modern combat tactics, flying air combat, air-to-air and air-to-ground gunnery, interception and close formation sorties, as well as receiving first-hand instruction on the use of radar and learning the capabilities of enemy aircraft.

In Brazil, the lists of volunteers were quickly wrapped up with the selection of 40 men, and the group began taking shape. Pilots serving at the Aviation School in Rio de Janeiro were sent to Recife and Natal Air Bases where they flew some 20 hours on the Curtiss P-40Ks available to units operating there. On 18 March the small cadre from Florida arrived at Albrook Army Air Field in Panama where it was united with the growing contingent of pilots and ground personnel who arrived in several flights from Brazil. Some 350 men were flown from Brazil to the Canal Zone between February and

'Father' to 1º GAvCa was Nero Moura who led the Group from inception to war's end. He returned to command the wing in the Meteor era.

Below: To this day, the badge of the fighting ostrich (a reference to the poor food on the Italian bases) is proudly worn by 1º/1º GAvCa's F-5 pilots.

Eagle-eyed photographer

Despite the excellent gun camera footage that the pilots of the 350th FG brought back from each mission, Allied High Command decided to install high resolution K-25A oblique cameras on the bomb racks under the left wings of a few of the group's Thunderbolts for damage assessment after each attack. The 1o GAvCa received four of these cameras and lost no time using them after each strike, the tail-end Charlie executing an extra pass after the bombs had been dropped over the target. This mission was extremely dangerous, as it forced the number four pilots to fly once more against the now-alerted enemy gunners. The Brazilians were soon bringing back extremely valuable photography, which was passed to the Group Intelligence Section.

Among all the 1st BFG pilots, one was truly amazing, not only as a superb pilot but as an above average 'photographer'. 2nd Lieutenant Pedro de Lima Mendes, who finished the war with 95 missions had the eyesight of an eagle according to then 1st Lieutenant Rui Moreira Lima: "He saw what nobody else could see. Besides, he was extremely lucky. Among all 51 of us, he was the one with the greatest number of enemy AAA batteries to his credit, but his plane was never hit!" One day his flight was flying at 14,000ft when Lima Mendes called on the radio: "I see a truck, will be right back!" already diving towards the ground. His surprised companions watched in

awe having had no time to react. Then, they saw the small orange mushroom of an explosion on the road below and soon Lima Mendes was edging his Thunderbolt back into the formation as if nothing had happened! He had superb situational awareness and often found such improbable targets that people had trouble believing his reports. Moreira Lima tells another most impressive story: "Once we had a hard time believing him as he came in on the airwaves reporting that he had seen a destroyer in the fairgrounds of a castle below! We flew over the villas near Lake Garda but deep down we all knew it was impossible for an oceanic ship to be operating in that area. Our search was fruitless. Undaunted, Lima Mendes reported his sighting to intelligence after landing, and went to his tent. That afternoon, his report was the source of great amusement at the base and word soon spread that a young Brazilian had seen a warship near Lake Garda! During the following morning, however, word arrived at Pisa saying that what our friend had seen was in fact a destroyer which was given by Mussolini himself to his close friend, the great Italian poet and aviator Gabrielle d'Annunzio, which the latter had transformed into a wing of his castle in Laguna Veria! From then on, Lima Mendes' word became the law!"

To operate the K-25 camera, however, good eyesight was not enough. One had to have extraordinary flying abilities as the best results were had flying close above the ground. "When the K-25s were distributed among the squadrons of the 350th", recalls Rui Moreira Lima, "the USAAF High Command decided to award a weekly prize to the unit which was able to bring back the best operational photos of important targets for intelligence purposes. Week after week the prize was given to the 1st BFG. We had our secret weapon in Lieutenant Lima Mendes". Perhaps the most incredible K-25 story stems from a mission performed by Blue Flight over the Brenner Pass. As usual, the 'group photographer' flew as number 4 with the K-25 under his left wing. It must have been with shock that the young lab operator at Allied intelligence at Caserta saw the post-mission results in the rolls of film brought back from Lieutenant Lima Mendes' plane. For in one of them, filling the entire frame and with eyes as big as baseballs, a German soldier stared directly at him, paralysed by the shock of seeing a P-47 Thunderbolt passing a scant six feet away!

criss-crossed the sea lanes around them in search of enemy U-boats.

US Army food had been a source of curiosity and humour for the Brazilians ever since their arrival in Panama. Joking that they could eat just about anything the US mess chiefs threw at them, they began calling themselves ostriches. The moniker stuck and, soon enough, Captain Fortunato Câmara de Oliveira took inspiration from Lieutenant Pedro de Lima Mendes's accentuated nasal profile to design what is today the unit's well known badge: a gun-toting ostrich protected by a blue shield engraved with the Southern Cross, standing on a stable cloud in the red sky of war. On the cloud was the battle cry 'Senta a Pua', a typical expression from northeastern Brazil which means 'hit hard' or 'give it to them'.

On 6 October 1944, after a stop in Naples, the *Colombie* finally anchored near the war-torn port of Livorno. After disembarking in pouring rain, the 1st Brazilian Fighter Group was met by then-Colonel Nelson Lavenere-Wanderley, one of two Brazilian liaison officers already in Italy with the XXII Tactical Air Command to prepare for the unit's arrival. A small battered train awaited the Brazilian airmen for the next

leg of the trip, and after a full night on the tracks, they finally arrived at their new home, the small village of Tarquinia.

Located some 96 km (60 miles) north of Rome, the medieval town of Tarquinia is barely big enough to figure on any but the most detailed maps. However, to the 1st Brazilian Fighter Group, it is one of the most important of Italian cities. Tarquinia was home to the USAAF's 350th Fighter Group, a much-distinguished unit, part of the 62nd Fighter Wing of the 12th Air Force and comprising the 345th 'Devil Hawk', 346th 'Checker Board' and 347th 'Screaming Red Ass' Fighter Squadrons. These units had been fighting since the North African landings and had changed their aircraft from P-39 Airacobras to P-47s. A small runway, derelict hangars and control tower, bombed buildings and the busy servicing of US and British aircraft made up the scene that greeted the Brazilians on their arrival at their new home. During the course of the next week, the 1st Brazilian Fighter Group – now assigned as the fourth unit of the 350th and thus designated the 1st Brazilian Fighter Squadron (1st BFS) – began receiving its 30 P-47Ds already painted in olive drab with green and

yellow fin stripes and the Brazilian star on the rear fuselage. Alphanumerical A, B, C and D markings followed by individual aircraft numbers identified each aircraft in one of the four – Blue, Green, Red and Yellow – flights into which the 1st BFG was subdivided. The fighting ostrich unit badge was applied to the aircraft's cowlings by a small group of mechanics led by none other than Lieutenant Pedro de Lima Mendes himself. Only the aircraft of Lieutenant Colonel Nero Moura and his operations officer, Major Oswaldo Pamplona Pinto, had different markings: they were aluminium-finished and carried the numbers 1 and 2 in black on the engine cowling.

Gaining combat experience

One by one the Brazilian pilots flew alongside their USAAF comrades in arms, gradually gaining combat experience and operational know-how. On 6 November, First Lieutenant John Richardson Cordeiro e Silva was shot down by AAA while returning from a mission

1o GAvCa pilots crowd together for a mission briefing at Tarquinia, 1944. The heavy B-3 leather jackets, seen here, later gave way to the newer fabric B-15.

San Giusto Airfield on the outskirts of Pisa was the 1st BFG's first operational home. The airfield had been heavily bombed but many buildings, including the control tower, were usable.

Thunderbolt 'A4' of Red flight is seen in these photographs. This P-47 was the usual mount of 2nd Lt Alberto Martins Torres, who was to complete 99 combat missions. It became FAB 4106 in the post-war Brazilian air force and was eventually struck off charge after an accident at Santa Cruz in May 1946.

to the outskirts of Bologna. It was the first day on which the young lieutenants flew as 'tail-end-Charlie' for the afternoon flights of the 350th. Lieutenant Cordeiro e Silva was assigned to a flight of the 345th. Hit by flak on his return to Tarquinia, he advised his leader that he would attempt a belly landing in a valley amid the towering Apennine peaks. He continued talking to his flight leader throughout his approach. As his aircraft touched the ground, it erupted into a fireball. The reality of combat immediately became crystal clear to the pilots of the 1st Brazilian Fighter Group.

One day later, the men of the 1st Brazilian Fighter Group were still mourning their fallen comrade when another accident shook their morale even further. A pair of Brazilian Thunderbolts took off from Tarquinia in the late morning for a training run over simulated triple-A positions. The wingman was Second Lieutenant Oldegard Olsen Sapucaia. Upon completing his attack, he banked violently, simulating evasive action; almost immediately, he lost control of his aircraft, which turned upside down and entered an irrecoverable inverted spin. Lieutenant Oldegard was still able to eject the canopy and free himself from the cockpit of his stricken aircraft, but he was too low for his parachute to open effectively. He hit the ground at more than 400 km/h (250 mph). Two days later, all units operating Thunderbolts received a technical order informing them that the new P-47D, equipped with a bubble canopy that provided improved all-around visibility, was severely susceptible to compressibility. All Ds were immediately

modified, receiving dorsal fins in kits from the United States. The notification stipulating the use of these kits had arrived two days too late at Tarquinia.

JAMBOCK

On 11 November the Brazilians began flying by themselves. For the first time, the callsign JAMBOCK appeared on the airwaves. It was assigned to them by 350th FG operations, and it was only long after the war that the Brazilians discovered it was a name given to a small South African whip made of rhinoceros tail hair!

Other casualties marked the early days of the 1st Brazilian Fighter Group in the MTO. On 16 November a public relations stunt claimed two more pilots in an air-to-air crash between a USAAF C-47 transport carrying a film crew and a 1st BFG Thunderbolt flown by First Lieutenant Luiz Felipe Perdigão Medeiros da Fonseca. A slight left slide caused by the C-47 pilot momentarily looking toward the aircraft

flying off his left wing was enough to cause the collision, which sent both aircraft plummeting down. Lieutenant Perdigo was able to bail out to safety, but the C-47 entered a spin and exploded on the ground. Inside, along for the ride, were Second Lieutenants Rolland Rittmeister and Waldyr Pequeno de Mello. Each had flown just one combat mission.

Tarquinia was proving an unlucky venue for the 1st Brazilian Fighter Group, but the setbacks of the first few weeks were not enough to bring down the unit's morale. By the third week in November, the fighter sweeps became dive-bombing missions followed by sweeps against targets of opportunity, and soon the once-fledgling warriors began collecting results.

Tarquinia was 45 minutes from the bomb line as the crow flies, so it came as no surprise that on 2 December the entire group moved to San Giusto Airfield on the outskirts of Pisa, some 320 km (200 miles) farther northwest. Despite having been massively bombed, the

Above: An enemy convoy comes under attack in the middle of an Italian village. With air superiority achieved, the full weight of 1º GAvCa could be brought to bear on ground targets.

One of the weapons used successfully by the Brazilians was the 4.5-in (114-mm) M10 triple 'bazooka' rocket launcher. In all, 850 rockets were launched by 1º GAvCa P-47s. This aircraft became FAB 4110 in the post-war air force and survives today as a monument at Curitiba AB.

airfield was still operational, and the concrete and steel matting runway had recently been repaired. Without a pause in their operations schedule, the aircraft lined up on the muddy runway of Tarquinia and took off for their daily missions, but returned directly to their new home where advance parties were already waiting to recover each flight. At Pisa, the officers of the 350th were billeted at the Albergo Nettuno, a five-story hotel that provided much better living conditions than the windswept canvas tents of Tarquinia.

With the arrival of the severe winter of 1944, the Allied offensive bogged down and fighting was reduced to skirmishes between Allied patrols probing the German defences of the formidable Gothic Line on the slopes of the Apennines. In the air, however, the pace of operations never faltered, as the main targets were far behind enemy lines, where any efforts to reinforce the front were taken out by the roving flights of fighter-bombers from the XIIth AF.

During the cold clear winter days that marked the end of 1944, the young Brazilians flew mission upon mission, rapidly gaining combat experience. Armed with two 500-lb bombs and eight 0.50-in Browning machine-guns with tracer, incendiary and armour-piercing rounds, the 1st BFS's P-47s were a formidable foe for the German ground troops hiding in the snow. In addition to ground attack sorties, the Brazilians flew top cover for Allied bombers, mostly North American B-25s on missions against targets in northern Italy. By the end of the war, nine Brazilians had flown over 90 missions, four had flown more than 80, four more than 70 and 14 more than 40 combat missions. Throughout the whole Italian campaign, only six pilots arrived to replenish casualties among the now-veteran flyers.

Operational accidents and German triple-A had inflicted a fair number of casualties on the 1st BFS. With only five replacements arriving from USAAF training bases, Lieutenant Colonel Nero Moura decided to train three flight controllers who had completed training in P-40s in Panama but were not considered suitable for conversion to the P-47. After being led through the P-47 instruction syllabus, the three controllers were finally included in the 1st BFS flight list.

Despite the excellent gun camera footage that the pilots of the 350th FG brought back from each mission, Allied High Command decided to install high resolution K-25A oblique cameras on the bomb racks under the left wings of a few of the group's Thunderbolts for damage assessment after each attack. The 1º GAvCa received four of these cameras and lost no time using them after each strike, the 'tail-end Charlie' executing an extra pass after the bombs had been dropped over the target. This mission was extremely dangerous, as it forced the number four pilots to fly once more against the now-alerted enemy gunners. The Brazilians were soon bringing back extremely valuable photography, which was passed to the Group Intelligence Section.

Rocket-equipped

In the beginning of February, the first of 28 Thunderbolts was sent to the XXII TAC depot in Naples to be fitted with M8A2 4.5-in rocket launchers. It was not long before the 1st BFS pilots hated the large, cumbersome contraptions, which increased drag and were extremely unreliable. It was also in February that Lieutenant Colonel Nero Moura was forced to stand down Yellow Flight due to that flight's particularly high operational losses. For health reasons Blue and Red Flight leaders, Captains Fortunato and Lafayette, as well as the operations officer Major Pamplona Pinto, were sent home with a fourth pilot, First Lieutenant Ismar Ferreira Costa. Captain Lagares became the new operations officer while Captains

Roberto Pessoa Ramos, Kopp and Horácio Monteiro Machado became the new leaders of Green, Red and Blue Flights, respectively.

There were few enemy aircraft in northern Italy by then, but flak batteries abounded. German gunners were extremely experienced and daily duels against enemy flak were the norm.

While the pilots of the 1st BFG flew against enemy targets, ground support personnel worked at a frenzied pace to restore damaged aircraft to the flight line. Long cold nights and sleepless

P-47D Thunderbolt
Rui Moreira Lima's Thunderbolt was one of the Group's original aircraft, handed over on 28 October 1944. Lima flew 94 combat missions with the 1st BFG.

Strange encounter

1st Lieutenant Rui Moreira Lima recalls a mission to the Casarsa rail lines that ended in a very peculiar way: "Casarsa was a difficult target, a railway bridge heavily defended by flak. When we arrived the sky lit up with 88-mm, 37-mm and 20-mm shells bursting around us throughout the dive. As the leader attacked a large convoy moving up a nearby highway I took my wingman and attacked a flak position, which was giving him a lot of trouble. Suddenly my plane shuddered and I knew that I was hit, although I was able to destroy the gun emplacement in the pass. As I struggled to control my plane, I still had to fly through an explosion which had been caused by the other attacking planes. I was able to regain height but my Thunderbolt was spewing thick black smoke and my canopy was rapidly filling with oil. I had to dive to extinguish the fire and then re-started my engine to re-gain height and try to make it back to Pisa.

"I finally belly landed at Forli, an RAF-occupied base. As soon as the plane stopped I jumped out fearing an explosion and ran towards where I would be safe from flying debris, but the plane did not explode. I was wiping my left eye from all the hot oil that had impaired my vision when a jeep drove up to me with an impeccably clad RAF pilot standing by the driver. When it stopped, he walked over to where I was and asked me in perfect Portuguese: "What the hell happened to you? And by the way how are those girls in Copacabana?" As there was no way he could be speaking my native tongue I began to reply in English but was immediately cut off by a string of swear words and more Portuguese! Fate had brought me to the airfield where Robert Tate, a Brazilian of English descent born in Curitiba, as I later learned, commanded an RAF Polish recce squadron!

As soon as I was dismissed by Forli's medical staff, the British and Polish pilots treated me to their own brand of medicine – vodka in large healthy doses. Needless to say, I was only back at Pisa two days later with a monster headache!

Lt Lima (left) poses with Lt Roberto Tormin Costa in front of a 'Jambock' Thunderbolt. Post-war, Rui Lima became a major with 1º GAvCa during the Meteor era.

hours were spent patching fuselages torn by flak, engines with peculiar problems and cockpits with glitches and faults. At dawn, as soon as the day's missions were posted, the P-47s were armed accordingly. Bands of 0.50-in ammunition were carefully prepared for the upcoming mission, the 1,920 shells aligned in the correct order: tracer, incendiary, armour-piercing, incendiary. Bombs were attached to the racks, and the rocket pods were strapped under each wing. These could be fired individually or in salvos of six, after which the three canisters under each wing could be ejected. In their free time, the 1st BFG ground personnel and assorted soldiers and NCOs gathered at their Clube Copacabana, which soon became one of the most vivacious spots in Pisa.

Spring offensive

The snows began to thaw in northern Italy with the coming of spring, and the Allied High Command was itching to unleash the long-awaited spring offensive which would roll down the slopes of the Apennines into the Po river valley and the Italian industrial heartland cities of Milan, Bologna and Turin. The American 5th Army had achieved a series of hard-fought successes that placed it in a very favourable position to begin moving rapidly towards the Po once the ground was free of snow. The British 8th Army had arrived at the Senio river and was regrouping to advance in a

Using a makeshift platform, Brazilian mechanics carry out repairs on one of the Group's jeeps.

co-ordinated move northward. Throughout the winter, flights of Allied fighter-bombers and large formations of bombers relentlessly searched for industrial and military targets in a never-ending campaign to weaken the German enemy. Railroad junctions and stretches of track, motor pools, ammunition dumps, enemy occupied buildings, convoys of trucks and animal-drawn transport, bridges and troop positions were the main targets assigned to the Allied fighter-bombers throughout the long winter of 1944/45.

On 9 April tanks and troops began to move north. Mark Clark's American 5th Army drove towards the Po on the west while General McCreery's Eighth British Army sprang toward the Austrian and Yugoslav borders on the east. All along the front, German defences began to collapse and a hasty but organised retreat was set in motion to cross the Po and regroup on the northern bank. Air operations increased, and on 14 April Allied aircraft pounded the enemy.

In the second week of April, two pilots arrived at Pisa as replacements, a welcome relief but far below the numbers needed to refresh the unit. Throughout that week, aircraft and crews worked double time to hit the retreating enemy

Accommodation at Tarquinia was spartan, to say the least. The pilots nicknamed their quarters 'The Waldorf Astoria'.

Taking an opportunity to see the sights of Pisa are 1st BFG pilots including (left to right), Theobaldo Kopp, Rui Lima and Jose Vasconcelos.

with everything they had. On 15 April strong enemy positions blocking the advance of the 6th South African Armoured Division atop Monte Sole were attacked by eight Brazilian Thunderbolts armed with 500-litre (110-Imp gal) napalm bombs and M8A2 4.5-in unguided rockets. The heavily armed aircraft swooped in low, dropping their incendiaries and turning the crest of the mountain into a scorching inferno. A few days later, 350th FG headquarters received written appreciation from the Commander II Allied Corps, responsible for the South African advance in that area. On 19 April, trained Brazilian eyes averted what could easily have become a major blue-on-blue massacre on the Via Emilia near Casalechio. Blue Flight leader Captain Horácio Machado Monteiro on an armed reconnaissance mission located enemy tanks; their absence of pre-arranged identification panels indicated they were enemy, but closer inspection revealed that

Behind enemy lines

Captain Theobaldo Antonio Kopp was in a dangerous position. A Brazilian of German extraction from the southern capital of Curitiba, he risked a traitor's reception if shot down behind enemy lines. To make matters worse, his mother, sister and brother-in-law had been trapped in northern Italy during a visit before the opening of hostilities between Brazil and the Axis. They lived at Torre del Benco on the shores of Lake Garda, and it was a recurring joke every time an 88-mm projectile exploded near a Brazilian aircraft that "Kopp's mother shooting at us", until Lieutenant-Colonel Nero Moura prohibited the joke before it got out of hand!

With this information in their possession, the Gestapo would have had an ace up its sleeve to extract intelligence from the young Brazilian flight leader were he shot down behind the lines. On 7 March, Red Flight attacked ammunition dumps near the small town of Suzzara. 7.92-mm and 13-mm machine-gun rounds hit Kopp's supercharger and wing and soon enough, the man who couldn't be shot down was floating gently towards occupied Italy. He landed in a field north of Bagnolo and was soon joined by two Italian cyclists who hid him in a small grove. One of them removed his flight jacket and placed a small cap on his head. Immediately they moved further away from the wreckage. "During moments like this," remembered Kopp, "nothing comes to your head except escape, escape, escape!"

During their flight a roving band of Black Brigade motorcyclists passed next to the three men who hid in a ditch beside the road. The two men now identified as partisans walked calmly on the road and Kopp began wondering about their very exposed situation. It was then that he noticed that some 50 yards in front walked two small children who reconnoitred the terrain ahead and let the men know that the road was clear. They finally reached a small hamlet where the Brazilian pilot

was fed and given local clothes. Their stop was brief and soon they were walking in the night trying to place as much distance as they could between the crash site and the German pursuers who were surely searching in ever growing concentric circles from the wreckage. Finally Kopp was delivered to a group of well-armed partisans in the village of Boretto, near Santa Vitoria. He was hidden at the home of a local partisan who insisted in challenging the local curfew to meet his girlfriend. Kopp would hide in a haystack every time his host left at night returning to the warmth of the house only when his Italian friend returned.

One day, he was hiding in the attic when German motorcyclists arrived to search the house. His heart almost jumped a beat when his host invited them in for some of the excellent wine produced in the region. After the customary toasts, the Italian partisan invited the German soldiers to search his home at will, but they declined and left to resume their search elsewhere. On 11 March, he was taken to Fabrico where the partisans had larger numbers. He remained at Fabrico for over a month where he met among other freedom fighters, a Russian aviator and a German who despised the Nazi regime. He moved from house to house and accompanied the partisans in several forays against enemy targets and in fights against foraging groups of Tartar deserters. Finally he was told that he could try to cross the lines into Allied territory, but his nighttime attempt failed and he was forced to return to Fabrico where he would wait for a new opportunity.

A German attack on the city forced his hasty escape to another location where he learned about the great spring offensive through the BBC. Sensing that help was near, Kopp decided to wait for the Allied troops to catch up with him and remained in hiding. On April 21, the first US Army tanks began appearing a few kilometres south of Fabrico. With five partisans, Kopp left on bicycles to regain the allied spearhead. When they were almost safe, they were spotted by a small group of SS troops who promptly opened fire.

Theobaldo Kopp smiles from the cockpit of his Thunderbolt. He was to spend six weeks on the run with Partisans.

The six men hid in a roadside ditch as bullets grazed the crest just inches from their heads. Soon one of the partisans was dead. Kopp was given a revolver and asked to keep the enemy at bay while the partisans went off for help. During 15 long minutes, the young Brazilian captain made sure the enemy stayed inside the small house they occupied, until some 50 partisans arrived from the nearby town. At this moment an American tank appeared down the road and was soon flagged to join the fray. After a few shells the enemy surrendered and there was nothing Kopp and the US Army tank crew could do to keep the Italians from executing the small band of German soldiers. Kopp then hitchhiked south until he reached Florence where he was interrogated by intelligence before returning to Pisa and the 1st BFG.

As soon as the Italian campaign was over, Theobaldo Antonio Kopp was given a jeep with which to search the north of Italy for his family. A few weeks later he rejoined his mother, his sister and brother in law in Milan.

---

the tanks were actually American Shermans – one of which did sport the mandatory yellow identification panels – which for some reason were far beyond their supposed position. Blue Flight leader radioed for instructions and was told to engage the 'enemy' tanks. Refusing to attack what he was sure were friendly forces, Captain Horácio returned home. His decision was confirmed when the tanks were identified as a vanguard force of the US 1st Armoured Division that had breached enemy lines and

decided to capitalise on their initiative by racing toward the valley.

Fighter Aviation Day

For the Brazilians of the 1st BFG, the most significant day of the great spring offensive was 22 April 1945, a date still marked as the Brazilian air force's Fighter Aviation Day. That day dawned cloudy and grey, and the 22 pilots capable of flying arrived at Pisa San Giusto from the Albergo Nettuno early in the morning. The

mission rate of the previous days and the need to block the German escape through the northern passes promised another busy day for the 1st BFG. On the other side of the Apennines, Feldmarschall Albert Kesselring's forces retreated rapidly, trying to find a safe place to regroup and block the Allied advance. Air power would have to catch them from the rear. The low ceiling had cancelled the dawn flight, but at 08.30 the first four JAMBOCK aircraft armed with two 500-lb general-purpose

'Jambock Jugs'

P-47D Thunderbolt
The P-47s of the 1st Brazillian Fighter Group in Italy were initially painted in standard olive drab and neutral grey with the exception of those flown by the group commander and his deputy. '1' was the aircraft of Lieutenant-Colonel Nero Moura, who eventually flew 65 combat missions.

P-47D Thunderbolt
More typical of 1º GAvCa Thunderbolts was 'C3' of Blue flight, whose most experienced pilot was Pedro de Lima Mendes with 95 combat missions. This aircraft has a different style of national insignia to that of the group commander. The group badge and mission markings were usually carried on the port side of the fuselage only.

The gun camera of Lt Jose Robelo Meira de Vasconcell catches two German tanks trying to cross to the northern bank of the river Po , 22 April 1945. The successes of this day became legend in the FAB.

Above: Thunderbolts pour fire on an enemy command post, 18 April 1945. On a few occasions, the 1st BFG was able to lend close air support to Brazillian ground troops fighting in Italy.

A munitions depot goes up in smoke after a attack by the Brazilians. One pilot, Fredrico Gustavo dos Santos, was killed when caught in such an explosion on 13 April 1945.

bombs each left the tarmac, heading north. Five minutes later another flight followed, both assigned to look for trade between highways 40 and 70, north of the River Po. Another five minutes went by and the third flight rose to the skies. The base was momentarily quiet while 12 bomb-laden Thunderbolts formed high in the cloudy sky for a momentous day. As they approached the Po valley, weather improved to scattered clouds at 7,000 ft (2134 m) with unlimited visibility. It did not take long for the first flights to realise they had caught the enemy in the open. Throughout the day, German targets were pounded by the 1st BFG. At 15.45 Green Flight took off for the last armed reconnaissance mission of the day. By then, over 100 vehicles, three pontoon bridges, 14 enemy-held houses, three flak batteries, a railway station, six barges and several lesser targets had been destroyed by the Brazilians. Eleven missions had been flown, totalling 44 sorties. Allied troops were capable of assembling a bridgehead on the Po and advancing to the northern bank without being opposed by regrouped German forces.

The war in Italy was drawing to a close but the tempo of operations remained unaltered. In the last week of fighting, the 1st BFG lost another two aircraft.

Shot down by flak on 4 February 1945, Lt Danilo Marques Moura, the younger brother of the group CO, barely managed to parachute safely and walked for 24 days through enemy-held terrain. After many adventures, he met up with US forces and returned to his unit on 2 March. Later he returned to visit Signore Pasqualini who helped him to cross the Po.

On 2 May Lieutenant José Rebelo Meira de Vasconcellos and Aspirante-a-Aviador Roberto Tormin Costa took off on an armed reconnaissance flight to the Brenner Pass area, with orders not to fire unless fired upon. What they saw filled their hearts with joy: throughout northern Italy, people ran outdoors waving white handkerchiefs. For almost two hours the two Brazilian Thunderbolts flew low over northern Italy, their pilots waving happily and savouring a moment they would never forget.

With the armistice in Italy signed, Lieutenant

Right: The aircraft of Aspirante-a-Aviador Raymundo da Costa Canario is seen after its collision with a factory chimney at Casarsa. With 1.28 m of wing missing, the return flight was long and arduous, but ultimately successful.

The Thunderbolt was a famously tough bird, and had to be in the ground attack environment in which the Brazilians operated. Here a groundcrewman lends size to a flak hole.

Unit Heritage

For a period post-war, the flights of 1º GAvCa adopted card suits as identifying markings. The club signified 'Club' Flight. 'Club 5' is shown over the island of Santa Catarina during 1951.

Below: Natural metal 'Diamond 2' taxies at Santa Cruz, post-war.

Colonel Nero Moura sent out search parties to find and bring back the pilots who had been shot down or had been taken prisoner. In jeeps or flying in the unit's single transport, a B-25 Mitchell that bore the name *Desert Lil* on the port side and *Earthquakers* on the starboard front fuselage, the men were slowly returned to Pisa. With all of its pilots back, the 1st BFG began to evaluate the 184 days of non-stop combat against the Germans. Of the 51 pilots who flew during the war, only 22 were there to see it end. While their XXII TAC counterparts had replacement pilots flown in from the USA in a continuous basis, the replacements from Brazil were few and far between. Therefore, the 1st BFG often flew two and sometimes even three missions daily, fulfilling their orders without complaint. The maintenance personnel on the ground consistently topped the availability rate on the XXII TAC roster, providing their pilots with aircraft they could trust. 1st BFG availability rates never dropped below 77 per cent throughout the campaign, and often sat at around an 81 per cent daily rate.

The 1st BFG flew 2,546 offensive and four defensive sorties, which amounted to 5,465 hours in combat. Some 4,442 bombs were dropped (4,180 AN/M43, 88 260-lb. and 90-lb fragmentation bombs, and 166-, 90-, 110- and 165-US gal fuel tank incendiaries), 1,180,200 machine-gun rounds were fired, as well as 850 rockets. These destroyed 2,511 enemy targets of

Above: The Thunderbolts allocated to 2º/1º GAvCa retained wartime code markings. this one is passing the famous Santa Cruz Zeppelin hangar circa 1946.

Below and below left. Two views of smartly marked Piper Grasshoppers (designated L-6 in Brazillian service) used by 1º GAvCa in the 1960s as communications aircraft. Both wear the unit title proudly on the fuselage and the same cartoon and inscription. Aircraft 3107 also sports the 'James Bond 007' film logo. Movie stars and cartoon characters were popular decorations on FAB aircraft of the period.

Post-war Thunderbolt

P-47D Thunderbolt
This illustration shows typical markings for a 1º/1º GAvCa P-47 in 1946 at Santa Cruz, in this case a 'Clubs' flight machine. Post-war, the national insignia lost the 'bars' and soon disappeared from the fuselage sides altogether. FAB 4142 was one of 19 replacement Lend-Lease P-47s allocated to the Forca Aerea Brasileria in January 1946. It was written off in an accident at Septiba in April 1948.

all kinds and damaged another 1,947, among them aircraft, locomotives and railroad cars, motor transport and tanks, bridges, portions of road and railroad, enemy-held buildings, artillery positions, refineries, and boats. Of the 51 pilots who flew in Italy, 16 were shot down. Five died in combat, another five were captured by the enemy, three were able to make it back through enemy-held territory, and another three landed behind Allied lines. Three other pilots were wounded by flak and another four died in accidents. Of the 48 P-47D-25-RE, P-47D-27-RE, P-47D-28-RA, P-47D-28-RE and P-47D-30-RE Thunderbolts used throughout the campaign, 16 were lost to flak and another six in operational accidents.

The 1st BFG was small in numbers but enormous in results. According to a US Army Air Forces report ordered by the 350 FG commander, Colonel Ariel W. Nielsen, the Brazilian pilots flew only 5 per cent of the unit's missions between 6 and 29 April (the spring offensive), but in that time they destroyed 15

per cent of the vehicles, 28 per cent of the bridges, 36 per cent of the fuel depots and 85 per cent of the ammunition depots accounted for by the 350th FG. The 22 pilots who flew during the spring offensive made sure the 1st BFG completed the same number of missions as their comrades in the 345th, 346th and 347th Fighter Squadrons. For these results, Colonel Nielsen recommended the Brazilian unit for the Distinguished Unit Citation. His recommendation was sent to Washington but was probably lost in the pile of post-war documents in the rush to demobilisation. Finally, 41 years after the end of hostilities, President Ronald Reagan bestowed the now-renamed Presidential Unit Citation on the 1st BFG, allowing the Brazilian unit to join the two other foreign recipients of that prestigious medal, Nos 2 and 13 Squadrons of the RAAF.

The 1st BFG remained in Italy for two months after the end of the war, and on 2 June it flew the remaining 26 aircraft to Capodichino depot near Naples, where one was damaged in a landing accident. On 6 July 1945 all support personnel boarded the US transport *General Meigh* along with the 1st Echelon of the

Brazilian Army Expeditionary Force, which had also fought in the Italian campaign. Of the 48 aircraft allotted to the Brazilians, 26 were sent to Brazil on another ship with all the vehicles used by the unit in Italy.

Returning home

Twenty pilots boarded a ship for the United States, where 19 brand-new P-47D-30-RAs waited to be ferried to Brazil. After a long flight that took them over Mexico, Panama, several islands in the Caribbean and the jungles of Guyana, they finally crossed the Brazilian border, entering through the state of Amap in the Brazilian Amazon. On 16 July 18 P-47s – one had remained in Amap with engine problems – overflew a cloudless Rio de Janeiro in a fitting return home.

The experience gathered by the 1st Brazilian Fighter Group in the MTO was too valuable to simply forget so, upon arrival at Santa Cruz Air Base (an old airship station 80 km/50 miles

Jet 'Jambocks'

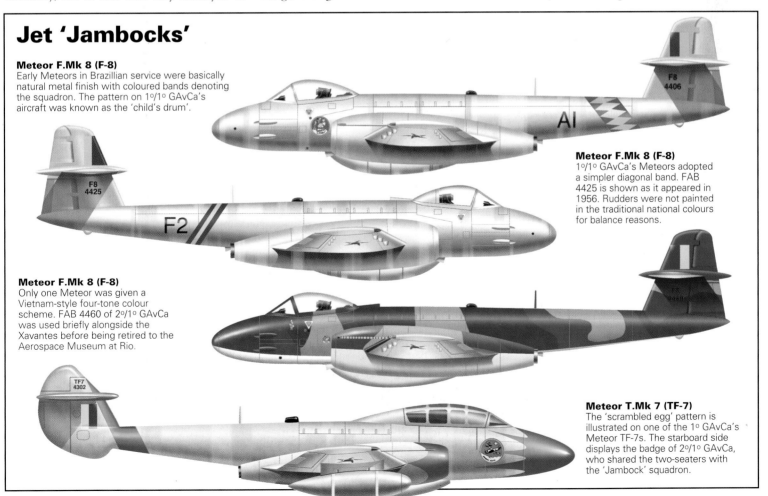

Meteor F.Mk 8 (F-8)
Early Meteors in Brazillian service were basically natural metal finish with coloured bands denoting the squadron. The pattern on 1º/1º GAvCa's aircraft was known as the 'child's drum'.

Meteor F.Mk 8 (F-8)
1º/1º GAvCa's Meteors adopted a simpler diagonal band. FAB 4425 is shown as it appeared in 1956. Rudders were not painted in the traditional national colours for balance reasons.

Meteor F.Mk 8 (F-8)
Only one Meteor was given a Vietnam-style four-tone colour scheme. FAB 4460 of 2º/1º GAvCa was used briefly alongside the Xavantes before being retired to the Aerospace Museum at Rio.

Meteor T.Mk 7 (TF-7)
The 'scrambled egg' pattern is illustrated on one of the 1º GAvCa's Meteor TF-7s. The starboard side displays the badge of 2º/1º GAvCa, who shared the two-seaters with the 'Jambock' squadron.

Unit Heritage

Above: This close-up view of a 2º/1º GAvCa F-8 shows details of the 20-mm cannon openings and the badge of the 1st Fighter Group's second squadron.

Left: The Meteors of 2º/1º GAvCa stand lined-up for inspection, circa 1956. The early marking of the 'child's drum' badge is visible here.

south of Rio), the group was divided into two squadrons. The 1º/1º GAvCa maintained the callsign JAMBOCK, the fighting ostrich badge and most of the veteran pilots of the Italian campaign, and the new 2º/1º GAvCa, christened Pif-Paf (after a popular Brazilian card game), included a few of the veteran pilots and would serve as a training unit. The 'Jambocks' received the new P-47D-30 fighters they had ferried from the United States, including such state-of-the-art equipment as the AN/APS-13 rear quadrant alert system, and 2º/1º flew the 25 Thunderbolts that had seen combat over Italy.

While the 1st BFG was flying missions off Pisa San Giusto, several groups of Brazilian pilots were sent to the United States to undergo fighter training. By the time the first of these groups was ready to embark for Italy, however, the war had ended, and they returned to Brazil. Santa Cruz Air Base became the birthplace of Brazil's modern fighter aviation. The 1st BFG

Above: 1º/1º GAvCa's Meteor TF-7 is seen in post-1965 markings undergoing maintenance inside the Zeppelin hangar at Santa Cruz.

Below: In recognition of the 1st BFG's 1945 exploits, 22 April was declared Fighter Aviation Day. Part of the 1965 ceremonies are shown here.

Right: Seven Meteors of 1º GAvCa 'give it hell' to a mock target with napalm at Santa Cruz, 1965. Stress caused by low-level flying hastened the retirement of the Meteor in FAB service.

and the 2nd Fighter Group composed of P-40E/K/M/N Warhawks were grouped under the 1º Regimento de Aviação (1st Aviation Regiment). This status was soon changed, though, the P-40s being passed to the newly formed 3º Grupo de Caça and sent to Gravata Field in the southern-most Brazilian state of Rio Grande do Sul. Thunderbolts and North American AT-6Ds used in the ESPC – Estagio de Seleçio de Pilotos de Caça, an eight-month (120-hour) training stage used to select the best candidates for the front line – were a familiar site around the base's huge Zeppelin hangar on any day. The extremely experienced veterans of the Italian campaign flew endless training sorties with the young hopefuls. In 1946 three AT-6D accidents claimed the lives of three of the best original 'Jambocks', First Lieutenant Pedro de Lima Mendes, and Aspirantes-a-Aviador Diomar Menezes and Roberto Tormin Costa. A temporary pause in the training syllabus allowed the instructors to review events, and it was decided that perhaps they were pushing the young hopefuls too hard. A slackening of the pace reduced the accident rate and the flight schedule returned to normal.

In 1947, the Brazilian air force went through a complete reorganisation process that renumbered units by geographical location from Belém southward. Thus, the 1st BFG and the 2nd FG were renamed the 1º/9º Grupo de Aviação and 2º/9º GAv – 1st/9th and 2nd/9th Aviation Groups. Immediately, veterans and novices alike began protesting vehemently against the unit's new status, until the original designations were restored in 1949.

During the late 1940s, jet aircraft captured the imagination of air forces around the world. Other South American countries began acquiring modern jet fighters, forcing the Brazilian air force to look into the matter. When the opportunity arose to check out the new aircraft, the air force high command selected four 1º GAvCa officers to fly the jets.

Despite the experiences these pilots brought back, F-80s in the C version were not delivered to Brazil until 11 years later, and they never flew in 1º GAvCa colours.

The Group goes British

By 1952, Nero Moura had risen to the rank of brigadier general and was also Minister of Aeronautics. A staunch believer in air defence, he was instrumental in acquiring Brazil's first jet fighter aircraft: 70 Gloster Meteors, costing £4,115,000 in Brazilian cotton. A small cadre of pilots was sent to the United Kingdom to train in the new fighters, and became known throughout the Brazilian air force as 'The Queen's Soldiers'. In April 1953 the first aircraft arrived in Brazil by ship and was unloaded at Rio de Janeiro. A total of 60 single-seat F.Mk 8s (designated F-8 in Brazil) and 10 T.Mk 7 twin-seaters (TF-7) began to enter service after the first flight in May that year. The Gloster Meteors came with four 20-mm guns and racks capable of accommodating 10 5-in HVAR rockets or two 1,000-lb bombs as well as two 454-litre (100-Imp gal) wing tanks and a 794-litre (175-Imp gal) belly tank. The fighters were distributed to the two squadrons of the 1st BFG at Santa Cruz and to the 1º/14º GAv Esquadrão Pampa based at Canoas Air Base near the city of Porto Alegre in Rio Grande do Sul.

For a brief period beginning in 1951, the ESPC course became the 3º/1º GAvCa. With the delivery of the Gloster Meteors to the 1st and 2nd Squadrons of the 1o Grupo de Aviação de Caça, all F-47 Thunderbolts in use by those units were transferred to the 3º/1º GAvCa. This unit, in turn, was dissolved in 1953, all F-47s being transferred to new units in the Brazilian northeast.

Although the Gloster Meteor was originally developed to perform high-altitude interception missions, the lack of a specialised net of air defence radars invariably forced the TF-7s and

F-8s towards specialising in interdiction and close air support missions. Air superiority missions were also practised by the pilots of the two Santa Cruz-based squadrons, but most sorties resulted in air combat proficiency training rather than GCI-guided interception. For ground attack training, the aircraft were armed with AN/M38A2 100-lb training bombs filled with sand, sawdust or ashes. For operational use, the Brazilian air force used 250-, 500- and 1,000-lb general-purpose bombs. Unguided Mk 3TH and Mk 4TH rockets were also widely used.

In 1956, the aircraft based at Santa Cruz sported an alphanumerical coding system on the fuselage to aid pilots in identifying their foes in mock combat. The 1º/1º GAvCa painted an easily recognisable diagonal green-yellow-green stripe on the rear fuselage, while those of the 'Pif-Paf' squadron opted for a diagonal light blue stripe containing green diamonds – this stripe soon became known as the Child's Drum Pattern. Despite the new markings, air-to-air missions continued to cause confusion between friend or foe, and in 1963 the 2º/1º GAvCa introduced a colourful red 'explosion' on the nose of their aircraft, the rays reaching all the way to the first quarter of the fuselage. The leading edge of all tail structures was also painted bright red, and in no time the 2º/1º GAvCa aircraft became quite distinguishable in the skies. This particular paint scheme earned the moniker Ovo Estalado, or Scrambled Egg.

Soon after, the pilots of the 1º/1º GAvCa began applying a similar scheme in dark blue, and the squadrons immediately were able to distinguish one another in the several dogfights that took place a few miles around Santa Cruz.

From June 1961, the Gloster Aircraft Company began issuing a series of precautions regarding low-level flight in TF-7s and F-8s. In January of 1962, another warning was issued, this time recommending the grounding of any TF-7 aircraft with more than 2,280 cell hours and any F-8s that had bypassed the 1,750-hour mark. As none of the Brazilian aircraft had reached those limits, operations continued at their normal pace. The early 1960s saw the entrance of other jet types in the FAB inventory. The 1º/4º GAv based at Fortaleza, in the northeastern state of Cear, received Lockheed F-80C and T-33A aircraft and shortly afterward a new mentality began to permeate the fighter ranks. Soon, the 1st and 2nd Squadrons began hoping for aircraft of a more modern generation with which to improve their capabilities.

The Brazilian air force high command had already been working on replacing their aircraft with 12 Northrop F-5A and four F-5B Freedom Fighters, aiming to equip the 2º/1º GAvCa with these aircraft by 1966. A year earlier, new directives issued by the British factory had alerted all Gloster Meteor operators to the possibility of severe structural problems if the aircraft exceeded g loadings of +5 and -3, or if they flew large portions of their operational lives at low altitudes. Upon inspection, the Brazilian air force with the help of British technicians found that most of the FAB Meteor fleet was compromised by fissures in the longeron. Almost 60 per cent of the fleet were immediately grounded, forcing the FAB to look for an immediate substitute or risk the paralysis of three front-line fighter squadrons. The intended buy of Freedom Fighters proved impossible for political reasons and, for a brief period, the Brazilian air force was forced to make do with a very unpopular solution.

For six years, the 1º GAvCa operated Lockheed T-33As in their AT-33A-20-LO version in place of the Gloster Meteors, a few of which were still operational for target towing. By late 1967, the 2º/1º GAvCa was receiving its first TF-33s and, by the end of the year, the whole group was flying the American trainers configured to perform minimally as fighters. They differed from the training versions of the T-33 'T-birds' in being fitted with hardpoints under each wing and the fuselage and racks for bombs and unguided rockets; however, these jets were far from performing the missions envisaged by the Brazilian air force to guarantee a minimal level of air defence. They carried a smaller payload than the F-8s, were armed with just two 0.50-in machine-guns and operated at lower speeds than most commercial jets already flying over Brazilian airspace. Morale in the 1º Grupo de Aviação de Caça had seldom sagged so low.

Phantoms vetoed

1967 also marked the beginning of a project intended to provide the country with an integrated air defence and traffic control system, for which a supersonic high-performance interceptor would be needed. After serious evaluation, the FAB committee ordered the selection of the McDonnell-Douglas F-4E Phantom II as the ideal fighter for Brazil. It possessed extraordinary

---

Tiger IIs and Freedom Fighters

F-5E Tiger II
In 1999 1º 'Jambock'/1º Grupo de Aviação de Caça at Santa Cruz was equipped with F-5Es and two-seat F-5Bs, as well as a handful of AT-27 (EMB-312) Tucanos. F-5E 4820 (USDoD serial 74-1582) was the FAB's first F-5E, delivered in 1975. Note the in-flight refuelling probe, fitted to allow refuelling from FAB KC-130s. Further upgrades to the F-5 fleet were announced in 1995, incorporating a new fire-control radar, avionics and related structural components to extend their useful lives well into the next century.

F-5B Freedom Fighter
On the occasion of a visit made by the late Formula One motor racing world champion Ayrton Senna to Santa Cruz, the Brazilian driving ace was flown in 1º GAvCa F-5B 4803 (74-1579), which was marked with his name to commemorate the occasion. The F-5Bs were retired in 1997.

Above and right: The F-5Es and Fs of 1o GAvCa are distinguishable from those of 14º GAv (the other FAB F-5 unit) by their three-tone (as opposed to grey) colour scheme and their refuelling probes. Today, the aircraft of 1º/1º and 2º/1º 'Pif Paf' are pooled, normally wearing the badge of the former on the port and the latter on the starboard side of the fin.

air-to-air characteristics, good air-to-ground capabilities and could carry a heavy payload.

The US State Department, however, vetoed the Phantom, offering instead the Northrop F-5C, which was turned down by the FAB. In 1970 Brazil announced the purchase of 13 Dassault Mirage IIIEBRs and three Mirage IIIDBRs, and by 1972 a new squadron had been formed to operate the new jets at Anapolis, near the capital of Brasilia.

The 1º GAvCa, however, toiled on with its TF-33s. In April 1972 a respite came in the form of brand-new EMBRAER EMB-326GB Xavante light trainers, the Brazilian-assembled version of the Aermacchi MB-326 which was designated by the FAB as the AT-26. Better than the TF-33s, these jets were distributed to the 2º/1º GAvCa while the 'Jambocks' kept on flying the 'T-Birds'. Later, both squadrons were equipped with the new Brazilian trainers.

By 1971, studies at FAB high command were well advanced to provide the Santa Cruz- and Canoas-based squadrons with a modern fighter capable of providing comprehensive air defence for Brazil's vast territory. Several aircraft were evaluated, such as the BAe Harrier Mk 50, the SEPECAT Jaguar GR.Mk 1, the FIAT G91Y, the Aermacchi MB-326K and the McDonnell Douglas A-4F Skyhawk. In the event, the Northrop F-5E Tiger II was chosen and a $115 million contract was signed in 1973 for 36 F-5Es and six F-5B twin-seaters, as well as parts,

ground support equipment and instruction packages. In 1974, a small cadre of pilots from both the 1º GAvCa and the Canoas-based 1º/14º GAv received instruction from USAF pilots of the 425th Tactical Fighter Training Squadron at Williams Air Force Base, Arizona. Throughout the next three years the FAB undertook Operation Tiger, the ferrying of the F-5E/Bs to Brazil. Two flights initially ferried three F-5Bs each, followed by another nine flights of four F-5Es each.

As soon as all the aircraft were at their bases – the operation suffered a single accident at Galeão Air Base adjacent to the Rio de Janeiro International Airport – the initial cadre of F-5E-proficient pilots immediately began forming new crews. The aircraft initially equipped the 1º GAvCa, but were not individually divided between the two squadrons. Instead, 1º/1º GAvCa badges were painted on the left side of the tail and the 2º/1º emblem was placed on the right. The two squadrons share the aircraft to this day. The F-5Es introduced several new doctrines to the 1o GAvCa, perhaps the most important of which was the capability to perform air-to-air refuelling, which was made possible by the arrival of the first Lockheed KC-130H Hercules in 1975. By the end of 1976, the 1º/14º GAv had also re-equipped with the F-5E/B.

In the early 1980s, attrition replacements were sought and contacts between the Brazilian

and US governments were signed, resulting in the sale of 22 second-hand F-5Es and four F-5Fs for $13.1 million. These aircraft came from the 57th Tactical Training Wing based at Nellis AFB, Nevada and the 58th TTW initially based at Luke, then at Williams AFB, both in Arizona. These aircraft had flown with the 64th and 65th Fighter Weapons Squadrons in the aggressor role and came to Brazil in their original camouflage patterns, displaying the colours of aircraft potentially hostile to the USAF. These aircraft did not have a VHF antenna or the dorsal fin housing the ADF antenna, nor were they equipped with air-to-air refuelling probes like those of the initial F-5E batch. In 1989, the last of these aircraft arrived at Canoas AB where they equipped the 1º/14º GAv, whose original F-5Es were transferred to the 1º GAvCa at Santa Cruz. This distinctive separation of batches led to a very clear difference in the way each of the two F-5E-equipped bases operated their aircraft. While the Santa Cruz unit flew very diverse sorties alternating air defence and interdiction, with long range air-to-air refuelling-assisted detachments, the Canoas squadron specialised in air defence to a greater extent, perhaps due to its strategic location near Brazil's southern borders.

RAF Vulcan escort

During the 1982 Falklands War between Argentina and the UK, the 1º GAvCa maintained a higher state of readiness than in normal peacetime periods. On 3 June 1982 a single Avro Vulcan of the RAF, piloted by Squadron Leader Neil McDougall developed serious problems off the Brazilian coast when its refuelling probe broke on contact with the drogue trailing behind a Victor tanker, following an attempt to hit Argentine air defence radars around Port Stanley. With fuel levels rapidly decreasing and a Shrike missile hung up on its pylon, the Vulcan had no other option but to try to reach the Brazilian coastline. McDougall dipped his left wing and headed for Rio de Janeiro. The British crew hastily tried to rid itself of all important documents and maps but damaged the door to the underside hatch, which made the emergency worse as they could no longer pressurise the cockpit and would have to fly at lower, less-economical altitudes. As it approached Brazilian airspace, the RAF

Pilots of 1º and 2º/1º GAvCa carry on the traditions of their illustrious forebears today. Among the reminders of the original 'Senta A Pua!' squadron is a street on Santa Cruz AB named 'Place Tarquina'.

The F-5s of 1º GAvCa are tasked with ground attack and the air defence of Rio de Janeiro, flying from the nearby base of Santa Cruz.

aircraft called Rio control and was cleared for a direct approach into Rio de Janeiro International Airport. It had already been monitored by radar and as soon as the emergency was declared a pair of 1º GAvCa F-5Es was diverted from Santa Cruz to escort the damaged Vulcan. The British aircraft was able to land in one piece and after nine days in Rio it returned to the UK.

In 1997, the remaining F-5Bs were taken out of commission and operational conversion of 1º GAvCa pilots had to be undertaken at Canoas with the 1º/14º GAv's F-5Fs, while Brazil began a programme to upgrade its fleet of some 50 Tigers. The upgraded aircraft should have entered service by early 2001, providing the two Santa Cruz squadrons with an aircraft capable of performing its missions until the arrival of a new-generation fighter in approximately 2010.

Today, the 1º GAvCa provides the backbone of the country's air defence system, overlooking the industrial regions comprising the sprawling megalopolis of São Paulo, the urban centres of Rio de Janeiro and Belo Horizonte, the aerospace heartland at São José dos Campos, and the oceanic approaches to the country's southeast area. On the sleek F-5Es that take to the skies patrolling the seemingly endless vastness of Brazil, the red badge of the fighting ostrich lends its testimony to the courage of the few young volunteers who flew in combat over northern Italy, almost 60 years ago.

Carlos Lorch

Preserved FAB P-47s

A surprising number of the Força Aérea Brasileira's Thunderbolts survived to be preserved as gate guardians or as exhibits by the Museu Aerospacial at Rio. A number of others have been acquired by US warbird operators.

FAB 4175 (44-90460) was displayed at Guararapes AB, Recife from 1970 to 1987 when it was sold in the USA. It is now registered N9246B to Neal Melton of Lutteral, Tennesee.

Seen in October 1995, '42-26766' is seen in October 1995. Actually 45-49151/FAB 4184, it has been restored to flying condition and is known to have made at least one flight.

P-47D-30 42-26757 (FAB 4107) was painted to represent the aircraft (44-19662/ 'D5') flown by Jose Rebello Meira de Vasconcelos of Green Flight. It was displayed for many years on a pole at Santa Cruz, previously as 'C3' and 'C5'.

42-19663 (FAB 4120) now belongs to the Museu Aerospacial collection, but for many years was displayed at Guaratingueta AB. It is a genuine Italian campaign veteran, having been taken on charge in October 1944.

'T-birds' & Silver Stars

Lockheed T-33/T2V Variants

The Lockheed T-33 flew at training bases in the American Southwest, where a blinding sun danced against metal in motion, and it was always a flash in the sky – so the 'Shooting Star' nickname was not an accident but a stroke of inspiration. It was the first jet aircraft flown by generations of pilots. All moved on to some other aircraft and never looked back, so when they thought about the T-33 years later they remembered a utilitarian, working hunk of machinery that reliably performed an everyday job – not the glint of steel against sun or the fact that, for many of them, the T-33 marked the first time they experienced high-performance flying.

They thought it was ordinary. They were right and they were wrong: yes, it was an unremarkable aircraft in many respects, one that evoked little emotion while soldiering at the job one instructor called "training green kids for jet combat", but those fledgling kids who earned their spurs in the Lockheed T-33 Shooting Star eventually flew every aircraft in American and Canadian inventories and bulwarked the air forces of three dozen other countries. "We never thought much about the T-33," says Colonel Charles Vasiliadis, who later flew Skyraiders and Thunderchiefs in Vietnam. "It was a little like my mother, or my car, or my house. It was just there." So unremarkable was the T-33 that it rated only an unremarkable nickname: 'the T-bird'.

Possibly a quarter of a million pilots alive today flew this peppy but prosaic training aircraft. The T-33 existed in far greater numbers than its stablemates from the Burbank, California manufacturer, the F-80 and F-94 fighters, and became one of the most numerous aircraft ever manufactured in the West. Lockheed built 5,691; Canadair replaced the reliable J33 engine with the equally reliable Nene and built 656 more; Kawasaki turned out 210 of these jet trainers, for a worldwide total of 6,557. Not merely plentiful, the T-33 was all but universal. It is nearly impossible to find a military pilot in the West who has not strapped into the venerable 'T-bird' at one time or another.

One pilot called the T-33 "forgiving". Vasiliadis said, "It treated me like an old woman." According to Lieutenant Colonel Robert Dwan, the 'T-bird' was "a pushover",

An instructor and student prepare to board their Kawasaki-assembled T-33A. While the T-33 has now largely passed from the inventories of most operators, a handful of air arms continue to use the type, often in the COIN role.

Above: The 'Acrojets' were re-equipped with T-33As around 1952, having earlier flown F-80s. Based at Williams AFB, Arizona, the Air Training Command display team disbanded the following year after it was decreed that their routine should be flown with tip tanks fitted.

Left: No. 417 'City of Windsor' Combat Support Sqn, CAF marked the 50th anniversary of the March 1948 first flight of the first TP-80C by painting CT-133 133299 in this silver/grey colour scheme, with appropriate branding. Canada operated the largest remaining fleet of 'T-birds' in the late 1990s.

Below: A 1st Air Force T-33A poses for the camera in June 1986. The USAF's last examples were mainly employed as 'hacks' and target aircraft, the last of these aircraft finally retiring in 1988.

and said, "Even the rawest recruit was unlikely to do anything terribly wrong in it." For every pilot who testifies to the roster of superb qualities of the T-bird, another remembers the its other side. In a hard-pressed operational setting, pilots and maintainers were furious about the doors to the nose compartment, which one called a "bad feature" because they had a tendency to pop open in flight when a latch came loose, rendering the 'T-bird' almost uncontrollable. A hinge at the forward edge would have kept the doors closed in flight no matter what happened, but that alteration was never made, even after an instructor pilot was killed trying to fly a T-33 with the doors out. Pilots also wondered why the nose gear of the T-33 was designed so that it closed the doors as the gear came up.

'Flying Blowtorches'

Powerplant of the T-33A was the 4,900-lb st (21.8-kN) Allison J33-A-35 centrifugal-flow turbojet engine (except for the Nene-powered examples built in Canada). Few engines were more widely used at the time, and to most people the powerplant was like the aircraft itself – pedestrian and unremarkable. Nonetheless, on early examples – at the time when jet aircraft were still dubbed 'flying blowtorches', and deserved the name – the pilot had to simultaneously manipulate fuel pump and throttle, a tedious and time-consuming process which, when rushed, could lead to a sudden and unwanted 30-ft (9-m) stream of flame shooting back from the engine.

One pilot described it this way: "It was late one afternoon and I was walking across the ramp between rows of T-33s en route to the trolley for a ride back to the flight shack. As I passed behind one T-33, I noticed an Iranian student beginning to start the engine on a bird

just to the left of me. A cloud of fuel began to erupt from the tailpipe and I began to run – which isn't too easy with a seat pack parachute hitting you behind the knees. As I got 50-75 ft away, the Iranian hit the ignition switch and a enormous 'explosion' occurred and fire erupted from the tail for around 20 ft – like one huge blow torch. I fully expected to see the tailpipe fly off of the T-33. This immediately brought to mind the great truism and admonition, 'Ignition, then fuel, ignition, then fuel.'"

The start-up process was improved, first with a cartridge, then with an automatic system, but centrifugal-flow engines were regarded by maintainers as an invitation to trouble unless properly fed and cared for. It was convenient

that the rear fuselage of the T-33 'broke' for easy engine removal.

Like its stablemate, the F-80 Shooting Star fighter (*Wings of Fame* No. 11), the 'T-bird' began with teardrop wingtip tanks but soon used as standard the 230-US gal (871-litre) Fletcher tanks that mounted at mid-wingtip. Early T-33s had a one-piece canopy which on later aircraft was broken by a canopy bow at the mid-point.

The 'T-bird' was, and will always be remembered as, the US Air Force's primary jet trainer of an era, but it flew also many other missions. Attack, reconnaissance, drone, and target-towing versions were numerous. Back-up duty with the US Air Force 'Thunderbirds' and US Navy 'Blue Angels' flight demonstration

Both the T-33 and F-94 started with the same airframe – 48-356. Known initially as the TP-80C, then the TF-80C and finally the T-33A, the 'T-bird' was derived, as its designations suggest, from the P-80C, 48-356 being taken from the P-80C production line to serve as a prototype. In its new guise, '356 took to the air, with Tony LeVier at the controls, on 22 March 1948. Both this airframe and the second example (48-357) went on to serve as YF-94s, prototypes for the USAF's first all-weather jet fighter. In these views of the TP-80C prototype, the original framed cockpit canopy is clearly evident.

teams was *de rigueur*. An experimental T-33 pioneered variable-stability flight research for more years than some of its pilots had been alive, and an offshoot called the T2V-1 SeaStar went aboard aircraft-carrier decks. Ultimately, there was a final grab for glory by a variant called the Skyfox, which had interesting possibilities but arrived on the scene when the T-bird's story was winding down.

When the prototype for the 'T-bird' series went aloft on 22 March 1948 piloted by Lockheed's Tony LeVier, the United States held world supremacy in science and technology – it possessed the only atomic bombs and was developing television as a household amusement – but America was only about even with, or perhaps slightly ahead of, other industrial states when it came to developing a jet trainer. Gloster's Meteor T. Mk 7, originally developed as a private venture tandem two-seat conversion training variant of the Meteor F.Mk 4, was neck-and-neck with the Lockheed trainer and made its maiden flight three days earlier, on 19

March 1948. Another British private venture, the Vampire T. Mk 11 side-by-side jet trainer – again, as was so common, based on a fighter design – did not fly until 15 November 1950.

Russia's 'Midget'

In the Soviet Union, the prototype UTI-MiG-15, otherwise known as ST-1 Sparka, was rolled out on 9 May 1949 and took to the air for the first time at Kuibyshev, apparently on 6 June 1949. The slightly different, production-model MiG-15UTI became the first swept-wing jet trainer in widespread use. It was never a very good trainer, with perhaps the most uncomfortable seating and worst visibility of any aircraft in its category, but it was about as numerous as the T-33, although accounts differ as to the total built. When Air Standards Co-ordinating Committee nicknames were assigned to Soviet aircraft in 1956, the MiG-15UTI became the 'Midget', which might have had symbolic significance had there not been so many of them.

T-33, Meteor, Vampire, MiG and Fokker S.14 were more or less contemporaries and, perhaps because the T-33 was so suitable for its mission, the US was slow to develop a swept-wing trainer. By the time a TF-86F Sabre two-seat trainer appeared, it was not a contemporary, had not been requested by the US Air Force, and was no longer needed – there being no need, by that late date, to replace the maturing T-bird. The first TF-86F was flown on 5 August 1954. A second ship was eventually built, but by then no one cared: the T-33 was in service, its minor teething problems were history, and it was performing well.

The first jet aircraft to be designed from the outset for instructional purposes, the Netherlands' Fokker S.14 Mach Trainer (itself only capable of getting about two-thirds of the way to Mach 1.0) was just two years behind Tony LeVier's maiden 'T-bird' hop, making its initial flight on 20 May 1951. At one point, 20 of these simple, clunky, side-by-side trainers were on order for the Royal Netherlands Air

Shooting Star: trainer to the world

As the 20th Century drew to a close, T-33s remained in service with a handful of countries in Europe and the Americas. This selection of photographs depicts aircraft in service with most of the many nations that have flown the type since it was introduced in mid-1949.

Above: Canada has used the Silver Star since May 1951 and examples are still going strong in the combat support role. This example belonged to No. 414 Electronic Warfare Sqn, CFB North Bay.

Burma received at least 12 and possibly as many as 32 AT-33As. UB511 (above) displays a prominent scorpion badge. The Canadian navy used Silver Star Mk 3s (below), initially to train F2H pilots.

Belgium acquired its 38 T-33As (above) from March 1952. They were operated as trainers by 11 and 31 Smaldeels. Bolivia (below) continues to use the type with Escuadrón 310 based at El Alto, La Paz.

56-3659 was the first of the Fiscal Year 1956 T-33A-5-LOs. The Lockheed construction number 1143 appears on the nose of the aircraft and (in the shortened form of '43') again on the tail. The Dash 5 Shooting Stars lacked the armament options available to the Dash 1 aircraft.

Force. Apart from its interest value, the S.14 had little true significance – it was a slow gas-guzzler with a sensible side-by-side seating arrangement and mediocre performance – but it did usher in a new era. The 'T-bird' symbolised the end of a day when an offshoot of a fighter design would suffice for training, while the S.14 foretold a future of aircraft that would begin at the blueprint stage as trainers, among them the Cessna T-37 'Tweet' and the Northrop T-38 Talon.

In the meantime, the T-33 Shooting Star went into production and into service. As a 'schoolhouse in the sky', it had both the advantages (centreline seating) and drawbacks (indirect contact) of the tandem configuration, it was as stable as a brick, and it was almost as forgiving as every trainer ought to be. It is easy to forget that the T-33 was very much a creature of the USAF's Air Training Command, headed up during the critical 1948-54 period by Lieutenant General Robert W. Harper. The 'T-bird' era truly began when ATC introduced T-33s with the 3525th Flying Training Group – later Flying Training Wing (FTW) – at Williams AFB, Arizona in June 1949.

Just when it looked like Flying Class 49-C would become the first to cut its teeth on the new trainer, a 3525th memorandum of 9 June 1949 noted that there were still too few of the new trainers. Still using the designation TF-80C (although the trainer had been redesignated T-33A on 5 May 1949), this memo may have been the first of hundreds over the years to set rules for joy rides in the new jet: "It is recommended that TF-80C aircraft assigned to this station be restricted from use as administrative aircraft except in the most extreme emergency or during periods when no student flying is being performed." At the time, Williams was struggling to attain an operational fleet of 16 T-33As and was also plagued by parts shortages. Apparently, this initiated a long-standing policy of only one T-33A being away from home station at a time for any non-training purpose. The question of who was to fly a T-33A, and when, persisted as long as the aircraft flew, because there were almost unlimited practical applications for a (relatively) high-performance jet with two seats.

After Williams, units that followed quickly as T-33 operators included the following FTWs and bases: 3605th, Greenville AFB, Miss., 3510th, Randolph AFB, Texas, 3530th, Bryan AFB, Texas, 3540th, Pinecastle AFB, Fla., 3560th, Webb AFB, Texas, 3565th James Connally AFB, Texas, 3580th, Foster AFB, Texas, 3615th, Craig AFB, Ala., 3640th, Laredo AFB, Texas, and 3645th, Laughlin AFB, Texas. In the early to mid-1950s, other units were added to this roster. As always, ATC trained American and international student pilots in the sunny south, where weather conditions offered good flying for most of the year.

Four-phase training syllabus

As late as 1952, some of the newly recruited pilots heading off to war in Korea had only the single-seat F-80 to introduce them to jet flying, but ATC made sweeping changes in November 1952 and adopted a four-phase pilot training programme.

The first phases was pre-flight, and lasted 12 weeks. Then came primary flight training

The majority of Danish T-birds (left) served with the Traeningsflight and various station flights. Colombia (above left) was the first South American nation to gain the type, from 1954. Ethiopian T-33 214 (above), ex-KLu M-58 and 52-9671) ended up dumped at Asmara, Eritrea, having been withdrawn by 1984. Chile's T-33As (above right) operated alongside the F-80Cs of Grupo 12 from Punta Arenas. Ecuadorian air force examples (right) remained in service until 29 April 1996.

lasting 18 weeks, highlighted by 120 flight hours in that prized wartime veteran, the T-6 Texan. Next was the basic flight phase lasting 16 weeks and including 130 hours in both the T-6 and the spanking-new T-28 (later named Trojan in its Navy guise only) plus the equally new T-33. Using the 'T-bird' meant that a student did not have to solo to make his first jet flight, and could learn jet principles with a seasoned instructor in the back seat. The fourth phase consisted of crew training and covered an average of 12 weeks – the route to a pilot's silver wings lasting a total of nearly 16 months. The Air Force had begun numbering its flying classes with Class 40-A in 1940, and the first to use the new training scheme was Class 53-H in

1953. For nearly 15 years to follow, every flyer in USAF uniform cut his teeth on the T-33. To give some sense of the numbers involved, in 1953 the USAF narrowly missed its goal of training 10,000 pilots (in a single year) and reaching a strength of 143 combat wings.

Foreign trainees and the T-33

An intriguing sidebar to the T-33 story involves pilots from overseas who trained in the US. When ATC introduced the T-33 as its basic single-engined trainer, it created a curious anomaly – pilots qualified to fly jet aircraft who came from countries that had no jet aircraft. To rectify this, ATC created a propeller-driven T-28 training programme for international

pilots, including some from a country of which almost no American had ever heard – Vietnam.

As early as 1954, with supersonic 'Century Series' fighters such as the F-100 Super Sabre soon to enter the inventory, ATC recognised that its traditional pilot-training aircraft (the ageing T-6G, which had replaced the T-6, followed by T-34 Mentor which was beginning to replace the T-28 as the second-phase aircraft, followed by the T-33) were not adequate for proper training. Already, the service was making plans to replace the new and much-admired T-34 with the T-37 Tweet, which would begin its duties as the second-phase trainer but would later become a primary trainer, enabling pilots to begin their flying experience in jet-powered aircraft. Above all, ATC saw the need to replace the T-33 with a supersonic trainer. Major General Glenn O. Barcus, who had commanded air forces in the Korean War and now took the helm at ATC, made a supersonic trainer "a top priority". His successor, Lieutenant General Charles T. Myers, agreed but a document from the area says that, "while a T-33 replacement is essential, what that aircraft will be is still to be determined".

On 1 July 1956, ATC replaced its last T-28 and was then operating five single-engine pilot training bases (Bryan, Greenville, Laredo, Webb and Laughlin, all in Texas) equipped with T-33s. Pilot training, which had fallen to about 7,000 per year, now plunged to 2,700 in 1957. Two years later came a major change when the USAF shifted from specialised to generalised training. As part of the change, the USAF established UPT (undergraduate pilot training) under which all students would train in the same aircraft. Gone were multi-engined aircraft

The AMI received 75 T-33As (such as MM51-9145 of the Scuola Volo Basico Avanzato Aviogetti, above) and 15 RT-33As from 1952. France (below) was the largest European T-33/CT-133 operator.

Below: Greece is the last European operator with about 30 T-33s in service in 1999, in combat support and training roles.

Guatemalan examples (above) served with the Escuadrón de Caza-Bombardeo until 1997. The IRIAF (below) continues to train pilots at Shiraz with a handful of T-33s.

Right: Having adopted the F-80C (as the TO-1, later TV-1) in the advanced jet training role, the US Navy eventually picked up T-33As from USAF production, designating these TO-2 (later TV-2). This is BuNo. 137936 (USAF serial 53-5243).

Below right: Here a TV-2 is seen on the wing of N125D (foreground), the carrier-capable Model 245 (T2V-1) prototype.

like the TB-25 Mitchell (which had trained 30,000 pilots and logged 2.5 million flight hours); now, a pilot would conclude his training experience in the T-33, even though the need for a more advanced trainer was more evident than ever.

The T-33 was the most widely-used aircraft in ATC, even as late as September 1959, shortly before production of the aircraft ended and ATC took delivery of its last ship at James Connally AFB, Texas. The final T-33 to come from the Lockheed line emerged in August 1959 and was named, suitably enough, *Exodus*. Two years later, on 17 March 1961, at Randolph AFB, Texas, ATC took delivery of its first T-38 Talon, the supersonic trainer intended to replace the T-33. The first Talon students were in Flying Class 62-F. The T-33 soldiered on as the training command's most numerous aircraft, however, and although its future as a trainer was limited, it had more years of service to provide in other missions. When Lieutenant General William W. 'Spike' Momyer (a future commander in the coming war in Vietnam) took the ATC helm in 1964, the training command disposed of a few T-33s which, along with twin-engined T-29s, had been used solely for instrument pilot instructor training. By then, ATC was also vigorously replacing T-33 pilot trainers with T-38s.

Another small, specialised mission reached a critical point in 1964: weapons controller training. From 1953 until 1958, a course at Tyndall AFB, Fla. had used T-33s to conduct GCIs (ground control intercepts) to train those who would guide interceptors on their missions against enemy bombers. After 1958 ATC placed

In Japanese service (above) the T-33A became the Wakataka or 'Young Hawk'. 51-5648 is a Lockheed-built example. JE-014 (below) belongs to the original batch of 15 aircraft supplied to 202 Escuadron Aereo Jet de Pelea of the Mexican air force from 1961. Forty more were obtained in 1987.

Libya (above) used T-33As until 1979 at least, while Singapore only gained its ex-French 'T-33Fs' in 1980 (below). The golden era for the type in Europe was the late 1950s and 1960s. The last flight of a Dutch example (right) was in June 1972 while Norway's were retired in 1968 (below right).

Civil Stars

less emphasis on live aircraft support for GCI training and by early 1963 only 10 T-33s remained in the 3625th Technical Training Group's inventory. Following a disagreement between ATC and Air Defense Command, on 1 April 1964 ATC transferred these T-33s to ADC, which was to use these and other T-33s for this and other missions for many years. As the Vietnam war was heating up, the T-33's role as a pilot trainer was ending. In 1967, ATC released the last of its T-33s, the final one departing Craig AFB, Alabama in February 1967.

Air Defense Command service

Outside the training world, the US Air Force's largest – and longest – user of the 'T-bird' was Air Defense Command, which hit upon the two-seat jet aircraft as a utility hack, a VIP transport, and a mock enemy flying 'faker' missions with both electronic and manual radar jamming equipment.

Over the years, thousands of Air Force pilots flew the 'T-bird' not as a trainer but as a small, fast utility transport, a 'hack'. Many referred to this as 'bug smasher' flying. A staff officer in the Pentagon or at SAC headquarters could get to a meeting more quickly, and keep up pilot proficiency, by using a T-33. However, the 'T-bird' was a jet, and an aircraft with little forgiveness for a mistake at low speed or around the airfield pattern, so the rules for 'hack' flying were inviolable. In order to make a trip anywhere in a T-33 – that is, to fly anywhere except in the local pattern – an officer had to fly the aircraft at least once every 15 days and to log at least 10 hours per month. Many believed this was not enough, and more than a few pilots relinquished the opportunity for speedy and efficient transportation, feeling that keeping current in the T-33 was simply more trouble than it was worth.

When the Royal Canadian Air Force

identified a need to switch to jets in its training operations, the still-evolving 'T-bird' was the obvious choice and was announced to the public on 13 September 1951. Under the plan, Canadair would build 576 of the jet trainers at its busy Cartierville facility and would redesign the engine housing to accommodate the preferred engine. The popular Rolls-Royce Nene became the powerplant of choice for the Canadian T-bird.

What looked like a straightforward engine switch proved to be a larger technical problem than expected. Canadair had to design new forgings for the engine support structure and experimented with three tailpipe designs before satisfied. A labour dispute killed plans for the wings to be manufactured under sub-contract by Ford of Canada, and Canadair took over this job. Ultimately, early production problems were resolved and the Cartierville factory was turning out one aircraft per day by the end of

the first year. The RCAF approved purchase of an additional 80 aircraft, bringing the total number of Canadian-built T-birds to 656.

Canada has always conducted a great deal of flying training, not merely of its own pilots but also of those from allied nations, and was one of the most important builders and users of the Harvard, alias the AT-6 Texan. In RCAF service, the 'T-bird' upheld this tradition. In the 1950s, Canadian pilots and those from NATO nations received a minimum of 80 hours in the Nene-powered Shooting Star. The Canadian model served in the training roll for nearly three decades, then continued as an electronic warfare decoy aircraft.

Japanese production

The 'T-bird' enjoyed equally long and successful service in Japan, the only other nation to manufacture it. Finding a nation that did not use the T-33 was a challenge, even outside the West. (Yugoslavia trained pilots in T-33s adorned with its version of the red star of the Soviet bloc.) Ultimately, just about every nation that was ever friendly to the US or Canada – and some that were not – became 'T-bird' users.

It would be almost impossible to set forth a precise list of nations that flew the T-33 in their inventories. Indeed, many aspects of the 'T-bird' story – including virtually every detail of its use as a drone and drone controller – have failed to surface, although much new information is contained in the variants list which follows. At risk of incompleteness (for example, Sweden nearly confiscated a USAF T-33 that landed on its soil in error in 1963, and one source says that a T-33 was sighted at the Soviet airfield of Akhtubinsk in 1970), the following is a partial (alphabetical) list: Belgium, Bolivia, Brazil, Canada, Chile, Colombia, Cuba, Denmark, Ethiopia, France, (West) Germany, Greece, Indonesia, Iran, Italy, Japan, Korea, Netherlands, Norway, Pakistan, Peru,

Philippines, Portugal, Saudi Arabia, Spain, Taiwan, Thailand, Turkey, Uruguay and Yugoslavia.

Literally hundreds of T-birds are on display in campgrounds, school yards and museums around the United States and abroad (many, sadly, derelict or reduced to serving as children's playthings) while more than a dozen fly in civilian guise as 'warbirds' at air shows around the world.

Robert F. Dorr

Above: The by-then long-in-the-tooth T-33 was offered a new lease of life in the early 1980s, when Skyfox Corporation launched their extensively rebuilt derivative – about 70 percent of the structural core being retained. Deciding that a market for the aircraft existed, Boeing took over the project, but failed to secure any orders.

Below: The last airworthy T-33 on the USAF books was the unique NT-33A, operated by Calspan. The aircraft was modified to reproduce the control characteristics of other aircraft types, usually before a prototype had flown. It was replaced in this role by the NF-16D VISTA.

Taiwan (above) and Thailand (below) received T-33As to complement the delivery of F-84G Thunderjets from 1953 and 1957, respectively. The Shooting Stars were required to ease the jump from piston fighters (CNAF F-47s and Thai F8Fs).

Turkey (above) operated the T-33 until the end of 1997. The Uruguayan air force retired its AT-/T-33As (below) in June 1996 having received two batches of four in 1956 and 1969, repectively and five more in 1989.

West Germany's first generation of pilots were trained on the T-33 (above), while Yugoslavia used T-33As (below), RT-33As and a batch of ex-US Navy TV-2s.

Lockheed T-33/T2V Variants

TP-80C

TP-80C was the initial designation of the two-seat trainer version of the P-80 Shooting Star fighter, also known as the Model 580 in Lockheed jargon. The design emanated from the very familiar single-seat P-80 (later F-80) jet fighter that became operational only days too late for World War II, established numerous speed and endurance records in the late 1940s, achieved history's first jet-versus-jet aerial victory in 1950, and flew thousands of fighter-bomber missions in the Korean War.

Working from the single-seat P-80 design, Lockheed engineering team leader Don Palmer revised the familiar fighter design by inserting a 38.6-in (98-cm) plug forward of the wing and a 12-in (30.5-cm) plug aft, and reduced fuselage fuel-tank capacity from 207 US gal (784 litres) to 95 US gal (360 litres). The Lockheed team offset the reduction in fuel capacity by installing nylon cells in the wings in place of the P-80's self-sealing fuel tanks. This left total fuel capacity at 353 US gal (1336 litres), still some 30 per cent less than in the P-80. The first aircraft in the series (48-356) was fitted initially with two standard 165-US gal (625-litre) drop tanks beneath the

wingtips. The first aircraft in the series were manufactured and delivered without ejection seats, although Lockheed routinely installed seats later on the T-33 series. The TP-80C introduced the AN/A1C intercom set which was, of course, unneeded on the single-seat fighter but became standard on the trainer.

Piloted by Tony LeVier, the TP-80C made its initial flight at Van Nuys, Calif. on 22 March 1948. The first ship (48-356) appears to have been the only one to fly under the TP-80C designation. This aircraft later was designated TF-80C, T-33A, YF-94, F-94A and F-94B, serving as the 'dogship' for virtually the entire series of two-seaters in the Shooting Star family. On 11 June 1948, the Air Force's 'P' for 'pursuit' aircraft acquired new designations in the 'F' for 'fighter' series, and both the prototype and the series were redesignated TF-80C (separate entry).

TP-80C serial:
48-356 (one conversion)

The first of over 5,000 Shooting Stars, TP-80C 48-356, is seen on its maiden flight on 22 March 1948. Note the framed cockpit canopy.

TF-80C

TF-80C was the designation for the two-seat trainer based on the F-80 Shooting Star fighter – that is, the prototype later redesignated T-33A – after 11 June 1948 when 'P' for pursuit was replaced by 'F' for fighter. Lockheed converted/built 128 TF-80s before the official designation was changed to T-33A on 5 May 1949. Of the first two TF-80Cs, one (48-356) became the prototype for the F-94 interceptor, flying as a TP-80C, TF-80C, T-33A, YF-94, F-94A and F-94B; the second TF-80C (48-357) became the sole ETF-80C (separate entry). The 18th

TF-80C (48-373) was converted to become the second YF-94 service-test prototype.

TF-80C serials (includes aircraft 48-356 delivered as TP-80C; 48-357/375 delivered as TF-80C; aircraft 49-2757 and 50-320/416 also listed in T-33A entry):
48-356/48-375 (20), 49-2757 (1), 50-320/416 (107)

Right: The sixth TF-80C displays the 'FT' buzz-code of the F-80, carried until the type was redesignated T-33 and recoded 'TR', in the 'T' for 'Trainer' range.

Below: An aircraft of the first TF-80C batch, 48-370 is seen at Williams AFB in the colours of the 3525th PTW 'The Fighter School' during December 1948.

Below: The original small 165-US gal (625-litre) tip tanks were replaced by 250-US gal (946-litre) Fletcher units with the small fin to stabilise the tank during flight, preventing wing twisting, a contributing factor in wing fatigue.

T-33A-1

T-33A was the designation of the basic T-33 Shooting Star trainer, and applied to most of the aircraft used for flight training by the USAF and other nations. The designation was adopted on 5 May 1949, changing the name of the US Air Force's first jet trainer from TF-80C (separate entry). Powerplant of the T-33A was the 4,900-lb (21.8-kN) Allison J33-A-35 centrifugal flow turbojet engine. At the time, Allison was a division of General Motors. The T-33A-1 variant differed from the subsequent T-33A-5 in being armed with two 0.50-in (12.7-mm) Browning M3 machine-guns, each with 300 rounds of ammunition.

A USAF T-33A-1-LO (51-4198) went to Canada to become the flying prototype for the Nene-powered Canadair T-33 Silver Star and was known in this role as the T-33ANX (see entry). Canada also borrowed 20 J33-powered USAF T-33As as the Silver Star Mk 1 (see entry), and subsequently borrowed 10 additional T-33As.

Countries which used the T-33A trainer included Bolivia, which received 38 in 1952-56; Brazil, which had a 'mix' of 58 AT-33 attack craft and T-33A trainers; Chile, with at least eight examples some plus three RT-33As; Colombia, which also had T-33ANs and RT-33As; France, which applied the designation T-33S-US to Lockheed-built machines and T-33S-C to Canadair models; Germany (Federal Republic of Germany), which had 192 T-33 trainers; Greece, where the eventual replacement was the T-2E Buckeye; Guatemala, which operated five from 1971; Honduras, which was also an RT-33A user; Indonesia, which replaced the 'T-bird' with the British Aerospace Hawk; Iran, which still flies five in 1999; Italy, which flew 75; South Korea, which may have had as many as 80 aircraft in two training squadrons; Japan, which manufactured the type; Libya, which acquired a small number of examples from various sources; Mexico, which had at least 15 trainers and also flew the attack variant; Norway, which flew 22 T-33As at Skv. 718 at Sola from 1953 to 1968; Singapore,

This view shows T-33A-1-LO 49-1006 in 'clean' configuration, without wing tanks and with a frameless cockpit canopy. The placement of national markings and serial numbers was standard for the period.

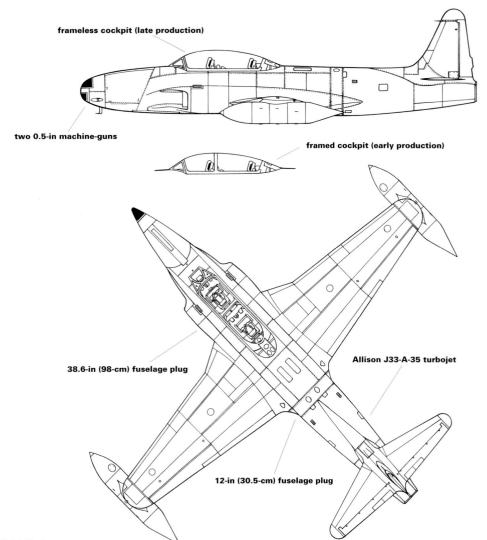

frameless cockpit (late production)

two 0.5-in machine-guns

framed cockpit (early production)

38.6-in (98-cm) fuselage plug

Allison J33-A-35 turbojet

12-in (30.5-cm) fuselage plug

which acquired eight ex-French examples in 1980; Spain, which gave this aircraft the designation E.15 and operated 58 examples; Taiwan (Nationalist China), where few details are available but aircraft may have numbered 50; Thailand, which had at least 20 trainers in addition to reconnaissance variants; Turkey, which operated over 100 but retired most relatively early, beginning in 1957; Uruguay, which appears to have employed primarily attack variants but used some for training; and Yugoslavia, which had a long history with 'Tegliacs' (tugboats), its term for a trainer. With 224 examples of all variants, France was the largest user of the T-33 that did not manufacture the type, and fourth-largest behind the US, Canada and Japan.

In August 1959, when production ended, Lockheed had built 5,691 aircraft in the T-33 family. One aircraft (51-4263) was fitted with a twin tail in a search to find ways to improve the 'T-bird''s less-than-satisfactory performance in the post-stall regime. Published works have identified this aircraft as an NT-33A (the 'N' signifying a temporary modification) and have indicated that the twin tails were the work of the US Navy, which was concerned about operations in the aircraft-carrier pattern. Lockheed never publicised this project and the Naval History Office has no record, but two people who worked on design efforts in the Navy's Bureau of Aeronautics say that the aircraft was simply called a T-33A and that work on the twin tail, in which the Navy was 'very interested', was carried out by Lockheed and the Air Force. The effort was a prolonged one which explored various shapes and materials. Ultimately, the twin-tail configuration was not chosen for a production aircraft and some pilots say the inadequate performance of the T-33 at low speeds was never fully rectified. Eventually, the aircraft reverted to single-tail configuration.

T-33A-1-LO serials (not including RT-33A-1-LO or Navy TV-2, but including initial 128 aircraft – beginning with 49-2757 – delivered under the designation TF-80C): 48-913/920 (8), 49-2757 (1), 49-879/1006 (128), 50-320/421 (112), 50-432 (1), 50-433/444 (12), 50-1272/1276 (5), 51-4025/4030 (6), 51-4037/4051 (15), 51-4058/4077 (20), 51-4084/4103 (20), 51-4110/4136 (27), 51-4143/4173 (31), 51-4180/4233 (54), 51-4234/4236 (3), 51-4244/4287 (44), 51-4295/4297 (3), 51-4298/4354 (57), 51-4365/4424 (60), 51-4435/4514 (80), 51-4525/4533 (9), 51-6497/6577 (81), 51-6588/6664 (77), 51-6675/6957 (283), 51-8506/8517 (12), 51-8542/8635 (94), 51-8652/8728 (77), 51-8750/8835 (86), 51-8871/8939 (69), 51-8954/9039 (86), 51-9076/9149 (74), 51-9168/9310 (143), 51-16976/16995 (20), 51-17388/17556 (169), 52-9129/9975 (847), 53-4886/5089 (204), 53-5091/5173 (83), 53-5175/5208 (34), 53-5210/5236 (27), 53-5240 (1), 53-5244/5256 (13), 53-5258/5272 (15), 53-5274/5290 (17), 53-5292/5307 (16), 53-5309 (1), 53-5318/5321 (4), 53-5323/5334 (12), 53-5336/5346 (11), 53-5348/5350 (3), 53-5364/5370 (7), 53-5372/5374 (3), 53-5388/5395 (8), 53-5397/5408 (12), 53-5410/5419 (10), 53-5421/5429 (9), 53-5431/5436 (6), 53-5461/5465 (5), 53-5467/5473 (7), 53-5475/5481 (7), 53-5483/5490 (8), 53-5492/5498 (7), 53-5500/5504 (5), 53-5535/5538 (4), 53-5540/5545 (6), 53-5547/5552 (6), 53-5554/5559 (6), 53-5561/5566 (6), 53-5568/5569 (2), 53-5604/5606 (3), 53-5608/5612 (5), 53-5614/5618 (5),

T-33A-1

53-5620/5625 (6), 53-5627/5630 (4), 53-5632/5637 (6), 53-5639/5641 (3), 53-5720 (1), 53-5722/5726 (5), 53-5728/5732 (5), 53-5734/5738 (5), 53-5740/5744 (5), 53-5746/5750 (5), 53-5753/5755 (4), 53-5757/5762 (6), 53-5764/5767 (4), 53-5769/5772 (4), 53-5774/5778 (5), 53-5780/5784 (5), 53-5786/5789 (4), 53-5791/5794 (4), 53-5796/5918 (120), 54-1523/1526 (4), 54-5128/5131 (4), 54-1533/1536 (4), 54-1538/1539 (2), 54-1544/1547 (4), 54-1549/1552 (5), 54-1554/1618 (65), 54-2950/2955 (6), 54-4035/4036 (2), 55-2979/2983 (5), 55-3029/3049 (21), 55-3074/3115 (41), 55-4425/4456 (32), 55-4807/4810 (4), 55-4945/4962 (18), 56-1573/1646 (74), 56-1648/1650 (3), 56-1652/1654 (3), 56-1656/1658 (3), 56-1660/1662 (3), 56-1664/1666 (3), 56-1668/1670 (3), 56-1672/1674 (3), 56-1676/1678 (3), 56-1680/1682 (3), 56-1684/1686 (3), 56-1688/1690 (3), 56-1692/1694 (3), 56-1696/1698 (3), 56-1700/1702 (3), 56-1704/1706 (3), 56-1708/1710 (3), 56-1712/1714 (3), 56-1716/1718 (3), 56-1720/1722 (3), 56-1724/1726 (3), 56-1728/1730 (3), 56-1732/1734 (3), 56-1736/1738 (3), 56-1740/1742 (4), 56-1745/1747 (3), 56-1749/1751 (3), 56-1753/1755 (3), 56-1757/1759 (3), 56-1761/1763 (3), 56-1765/1767 (3), 56-1769/1771 (3), 56-1773/1775 (3), 56-1777/1779 (3), 56-1781/1783 (3), 56-1785/1787 (3), 56-1789/1792 (4)

Above: 51-4226 of the 176th Instrument School is fitted with a blind flying hood, seen here in the folded position.

Above: This view gives an impression of the underside of a typical T-33A-1-LO of Air Training Command, fitted with Fletcher tip tanks.

Left: T-33A-1-LO 49-0914 was used in experimental testing of the XLR53-AJ-1 liquid rocket in a modified 165-US gal (625-litre) tip tank during 1958.

T-33/T2V Variants

Below and below right: During the definition phase of the naval T2V-1 SeaStar, T-33A-1-LO 51-4263 was fitted with an experimental twin tail assembly to improve directional stability. The rear fuselage was also modified to contain what appears to be a form of arrester system, a cable being stretched under the fuselage. Also, a large anti-dazzle panel was painted behind the rear cockpit. The twin-tail idea was not proceeded with, Lockheed instead increasing the size of the empenage and raising the tailplane onto the fin itself.

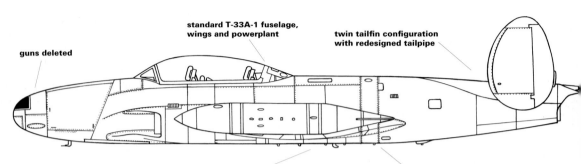

standard T-33A-1 fuselage, wings and powerplant

guns deleted

twin tailfin configuration with redesigned tailpipe

T-33A-1 (51-4263)

standard T-33A-1 fuselage, wings and powerplant

250-US gal (946-litre) Fletcher tiptanks

T-33A-5

Aircraft in the T-33A-5 block (USAF blocks began with '1' and were applied by a manufacturer in increments of five, making this the second block) were initially meant to be 'navigation trainers' and lacked the armament found on T-33A-1 aircraft. A number of T-33A-5 trainers were modified to T-33A-10 standard with installation of AN/ARN-21 TACAN and removal of VOR and ILS equipment.

T-33A-5-LO serials: 53-5919/6152 (234), 55-3017/3049 (33), 55-3116/3117 (2), 55-4332/4424 (93), 56-3659/3694 (36), 57-530/769 (240), 58-450/710 (261), 58-2094/2106 (13)

Seen landing at an airfield on Malta in the early 1970s, T-33A-5 57-593 was based at Ramstein AB, West Germany with the 7230th Combat Support Wing. Note the lack of any evidence of nose armament – an identification feature of the 'Dash-5'. This aircraft also carries a luggage pod in the standard position, under the rear fuselage.

AT-33A (T-33A-20)

The AT-33A attack aircraft, also identified in some records as the T-33A-20, differed from the standard 'T-bird' trainer in being equipped to carry two M116A 690-lb (313-kg) or two 1,000-lb bombs or eight 5-in HVARs (High Velocity Aircraft Rockets) on MA-2 launch rails. Aircraft brought to this standard from T-33A-1 airframes (separate entry) retained the two nose 0.50-in

machine-guns associated with the 'dash one' model, while those modified from unarmed T-33A-5s (separate entry) were equipped with a similar gun under each wing in an LAU-59 external pod.

Countries that flew the AT-33A include Brazil, whose attack-model Shooting Stars were known as FT-33s according to that country's air force and as AT-33A-20s

Right: 2°/1° GAvCa, Força Aérea Brasileira, used the AT-33A in both the pilot and tactical training roles. This example displays the underwing racks and pylons that distinguished the variant from the T-33A-1.

Left: In this view of another 1° GAvCa machine, the gun ports in the nose are visible, suggesting that it was converted from a T-33A-1-LO. Note also the Fletcher tip tanks.

according to another source; they served from the late 1950s until April 1972, when they began to be withdrawn in favour of the EMBRAER-built Aermacchi MB-326GB. Ecuador, according to the US Library of Congress, has no fewer than 30 AT-33As operational today, although another source implies that the inventory may be smaller. Nicaragua converted at least five of its 'T-bird' trainers to AT-33A attack aircraft,

with an armament package that has not been disclosed; in 1979 these warplanes saw action against the Sandinista forces, which were then the country's rebels. Uruguay has four AT-33As which remain operational today. Burma also flew AT-33As.

AT-33As were created by modifying airframes during depot inspection, and there exists today no authoritative listing of these airframes.

DTF-80C

Apparently, just one DTF-80C (48-360) flew as a drone controller (the 'D' prefix) before this family of Lockheed jets was reclassified

in the trainer category. The aircraft was part of the initial batch of Shooting Star trainers and was delivered on 27 September 1948. It was assigned to the 2754th Air Base Group at Holloman on 31 March 1949, thus enjoying its initial designation for less than

five weeks. It was very much the first of many, as additional drone controller 'T-birds' followed in several batches over many years. A surviving photo appears to show none of the external changes in the form of antennas found on drone controllers that

flew later. This ship became a DT-33A (at the time, apparently the only one) on 5 May 1949.

DTF-80C serial: 48-0360 (one conversion)

DT-33A

The DT-33A nomenclature identified 'T-birds' converted to the drone controller mission. Nearly half a century after Shooting Stars were employed as drones and drone

controllers in numerous locations and for several purposes – some drones were aerial targets, some were collectors of radioactive samples; some drone controllers had no other mission, others performed the task as a secondary duty – it has not proven possible to locate records of the

Above: Though of poor quality, this interesting photograph shows a DT-33A bringing a QB-47E target aircraft into land at Eglin AFB.

remanufacturing programmes that produced these aircraft in several batches. DT-33As controlled all manner of unpiloted drones, not merely other T-33s. For example, two were used for an extended period in operations with the QB-47 Stratojet drone bomber. An early example in USAF service was aircraft 50-383, assigned to the 3205th

Drone Group at Holloman AFB, New Mexico on 4 June 1952 and sporting a distinctive blade antenna above the nose and smaller antennas on the rear fuselage, characteristic of some, but not all, DT-33As. At least one DT-33A began its career as a DTF-80C (separate entry). At least one other (49-920) was designated ETD-33A (separate entry).

DT-33A 'DTR-913' formates with a QF-80F, both of which are manned. External features were confined to a pair of antennas on the nose.

EDT-33A

The EDT-33A term (the 'E' prefix meant 'exempt from technical orders'; the 'D' signified drone controller configuration)

applied to at least one aircraft (49-920). It was used to direct drones (QF-80s and QT-33s) in nuclear tests at Eniwetok in 1954 and later was noted with the 3200th Target and Drone Squadron at Eglin AFB, Florida.

ETF-80C (ET-33A?)

The ETF-80C appellation went to the second prototype TF-80C trainer (separate entry). This airframe (48-357) was used for ejection seat development work by the 2750th Air Base Wing at Wright-Patterson AFB, Ohio. The 'E' prefix denoted an aircraft with modifications not found on the rest of the fleet, including installation of a different canopy design so that the pilot in the front

seat could remain enclosed while an ejection could be accomplished from an open-canopy environment in the back seat.

If the USAF had followed its own logic, the aircraft would have been redesignated T-33A or ET-33A on 5 May 1949, but it is unclear whether this occurred.

ETF-80C serial: 48-357 (one conversion)

The single ETF-80C displays calibration marks below the rear cockpit, and a nose fairing housing a rear-facing camera to record ejection seat tests.

NT-33A

NT-33A was the designation assigned to a T-33A-1 (51-4120) modified as a flight control and handling qualities research aircraft in 1954-57 by Cornell Aero Lab (the forerunner of Calspan SRL Corporation), with a distinctive nose making it resemble an F-94B Starfire. The 'N' prefix supposedly means a permanent modification, making the aircraft unable to resume its original mission.

The aircraft, accepted by the USAF in October 1951, was owned by the USAF's Wright Laboratory although it was operated and maintained by Calspan of Buffalo, New York. Modifications included relocating internal systems and installing a data recorder, sensors and computers into which desired flight characteristics could be programmed, a fly-by-wire front cockpit, and a programmable HUD. Also installed in this NT-33A was an independently controlled centre stick whose input went into the computer, together with hydraulic actuators controlled by the computer on all primary control surfaces. These variable flight controls enabled its use as an inflight simulator for flight control systems (FCS) research for a variety of aircraft, one of the

first programmes being to simulate re-entry characteristics for the X-15.

The NT-33A undertook other simulations for the YF-16, YF-17, F-18, A-9, A-10, F-117 and F-22 plus the IAI Lavi and Saab JAS 39 Gripen. In most cases, these simulations were done before the aircraft themselves made their first flights, although in the case of the Gripen it was used to determine a solution to FCS problems encountered after the aircraft had flown.

The final assignment of the NT-33A, involving the flight characteristics of advanced aircraft, was undertaken at Edwards AFB, California. The senior class at the USAF Test Pilot School flew the last sorties, the final test flight taking place on 16 April 1997. The NT-33A is slated for display at the USAF Museum at Wright-Patterson AFB, Ohio.

Right: NT-33A 51-4120 here demonstrates its unique tiptank-mounted air brakes.

Below: This 1974 'hook-up' between NT-33A 51-4120 and a VAQ-33 EKA-3B Skywarrior was the first in-flight refuelling of an aircraft flying under fly-by-wire controls.

T-33A-1-LO 49-0913 was another aircraft re-designated NT-33A while with Air Research & Development Command's Wright Air Development Center around 1960. The aircraft appears to have been fitted with nose-mounted camera windows and a small thimble fairing on the extreme nose.

QT-33A

The QT-33A drone version of the 'T-bird', together with its close cousins in the drone (QT-33B, QT-33C, TV-2K) and drone control (DT-33A, DT-33B, TV-2KD) families, has a convoluted history which encompasses several manufacturers and users, at different periods. Every element of the drone story has one common point: no comprehensive history has ever been published, and most of the documentation that would permit a thorough history no longer exists.

Sperry Flight Systems modified QT-33A drones for the US Air Force and Navy at Marana Air Park near Phoenix, Ariz. All of the company's records have since been destroyed. Some sources also suggest that Sperry and other companies modified QT-33As at other locations. Most of these aircraft were intended for Navy use at the Pacific Missile Test Center, Point Mugu, Calif., and the Naval Weapons Center, China Lake, Calif. Sperry also manufactured the DSCE-33N drone stabilisation and control bench, a ground-based operator position for controlling drones in flight.

Documents from the Honeywell Corp., which apparently refer to work performed under the Sperry name, says that Honeywell was also involved in the drone business. The company produced 107 QB-17 Flying Fortresses over 1948-54, identified today as the 'first FSAT' (Full-Scale Aerial Target). They were followed by 107 QF-80 FSATs over 1948-60 and 75 QT-33A FSATs over 1950-60. Despite their name, these aircraft were not initially intended as gunnery or missile targets. Their first job was to test the effects of an atomic cloud on aircraft and to collect samples of radioactive fallout. In the 1950s, the US detonated dozens of atomic and hydrogen bombs in the Pacific and at the national test site in Nevada. A separate document indicates that Honeywell produced 81 QT-33As, six for Air Force use in nuclear tests and 75 for the Navy to be used as targets, and that the Air Force operated no targets and the Navy no sampling aircraft. Yet another Honeywell document makes these figures 84, 85 and nine.

When Sperry received an ex-USAF T-33A for conversion to a 'QT' drone, it installed a 400-amp DC generator, nosewheel steering and an arrester hook. The conversion to drone configuration also involved instrument panel modifications, fuel tank changes, automatic fuel-management switching, installation of an anti-skid brake system, and installation of a camera scoring system.

Controls installed by Sperry, and developed originally for the QF-80, included vertical gyro, turn and pitch controller, flight control system amplifier, servo control (amplidyne), altitude integrator, air speed reference unit, surface actuators, trim tab control adaptor, trim tab limit switch, airspeed amplifier, airspeed follow-up unit and throttle servo. On QT-33A drones for the Air Force, an automatic pilot was included and a flight controller unit was provided for this purpose. Navy QT-33As did not have an autopilot, but they did have primary and secondary control panels to permit a safety pilot to simulate command receiver inputs to the drone stabilisation and control equipment.

The QT-33A was capable of being controlled remotely either while manned or unmanned. Dual AN/DRW-29 command receivers (audio tone) were used for receipt and decoding of guidance commands. An AN/AKT-2 telemetry transmitting set (audio tone) was used for data transmission to the guidance and command station.

Above: In the QT-33A the space in the rear cockpit normally occupied by the trainee pilot was filled with electronics. BuNo. 155925 was used by the Naval Weapons Center, China Lake.

Below: Resplendent in high-visibility red, QT-33A 155946 sits among QF-9 Cougars awaiting its fate. Both types later gave way to QF-86 Sabres in the USN drone programme.

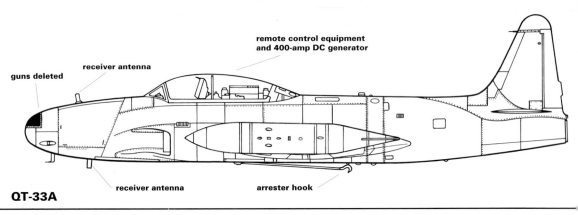

QT-33A

guns deleted · receiver antenna · remote control equipment and 400-amp DC generator · receiver antenna · arrester hook

EQT-33A (JT-33A)

The EQT-33A designation (the 'E' prefix meant 'exempt from technical orders'; the 'Q' signified drone configuration) was assigned to a single aircraft (48-919) which subsequently was known as a JT-33A.

A JT-33A (48-919) was employed by the USAF in a number of different research duties. The 'J' prefix was meant to identify a temporary modification (an aircraft with a more 'permanent' change being an NT-33A), but this airframe was never used operationally as a trainer. At one juncture in a long career of flying various experiments, this aircraft was designated EQT-33A. Near the end of its service life, it flew with a nose having the shape of the Martin TM-76 Mace surface-to-surface missile, a jet-powered forerunner of the cruise missiles of a later era.

The JT-33A designation has been applied to a number of aircraft of varying configurations. This example (53-5404) was used for thunderstorm and squall research as part of Project Rough Rider (and displays nose art to this effect). For this task it was fitted with a nose mounted yaw/pitch boom and a atmospheric pressure sensor under the wing.

RT-33A

The RT-33A photo-reconnaissance version featured vertical and oblique cameras in a nose of modified contour and carried electronic and recording equipment in the rear cockpit, displacing the second seat. Some 85 aircraft were manufactured in this configuration, taken from selected slots in the T-33A production line. The purpose was to provide an affordable reconnaissance capability to allies who were unlikely to invest in a more costly system like the RF-101 Voodoo.

No authoritative description of RT-33A camera installations has been found. One source says that the cameras were usually K-14 and K-18 models with different focal lengths. According to the recollection of one reconnaissance pilot, the installation usually consisted of two camera sets, a KS-6 for oblique shots to the left or right of the aircraft and a KS-8 framing camera for direct overhead shots. The RT-33A was a single-seater and carried a forward fuselage tank in lieu of an aft pilot's seat. Mounted on top of the tank in the position originally meant for a back-seat instructor was an ARC-3 VHF radio for use in locations that did not have USAF-standard UHF radios, plus an ARN-6 automatic direction finder. It should be noted that some overseas operators created their own RT-33As, in addition to those listed by serial below which came from the factory, by converting trainers. In both the new-build and the modified RT-33As there may have been several kinds of camera installations.

American pilots flew at least one RT-33A (53-5347) in the Field Goal effort, flying from Don Muang Airport, Thailand, over Pathet Lao installations in Laos in the early 1960s.

At Wiesbaden AB, Germany in the late 1950s and early 1960s, the USAF's 7499th Support Group flew an assortment of (somewhat odd) aircraft with no military markings. The unit was overseen by Colonel Ralph Steakley, who later formed and headed the National Reconnaissance Office. A former member of the unit recalls that among its aircraft were RT-33As used for reconnaissance missions along the East German border.

Countries which have operated RT-33As include Chile, Colombia, Ecuador, France, Honduras, Iran, Iraq, Italy, Philippines, Thailand, Turkey and the USA. Rather incredibly, as late as 1990 three RT-33As were active in the Philippines. Mexico modified 30 of its T-33A trainers to RT-33A standard, using a different 'fit' than on other reconnaissance 'T-birds'. Given serials JE-017/056 and assigned to 210, 211 and 212 Escuadrones, they carried underwing 0.50-in (12.7-mm) machine-gun pods; they are operational today.

In addition to the Lockheed RT-33A, 10

Canadair T-33AN Silver Star Mk 3 trainers (separate entry) were modified to RT-33A standard (albeit with Nene rather than J33 engines). They were equipped with Vinten camera and served with 408 Squadron at Rockliffe, Ontario.

USAF serials: 53-5090, 53-5174, 53-5209, 53-5237/5239, 53-5257, 53-5273, 53-5291, 53-5308, 53-5322, 53-5335, 53-5347, 53-5359, 53-5371, 53-5384, 53-5396, 53-5409, 53-5420, 53-5430, 53-5441, 53-5449, 53-5457, 53-5466, 53-5474, 53-5482, 53-5491, 53-5499, 53-5508, 53-5517, 53-5525, 53-5533, 53-5539, 53-5546, 53-5553, 53-5560, 53-5567, 53-5574, 53-5581, 53-5587, 53-5594, 53-5600, 53-5607, 53-5613, 53-5619, 53-5626, 53-5631, 53-5638, 53-5644, 53-5650, 53-5656, 53-5662, 53-5668, 53-5675, 53-5681, 53-5687, 53-5693, 53-5699, 53-5705, 53-5710, 53-5716, 53-5721, 53-5727, 53-5733, 53-5739, 53-5745, 53-5751, 53-5756, 53-5763, 53-5768, 53-5773, 53-5779, 53-5785, 53-5790, 53-5795, 54-1522, 54-1527, 54-1532, 54-1537, 54-1540/1543, 54-1548, 54-1553 (85 aircraft)

Right: This view of the forward fuselage of an Italian RT-33 shows the redesigned nose of the aircraft and equipment crammed into the rear cockpit space.

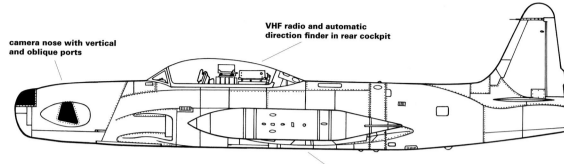

camera nose with vertical and oblique ports

VHF radio and automatic direction finder in rear cockpit

RT-33A

230-US gal (871-litre) Fletcher tiptanks

Left: 53-5090 was the first RT-33A conversion. Most RT-33As were delivered to foreign operators under various military assistance programmes. USAF PR squadrons employed the RF-101 Voodoo.

Above: RT-33A 53-5237 peels away from the camera ship to display its nose camera ports. Lockheed-produced machines had five ports; overseas conversions and those done 'in the field' often differed.

'T-33F'

The 'T-33F' designation, with the 'F' suffix perhaps signifying France, has been used to refer to 'T-birds' re-exported from France to other countries, such as 18 aircraft transferred from France to Bolivia in the 1970s. The so-called 'T-33Fs' in Bolivia are the survivors of 18 (the most-frequently cited number) ex-Armée de l'Air T-33As/CT-133s delivered from June 1985. All were assigned to the FAB's Grupo Aéreo de Caza 31 and Grupo Aéreo de Caza 32, split between La Paz/El Alto and Santa Cruz.

With no other identifying marks, other than its French delivery registration F-ZVLI, this camouflaged aircraft was destined for the Fuerza Aérea Boliviana when photographed at Quebec City airport in June 1985. Its original identity is believed to be CT-133 21042 or 21247; the re-use of delivery registrations makes it difficult to be certain.

Naval variants

TO-2/TV-2

TO-2 was the initial US Navy designation for its T-33 aircraft. The 'T' indicated a trainer, the 'O' was the letter assigned to Lockheed-built aircraft, and the '-2' indicated the second variant (the TO-1 designation went to the single-seat F-80 fighter).

It does not appear that the TV-2 was ever actually used in the Navy's pilot training programme, which employed single-seat F9F-6 and -8 Cougars and (after 1956) single-seat F11F-1 Tigers and two-seat F9F-8T Cougars in advanced pilot training.

Yugoslavia operated 52 TV-2s, the only country to receive these aircraft in export. Reports of TV-2s operated by Nicaragua are inaccurate.

Six TV-2s (typified by BuNo. 128671/ 51-4293) were operated by the FAA (Federal Aviation Administration) for high-altitude flight checking of navigational aids. The FAA acquired 12 aircraft in 1959 with

the following Bureau numbers and civil registry numbers: 126583 (N151), 126585 (N9126Z), 126589 (N9125Z), 128671 (N152), 128700 (N9123Z), 128705 (N156), 128706 (N9124Z), 128719 (N154), 131729 (N9122Z, later N592W), 131770 (N9121Z), 131787 (N153) and 131804 (N155, later N15511). One of these TV-2s was later noted as N85. The aircraft were picked up from storage at Litchfield Park, Arizona and some flew only once, from there to the FAA facility at Oklahoma City, Oklahoma, where about half were used for spare parts to keep the others flying. Some were also assigned to NAFEC (National Aviation Facilities

The Navy's TV-2s (of which the first 26 were delivered under the TO-2 designation) were diverted from batches ordered by the USAF. This late production aircraft is seen on a pre-delivery test flight.

T-33/T2V Variants

Experimental Center), Atlantic City, New Jersey. It appears that the flying examples were N151/156. The FAA lost several TV-2s in mishaps before the FAA retired its last 'T-bird' in 1973.

TV-2 BuNos (and USAF serials):
124571/124585 - 49-2758/2772 (15),
124930/124939 - 50-445/454 (10),
126583/126588 - 51-4019/4024 (6),
126589/126594 - 51-4031/4036 (6),
126595/126600 - 51-4052/4057 (6),
126601/126606 - 51-4078/4083 (6),
126607/126612 - 51-4104/4109 (6),
126613/126618 - 51-4137/4142 (6),
126619/126624 - 51-4174/4179 (6),
126625/126626 - 51-4237/4238 (2),
126661/128665 - 51-4239/4243 (5),
128666/128672 - 51-4288/4294 (7),
128673/128682 - 51-4355/4364 (10),
128683/128692 - 51-4425/4434 (10),

128693/128702 - 51-4515/4524 (10),
128703/128712 - 51-6578/6587 (10),
128713/128722 - 51-6665/6674 (10),
131725/131748 - 51-8518/8541 (24),
131749/131764 - 51-8636/8651 (16),
131765/131785 - 51-8729/8749 (21),
131786/131820 - 51-8836/8870 (35),
131821/131834 - 51-8940/8953 (14),

131835/131870 - 51-9040/9075 (36),
131871/131888 - 51-9150/9167 (18),
136793/136886 (94), 137934/138097 (164),
138977/139016 (40), 141490/141501 (12),
141502/141558 - 55-2984/3016,
55-3050/3073 (57), 143014/143049 (36)
Total built: 699

*USMC units used a number of TV-2s as communications aircraft and continuation trainers. This **HEDRON 12** example is a **TO-2**. The aircraft's data panel displays both its **USN Bureau Number** as well as its **USAF Fiscal Year** serial number.*

TV-2D (DT-33B)

The TV-2D designation was assigned to Navy drone-controller aircraft, apparently redesignated DT-33B on 1 October 1962.

These aircraft were configured differently than the TV-2KD model.

*Two early model **TV-2KDs** with nose-mounted whip antennas escort an early KDU-1 Regulus I drone. **TV-2KD BuNo. 131884** (left) has a blade aerial fitted.*

*Above: Controlled by the **TV-2KD**, a **KD2U-1 (Regulus II)** drone is launched at the Naval Missile Center, Point Mugu, while a F8U-1P Crusader acts as camera ship.*

TV-2KD (QT-33C)

The TV-2KD designation went to US Navy drone aircraft modified as radio-controlled aerial targets, apparently in a configuration somewhat different from the Air Force DT-33A. These aircraft were intended to operate as both drones and drone controllers, the only ''T-birds' so configured, and also were used for utility transport or 'hack' duties. The Navy reportedly operated at least 32 of these aircraft, redesignated QT-33C on 1 October 1962.

QT-33B

The QT-33B designation was assigned to Navy TV-2KD dual-role director/drone aircraft when they were operated as drones after 1 October 1962. In addition, this designation was probably intended for 252 former US Air Force T-33A trainers which were assigned Navy BuNos 155918/156169. Conventional wisdom has long held that the conversion to drone status never took place and nearly all of these aircraft instead went to the 'boneyard' in Tucson, Arizona; however, a photo shows an aircraft flying with BuNo. 155920, wearing the red-orange paint scheme associated with drones, with a blade antenna near the tip of the nose and a tail hook installed. One source refers to these unconverted drones by the QT-33A designation, which appears unlikely. The Bureau numbers were never painted on, and the 'T-bird's retained their Air Force serials. The aircraft arrived at MASDC (Military Aircraft Storage and Disposition Center) between August 1964 and December 1970.

L-245

The company-funded L-245 prototype (which led eventually to the T2V-1 SeaStar) was also known simply as the 'Lockheed Trainer', and unofficially as the T-33B in some documents, the T-33D in others. Later, it was also dubbed the company Model 1080-91-08.

The L-245 was an attempt to bring together the qualities of the 'T-bird' design with a *bona fide* capability for aircraft-carrier operations. Lockheed's Clarence 'Kelly' Johnson also felt a strong need to improve the working environment of the back-seat flight instructor. The poor performance of the 'T-bird' at low speeds and especially in the post-stall mode was another problem that Johnson and the Lockheed team sought to resolve in the L-245. These

concerns led to a decision to elevate the instructor's rear seat by 6 in (15 cm) and to redesign the windscreen (which became single-piece) and canopy. To enhance low-speed performance, the L-245 acquired leading-edge slats, and boundary layer control (BLC) with its flaps, and bigger, redesigned vertical and horizontal tails.

The BLC system was advanced for its time and used bleed air from the engine compressor section. A circular manifold collected air from compressor chambers and discharged it over the top of the flap leading edge along the entire flap span. This led to a reduction of about 10 mph (16 km/h) in landing speed, a slightly larger reduction in take-off speed, and economies of operation in the aircraft-carrier pattern.

The L-245 introduced other improvements including single-point refuelling, which was expected to cut turn-

around time by 66 per cent, and strengthened landing gear.

The sole L-245 (registered N125D) made its initial flight on 16 December 1953, piloted by Tony LeVier.

Suitably labelled on the rear fuselage as the 'Lockheed Trainer', L-245 N125D was the first of the 'humped-back' naval aircraft.

Redesigned airframe
A substantial redesign of the TV-2 (T-33B) was necessary to produce an aircraft more suited to the naval training role. Among the changes was the incorporation of a stepped cockpit to improve the instructor's view from the rear cockpit. Blind flying curtains could be fitted in the rear cockpit for instrument training flights (the instructor sitting in the front seat on these occasions). For the navigator training role, new navigation and communications equipment was housed in the nose.

Powerplant
The SeaStar was equipped with a more powerful version of the Allison J33 turbojet found in T-33s and the TV-2. Initially T2V-2's were equipped with the J33-A-24, rated at 6,100 lb st (27.13 kN); later production aircraft had the 6,350-lb st (28.25-kN) Dash-16A.

Delivered in 1956, 142266 was the sixth of 149 production T2V-1s, the first operational examples of which equipped Naval Air Advanced Training Command at NAS Corpus Christi from May 1957. This aircraft was among those employed by the NATC in carrier qualification trials for the type aboard USS *Antietam* (CV-36) later that year.

Tailhook
An obvious modification for this carrier-capable aircraft was the addition of a tailhook, hinged in line with the wing trailing edge. This was hydraulically extended and maintained in position pneumatically.

Lockheed T2V-1 SeaStar Flight Test Division NATC Patuxent River 1957

Fuel capacity
To provide a range in the order of 900 miles (1448 km), the SeaStar had increased fuel capacity over that in the T-33. Internally, an enlarged tank behind the cockpit and tanks in the wings provided a 300 US gal (1136.5 litre) capacity to which was added the 460-US gal (1741-litre) in the non-jettisonable tiptanks.

Colour scheme
When delivered, the T2V-1s were finished in the standard US Navy high-visibility international orange/insignia white trainer scheme. Lettering was in black, along with the aircraft's nose and the anti-glare panel forward of the cockpit.

BLC and slats
To lower the aircraft's landing speed, Lockheed added boundary-layer control (BLC, using air bled from the engine and blown over the flaps) and leading-edge slats. A lower landing speed (97 mph/156 km/h) than any other jet aircraft was claimed.

Undercarriage
For carrierborne operations, the T2V was equipped with considerably strengthened undercarriage, able to withstand a sink rate of 20.8 ft (6.34 m) per sec – more than twice that permitted in a T-33A. The nose gear could be hydraulically 'lengthened' to raise the nose for catapult take-offs.

Left: Lockheed's L-245 was initially finished in the standard USN trainer scheme. It is seen on its first flight on 15 December 1953.

Above: The SeaStar's main airframe differences were directed at making the 'T-bird' more suitable for operations from a carrier.

T2V-1 (T-1A) SeaStar

The T2V-1 SeaStar was Lockheed's follow-on to the ubiquitous 'T-bird', powered by a 6,100-lb st (27.13-kN) thrust Allison J33-A-24 centrifugal-flow turbojet, virtually the most powerful engine on any member of the T-33 family. The T2V-1 was designed to take students aboard aircraft-carriers and was equipped with a tailhook as well as a hold-back catapult bridle just forward of the arrestor hook and a catapult attachment in front of its dorsal speed brakes. With a length of 36 ft 7 in (11.45 m), the SeaStar (also called Sea Star and Seastar) was more than 12 in (30 cm) shorter than the standard 'T-bird', but its wing span of 42 ft 11 in (13.06 m) was 5 ft (1.52 m) greater than the span of a typical Shooting Star trainer. The T2V-1 was about 3,300 lb (1497 kg) heavier than a 'T-bird' and incorporated tandem Martin-Baker Mk L-5 ejection seats, considered to be an improvement over the Lockheed seat.

T2V-1 BuNos: 142261/142268 (8), 142397/142399 (3), 142533/142541 (9), 144117/144216 (100), 144735/144764 (30) Total built: 150

Below: The new raised rear cockpit provided better forward vision for the instructor, vital during deck landing training.

Below: From below the SeaStar's shorter nose (compared to the T-33A), redesigned rear fuselage and tail-plane assembly were prominent. Less visible was the increased wing span.

Right: Small numbers of SeaStars were allocated to the Marines for use by Headquarters & Maintenance Squadrons. T-1A BuNo. 144144, was with H&MS-24 in May 1967.

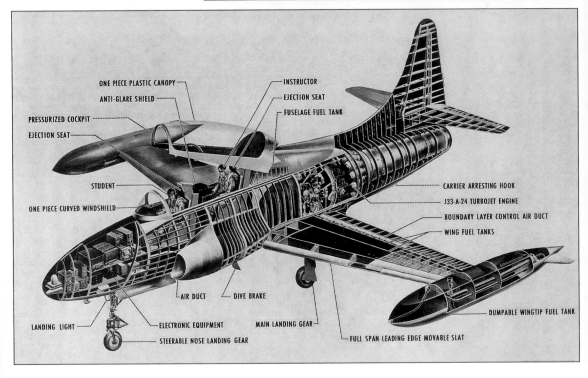

ONE PIECE PLASTIC CANOPY
INSTRUCTOR
ANTI-GLARE SHIELD
EJECTION SEAT
FUSELAGE FUEL TANK
PRESSURIZED COCKPIT
EJECTION SEAT
STUDENT
CARRIER ARRESTING HOOK
J33-A-24 TURBOJET ENGINE
ONE PIECE CURVED WINDSHIELD
BOUNDARY LAYER CONTROL AIR DUCT
WING FUEL TANKS
AIR DUCT
DIVE BRAKE
LANDING LIGHT
ELECTRONIC EQUIPMENT
MAIN LANDING GEAR
DUMPABLE WINGTIP FUEL TANK
STEERABLE NOSE LANDING GEAR
FULL SPAN LEADING EDGE MOVABLE SLAT

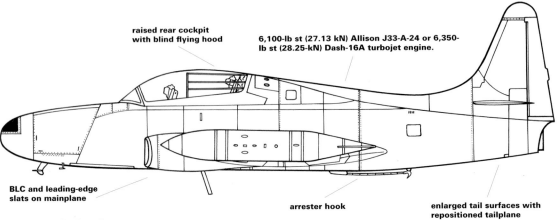

raised rear cockpit with blind flying hood

6,100-lb st (27.13 kN) Allison J33-A-24 or 6,350-lb st (28.25-kN) Dash-16A turbojet engine.

BLC and leading-edge slats on mainplane

arrester hook

enlarged tail surfaces with repositioned tailplane

T2V-1 (T-1A) SeaStar

Above: *From above, the SeaStar's redesigned and enlarged control surfaces may be seen.*

Left: *Marked as a YT2V-1, the first production aircraft approaches USS Antietam for the first deck landing.*

Foreign variants & production

T-33A Silver Star Mk 1

The Silver Star Mk 1 designation applies to the Royal Canadian Air Force's first 'T-birds', a batch of 20 Lockheed-built T-33As provided on loan in May 1951 with deliveries ending in January 1952. Supplied so that Canada could prepare to employ its own Canadair-built Shooting Stars, these aircraft had underslung tip-tanks and no ejection seats. They were initially assigned to No. 416 Squadron, an F-51 Mustang unit at Trenton scheduled to receive Canadair Sabres.

Later, another 10 were supplied, again 'on loan', though these aircraft did not receive RCAF designations or serial numbers and retained standard USAF markings, except for the maple leaf national insignia. Survivors of the 30 aircraft were returned to the USAF, at least on paper, a number going to NATO allies.

Left: *The Silver Star Mk 1s served with No. 416 Sqn and No. 1 (F)OTU. Note the tip tanks on 14679; aircraft from the later batch of loaned aircraft had centre-mounted Fletcher tanks.*

Above: *T-33A 51-6715 (of the second batch) is seen soon after delivery to the RCAF, retaining both its USAF serial and buzz codes.*

Silver Star Mk 1 serials: 14675/14694 (US serials of known aircraft in first batch were: 50-430, 50-433, 50-1275/1276, 51-4063/4065, 51-4091/4093, 51-4119, 51-4121, 51-4146, 51-4156 and 51-4198. The second batch of 10 aircraft comprised 51-6713/6717 and 51-6743/6747).

(Canadair) T-33ANX Silver Star Mk 2

T-33ANX was the term used to refer to an American T-33A (51-4198) modified to serve in Canada as a flying prototype for the Canadair CL-30 Silver Star 3 trainers manufactured in Montreal. The sole T-33ANX was given RCAF serial 14695.

Known as the Silver Star Mk 2, this aircraft first flew in its revised configuration on 28 October 1952. Re-engined with a 5,100-lb st (22.69-kN) Rolls-Royce Nene Mk 10, this test ship began engine runs at the Canadair factory on 13 September 1952 and flew on 28 October 1952, piloted by Hedley Everard.

The sole T-33ANX (left) was used to test the engine and associated systems for the Silver Star 3 – the 'NX' in its designation standing for Nene (in place of the Allison J33-A-25) and 'experimental'. It was the last of the original batch of T-33As delivered to the RCAF by the USAF. After testing the Rolls-Royce engine, 14695 was used at NAE Uplands for various test programmes. Here it is seen with vortex generators on its outer wings in July 1955 (below).

(Canadair CL-30) T-33AN Silver Star 3 (CT-133)

T-33AN was the designation for the production Canadair CL-30 Silver Star 3 trainer (note that use of the 'Mk' prefix had been abandoned by this time) manufactured by Canadair (the 'N' prefix denoted the Nene engine). The first aircraft completed its maiden flight on 22 December 1952 with Bill Longhurst at the controls. Between 1952 and 1959, Canadair built 656 of these aircraft, almost identical to the Lockheed product but powered by a 5,100-lb st (22.69-kN) thrust Rolls-Royce Nene Mk 10, which proved to be a heavier engine in weight but developed more thrust than the Allison J33 installed on American 'T-birds'.

Most initially went to the Royal Canadian Air Force and included three sub-types: the Silver Star 3PT pilot trainer (the most numerous variant); 3AT (armament trainer; equipped with two 0.5-cal machine-guns, as per the T-33A-1); 3PR (three aircraft with nose-mounted cameras).

There were also a number of conversions for the search-and-rescue role – the Silver Star 3PTS(SARAH), with search-and-rescue homing gear and the 3PT(Search).

The Royal Canadian Navy began receiving examples in January 1955 with squadron VT 40 at HMCS Shearwater, where they were used to train F2H Banshee pilots. Later, the squadron became VU 32 and still later these aquatic Silver Stars became maritime aggressors, hack utility craft and target tugs. Other examples flew with VX 10 and VU 33. The Canadian armed forces were unified in 1968 and, on 11 November 1970, the aircraft were redesignated CT-133.

The contract for manufacture of these 'T-birds' was inked in April 1952. Of Canadair's 656 trainers, 148 aircraft (21051/21199) corresponded (except for engine and some other features) to the T-33A-1 from Lockheed and carried standard armament for the type. All remaining Canadair trainers corresponded to the T-33A-5 navigation trainer from Lockheed.

Nations which received Canadair T-33AN trainers retired from Canadian service were Bolivia, France (which applied the designations T-33S-US to its Lockheed-built examples and T-33S-C to Canadair ships), Greece, Portugal and Turkey.

Canadair T-33AN serials: 21001/21656 (656), later changed to 133001/133656 Total built: 656

Known serials of Silver Star 3PTS and 3PT aircraft include '119, '176, '190, '287, '303, '304, '393, '398, '423, '452, '468, '490, '512, '546, '560, '572, '577, '581, '599, and '625.

Above: By the end of the Korean War Silver Star 3s were coming off the Canadair production lines at the rate of two a day. Production ran from November 1952 until March 1958.

Canada's huge purchase of Silver Star 3s was intended to help establish and equip a large training organisation to provide NATO countries with jet-trained pilots. 21085 (left) is configured as Silver Star 3PT pilot trainer, with its nose-mounted machine-gun ports faired over, while 21075 (right) is a Star 3AT, with guns and underwing stores pylons.

Above: The Red Knight aerobatic routine was performed at small events between 1958 and 1969 flying one of several specially painted Silver Star Mk 3.

Camera-equipped RCAF CT-133

In 1962, the RCAF's No. 408 Squadron at Rivers, Manitoba began to receive Canadair-built T-33 Silver Star Mk 3s modified with a camera nose and referred to as 'armed trainers', with a secondary capability to conduct chemical warfare. CARDE (Canadian Armament Research and Development Establishment) had used a T-33 equipped with a forward-facing nose camera to record the firing trials by F-86 Sabre and CF-100 Canuck aircraft of Canada's Velvet Glove missile programme in 1957. A development of this nose system was a nosepiece equipped with forward and vertical cameras that replaced the gun muzzle segment of the nose and redesigned gun bays to hold two oblique cameras with associated hardware. The wing pylons could also be fitted with camera pods.

The camera-equipped 'T-birds' were used to support Army exercises. They served for almost a decade until Ottawa disbanded No. 408 Squadron in April 1970. Two of these aircraft crashed, the first (21565) on 12 October 1967 (being struck off charge on 24 October 1967) and the other (21633) on 16 June 1969 (struck off charge on 15 September 1969). One ship (21257) later went to France and is now on display at a museum there. The remaining two (21556/21557) were struck off charge on 10 November 1970 but 21556 continues to fly as N99179 with PLR Aircraft Leasing in Los Angeles, Calif., and 21557 is privately owned as N99175 in Salt Lake City, Utah. Both civil survivors have their camera noses intact.

The five aircraft modified to this configuration were 21257, 21556/21557, 21565 and 21633.

Camera-equipped NAE CT-133

In 1953 and 1954, this aircraft was used by the Canadian Armament and Research Establishment and the National Aeronautical Establishment for photographic pacer duties to record details of the air firing trials of the Canadair/Westinghouse CL-20 Velvet Glove air-to-air missile test vehicles.

Modifications were made to the forward nose compartment and a nosepiece was added to house two tracking cameras for the recording of the Velvet Glove's boost phase trajectories when air launched from RCAF's CEPE F-86 Mk 2 and CF-100 Mk 3A test aircraft. A 35-mm EYEMO camera faced up at 45° to record pre-launch, up to the initial part of the missile trajectory, while a 70-mm HULCHER camera faced up at 8° to photograph the later part of the trajectory until the end of the boost phase.

This was a one-off aircraft modification and is not to be confused with five modified camera-equipped Silver Stars of No. 408 Squadron. This aircraft is presently preserved at the CAE plant at Edmonton's International Airport.

The first Canadair-built T-33AN (21001) carried camera equipment in a heavily modified nose section to record the flight of the CL-20 Velvet Glove vehicles.

'TE-133'

'TE-133' is an unofficial designation used to identify CT-133 trainers used to simulate anti-shipping threats. These aircraft were known as 'TE-133s' for scheduling purposes and are equipped with the AN/DPT-1 threat emitter in the nose, making them readily distinguishable by the small black bump on the nose. The system is used to simulate radar emissions from sea-skimming anti-shipping and other missiles.

Some of these aircraft were also equipped to carry the Del Mar Radop target-towing system, consisting of two styrofoam targets (containing a radar reflector) towed behind the 'T-bird' at a range of up to 10,000 ft (3048 m) allowing gunners from frigates and destroyers to hone their skills.

Aircraft carrying the Radop system usually had Dayglo-coloured tip tanks and, during the period when the CT-133s were finished in natural metal, also carried that colour on the nose and tail. As one pilot said, "it was to remind ships' gunners that the aircraft was in front towing rather than in the rear pushing".

'TE-133s' also worked with a shore-based training turrets and with Army air

defence troops.

These aircraft were initially assigned to Canadian Navy squadrons VU 32 (on the east coast) and VU 33 (on the west coast). After Canadian service branches were unified in 1968, these aircraft continued their threat duties as part of Maritime Command. When VU 32 and VU 33 were disestablished in 1992, 'TE-133s' went to Canada's two combat support (CS) squadrons, No. 434 Squadron 'Bluenosers' with 12 Wing at Shearwater, Nova Scotia and No. 414 Squadron 'Black Knights' with 19 Wing at Comox, British Columbia.

In January 1999, six 'TE-133' were extant. 'TE-133' 133102, 133119 were flown by No. 414 Sqn (the latter aircraft having a secondary SAR role), while with No. 434 Sqn were 133389, 133402, 133593 and 133656.

Known serials of those fitted with the Del Mar Radop include 056, 077, 118, 120, 130, 167, 179, 180, 189, 196, 247, 303, 371, 423, 446, 461, 465, 487, 583, 585, 610, 613, 629, 641, 642, 643, 644, 645, 646, 647, 648, 649, 650, 651, 652, 653, and 656.
Known serials of those fitted with the DPT-1 include: 102, 266, 352, 389, 402, 441, 577, and 593.

Right: 'TE-133' 133402 of No. 434 Squadron carries a pair of Del Mar Radop towed targets.

Below: 133656 (the last T-33AN built) of VU 32 is equipped with the nose-mounted DPT-1 emitter.

'ET-133'/'EW-133'

The 'ET-133' designation, which is unofficial, applies to trainers modified and used to simulate an aerial threat to North American Aerospace Defense Command elements (including AWACS, GCI and fighter interceptor crews), and ground and naval forces.

Sometimes also known as the 'EW-133', this variant is equipped to carry a selection of USAF jamming pods and, apart from a small amount of control equipment in the rear cockpit, are standard CT-133s.

Equipment carried has included ALQ-71 (used against ground-based radars, AWACS and ships), the ALQ-176/1761 (used against ships, fire-control platforms and AWACS), and the ALQ-188 pod for use against low-level air defences and modern fighter types such as the CF-18, F-15 and F-16. The

variant is also capable of carrying the ALE-2 and ALE-502 chaff pods, which are used to deflect radar energy and mask incoming threats.

All 'ET-133s' were assigned to No. 414 Sqn during the unit's time at CFB North Lake and later by both Nos 414 and 434 Sqns after the former was divided between east and west coast bases. Both units therefore operated 'TE-133s', 'ET-133s' and standard CT-133s at this time.

Known serials of 'ET-133s' include: '083, '119, '479, '483, '560, '571, '573, '576, '604, and '615.

'EW-133' 133560 of No. 414 Squadron carries a jamming pod (starboard wing) and a chaff tank.

CE-133

Advancements in radar and weapons technology and the phase-out of older ram-air driven EW pods by US forces required the CAF to undertake an update of its electronic support and training (EST) systems for its CE-133 and CE-144 Challenger EW platforms. In 1995 the Ericsson A100 Erijammer ECM pod was acquired, offering not only an extensive selection of ECM modes and a built-in radar warning receiver, but also 360° of coverage. The Lundy AN/ALE-503 chaff dispenser was acquired, allowing the EW officer to select chaff lengths to match the frequency being jammed. The EST fit on the CE-133 included two 3-kV inverters to supply AC power to each pylon-mounted pod, a cockpit avionics update, and RWR, EW and chaff controls in the EWO rear cockpit. In 1996 consideration was given to removing the flying and engine controls from the rear cockpit of the CE-133s, though it is unclear whether this

was carried out.

Along with the avionics/cockpit upgrade planned for all operational 'T-birds', the decision was made to redesignate nine, later 10, CT-133s as CE-133s. The new designation was deemed appropriate given the extent of changes to the aircraft, notably in, but not limited to, the rear cockpit.

The new designation took effect when the aircraft were selected for conversion, choice of airframe being based primarily on its state of repair and number of airframe fatigue hours remaining. For this reason, not all CE-133s were necessarily conversions of existing 'ET-133s'.

The initial nine officially redesignated as CE-133 are 133083, 133441, 133479, 133483, 133560, 133571, 133573, 133604, and 133615. Later, 133446 was added and it served with AETE as the conversion prototype. As of January 1999, No. 414 Sqn flew CE-133 '615*', while No. 434 Sqn operated '083*, '441, '446*, '479*, '483*, '560, '571, '573, '604* (those aircraft marked * having received the EST upgrade).

Above: CE-133 133615 was in service with No. 414 (Combat Support) Squadron in 1999. External differences between the CE-133 and CT-133 are minimal, grey being the standard colour of the CT-133 fleet.

Below: Unlike No. 414 Sqn, CFB Greenwood-based No. 434 (Combat Support) Squadron's Silver Stars operate alongside EW-tasked CE-144 Canadair (Bombardier) Challengers.

Left: The return of loaned USAF jamming pods resulted in a CAF programme to purchase its own Ericsson A100 Erijammers, ordered in June 1993. Unlike older, less-capable pods, the A100 is completely self-contained, requiring only a power supply from its carrier aircraft.

'CX-133'

'CX-133' is the unofficial designation for a specially instrumented pacer/calibration/test aircraft operated by the Aerospace Engineering and Test Establishment at CFB Cold Lake for experimental duties such as ejection seat testing. The sole 'CX-133' aircraft (133613) is currently with the AETE operating alongside four standard CT-133s, all carrying a distinctive 'X' on their tails.

From 1955 to 1989, T-33AN 21505, later CT-133 133505, served as an ejection seat test aircraft for CF-100, CF-104 and CT-114 seats but, despite its extensive modifications, was never designated 'CX-133'. Several requests to designate this AETE aircraft as 'CX-133' were turned down (at the same time as efforts to apply designation CE-133 to the EW-modified aircraft of No. 414 Sqn). This aircraft was seen stored at AMDU, CFD Mountainview in 1990.

Above: Given its role and modifications, it was intended that 133613 be officially redesignated a CX-133, but CAF approval was not forthcoming.

Right: With the 'X' marking on its tailfin, 'CX-133' 133505 conducts another ejection seat test over Primrose Lake, Saskatchewan.

Atmospheric research CT-133

Two T-33AN aircraft (prior to redesignation as CT-133) are operated by Canada's NAE (National Aeronautical Establishment) for atmospheric research and microgravity experiments. The two 'T-birds' were acquired in 1968 and 1970 by the NAE – since renamed first the National Aeronautical Establishment and then the National Research Council Flight Research Lab – at Uplands Airport, Ottawa.

The primary aircraft, ex-21379, acquired from the RCAF/CEPE in 1965, was originally registered as CF-SKH, then as CF-SKH-X and is currently C-FSKH. Among its varied tasks, it was the original NRC microgravity research vehicle and the NRC Atmospheric Research Aircraft (NTRA). In its role as an atmospheric research aircraft in the last half of the 1970s, for various cloud seeding experiments into forest fire suppression, it carried on the underwing pylons NRC-modified flare-launcher pods to dispense silver iodide from end-burning flares. A Doppler radar, to measure aircraft velocity relative to the terrain along each of its three axes, was mounted in a special pod under the fuselage. A variety of nose pitots and specialised long static boom

were also carried. This instrumented Silver Star participated with the FAA and NASA in the study of Convair 880 wake characteristics in November 1967, intended to analyse flight measurements in the wake of a large jet transport aircraft.

The other aircraft, ex-21590, was acquired from the RCN VU-32 in 1967. Original registry was CF-WIS, then CF-WIS-X and currently C-FWIS. Used principally for pilot training and proficiency, a modified nose and radome housed a Bendix RDR-11 radar antenna and was employed to study the effects of clear air turbulence (CAT) in 1970 along with other turbulence research projects and cloud physics studies.

C-FWIS (ex-21590) is used for pilot/astronaut training and special projects. C-FSKH (ex-21379) is fitted with an instrumented nose boom and used to support atmospheric, flight dynamics and defence projects (such as the MAWS – missile approach warning system), and microgravity experiments.

Below: C-FWIS (formerly CF-WIS and CF-WIS-X) has served the NAE for over 30 years.

Above: CF-SKH-X is seen here with underwing flare pods and a centre-line cloud seeding equipment.

Below: CAT research aircraft CF-WIS carries evidence on its starboard wing that it is an ex-RCN aircraft.

Kawasaki T-33A

Kawasaki T-33A production began in 1953 when two nearly-complete, Lockheed-built 'T-birds' (USAF serials 54-1584/1585) were shipped to Kawasaki for assembly as pattern aircraft. In 1955, 18 more 'knocked down' followed. These 20 aircraft are included in the total of Lockheed aircraft manufactured. Powerplant of the Kawasaki-built 'T-bird', like its American counterpart, was the 4,900-lb st (21.79-kN) Allison J33-A-35 centrifugal flow turbojet engine.

The JASDF also operated 68 Lockheed-built T-33s which were assigned JASDF (not USAF) serials 51-5601/5668.

Kawasaki T-33A serials: 61-5201/5230 (30), 71-5231/5326 (96), 81-5327/5397 (71), 91-5398/5410 (13)
Total: 210

Right: 51-5610 was among the 68 T-33As supplied to the JASDF from Lockheed via the USAF.

Right: An overall silver finish has adorned Japanese T-33s throughout their 40-year career, with the aircraft's 'last three' repeated on the nose, in black.

Below right: As the script on the flanks of 61-5201 proclaims, this was the first of 210 T-33As assembled in Japan by Kawasaki. The first figure in JASDF serial numbers equated to the fiscal year (i.e. '6' is FY1956)

Aérospatiale T-33AN Pégase

The Aérospatiale Pégase T-33 was an aerodynamic test vehicle developed in the mid-1970s by Aérospatiale along with France's CEV (Centre d'Essais en Vol, Flight Test Centre, a government test unit) and ONERA (Office National d'Etudes et Recherches Aérospatiales, National Aerospace Study & Research Committee). SNIAS (Aérospatiale) had been engaged since 1972 with research regarding a subsonic supercritical wing, intended – rather remarkably – for civil application. (Sources do not specify the use, but candidates for such a wing might have included the Airbus family of jetliners.) The name for the programme and the aircraft was itself an acronym, 'Pégase' standing for Programme d'Etude Générale d'une Aile Supercritique Epaisse (Thick Supercritical Wing General Study Programme).

The aircraft, a Canadair T-33AN (Canadian serial 21064), was modified to test a wing with thick supercritical airfoil. The aircraft was bailed from the Armée de l'Air to CEV and made its first flight with the new wing on 13 April 1977, piloted by Alain Guillard. It carried out 74 flights with the supercritical

wing, ending its final sortie on 2 May 1978.

The Pégase 'T-bird' had no markings other than a red winged-horse (Pegasus) motif on its nose and the CEV logo on its tail. The rest of the aircraft was deep blue and white, with red wings and fin-tip. It flew in standard Armée de l'Air colours when first fitted with a supercritical wing.

Engineers determined that a supercritical airfoil would increase flight performance within a wide range of supersonic air flow conditions and would make it possible at high Mach to employ thicker wings, thus allowing greater fuel load and range. As affixed to the T-33 testbed, the supercritical wing was made of balsa, textile and resins. Flight test data showed that, despite the increased thickness of the wing (17 per cent of chord instead of 13 per cent), low-speed performance was greatly improved and high-speed performance was virtually unchanged.

This unusual Shooting Star apparently was never returned to l'Armée de l'Air. Today, it is in storage for the Musée de l'Air et l'Espace at Dugny, on the western side of Paris's Le Bourget airfield.

The T-33AN (top right) was chosen to test the supercrical wing as it had a straight wing and could fly level at near Mach 0.8. 21064 had previously served with GE 314 at Tours as '314-VP' and then '314-UP' (left), retaining its basic metal scheme during the early test phase, before being sprayed in the special CEV/Aérospatiale scheme (right and below).

Upgrade programmes

T-33SF

In 1961, the Armée de l'Air decided to bring its T-33S-US (T-33A) and T-33S-C (CT-133) aircraft up to a common standard with a view to not only simplifying maintenance practices but also lessening the confusion that reigned among pilots of the differently equipped and instrumented aircraft.

Initially, one aircraft of each type was re-engined, with an Hispano-Suiza licence-built Rolls-Royce Nene engine, and fitted with new ejection seats, navigation and radio equipment. The first rebuilt aircraft was flown in March 1961 and after successful flight testing it was decided that another 83 aircraft would be put through the

programme. Designated T-33SF, the first of these 'production' conversions was completed on 7 April 1964.

By 1978, 58 T-33SFs and T-33S-USs remained in French service. As their Alpha Jet replacements were delivered, unmodified T-33S-USs were returned to the USAF for disposal, while T-33SFs were sold on to various air arms, including those of Singapore, Turkey, Thailand and Bolivia.

Above: 53093, a T-33S-US (T-33A) re-engined under the T-33SF programme, and seen here circa 1972, carrying the markings of EC 11/SLVSV (liaison and instrument flight), was later sold to the Turkish air force.

Right: Republic of Singaporean Air Force T-33SF '369' (formerly coded '910') was built as T-33A-1-LO 51-4385 and was among about 15 T-33SFs sold to the RSAF in 1980 after retirement by the Armée de l'Air.

Kelowna FlightCraft

In 1997 it was reported that Kelowna FlightCraft of Canada had received a US$15 million to upgrade 19 T-33s (12 T-33Fs and seven Silver Star Mk 3s) for the Bolivian air force. Employed in the COIN role, the aircraft were to receive structural and avionics work based on that carried out by the same company on CAF CT-133s. A glass cockpit was to be installed during a depot-level inspection and repair, to be carried out at the company's Abbotsford, BC facility.

Flight Systems (FSI)

Flight Systems proposed a mid-1980s upgrade of the T-33 that would have used a single 5,800-lb (25.79-kN) Rolls-Royce Turboméca Adour turbofan, the most powerful engine ever to be installed on a

Below right: Ecuador's FAE took delivery of AT-33s refurbished by Sabreliner in the 1980s. All have since been withdrawn.

'T-bird' (when the very different T2V-1 variant is left aside). Like other, lesser-known proposals to keep the 'T-bird' alive for a generation longer, this plan did not materialise.

Sabreliner Corporation

Sabreliner Corporation of St Louis, Missouri developed an upgraded 'AT-33A Attack Trainer', as prime contractor to the USAF, in the 1980s. Between 24 and 40 aircraft had been refurbished for the Ecuadorian air force by 1989, the work including structural, avionics and armament upgrades. However, these aircraft were finally withdrawn in 1996.

(Boeing) Skyfox

The Skyfox was a mid-1980s' effort to modernise the 'T-bird' design. Had the concept succeeded, there might have existed a worldwide market for hundreds of rebuilt T-33 trainers, reconnaissance ships or light attack aircraft, to be used by a dozen or more air forces. Although its 'T-bird' lineage was evident at a glance, the Skyfox had many sharp external differences, including a different-shaped nose and tail, a 'bullet' on the leading edge of the horizontal stabiliser to control airflow over empennage control surfaces, and external pods for its

twin Garrett TFE731-3 turbofan engines of 3,700 lb st (16.46 kN) thrust each. The fuselage had a smoother shape, with the original T-33 air inlets faired over, and the wingtips featured downward winglets in lieu of tip-tanks.

Initially offered by the Skyfox Corporation of Los Angeles, and later by Boeing-Wichita, Skyfox prototype N221SF made its first flight on 23 August 1983 with Pat Quinn at the controls. Portugal expressed an intent to manufacture 20 examples under licence, but the plan never materialised.

After initial flights in a Skyfox corporate colour scheme (left), N221SF was repainted in this tactical finish (above). Boeing-Wichita acquired an exclusive licence to produce the Skyfox in 1986, having test flown the prototype the year before. Comparison with a standard T-33 (above) shows the extent to which the Skyfox was rebuilt. In rebuilt form the aircraft was some 6 ft 3 in (1.9 m) longer than a T-33A.

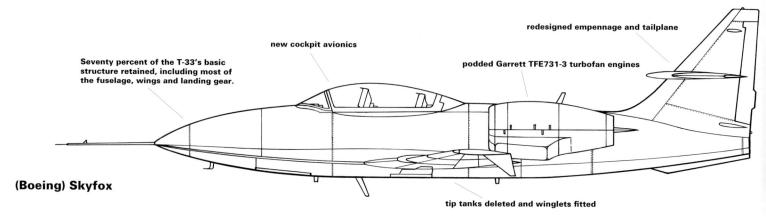

new cockpit avionics

redesigned empennage and tailplane

Seventy percent of the T-33's basic structure retained, including most of the fuselage, wings and landing gear.

podded Garrett TFE731-3 turbofan engines

(Boeing) Skyfox

tip tanks deleted and winglets fitted

Above and above right: The biggest change made in the transformation from T-33 to Skyfox was the replacement of the T-33's single J33 turbojet with a pair of podded Garrett AiResearch TFE731 turbofans.

'T-birds' today – Greek T-33s in service in the 1990s

The last military operator of the T-33 in Europe, the Elliniki Polimiki Aeroporia (Greek air force) operated just 18 examples (of over 150 originally delivered) in the late 1990s, in the target-towing and training roles with 222 MEE at Souda and 366 SEE at Tanagra, respectively.

Below: Very few current Greek air force pilots are older than the Shooting Stars they fly. In 1952, when the type entered Greek service, few would have expected the type to be in use in the late 1990s.

In 2002 the T-33A will have been in Greek service for 50 years. 222 Mira Epercherisiakis Ekpetheusis (Weapons Training Squadron) – part of the A-7H-equipped 115 Pteriga Mahis (Combat Wing) – operates orange target-towing aircraft (above, right and below), while 366 Sminos Ekpetheusis (Training Flight) has a training and liaison role and flies T-33s in a sand and brown camouflage. All aircraft retain underwing hardpoints and USAF-style buzz codes (left). 53-6000 was photographed in 1998 with a 'TR-6000' buzz code.

Royal Air Force Fighters 1930–1939

The period between 1 January 1930 and Mr Chamberlain's September 1938 meeting with Hitler in Munich marked the close of the peace which followed the end of the Great War. After Munich, the nations of Europe re-armed and began preparing for the war which had become inevitable. During those nine years until 1947, the Royal Air Force experienced a period of massive change, and its fighter force, in particular, underwent a major transformation. The force was expanded and reorganised, and was progressively re-equipped with a new generation of aircraft; still biplanes, and themselves soon superseded by new monoplanes, the technological leap which they represented has often been forgotten.

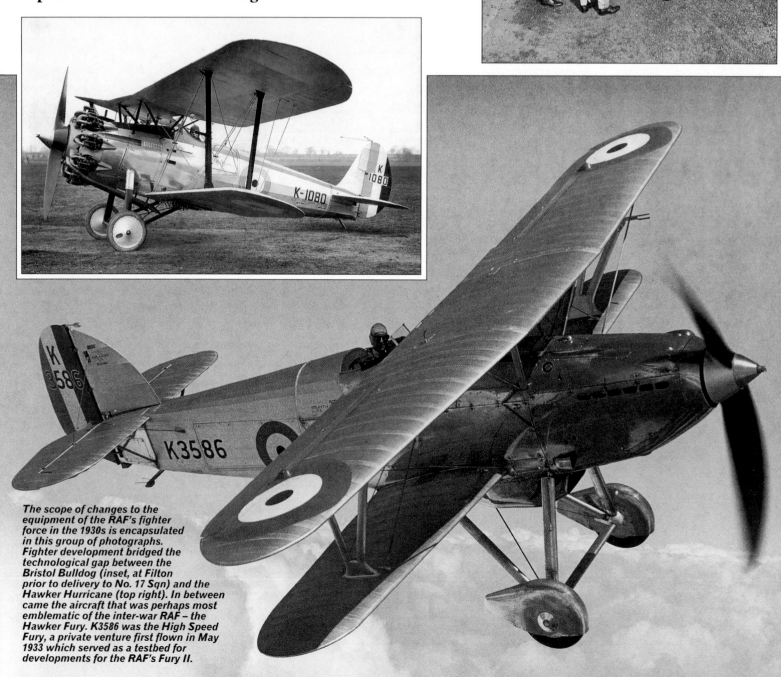

The scope of changes to the equipment of the RAF's fighter force in the 1930s is encapsulated in this group of photographs. Fighter development bridged the technological gap between the Bristol Bulldog (inset, at Filton prior to delivery to No. 17 Sqn) and the Hawker Hurricane (top right). In between came the aircraft that was perhaps most emblematic of the inter-war RAF – the Hawker Fury. K3586 was the High Speed Fury, a private venture first flown in May 1933 which served as a testbed for developments for the RAF's Fury II.

Above: Bulldogs served with ten front-line squadrons between May 1929 and March 1937, including No. 23 Sqn, operator of this aircraft.

Right: No. 3 Sqn became the first squadron to gain the Bulldog (Mk II), the type replacing its Gamecocks. As such, No. 3 was involved in establishing operational procedures for the type and was to be the last operational user of the type.

Below right: Two Bulldog-equipped flights of No. 56 Sqn used aircraft fitted with experimental cowlings and overwing gun cameras.

Below: Bulldog IIA K2168 served only with the Armament and Gunnery School (later Air Armament School) at Eastchurch from October 1931 until October 1936, becoming maintenance airframe 941M the following year.

The end of the 1920s brought the retirement of Lord Trenchard as Chief of the Air Staff. Trenchard was a bomber man and had always given priority to spending on strategic bombing aircraft. He left his post on the last day of the decade, to be replaced by his long-serving deputy, Sir John Salmond, who oversaw the first expansion in RAF fighter strength. The 12 long-standing home-based RAF fighter squadrons were augmented as soon as the decade began, with No. 54 Squadron reforming at Hornchurch on 15 January 1930 with Siskin IIIAs and IIIDCs. Hornchurch expanded from being a single-squadron aerodrome to housing a full fighter wing, though further expansion was slow to come. The next real evidence of expansion came in 1932, when Biggin Hill reopened after a major rebuilding programme.

The other front-line fighter squadrons were generally similarly equipped. Siskin IIIAs were nearing the end of their service lives, but still formed the equipment of Nos 1, 19, 25, 29, 32, 41, 43, 56 and 111 Squadrons. Although of metal construction, the Siskin was fundamentally old-fashioned, using heavy steel tube rather than the more modern pressed steel strip used in the lighter, cheaper Bulldog, which already equipped No. 3 and No. 17 Squadron, at Upavon, and, from April 1930, the newly formed No. 54 Squadron at Hornchurch. The highly agile wooden Gamecock served only

K3925 was one of a batch of 31 Bulldog Trainers delivered between October 1933 and May 1934. It served (coded '3') with the RAF College, Cranwell between November 1934 and March 1936.

with No. 23 Squadron, the other Gamecock units having already re-equipped.

Bristol's Bulldog

The success of the Bulldog was described in the 'RAF Fighters 1920-1929' article in *Wings of Fame* Volume 5. In that article, the Bulldog was likened to a radial-engined, metal-airframed Sopwith Snipe, whose maximum speed "had only increased by one-third, rate of climb by 1.5..." In fact, the Bulldog was a much more modern aircraft than the Siskin IIIA which it immediately replaced, let alone the ancient

Snipe, and compared favourably with its contemporaries. The Boeing F4B-1, for example, could manage 169 mph (271 km/h) – a full 10 mph (16 km/h) less than the Bulldog. It should also be remembered that even the 33 per cent increase in speed represents a considerable and worthwhile improvement, while the Bulldog's near-180 mph (290 km/h) top speed represented a 50 per cent improvement over the Snipe's 120 mph (193 km/h) performance. Similarly, the Bulldog reached 20,000 ft (6096 m) just under five minutes quicker than the Snipe could struggle up to 15,000 ft (4572 m), while

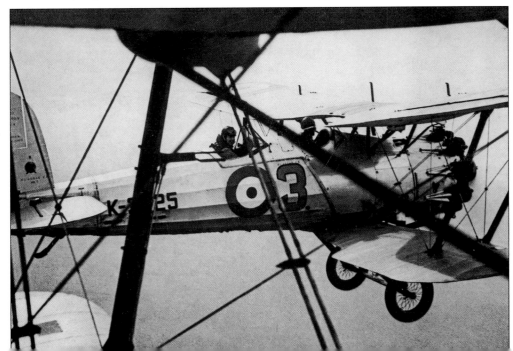

RAF fighter squadrons
1 January 1930 to 19 September 1938

DATE	BASE	TYPE
No. 1 Squadron		
to February 1932	Tangmere	Siskin IIIA
Feb 1932-Nov 1938	Tangmere	Fury I
Feb 1937-Mar 1937	Tangmere	Gladiator

Markings: Parallel red bars across upper mainplanes and on fuselage sides, tapering and meeting aft of the roundel. Munich crisis codes 'NA', probably not worn.

No. 3 Squadron		
to May 1934	Upavon	Bulldog II
May 1934-Oct 1935	Kenley	Bulldog IIA
Oct 1935-Aug 1936	Sudan	Bulldog IIA
Aug 1936-Jul 1937	Kenley	Bulldog IIA
Mar 1937-Jul 1939	Kenley	Gladiator
Mar 1938-Jul 1938	Kenley	Hurricane

Markings: Emerald green bar between roundels on upper mainplane and from engine to tailpost. Fuselage stripe later broadened and shortened, from tailplane leading edge to metal part of forward fuselage. Possibly not applied to Gladiators. Munich crisis codes 'OP'.

No. 17 Squadron		
to May 1934	Upavon	Bulldog II
May 1934-Aug 1936	Kenley	Bulldog II/IIA
Aug 1936-Jun 1939	Kenley	Gauntlet II

Markings: Two parallel black 'zig-zag' stripes between upper wing roundels and running along the fuselage from the serial to the centre section strut. Later shortened to stop at the metal forward fuselage section. Gauntlets had black top-decking to fuselage. Munich crisis codes 'UV'.

No. 19 Squadron		
to Sep 1931	Duxford	Siskin IIIA
Sep 1931-Jan 1935	Duxford	Bulldog IIA
Jan 1935-Mar 1939	Duxford	Gauntlet I
Sep 1936-Feb 1939	Duxford	Gauntlet II
Aug 1938-Dec 1940	Duxford	Spitfire I

Markings: Double row of blue and white checkers on upper surface of top mainplane and on fuselage side fore and aft of the roundel. Spitfires camouflaged with large yellow '19' on fuselage side.

No. 23 Squadron		
to Sep 1931	Kenley	Gamecock
Jul 1931-Apr 1933	Kenley	Bulldog IIA
Jul 1931-Jul 1932	Kenley	Hart Fighter
Jul 1932-Dec 1938	Kenley	Demon
Sep 1932-Dec 1936	Biggin Hill	Bulldog/Demon
Dec 1936-May 1938	Northolt	Demon
May 1938-Dec 1938	Wittering	Demon

Markings: Single row of alternate red and dark blue squares between the upper wing roundels and fore and aft of the fuselage roundel. Serial superimposed on silver dope rectangle. Munich crisis codes 'MS'.

No. 25 Squadron		
to Mar 1932	Hawkinge	Siskin IIIA
Feb 1932-1937	Hawkinge	Fury I
Nov 1937-Oct 1937	Hawkinge	Fury II
Oct 1937-Jun 1938	Hawkinge	Demon
Jun 1938-Feb 1939	Hawkinge	Gladiator

Markings: Parallel black bars across upper mainplanes and on fuselage sides, tapering and meeting aft of the roundel. Munich crisis codes 'RX' (possibly not applied).

No. 29 Squadron		
to Jun 1932	North Weald	Siskin IIIA
Jun 1932-Apr 1935	North Weald	Bulldog IIA
Mar 1935-Mar 1936	North Weald	Demon
Oct 1935-Sep 1936	Egypt	Demon
Oct 1936-Nov 1937	North Weald	Turret Demon
Nov 1937-Dec 1938	Debden	Turret Demon

Markings: Parallel red bars between the upper wing roundels, containing six red Xs (XXXXXX). Similar marking on the fuselage side with three red Xs (XXX). Markings revised on Bulldog and Demon with single X on each side of fuselage roundel, and with eight overwing Xs on the Demon. Munich crisis codes 'YB' probably not applied.

No. 32 Squadron		
to Jan 1931	Kenley	Siskin IIIA
Jan 31-Sep 1932	Kenley	Bulldog IIA
Sep 1932-Jul 1936	Biggin Hill	Bulldog IIA
Jul 1936-Oct 1938	Biggin Hill	Gauntlet II

Markings: Medium blue stripe between upper mainplane roundels and on fuselage side, with three thin white diagonal stripes on Siskin. On Bulldog blue fuselage bar extended from below cockpit back to tailplane leading edge, broken by narrow diagonal silver dope stripes. Serial outlined in silver on rearmost part of blue band. On Gauntlet blue band reduced in length, with vestigial 'stub' forward of roundel. Single silver diagonal on rear part, between roundel and serial. Munich crisis codes 'KT'.

No. 33 Squadron		
to February 1938-1940	Ismailia	Gladiator (re-roled)

Markings: No distinctive markings. Codes 'SO'.

Bulldogs of No. 3 Sqn are seen over the Sudan during the Abyssinian Crisis of 1935/36. Based at Port Sudan and Khartoum, the squadron joined five Hawker Demon squadrons deployed to the region – two to Egypt and three to Malta.

the Bulldog's ceiling was a whole 10,000 ft (3048 m) higher. These were more than merely "incremental improvements".

Bulldogs replaced most of the Siskins and the remaining Gamecocks rapidly during 1931 and 1932. Nos 32 and 111 Squadrons converted in January 1931, No. 23 in July 1931, No. 19 in September 1931, No. 41 in October 1931, No. 29 in June 1932, and No. 56 in October 1932. Although it enjoyed only a brief front-line career, the Bulldog proved popular and effective, and its passing was mourned.

The Bulldog was outshone by the Hawker Fury in service, not least because its inline Kestrel engine gave it more streamlined and rakish looks than the radial-engined Bristol, and perhaps also because the Hawker aircraft was the first RAF fighter able to crack the magical 200-mph (322-km/h) barrier. Some have opined that the Bulldog, with its beautiful wing, was prettier than any of the radial-engined Fury versions, and have speculated that a Kestrel-powered Bulldog would have exceeded the Hawker fighter in performance and in looks. The Fury was also the RAF's first

dedicated interceptor, equipping a small and distinctive 'elite force' of only three squadrons. In fact, the interceptor tag effectively meant only that the aircraft was lighter and shorter-ranged than the Bulldog, which was expected to mount long-endurance 'standing patrols', carrying a heavier load of fuel and ammunition.

Emblematic Fury

Fairly or unfairly, in many respects, the Fury (and especially the two Tangmere-based Fury squadrons) has since become emblematic of the RAF in the 1930s. Ironically, the Fury was probably never as important as the Bulldog with which it served, although the small three-squadron force almost certainly provided the RAF with a useful additional capability. Many have asked why so few Furies were purchased, when the aircraft demonstrated such an edge over the Bulldog. Apart from the difference in role (and thus in load), the Fury was considerably more expensive to build, (£700 more per aircraft, at £5,400) as well as being more costly and more difficult to maintain. The three original Fury squadrons converted from Siskins in May 1931 (No. 43 Squadron) and February 1932 (Nos 1 and 25 Squadrons).

The RAF's front-line home defence fighter squadrons had been entirely equipped with single-seat aircraft since the end of World

From October 1930 all RAF service aircraft were painted with fin flashes, with red nearest the rudder post to avoid confusion with French aircraft. This was discontinued in 1934, most fighters then acquiring large squadron badges on their tailfins. In 1935 another edict standardised wing roundel size, and decreed that they not overlap any control surface. These No. 1 Sqn Fury Is display pre-1934 markings.

Above: K1938 was one of the original batch of 21 Fury Is delivered in April 1931. It served with No. 43 Squadron until April 1935 when it was returned to Hawkers. Issued to No. 11 FTS in February 1936, it suffered a forced landing in August 1938.

Above: Furies of the Central Flying School, based at Wittering and, from late 1935, Upavon, displayed the CFS badge prominently on the fin.

Below: Fury Is of No. 1 Squadron were identified by red bars along the fuselage and on the top surface of the upper wing.

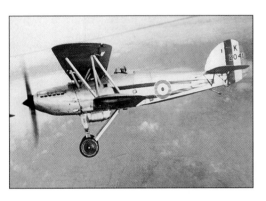

War I, though many senior RAF officers remembered the extraordinary success of the Bristol Fighter during that war. The 'Brisfit' had enjoyed a relatively long post-war career, albeit as a general-purpose machine in overseas commands. Many still believed that a two-seat fighter would be operationally useful. The advent of the Hawker Hart day bomber proved to be the catalyst for the development of a new fighter derivative in the mould of the Bristol Fighter, a two-seater with fixed forward-firing armament and a gunner with a single Lewis gun on a Townend ring. The Hart was breathtakingly fast, by contemporary bomber standards, and was versatile and adaptable, spawning a number of training, fleet and army co-operation derivatives. A Hart Fighter promised to be both fast and cheap to produce. Two converted Hart bombers served as prototypes, after which an initial batch of six Hart Fighters was built and delivered to Kenley, where they formed one flight of No. 23 Squadron, operating alongside two flights of single-seat Bulldogs. Renamed Demon in July 1932, the Hart Fighter proved fractionally faster than the Bulldog and, initially at least, the second crewmember appeared to impose no real penalty.

Demons for No. 23 Sqn

In April 1933 the Demon was judged to be a success, and No. 23 Squadron (by now at Biggin Hill) re-equipped fully with the two-seat aircraft. No. 41 Squadron at Northolt followed suit in July 1934. Some 232 Demons were destined to

be delivered before production finally ceased in January 1938, equipping seven Fighter Command squadrons and Auxiliary Air Force units.

Even with the Bulldog, Demon and Fury in widespread service, for the first few years of the new decade the RAF remained weak and relatively ill-equipped. It was only the rise of Hitler in Germany that switched attention away from the non-existent 'French threat' and prompted any meaningful expansion of the armed forces. This was a rather late response to German rearmament, which had begun in earnest seven years earlier. Such expansion as there was brought the forces to a level that was merely inadequate, which was at least an improvement over the dangerous state of neglect which had prevailed throughout the 1920s. An Expansion Programme for the RAF was formally promulgated in July 1934, with the stated aim of raising it from a total of 42 to 75 squadrons, and to 128 squadrons within five years. Even more significantly, work was begun on a series of new fighter and bomber aerodromes, and on significant improvements to most of the existing fighter stations. This programme saw the construction of RAF Debden as a No. 11 Group Sector Station covering the southern part of East Anglia, and of RAF Church Fenton in Yorkshire. Long disused aerodromes (or training airfields) were

improved for front-line squadrons, including the new fighter bases at Catterick and Digby.

The Expansion Programme began relatively slowly, although the Air Defence of Great Britain's Fighting Area (Fighter Command's precursor) gained another unit, No. 65 Squadron, in August 1934, equipped with Demons at Hornchurch. No. 29 Squadron traded its Bulldogs for Demons in March 1935. Another new Demon unit, No. 604 Squadron, formed at Hendon in June 1935. This was the first of the Auxiliary Air Force squadrons to convert to the fighter role, marking the beginning of a transition by most of the part-time squadrons from the light bomber/army co-operation role to fighter duties. This process continued even after the Munich crisis. No. 604 Squadron converted to the Demon from the lumbering Westland Wapiti, allowing it to continue to make full use of its highly motivated and enthusiastic air gunners – most of whom were members of the ground crew.

The slow speed of the RAF's expansion was criticised by some, but wiser heads prevailed,

No. 43 Squadron was the first unit with Furies. Apart from the black and silver checks on the fuselage and wings, flight commanders' aircraft sported a coloured tailfin, as seen on K1928 (second from the camera) in this photograph.

No. 41 Squadron

to Nov 1931	Northolt	Siskin IIIA
Oct 1931-Aug 1934	Northolt	Bulldog IIA
Jul 1934-Oct 1935	Northolt	Demon
Oct 1935-Sep 1936	Aden and ME	Demon
Sep 1936-Oct 1937	Catterick	Demon
Oct 1937-Jan 1939	Fury II	Fury II

Markings: Siskins marked with broad red band ahead of roundel on fuselage and on upper wing. Fuselage stripe later extended aft to leading edge of tailplane. Similar markings on Bulldog and Demon. Furies had red fin with squadron badge in standard arrowhead, but no fuselage or wing markings.

No. 43 Squadron

to May 1931	Tangmere	Siskin IIIA
May 1931-Jan 1939	Tangmere	Fury I

Markings: Double row of black and white checks on upper surface of top mainplane and on fuselage side from the cowling to immediately forward of the roundel, white checks replaced by 'hollow' black-edged silver dope squares on Fury. Munich crisis codes 'NQ', probably not worn.

No. 46 Squadron

Sep 1936-Nov 1937	Kenley	Gauntlet II
Nov 1937-Mar 1939	Digby	Gauntlet II

Markings: Hollow red arrowhead (pointing forward) on the fuselage side, bisected by roundel. Similar design on top of each upper wing, pointing inwards. Munich crisis codes 'RJ'.

No. 54 Squadron

Jan 1930-Dec 1930	Hornchurch	Siskin IIIA
Apr 1930-Sep 1936	Hornchurch	Bulldog IIA
Aug 1936-May 1937	Hornchurch	Gauntlet II
Apr 1937-Apr 1939	Hornchurch	Gladiator

Markings: Original marking was a yellow stripe on the fuselage and upper wings, probably not applied to the interim Siskins. Initially extended forward to the cockpit on the Bulldog, then reduced to aft of the roundel only. Replaced by red stripe of similar dimensions on Gauntlet (not on wings), with diagonal white bars added almost immediately. Fuselage and tail colours not applied to the Gladiator. Munich crisis codes 'DL' (possibly not applied).

No. 56 Squadron

to Oct 1932	North Weald	Siskin IIIA
Oct 1932-May 1936	North Weald	Bulldog IIA
May 1937-Jul 1937	North Weald	Gauntlet II
Jul 1937-May 1938	North Weald	Gladiator
Apr 1938-Feb 1941	North Weald	Hurricane I

Markings: Double row of red and white checks on upper surface of top mainplane and on fuselage side from forward of the roundel to cowling. Shortened on Bulldog, with 2½ squares forward of the roundel and 1½ aft. Reduced further on Gauntlet, with ½ a square in front of roundel, and 2½ aft.

No. 64 Squadron

Mar 1936-Sep 1936	Egypt	Demon
Sep 1936-May 1938	Martlesham Heath	Demon
May 1938-Dec 1938	Church Fenton	Demon

Markings: On return to the UK the squadron adopted an intersecting blue and red 'zig-zags' forming a 'trellis' pattern above wings and on fuselage sides from below the cockpit back to the tailplane leading edge. Munich crisis codes 'XQ' probably not worn.

No. 65 Squadron

Aug 1934-Jul 1936	Hornchurch	Demon
Jul 1936-Jun 1937	Hornchurch	Gauntlet II
Jun 1937-Apr 1939	Hornchurch	Gladiator

Markings: Unmarked Demons gave way to more colourful Gauntlets, which wore a series of forward-facing red chevrons along the fuselage from just aft of the cockpit to the tailplane leading edge. Similar outward-pointing chevrons were applied on the top of the wing. The Gladiators were similarly marked, perhaps with a red hexagon on the centre section between the wing chevrons. Munich crisis codes 'FZ'.

No. 66 Squadron

Jul 1936-Dec 1938	Hornchurch	Gauntlet

Markings: Two pale blue stripes were parallel above the wing and forward of the roundel, but tapered towards each other on the rear fuselage.

No. 72 Squadron

Feb 1937-Jun 1937	Tangmere	Gladiator
Jun 1937-May 1939	Church Fenton	Gladiator

Markings: Red/blue/red stripe overwing and on fuselage from cowling to roundel, then tapering back to serial and with vestigial red stripe from the serial to the tailplane. Munich crisis codes 'RN'.

No. 73 Squadron

Mar 1937-Jun 1937	Mildenhall	Fury II
Jun 1937-Nov 1937	Debden	Gladiator
Nov 1937-Jul 1938	Digby	Gladiator
Jul 1938-Sep 1939	Digby	Hurricane

Markings: Blue chevron (supposedly in sword-blade shape) with central yellow stripe on fuselage side, broken by roundel. Similar shaped chevrons pointing outwards on upper surface of top wing, joined at 'base'.

Above: The first production Hawker Hart, J9933, was re-engined with a 485-hp (362-kW) Kestrel II, its armament increased to two Vickers machine-guns and the gunner's field of fire improved. The result was known as the Hart Fighter prototype, forerunner of the Demon. Six Hart Fighters were built and trialled by No. 23 Sqn.

Right: No. 604 Sqn was the first Auxiliary squadron to convert to the fighter role with Demons.

Left: In October 1935 No. 29 Sqn with Demons was transported to Amriya, Egypt, in a show of strength to 'contain' the Abyssinian crisis. The unit had operated the type since March 1935, but at Amriya engine problems caused by the ingestion of sand resulted in the squadron re-equipping with Fairey Gordons in March 1936. On return to the UK in August No. 29 Squadron re-equipped with Turret Demons.

and great efforts were made to ensure that the RAF would not be expanded simply through the addition of units equipped with obsolete types.

In addition to the two-seat Demon, the backbone of the expansion was provided by the Gloster Gauntlet, which started to enter service in February 1935, when No. 19 Squadron at Duxford received its first example for trials, re-equipping fully from May 1935. Superficially less attractive than the Fury due to its radial engine and consequent 'snub nose', the Gauntlet was, if anything, even more gracefully proportioned, and its Mercury engine produced a delightful 'song'. Despite its heavy fuel and

ammunition load, the Gauntlet could outrun any Fury (even the improved Mk II). Quite apart from sheer straight-line performance, the Gauntlet was also a superb climber, hitting 20,000 ft (6096 m) in only nine minutes. Only 5 mph (8 km/h) slower than Boeing's monoplane P-26, the Gauntlet climbed higher and faster, and was easier and cheaper to manufacture than many of its rivals. The aircraft also inherited the superb handling characteristics and aerobatic 'flair' of the earlier Gloster Gamecock, yet shared none of the older type's more vicious or dangerous foibles.

No. 19 Squadron initially used Gauntlet Is from the first production batch of 24 aircraft.

Just visible on the fin of this Demon is the winged sword of No. 601 Sqn, Auxiliary Air Force. Based at Hendon, No. 601 'County of London' Sqn converted from Harts to Demons in 1936 and kept them until October 1938.

On 1 March 1936 No. 64 Squadron was re-formed with Demons at Heliopolis, Egypt, from 'D' Flight of No. 208 Squadron and an element of No. 6 Sqn. The squadron's war tasks would have been airfield attack and bomber escort duties.

Above: After a spell in Egypt, No. 29 Sqn returned to North Weald to re-equip with the Turret Demon, with its hydraulic Frazer-Nash turret. This featured a four-segment 'lobster-back' to protect the gunner from the slipstream.

Right: Turret Demon K5740 was one of 96 built by Boulton-Paul of Wolverhampton.

All 204 subsequent Gauntlets were Mk IIs, with revised structure, including redesigned wing spars and rear fuselage sections. The first Gauntlet IIs were delivered to Nos 56 and 111 Squadrons in May 1936, replacing Bristol Bulldogs. The 'ordinary' fighter units at last had an aircraft faster than the two-seat Demons, and better overall than the Furies of the 'elite' Tangmere interceptor wing.

In November 1935, RAF fighters had been deployed overseas in an ultimately fruitless and impotent show of force mounted in response to Mussolini's invasion of Abyssinia No. 3 Squadron's Bulldogs were sent to the Sudan, while No. 29's Demons deployed to Egypt, where another Demon fighter squadron, No. 64 Squadron, formed in March 1936. Two more two-seat fighter squadrons, Nos 23 and 65, went out to Malta, ready to join any operations, and yet another Demon squadron, No. 74, formed at Hal Far in September 1935. These deployments represented roughly half of the Demons available, and at one stage seemed to mark the beginning of a transition from fighter to colonial policing duties for the Demon – a role for which it was still well suited. Unfortunately, however, the RAF of the 1930s was firmly wedded to an inflexible set of set-piece tactics for use against incoming, unescorted enemy bombers (the so-called Fighting Area Attacks) in which the possibility of enemy fighter intervention (or even of energetic counter-manoeuvre by the target)

were not really considered. In such a scenario, the prospect of Demons drawing alongside enemy bombers (which would, of course, be no faster than the lumbering Demon) did not seem improbable. Back in Abyssinia, Mussolini took little notice of Britain's unilateral and empty gesture, and the Demon units all returned to the UK, where they bolstered Britain's air defences, taking up valuable airfield and hangar space which might have been better given over to more Gauntlet squadrons.

ADGB disbands

The expansion of the RAF was underpinned by a massive reorganisation, with the old Air Defence of Great Britain disbanding and being replaced by functional commands. Fighting Area gave way to Fighter Command on 14 July 1936, under Air Marshal Sir Hugh Dowding.

The formation of new squadrons, and the re-equipment of existing units, continued apace and the Gauntlet force, in particular, grew and grew. No. 66 Squadron formed from a nucleus provided by No. 19 Squadron's 'C' Flight in July 1936 at Duxford, operating the Gauntlet II, while No. 65 Squadron returned from Malta and also converted to the Gauntlet. No. 151 Squadron, provisionally classed as a reserve unit, formed from No. 56 Squadron's 'B' Flight in August 1936. The squadron operated Gauntlet IIs from North Weald, but flew fewer than the then-normal establishment of 14 aircraft. Most front-line units had 14 new aircraft, with five

high-hours aircraft used as a reserve. Gauntlets continued to be delivered both to newly-forming units and to existing Bulldog fighter squadrons, with No. 32 Squadron re-equipping in July, No. 54 in August, and with No. 17 converting to the Gauntlet II from August 1936. No. 17 Squadron's aircraft were decorated in the normal manner, with 'fighter bars' on the fuselage and upper wing but, unusually, flight colours were reportedly extended to include the entire upper fuselage decking. The re-equipment of Nos 54 and 17 Squadrons marked the end of

Below: Upper fuselage-decking colours denoted the individual flights of No. 17 Sqn's Gauntlet IIs – red, yellow and blue for 'A', 'B' and 'C' Flights, respectively. As one of the first squadrons to have an official badge approved in 1937, it chose a gauntlet, this appearing in a standard spearhead frame on the fin of each aircraft.

Below left: No. 111 Sqn at RAF Northolt was the first squadron to receive the Gauntlet II in mid-1936 and flew until January 1938.

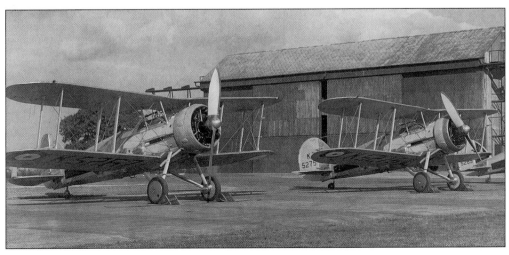

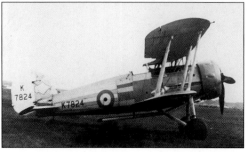

Above: The Munich Crisis of 1938 saw the hasty application of Dark Green and Dark Earth camouflage to RAF aircraft, including the Gauntlets equipping eight operational squadrons. Roundels were converted to Type B (without the white segment), while upper wing roundels were painted out in Night.

Left: This Gauntlet II K7824 of No. 66 Sqn has a (temporary) extra long exhaust pipe slung under its fuselage, a fitting made for the the last RAF Hendon Display in 1937, when No. 66's Gauntlets performed formation aerobatics using coloured smoke trails.

the line for the Bulldog as a front-line fighter, though the type soldiered on in a number of second-line roles.

The Gauntlet now represented the future, and the numbers in service grew rapidly. Just as No. 151 Squadron joined No. 56 at North Weald, No. 17 Squadron's 'B' Flight formed the basis of the newly-formed Gauntlet II-equipped No. 46 Squadron at Kenley in September 1936.

The two-seat Demon was already showing its age, but was still considered useful, especially for night-fighting, and the type remained in widespread use. No. 64 Squadron returned from Egypt in September 1936, taking up residence at Martlesham Heath. More Demons joined Fighter Command as the Auxiliaries began to swap roles. No. 607 Squadron traded its Wapiti bombers for Demon fighters in September 1936, at Usworth. No. 608 Squadron followed suit in January 1937, re-equipping with Demons at Thornaby in March 1939.

The Demon was significantly improved by the addition of a power-operated turret incorporating a four-section 'lobster back' fairing which protected the gunner from the slipstream. This improved gunnery accuracy at a stroke, not least by keeping the gunner comfortable, and by preventing goggle and helmet 'flutter'. So-called 'Turret Demons'

entered service with No. 29 Squadron at North Weald in October 1936, spreading to No. 23 Squadron in May 1937 and No. 64 Squadron in February 1938. This was too little, too late, though, and the Demon was little more than a gap-filler in the RAF's order of battle, and a useful machine for impressing the public at Empire Air Days.

Gauntlet and Gladiator

With its ability to reach speeds of 230 mph (370 km/h) in level flight, and to fly at an altitude of 33,500 ft (10668 m), the open-cockpit Gauntlet was clearly and demonstrably an anachronism, although it still presented a vaguely credible threat to any enemy. It was inevitable, however, that when a further improved derivative arrived, it would feature an enclosed cockpit. The Gladiator teamed the new enclosed cockpit with a powerful new 800-hp (596-kW) Mercury VI engine, aerodynamic refinements and a four-Browning machine-gun armament, and entered service with the newly formed No. 72 Squadron at Tangmere in February 1937. The new squadron formed around a nucleus provided by No. 1 Squadron, still going strong with its much-loved Furies.

The high profile enjoyed by the rival Fury squadrons at Tangmere and Hawkinge continued until Munich, even though (with the

The prototype SS.37 Gladiator was built as a private venture and submitted to meet Specification F.7/30. It first flew on 12 September 1934 without the enclosed cockpit later fitted to production aircraft and a two-bladed Watts wooden propeller. It was taken on Air Ministry charge under Contract 395996/35 in April 1935 and tested at A&AEE Martlesham Heath and by No. 1 Sqn. A production order soon followed.

Specification F.7/30

Six manufacturers built prototypes to specification F.7/30. The biplane designs included (clockwise from right) Bristol Type 123, Blackburn F.3, Hawker PV.3, Westland PV.4. There were two monoplane candidates – Bristol's Type 133 (below) and the Supermarine Type 224 (bottom).

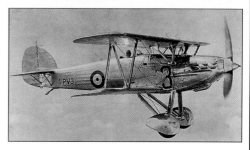

Air Ministry Specification F.7/30 called for a single-seat day and night 'interceptor' fighter with a high maximum speed in excess of 250 mph (402 km/h), superior range, manoeuvrability, rate of climb and service ceiling over existing fighters and a steep rate of climb for night interceptions. A low wing loading with a maximum landing speed of 50 mph (80 km/h) was also specified along with the provision of a two-way radio and full night flying equipment. The Air Ministry also stated a preference for the Rolls-Royce Kestrel IV powerplant, produced as the Goshawk with evaporative cooling. Prototypes were to be ready in 1934, and those firms not selected were encouraged to submit private venture prototypes for evaluation. Ultimately, the Goshawk proved a failure and the Bristol Mercury radial-engined Gladiator was chosen for production.

Left: No. 73 Sqn operated Gladiator Is for just over a year from June 1936, when they replaced Fury IIs, until July 1937, when the squadron received Hurricane Is. The Gladiators carried distinctive blue and yellow fuselage markings which were repeated on the top surface of the upper wing.

Right: Aerobatics by aircraft 'tied together' was a popular display item at the annual RAF shows. This formation is made up of No. 87 Sqn Gladiators.

disappearance of the last Bulldogs) they flew the slowest and oldest single-seat fighters in Fighter Command. In many ways the units were like the Auxiliary squadrons, high-spirited and (to a certain extent) exclusive and socially advantaged. High-speed runs to London night-clubs in powerful Bentleys and Lagondas were the norm, and the units continued to build on their near-legendary aerobatic prowess. It was widely reported that the efforts of No. 1 Squadron's aerobatic team at the International Air Meeting in Zurich drew the congratulations of General Milch of the Luftwaffe himself, though, since the Luftwaffe had Messerschmitt Bf 109Bs already in action in Spain, his true thoughts must have been more complicated. Not to be outdone, No. 66 Squadron's aerobatic team was already flying with coloured smoke, and another Gauntlet squadron, No. 32, had been busily engaged in radar-directed interception trials since November 1936.

Whatever was happening at Tangmere and Duxford and elsewhere with the Furies and Gauntlets, the Gladiator was seen as the future.

Some pilots missed the Gauntlet's crisper handling characteristics, and others flew their Gladiators with the hood 'slid back', but the aircraft's enhanced performance and firepower were an undoubted benefit. Gauntlets and Gladiators continued to enter service with new and re-forming squadrons as the RAF expanded in the run-up to war. Some observers have intimated that the Gladiator itself was obsolete even before it entered service, simply because of its biplane configuration, which was certainly becoming regarded as anachronistic by 1937, when the type entered service. Its qualities can be demonstrated by the simple fact that when war finally broke out, the supposedly 'obsolete' biplanes downed an estimated 450 enemy aircraft, and in overseas theatres had a vital role to play for most of 1940 and even into early 1941.

Fortunately, the Demon had disappeared from the front line by the time the shooting started, though, in 1937, new squadrons were continuing to form or convert. No. 600 Squadron swapped Hart bombers for Demons

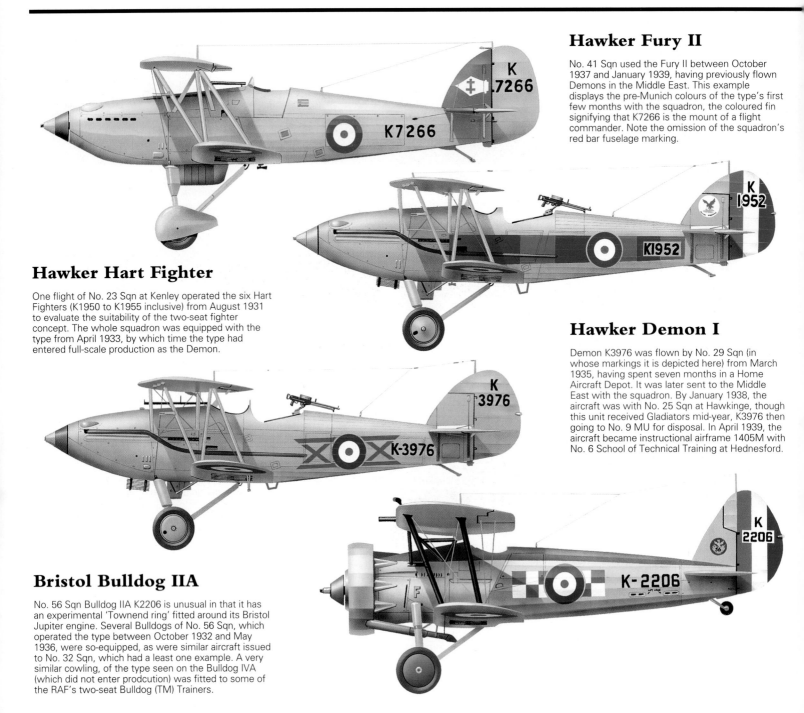

Hawker Fury II

No. 41 Sqn used the Fury II between October 1937 and January 1939, having previously flown Demons in the Middle East. This example displays the pre-Munich colours of the type's first few months with the squadron, the coloured fin signifying that K7266 is the mount of a flight commander. Note the omission of the squadron's red bar fuselage marking.

Hawker Hart Fighter

One flight of No. 23 Sqn at Kenley operated the six Hart Fighters (K1950 to K1955 inclusive) from August 1931 to evaluate the suitability of the two-seat fighter concept. The whole squadron was equipped with the type from April 1933, by which time the type had entered full-scale production as the Demon.

Hawker Demon I

Demon K3976 was flown by No. 29 Sqn (in whose markings it is depicted here) from March 1935, having spent seven months in a Home Aircraft Depot. It was later sent to the Middle East with the squadron. By January 1938, the aircraft was with No. 25 Sqn at Hawkinge, though this unit received Gladiators mid-year, K3976 then going to No. 9 MU for disposal. In April 1939, the aircraft became instructional airframe 1405M with No. 6 School of Technical Training at Hednesford.

Bristol Bulldog IIA

No. 56 Sqn Bulldog IIA K2206 is unusual in that it has an experimental 'Townend ring' fitted around its Bristol Jupiter engine. Several Bulldogs of No. 56 Sqn, which operated the type between October 1932 and May 1936, were so-equipped, as were similar aircraft issued to No. 32 Sqn, which had a least one example. A very similar cowling, of the type seen on the Bulldog IVA (which did not enter prodcution) was fitted to some of the RAF's two-seat Bulldog (TM) Trainers.

No. 33 Sqn was the first RAF single-seat fighter unit to be stationed outside the UK since No. 1 Sqn had left Iraq in 1926. It arrived at Ismailia (where these Gladiators were photographed) in March 1938.

in February 1937, at Hendon.

As the tempo of expansion gathered pace, airfield space became a limiting factor, and 1937 saw No. 73 Squadron (which formed on the Fury II in March 1937) spending its first three months at RAF Mildenhall, planned as a bomber aerodrome. Similarly, the formation of No. 79 Squadron at Kenley in March 1937 (from No. 32 Squadron's 'B' Flight) forced No. 80 Squadron to spend three months at Henlow before moving on to Debden on 9 June.

No. 74 Squadron was a former Malta-based Demon unit, which formed at Hornchurch from a nucleus provided by No. 80 Squadron in March 1937. Gauntlets were taken on charge as interim equipment, pending planned conversion to the more advanced Gladiator. Legend has it

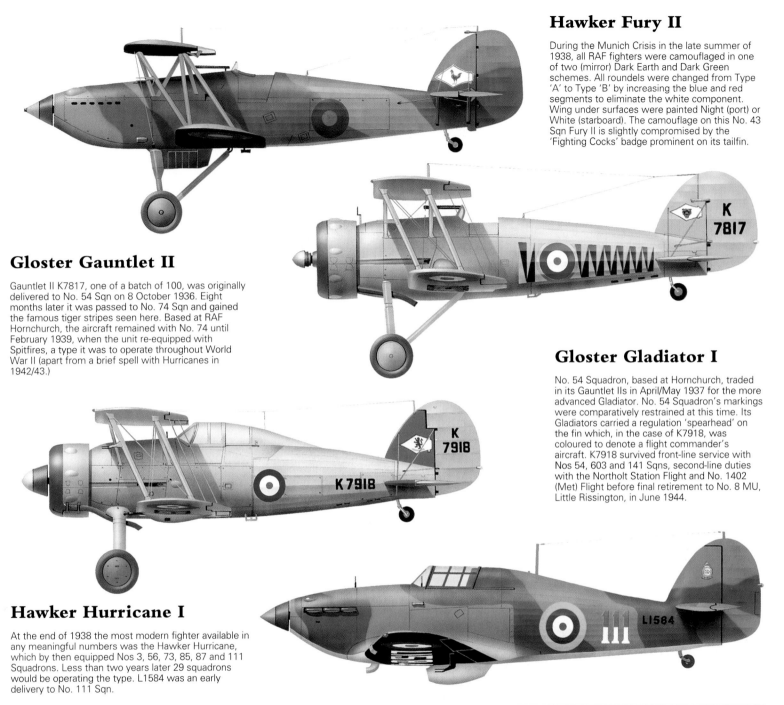

Hawker Fury II

During the Munich Crisis in the late summer of 1938, all RAF fighters were camouflaged in one of two (mirror) Dark Earth and Dark Green schemes. All roundels were changed from Type 'A' to Type 'B' by increasing the blue and red segments to eliminate the white component. Wing under surfaces were painted Night (port) or White (starboard). The camouflage on this No. 43 Sqn Fury II is slightly compromised by the 'Fighting Cocks' badge prominent on its tailfin.

Gloster Gauntlet II

Gauntlet II K7817, one of a batch of 100, was originally delivered to No. 54 Sqn on 8 October 1936. Eight months later it was passed to No. 74 Sqn and gained the famous tiger stripes seen here. Based at RAF Hornchurch, the aircraft remained with No. 74 until February 1939, when the unit re-equipped with Spitfires, a type it was to operate throughout World War II (apart from a brief spell with Hurricanes in 1942/43.)

Gloster Gladiator I

No. 54 Squadron, based at Hornchurch, traded in its Gauntlet IIs in April/May 1937 for the more advanced Gladiator. No. 54 Squadron's markings were comparatively restrained at this time. Its Gladiators carried a regulation 'spearhead' on the fin which, in the case of K7918, was coloured to denote a flight commander's aircraft. K7918 survived front-line service with Nos 54, 603 and 141 Sqns, second-line duties with the Northolt Station Flight and No. 1402 (Met) Flight before final retirement to No. 8 MU, Little Rissington, in June 1944.

Hawker Hurricane I

At the end of 1938 the most modern fighter available in any meaningful numbers was the Hawker Hurricane, which by then equipped Nos 3, 56, 73, 85, 87 and 111 Squadrons. Less than two years later 29 squadrons would be operating the type. L1584 was an early delivery to No. 111 Sqn.

In May 1938 Gladiator I-equipped No. 80 Sqn joined No. 33 at Ismailia, Egypt, as part of the Suez Canal defence force. The airship mooring mast on the airfield, prominent in this view, was a well-known landmark.

that the former Gauntlet pilots of No. 80 Squadron universally expressed their preference for the older fighter. Since Gladiator conversion took twice as long as Gauntlet conversion for the squadron's new pilots, and since a high proportion of the pilots required no formal conversion to the Gauntlet, conversion to the Gladiator was cancelled, and the five Gladiators delivered were diverted to No. 3 Squadron.

Like No. 73, No. 87 Squadron used the Hawker Fury only briefly, as an interim type pending conversion to the newer Gladiator. It formed from a nucleus provided by the Gauntlet-equipped No. 54 Squadron. The two newly-formed Gladiator units served together at Debden from June 1937, after converting to Furies in March. While No. 87 Squadron spent

A Decade of Air Power

Westland's Pterodactyl

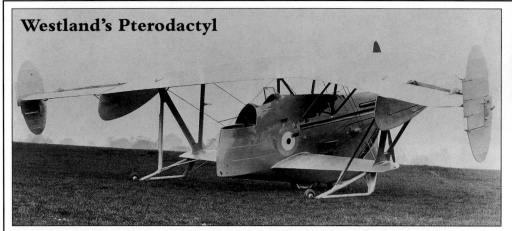

Without a doubt the most radical and outlandish fighter prototype of the 1930s, the Westland Pterodactyl V was designed as a two-seat fighter to Specification F.3/32. The aircraft first flew (as 'P-8') in May 1934, powered by a Rolls-Royce Goshawk II. The Air Ministry tested the aircraft as K2770 but as it did not offer any advantage over the Demon interest evaporated. It was planned to arm the Pterodactyl with two forward-firing Vickers guns, and a Lewis gun in the rear cockpit. Struck off in 1937, K2770 was destroyed during test flying by Westland.

its time with Furies at Mildenhall, No. 73 stood up at Tangmere.

The last front-line 'regular' home-based Gauntlet squadron to form was No. 213 Squadron, which formed from No. 111 Squadron's 'A' Flight at Northolt in March 1937. Demon units also continued to stand up, especially as Auxiliary bomber units transitioned to the fighter role. No. 601 Squadron converted in August 1937, at Hendon.

In October 1937, No. 25 Squadron gave up its last Hawker Furies, but instead of re-equipping with new Hurricanes or Spitfires found itself taking over No. 41 Squadron's ancient Demons at Catterick, while No. 41 itself took over the Fury IIs. Many on No. 25 Squadron would have preferred to retain the sleek Furies, and No. 41, as a two-seat unit, might have been better keeping its Demons until Blenheims were available, but it was not to be, and No. 41 Squadron began the process which would see it becoming one of the most successful single-seat fighter squadrons of World War II.

Fighter Command entered the monoplane era in November 1937, when No. 111

Squadron gained sufficient Hurricanes to equip one of its flights. The squadron was completely Hurricane-equipped by February 1938. This was a major step, and marked the service introduction of the world's first eight-gun fighter, though subsequent operational experience would show that this was itself something of a dead end, and that small numbers of heavy-calibre cannon represented a better fighter armament. The Hurricane was fast and undoubtedly modern, though, and No. 111 Squadron wasted little time in demonstrating its capabilities. On 10 February, for example, the CO, Squadron Leader John Gillan, flew an aircraft from Edinburgh's Turnhouse to London's Northolt at a ground speed of 408.75 mph (657 km/h), admittedly taking advantage of a hefty tailwind. Biplanes still had their part to play, and during the same month, No. 33 Squadron at Ismailia reroled as a fighter unit, equipping with the Gladiator.

No. 3 Squadron at Kenley re-equipped with the Hurricane in March 1938, though it subsequently converted back to the Gladiator in July, and was still operating the Gloster biplanes

by the time the Munich crisis broke. No. 56 Squadron received Hurricanes in April 1938, but its work-up was protracted, and the unit remained non-operational by September. No. 85 Squadron formed at Debden from No. 87 Squadron's 'B' Flight in June 1938, but never became operational on the Gladiator and converted to the Hurricane in September 1938.

Poor old No. 25 Squadron finally gained half-way modern equipment in June 1938, replacing its hated 'second-hand' Demons with slightly fresher Gladiators. The slow, unwieldy and underarmed Demons remained in use with a number of Auxiliary units.

While the Hurricane's Merlin engine, retractable undercarriage and eight-gun armament made it seem almost modern, it was in some respects still the 'Fury monoplane' envisaged when it had been ordered. The all-metal Spitfire, by contrast, was a genuinely state-of-the-art machine, and one which entered Fighter Command's rolls in August 1938 with No. 19 Squadron at Duxford. The unit had fully converted from the Gauntlet by 19 December.

Munich – shortcomings laid bare

As Chamberlain flew to Munich for his fateful meeting with Hitler, the RAF came to combat readiness. It was a useful opportunity to see the shortcomings in the RAF's mobilisation plans – not least because not one of the Gladiator or Gauntlet squadrons was available at combat readiness as the crisis began. The Gauntlet's long-running engine problems had by then been solved – but all of the Gauntlet squadrons (45 per cent of Fighter Command's strength) were on 'Block Leave'. All were recalled within four days, and most Fighter Command aircraft were immediately camouflaged in dark earth and dark green paint – sometimes drawn from official stocks and thus of the right shades, and sometimes simply bought locally. This happened at Tangmere, where the local builders' merchants provided an approximation of the officially laid down colours. Sometimes aircraft were painted according to official patterns, and sometimes according to local whim. Roundels were hastily overpainted to remove the white centres, and fin flashes were usually removed. Starboard wing undersides and fuselage undersides were painted white, with black to port. There were exceptions to the rule, of course, and No. 79 Squadron retained some of its aircraft in all-black night-fighter colours, with flight colours on the wheel disc and tailfin. Painting the highly-polished and

With its two-bladed, fixed-pitch, wooden propeller and 'non-blistered' cockpit canopy and original pattern radio mast, Spitfire I K9787 stands out as the first production example, first flown in May 1938. Whereas the Hurricane was in many ways a 'Fury monoplane', the Spitfire was thoroughly modern and unlike anything the RAF had flown hitherto.

Fighter development 1918-1938

	Snipe	Gamecock	Bulldog	Gauntlet	Hurricane I
engine power	230 hp (172 kW)	435 hp (324 kW)	490 hp (365 kW)	645 hp (481 kW)	1,030 hp (768 kW)
maximum speed	121 mph (195 km/h)	153 mph (246 km/h)	178 mph (286 km/h)	230 mph (370 km/h)	322 mph (518 km/h)
time-to-height	19 mins to	20 min to	14.5 mins to	9 min to	10.5 min to
	15,000 ft (4572 m)	20,000 ft (6096 m)	20,000 ft (6096 m)	20,000 ft (6096 m)	20,000 ft (6096 m)
ceiling	19,500 ft (5944 m)	23,000 ft (7010 m)	29,300 ft (8931 m)	33,500 ft (10211 m)	33,400 ft (10180 m)

Fighter performance 1930-1938

	Bulldog	Fury I	Demon	Gauntlet	Gladiator
maximum speed	178 mph (286 km/h)	207 mph (333 km/h)	202 mph (325 km/h)	230 mph (370 km/h)	254 mph
time-to-height	14.5 mins to	4.5 min to	8.8 min to	9 min to	4.75 min to
	20,000 ft (6096 m)	10,000 ft (4572 m)	15,000 ft (4572 m)	20,000 ft (6096 m)	10,000 ft (3028 m)
ceiling	29,300 ft (8931 m)	28,000 ft (8534 m)	28,580 ft (8711 m)	33,500 ft (10211 m)	32,800 ft (9997 m)

Specification F.5/34

F.5/34 called for a single-seat fighter with a rapid rate of climb, armament of six or eight Browning machine-guns each with 300 rounds of ammunition (enough for a 15 second duration of fire), a top speed of 275 mph (443 km/h) at 15,000 ft (4572 m) and 265 mph (426 km/h) at 20,000 ft (6096 m), a service ceiling of 33,000 ft (10058 m) and a 1-hour 30-minute endurance. Features specified by the Air Ministry included retractable undercarriage, an enclosed cockpit and an oxygen supply for the pilot. Four companies built prototypes (Martin-Baker as a private venture) while Fairey carried out a design study to the specification. Hawker's F.5/34 design remained unbuilt, Supermarine may have put in a proposal (records are unclear), while Westland worked on a Bristol Perseus-powered monoplane design to F.5/34, though this was not tendered.

F.5/34 candidates, clockwise from above: Gloster G.38, Vickers Type 279 Venom and Martin-Baker MB.2. The fourth completed submission was the Bristol Type 146.

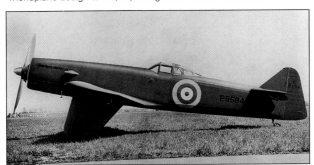

gaily-coloured Gauntlets and Furies in dull camouflage represented the end of an era and, at Tangmere in particular, the new reality dawned with a crash. The CO of No. 1 Squadron told his pilots that their Furies would not catch the German bombers, and that they would have to ram them!

Expansion after Munich

Expansion continued apace after Munich, and though the new monoplanes began to assume a greater importance, a number of new home-based squadrons stood up with Gauntlets and Gladiators, or converted from the last remaining Demons, including Nos 504, 601, 602, 615, and 616 with Gauntlets, and Nos 141, 152, 247, 263, 603, 604, 605, 607 and 615 Squadrons with Gladiators. The Gladiator and Gauntlet may have been obsolete by 1939, but

In April 1938 No. 56 Squadron was the third squadron to re-equipped with the Hurricane I (converting from the Gladiator I). L1599 had a comparatively short career with the RAF, serving only with No. 56 Sqn. The aircraft crashed on 24 April 1939, near Chelmsford, Essex, the pilot apparently losing control during an attempted aerobatic routine.

they were at least single-seaters, and there was some confidence that the aircraft would be able to give some kind of account of themselves. The Demon, on the other hand, was thoroughly anachronistic, and promised to be no more than cannon fodder. The type was formally declared obsolete in September 1939. For many squadrons, including the Fury-equipped Nos 1, 41 and 43, and for several of the more 'senior'

Gauntlet and Gladiator units, 1939 brought re-equipment with the Hurricane or even the superb Spitfire. Overseas, Nos 6, 33, 94, 112, 123, 127, 261 and 274 Squadrons were among the units which equipped with one or other of the Gloster biplane fighters; some found themselves involved in combat operations during World War II – but that is another story.

Jon Lake

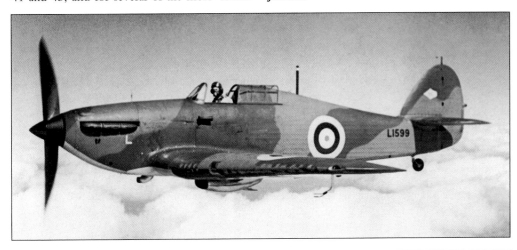

<table>
<tr><td colspan="2">Air Defence of Great Britain fighter squadrons, April 1932</td><td colspan="6">Fighter Command and overseas fighter units, September 1938</td></tr>
<tr><td colspan="2">Fighting Area, HQ Uxbridge</td><td colspan="3">No. 11 Group, HQ Kenley</td><td colspan="3">No. 12 Group, HQ Uxbridge</td></tr>
<tr><td>Biggin Hill</td><td>AACF</td><td>Biggin Hill</td><td>No. 32 Squadron</td><td>Gauntlet</td><td>Catterick</td><td>No. 41 Squadron</td><td>Fury</td></tr>
<tr><td>Duxford</td><td>No. 19 Squadron   Bulldog</td><td>Biggin Hill</td><td>No. 79 Squadron</td><td>Gauntlet</td><td>Church Fenton</td><td>No. 64 Squadron</td><td>Demon</td></tr>
<tr><td>Duxford</td><td>No. 29 Squadron   Siskin</td><td>Debden</td><td>No. 29 Squadron</td><td>Demon</td><td>Church Fenton</td><td>No. 72 Squadron</td><td>Gladiator</td></tr>
<tr><td>Hawkinge</td><td>No. 25 Squadron   Fury</td><td>Debden</td><td>No. 85 Squadron</td><td>Hurricane</td><td>Digby</td><td>No. 46 Squadron</td><td>Gauntlet</td></tr>
<tr><td>Hornchurch</td><td>No. 54 Squadron   Bulldog</td><td>Debden</td><td>No. 87 Squadron</td><td>Hurricane</td><td>Digby</td><td>No. 73 Squadron</td><td>Hurricane</td></tr>
<tr><td>Hornchurch</td><td>No. 111 Squadron   Bulldog</td><td>Hawkinge</td><td>No. 25 Squadron</td><td>Gladiator</td><td>Duxford</td><td>No. 19 Squadron</td><td>Spitfire/Gauntlet</td></tr>
<tr><td>Kenley</td><td>No. 23 Squadron   Bulldog</td><td>Hendon</td><td>No. 600 Squadron</td><td>Demon</td><td>Duxford</td><td>No. 66 Squadron</td><td>Gauntlet</td></tr>
<tr><td>Kenley</td><td>No. 32 Squadron   Bulldog</td><td>Hendon</td><td>No. 601 Squadron</td><td>Demon</td><td>Thornaby</td><td>No. 608 Squadron</td><td>Demon</td></tr>
<tr><td>Northolt</td><td>No. 41 Squadron   Bulldog</td><td>Hendon</td><td>No. 604 Squadron</td><td>Demon</td><td>Usworth</td><td>No. 607 Squadron</td><td>Demon</td></tr>
<tr><td>North Weald</td><td>No. 56 Squadron   Siskin</td><td>Hornchurch</td><td>No. 54 Squadron</td><td>Gladiator</td><td>Wittering</td><td>No. 23 Squadron</td><td>Demon</td></tr>
<tr><td>Tangmere</td><td>No. 1 Squadron   Fury</td><td>Hornchurch</td><td>No. 65 Squadron</td><td>Gladiator</td><td>Wittering</td><td>No. 213 Squadron</td><td>Gauntlet</td></tr>
<tr><td>Tangmere</td><td>No. 43 Squadron   Fury</td><td>Hornchurch</td><td>No. 74 Squadron</td><td>Gauntlet</td><td></td><td></td><td></td></tr>
<tr><td>Upavon</td><td>No. 3 Squadron   Bulldog</td><td>Kenley</td><td>No. 3 Squadron</td><td>Gladiator</td><td></td><td></td><td></td></tr>
<tr><td>Upavon</td><td>No. 17 Squadron   Bulldog</td><td>Kenley</td><td>No. 17 Squadron</td><td>Gauntlet</td><td></td><td></td><td></td></tr>
<tr><td></td><td></td><td>Northolt</td><td>No. 111 Squadron</td><td>Hurricane</td><td></td><td></td><td></td></tr>
<tr><td colspan="2">NB: Fighting Area also included some Communications, Army Co-operation and training units, not listed here.</td><td>North Weald</td><td>No. 56 Squadron</td><td>Hurricane</td><td colspan="3">Overseas units</td></tr>
<tr><td></td><td></td><td>North Weald</td><td>No. 151 Squadron</td><td>Gauntlet</td><td>Ismailia, Egypt</td><td>No. 33 Squadron</td><td>Gladiator</td></tr>
<tr><td></td><td></td><td>Tangmere</td><td>No. 1 Squadron</td><td>Fury</td><td>Amiriya, Egypt</td><td>No. 80 Squadron</td><td>Gladiator</td></tr>
<tr><td></td><td></td><td>Tangmere</td><td>No. 43 Squadron</td><td>Fury</td><td></td><td></td><td></td></tr>
</table>

Shahaks over the Sinai

101 Squadron, IDF/AF in the Six Day War

Part One: Rising tensions and Day One

During the Six Day War in June 1967, the Israeli Defence Force/Air Force (IDF/AF) fielded nine squadrons of front-line fighters plus a squadron of armed trainers. The spearhead of this small – but effective – force was three squadrons equipped with the Dassault Mirage III, known as Shahak (Skyblazer) in IDF/AF service. They flew a total of 1,107 sorties in those six days, claimed 48 air-to-air kills and lost nine Shahaks. The share of the IDF/AF's premier fighter unit, 101 Squadron, in that total was 337 sorties and 14 kills, for the loss of four Shahaks.

The Dassault Mirage IIICJ entered IDF/AF service in 1962 and by 1964 three squadrons were equipped with the Shahak. At first only experienced fighter pilots were streamed to fly the new IDF/AF fighter, but in 1965 it was decided to train younger pilots on the type. The first younger and relatively inexperienced fighter

pilots converted to the Mirage in the summer of 1965. A year later the IDF/AF Shahaks gained their first air-to-air victory and by the end of 1966 the three Shahak squadrons shared five confirmed kills, three of which were claimed by pilots of the IDF/AF's first fighter unit, 101 Squadron.

On 7 April 1967 the IDF/AF

Shahaks clashed with Syrian Air Force (SAF) MiG-21s and emerged victorious with six confirmed kills, including three by 101 Squadron pilots. This relatively routine border skirmish was the turning point in the development of the Six Day War. As the result of (false) Soviet intelligence information that Israel was concentrating its forces along the Syrian border, Egypt, in an act of Arab solidarity, expelled the UN forces from Sinai, the buffer zone peninsula between Israel and Egypt. The Egyptian Army entered Sinai on 15 May 1967 and the Egyptians began to mass their forces in Sinai. The UN forces completed their departure from Sinai on 19 May and on 22 May the Egyptian President announced the closure of the Strait of Tiran to Israeli shipping, thus reinstating the maritime blockade on the Israeli port of Eilat which had been lifted following the Sinai Campaign 11 years earlier.

The same day, while visiting an Egyptian Air Force (EAF) Su-7 squadron, President Nasser made his famous, provocative announcement: if Major General Yitszhak Rabin [the IDF Chief of Staff] wants war, then *ahalan va'sa'alan* ('welcome', in Arabic). Relations deteriorated to the point of war.

Reservists mobilised

To counter the Egyptian threat, Israel had no option but to mobilise its reserve units. During a period of three weeks, both sides massed their forces, every move by one side resulting in an escalation by the other. On 30 May King Hussein of Jordan joined Egypt and Syria and two days later, 1 June, an Egyptian commando regiment was flown to Jordan. In case of war it was speculated that the task of this commando force would be to attack the IDF/AF air

Above: Mirage IIICJ Shahak 15 was the mount of Major Oded Marom when he scored his first kill, an Egyptian MiG-19S on 6 June 1967. Marom went onto to score a further 10 air-to-air victories as an IDF pilot.

Below left: No. 101 Squadron scored five victories over the Egyptian air force's relatively small fleet of MiG-19s during the Six Day War. The small black triangle on the top right corner of each frame indicates that the cannon's trigger is being pressed.

A 'finger four' formation of 101 Sqn Shahaks over Israel taken exactly one month before the squadron went into combat. All carry two 1300-litre drop tanks and display red/white striped fins.

bases. There were also reports of an Iraqi expeditionary force which was to join the Jordanians.

Israel felt threatened and that its very existence was at stake. For three weeks the IDF mustered its units and waited for orders. The IDF/AF mobilised its reserves, practically stopped its routine training, and waited. Those three weeks became known as the waiting period but finally the order came, the safes were opened, the seals of the envelopes were removed and the operational orders were given.

Air superiority was the priority of the IDF/AF since it was formed in 1948. Its first fighter operation was planned to be an attack on the Egyptian El-Arish air base, although this had to be cancelled due to a much more urgent IDF requirement to attack an Egyptian column which was just 32 km (20 miles) south of Tel-Aviv. During the 1950s the IDF/AF practised achieving air superiority by attacking enemy air bases. The tactic was to use large formations which were to suppress the anti-aircraft ground defences of the air base, to bomb the runways and to attack the air base installations with rockets. It was basically the same tactic that the Anglo-French forces used to attack the EAF in the Sinai Campaign.

Changed thinking

By the early 1960s the IDF/AF had changed its thinking, and instead of using large formations the concept of small ones was introduced. The bombing of the runways was retained but the same aircraft which bombed the runways were now to return and strafe with their cannon, though not the air base installations; the target of the strafing was the enemy's aircraft. This new doctrine had its advantages but also its weaknesses: the enemy's air defences were completely ignored and there were no fighters devoted to protecting the attacking fighters from enemy interceptors. Moreover, the full force was utilised to attack the air bases, with only a token force being left behind in readiness to intercept any hostile intruder. It was a high-risk plan based on extremely accurate intelligence and on the element of surprise. When the planning was completed, the plan, known as Operation Moked (Focus), was placed in the safes of each squadron, though it was

constantly updated when new intelligence information emerged or when the IDF/AF order of battle was changed.

During the waiting period it was clear that if Israel was to strike first, the IDF/AF would be the spearhead of the pre-emptive strike with its Operation Moked. The achievement of air superiority was essential to secure any chances of success to the outnumbered IDF ground forces and, as such, it was vital to the very existence of the state of Israel. The pilots felt that they were the key element in their country's survival and this feeling was only emotionally heightened when the IDF Chief of Staff Major General Rabin visited 101 Squadron on 2 June – as Ilan Gonen, then one of the youngest 101 Squadron pilots, recalls.

"I remember Rabin arriving at the squadron before the war and saying to the pilots the famous sentence, 'You will be the decisive force. There will be war and you will be the decisive force!' He was smoking heavily. I was sitting in the first row and he took my cigarettes. I felt how much he was fearing the war and how much he was placing on our shoulders."

Yosef Arazi, who, like Ilan

Top: One of the first six IDF/AF Mirage pilots, Major Amos Lapidot was the commanding officer of 101 Sqn during the Six Day War.

Above: The first Israeli Mirage kill was an Egyptian MiG-21 which fell to Yoram Agmon in 1966. He added five others on the Mirage before transitioning to the F-4 Phantom. The symbol ahead of the engine intake shows the shatter pattern of the canopy during ejection.

Left: The senior deputy commander of the squadron during the conflict was Major Dan Sever. Post war he was its acting commander, between the departure of Major Amos Lapidot in the summer of 1967 and Lt Col Oded Marom's arrival in the autumn of 1967.

Four Shahaks, with 101 Sqn's two-seat Mirage IIIBJ 86 leading, taxi at Hatzor in June 1967. Note that the fourth Shahak is a 119 Sqn example.

Gonen, had been flying the Shahak since 1965 but unlike Gonen was a more experienced fighter pilot, recalls, "If there is an example of a just cause war then it is the Six Day War. The background was such that our level of anger at the squadron was unusual. I remember the build-up of the [Arab] forces all around us, the demonstrations in Cairo and Damascus and Amman [calling] to massacre the Jews. It was clear to us that we would not allow a second Holocaust to happen and that only we could do the job. We had a high level of self-confidence. I do not know if it was justified but it was out of all proportion.

"When Rabin came to visit the squadron before the war he was nervous and under pressure, and he was smoking heavily. He was unusually stressed. We sat in the briefing room and we told him, 'Yitzhak, do not worry. We will do the job for you!'"

Surprise was the key element to ensure the success of Operation Moked. The decision to launch the risky pre-emptive strike was taken on 4 June, and on that evening the IDF/AF base commanders were briefed by the IDF/AF commander, Major General Mordechai Moti Hod. When the base commanders returned from IDF/AF headquarters in Tel-Aviv they, in turn, briefed the squadron commanders.

0745 hours: H-Hour

H-Hour was 07.45 on the morning of 5 June 1967. The pilots were woken at 04.00 and the briefing began an hour later. Simultaneously, the families of the pilots left the air base and the fighters were prepared for the take-off. Everything had to be conducted without a word on the radio; the radio sets were switched off to avoid any accidental radio messages. The whole Hatzor wing, three squadrons, was to take off within about one hour in complete radio

silence and each formation was to set course to its target at an altitude not higher than 100 ft (30 m) above ground level. A pilot in distress was left on his own with no radio to advise of his position and very slim chances of survival from an ejection at such a low altitude.

Most of the 101 Squadron pilots were very experienced and confident. They had waited for this moment for three weeks. Still, they were all human and as expected they had their fears and worries. Ilan Gonen recalls the briefing.

"If I remember anything then it is the briefing. We came in the morning and we were told that this is it, the waiting period is over and we are going. H-Hour was written on the board. The secret was well kept. I had been on readiness the previous evening with [Lieutenant Colonel Arlozor] Zorik Lev, so I knew. Zorik received the message to prepare the squadron. He tried to keep it secret from me but he could not because we were both alone at the squadron.

The SAM threat

"At the morning briefing there was a feeling of apprehension because we did not know what those [surface-to-air] missiles were capable of. I do not know about the others, but for a young pilot it was a great fear. At one stage I left the briefing room to wash my face because I felt I could no longer maintain the required concentration and listen, with all those fears. For a young pilot like me, it was the brink of a great war for which we had waited so long, and it looked terrifying.

"I sat in the briefing beside [Captain Yair] Nueman who wrote

[that morning] in the squadron's book 'my hand is shaking, I can not write any longer'. He was killed the same day. He expressed the feeling of us all in that short sentence – or maybe just me, I felt the same. I remember [Binyamin] Beni Peled, the base commander, arriving full of self-confidence and saying 'we will show them', and I did not understand how could be so confident.

"We were to take off in a complete radio silence with the radio sets switched off. Someone asked what would happen if we had a problem after take-off – the air base would be busy with the take-offs and there would be a radio silence. He simply replied, 'You set course for the sea and eject.' So we said, 'That is fine, but no-one will know that we ejected, no one will find us,' and Colonel Peled replied, 'I hope that you will be lucky.' When you tell such a thing to a young pilot – if you have any problems then do not inform anyone, eject, if you are found it's fine, if not it's bad luck – it results in a very unpleasant feeling."

The 21 serviceable Shahaks of 101 Squadron were organised into seven formations in the early morning hours of 5 June 1967. Two pairs – Lieutenant Colonel David Ivry and Lieutenant Ilan Gonen, and Captain Avshalom Ran and Lieutenant Giora Epstein – were on immediate alert, ready to scramble to intercept any hostile intruder. The other five formations were to attack three targets: Beni Suef, Bir Tmada and Cairo West air bases. The latter air base was the home of the EAF No. 65 Air Brigade with Tu-16 bombers, including No. 95 Flight with

Above: This is the Egyptian Ilyushin Il-14 'Crate' shot down by Lt Ilam Gonen over the Sinai on 5 June 1967. It has suffered what seems to be extensive fire damage to the wing outboard of the starboard engine.

For the air-to-ground mission the Shahak's typical configuration consisted of a pair of iron bombs under the fuselage and two large 1300 litre external fuel tanks. Of note is the informal dress of some of the the ground-crew.

101 Squadron's personnel

Based at Hatzor air base, the IDF/AF's 101 Squadron on 5 June 1967 officially had 22 Shahaks and 33 pilots at its disposal. Like all other IDF/AF combat squadrons, the pilots of 101 Squadron fell into three categories: a skeleton of regular pilots, Hatzach pilots and reservists. The regular pilots comprised the experienced squadron's 'management' – the commander, his two deputies and the operations officer – plus relatively younger pilots. The Hatzach pilots were either staff officers, IDF/AF Flying School instructors or pilots on a study leave. Hatzach is the Hebrew acronym for Hatzavot Hirum (Emergency Posting) and under this unique IDF/AF arrangement the pilots on a non-operational assignment continue to fly with their operational squadrons for one day each week. The Hatzach pilots were also the first to be called back to their squadrons in times of tension, as their availability was higher than that of the reserve pilots. The later concept of fast-jet reserve pilots in regular squadrons was introduced in 1960, but by 1967 only a small number of reserve pilots flew with the three IDF/AF Shahak squadrons; however, they formed the backbone of the other six IDF/AF front-line squadrons and the armed trainer unit. This phenomenon arose from two factors: the Shahak was the newest fighter in IDF/AF service, having been introduced into service in 1962, and only the best pilots were streamed to fly the revolutionary delta fighter. Those pilots usually served longer, so by 1967 few had left the service. After 1967, however, the trend changed and the number of reservists in the Shahak squadrons rose sharply.

The squadron had been commanded since August 1965 by Major Amos Lapidot, a member of the first group of IDF/AF fighter pilots to convert to the Mirage III in France in 1961 and a future IDF/AF commander between 1982 and 1987. Each IDF/AF squadron commander had two deputies who were referred to as deputy commander A for the senior and deputy commander B for the junior. The two deputies of Major Amos Lapidot were the experienced Major Dan Sever and the future ace Captain Iftach Spector. Sever had been flying the Shahak since 1963 and had been the deputy of Amos Lapidot since 1964, when the latter commanded the IDF/AF Operational Training Unit (OTU) equipped with the Dassault Ouragan. In January 1966, four months after Lapidot left the OTU to command 101 Squadron, Dan Sever followed his lead and returned to 101 Squadron as the senior deputy commander. Spector, on the other hand, was a relative newcomer to the IDF/AF Shahak community, having converted to the type in 1966, but he was an experienced fighter pilot and had flown the Dassault Super Mystère B.2 since 1961, while he also served under the command of Major Amos Lapidot as an OTU instructor in 1964.

By June 1967 many of the squadron's pilots were very experienced, five having shared between them six confirmed kills and many others having participated in real air combats and operational missions. The squadron had a favourable ratio of 1.5 pilots per aircraft (33 pilots and 22 aircraft), although this was slightly disturbed in late May 1967 when the three youngest 101 Squadron pilots – Lieutenants Ron Holdai, Amnon Shadmi and Eli Zohar – were returned to neighbouring 105 Squadron to fly the Dassault Super Mystère B.2. Immediately after the Six Day War those three pilots returned to their unit, 101 Squadron, but during the war they flew only with 105 Squadron.

Among the 33 pilots were three lieutenant colonels on Hatzach: Arlozor Zorik Lev (101 Squadron commander in 1963-65), David Ivry (a Shahak squadron commander in 1964-66) and the IDF/AF chief test pilot Daniel 'Danny' Shapira. Another very experienced Hatzach pilot was Major Giora Furman, who was intended to succeed Major Amos Lapidot as the 101 Squadron commander later in the year. Furman completed his tour of duty as an Ouragan squadron commander in April 1967. After a month and a half long trip to Africa, Major Giora Furman returned to fly with 101 Squadron but he also flew with his previous Ouragan squadron, toward which he felt greater responsibility. During the war he flew with both squadrons: with the Ouragan squadron which he had commanded and with 101 Squadron which he was scheduled to command. Giora Furman remembers the squadron just prior to the Six Day War: "There was a lot of story-telling during the waiting period, like those about Danny Shapira whose instincts we admired. The preparations included a napalm bombing at the range. They explained to him how

Above: Pilots of 101 Sqn during the Six Day War pose in front of one of their Shahaks. From the left, standing are Lev, Lapidot, Haber, Slapak, Sever, Agmon, Aharon, G. Palter, Holdai, E. Palter and A. Palter. Seated are Spector, Barzilai, Arazi, Furman, Nevo, Ran, Zohar, Shadmi and Epstein.

Right: Taken during their 1965 Shahak conversion course are (left to right) Lt Itshak Barzilai, Capt Nissim Ashkenazi, Lt Avner Slapak and Lt Itshak Peer below 101 Squadron's famous 'skull' badge.

Below left: Taking a quick break in 101 Sqn's ready room are (from left to right) Capt Shlomo Levi (nine kills during IDF/AF career), Capt. Eitan Ben-Eliyahu (four kills and IAF CO from 1998), 1st Lt Giora Epstein (17 kills) and Major Oded Marom (11 kills).

to do it with the sight. All the pilots scored hits with the sight but he did not. Finally, he begun to score hits but he used his instincts [not the sight].

"There were several very aggressive pilots in the squadron like (Avner) Slapak with a lot of talent and aggressiveness. Giora Epstein was not very aggressive. He was relatively inexperienced in flying but he had a lot of experience in life. When he finished his OTU, Amos [Lapidot] said, 'He had just finished the OTU, but with such experience as his I can give him the command of a squadron.'

"Of the pilots in the 'first league', there were those who had deserved it and who were really at the top, especially in air combats, like (Avner) Slapak, (Iftach) Spector and others. Others were more gentle, more responsible, like Ezra Aharon, (David) Ivry, Amos Lapidot. Excellent pilots, but not necessarily for air combat. This mix was very successful."

These were the 101 Squadron pilots who were to take off in the early morning hours of 5 June 1967 as part of almost the entire IDF/AF front-line fighter force to launch Operation Moked.

Tu-16s equipped with AS-1 'Kennel' air-to-surface missiles, and as such was a top priority target. Three 101 Squadron formations were to attack Cairo West. The other two formations were to attack Beni Suef – the second EAF Tu-16 air base and the only EAF air base at Upper Egypt to be attacked during the first wave – and Bir Tmada in Sinai. Bir Tmada was known as the EAF 260 Air Base and was viewed by the EAF as a forward attack base. As such it was planned to contain a MiG-17 unit, No. 25 Squadron of the 2nd Air Brigade, and elements of the only operational EAF Su-7 unit, No. 55 Squadron of the 1st Air Brigade, but it seemed that the base housed no combat aircraft on the morning of 5 June 1967.

The first 101 Squadron formation to attack, exactly at H-Hour (07.45 Israeli local time), was the formation which had Bir Tmada as its designated target. The mission of that formation was to bomb the runway of the air base and then fly a combat air patrol (CAP) over the area from which the attacking IDF/AF formations turned to their targets. This formation consisted of three Shahaks: the leader was Major Dan Sever in Shahak serial number (s/n) 77 with Lieutenant Itshak Peer as No. 2 and Captain Guri Palter as No. 3 in Shahak s/n 06.

Dan Sever recalls: "Amos

Above: An early view of Shahak 09 carrying the 101 Squadron badge on the tail but without the red and white rudder stripes applied early-on in service to all 101 aircraft. The aircraft displays the designation Mirage IIIC on the nose instead of the full Mirage IIICJ titles.

Left: The end of a Tupolev Tu-16 'Badger-B' as captured by the gun-sight camera of Maj Amos Amir's Shahak 34 during the attack on Cairo West undertaken by the squadron on 5 June 1967. Beni Suef, the other Tu-16 base, was also attacked on the war's first day.

[Lapidot] asked which mission I preferred; he chose the first formation and I had second choice. We were an air-to-air squadron, the first IDF/AF fighter squadron. We operated the Rafael Shafrir and the MATRA R.530 Yahalom (Diamond) AAMs but all the Moked missions were air-to-ground. One formation's mission was to bomb a relatively close air base at H-Hour and then protect the IDF/AF turning point. It was a point roughly off Bardavil from which all the IDF/AF formations turned towards their targets. It was feared that if the enemy could get to this area it might cause a lot of damage, it would disturb the navigation of the formations, so they wanted air defence at this point. I saw it as my chance to get a MiG kill and I chose this mission.

"We were a three-ship formation: Peer was No. 2 and Guri Palter was No. 3. Our mission was to bomb Bir Tmada with 500-kg bombs and within five minutes or even less to reach the turning point. We bombed the runway and as we pulled out and flew north we saw pillars of black smoke coming from the nearby Bir Gafgafa air base. I looked at that direction and I saw an Il-14 flying slowly at about 3,000 ft. I reported to No. 2 and No. 3 and dived at him, full speed, but while I was several kilometres away from him I saw a MiG-21 turning to the east. I reported, got organised for the kill and at the range of 600 m, just as I was getting ready to squeeze the trigger, he entered a spin. Two turns and he crashed. I said, 'He crashed, we are returning to the Il-14,' but we could not see him. He disappeared and we had our mission, so we flew north to the turning point.

Haunted by an Il-14

"When we returned to the squadron I debriefed the mission with the Intelligence Officer. He grabbed me and said, 'Sever, do you know what that transport aircraft was? It was flying the high command of the Egyptian army, which was caught with its pants down. General Amer and his officers were visiting the front in Sinai. They were in that aircraft. You should have shot it down!' It was a story that haunted me for years. A fighter pilot goes after fighters, but in that particular scenario the right thing to do was to shoot down the transport aircraft!"

Guri Palter adds his own perspective of the same mission. "We bombed at H-Hour. As far as I can recall there was a strong crosswind and we missed the runway. We then strafed the aircraft, Mi-6s and an Il-14. Our mission was to patrol over the Mediterranean at the point where the formations turned. While en route we saw an Il-14 flying towards Bir Gafgafa but he disappeared in the smoke. We then saw a MiG-21. Sever followed him, with us in line astern. The MiG probably saw Sever at the last moment and tried to break, but he had no airspeed and he spun into the ground. We then looked for the Il-14 but it disappeared, and after a short patrol we returned home. Only then did we learn from the intelligence that the Il-14 was transporting the headquarters of Marshal Amer and that it was a much higher value target than the MiG, but who would follow an Il-14 when you have a MiG-21? Sever was justifiably credited with the kill because it crashed due to his threat."

Dan Sever does not believe that they missed the runway. When he visited Bir Tmada, less than a month after the war, he observed two direct hits on the runway, but it is difficult to connect these hits with the Shahaks since the 101 Squadron formation attack was followed by additional waves of attacks by Dassault Ouragans and Mystères. Actually, the 101 Squadron Shahaks dropped only five bombs. One of Major Sever's bombs did not release so he jettisoned it together with the bomb carrier by using the pyrotechnic emergency release device immediately after pulling out of the strike and prior to the engagement with the Il-14 and the MiG-21. Sever is also sure that they did not strafe Bir Tmada because they had to conserve their internal cannon ammunition for the air-to-air mission.

Five minutes after H-Hour –

Three generations of French-built Israeli air force combat aircraft (Ouragan 82, Super Mystére B.2 44 and a 101 Squadron Mirage IIICJ) are seen at Hatzor in June 1967.

07.50 - was the Time Over Target (TOT) of the first of three 101 Squadron formations to attack Cairo West. The leader was Major Amos Lapidot and the other pilots in this formation of three Shahaks were Captain Binyamin Romach and Captain Baruch Friedman. The formation bombed runway 16/34 and claimed that five of the six bombs which were dropped hit the target. In the ensuing strafing passes the three Shahaks claimed eight Tu-16s, one Il-28 and three MiG-21s as destroyed.

The second 101 Squadron formation to attack Cairo West was the third IDF/AF formation to attack that target. The leader was Major Amos Amir in Shahak 34 and the other pilots were Captain (reserve) Maoz Poraz, Captain Itshak Barzilai and Captain Yochai Richter. TOT was 08.10 and the target of the bombing was runway 28/10. Only the leader of this formation carried the first runway-piercing bombs to be dropped on Cairo West. This specially designed weapon, dropped from low altitude, was equipped with a parachute to slow it down and stabilise it before a rocket was fired to bury the bomb as deep as possible in the runway's concrete. It produced considerably more drag than the regular 500-kg GP bombs used by the previous formations, as Amos Amir explains.

Runway-piercing bombs

"The heavier 250-kg bombs were carried under the fuselage and these smaller, 150-kg bombs were carried under special racks near the wingtips where the AAMs were usually carried. It was a very special installation and as such it was very draggy, hence the higher fuel consumption. I did not realise it, I figured it was just two additional small unimpressive bombs, but they sure impressed the wing. We did the bombing run and in the second pass, when they (the other Shahaks) strafed, I passed over the runway. I had to release the bombs and I thought I released them, since I could not see them from the cockpit (but the special bombs were not released). On our way back I realised that I would not make it – it was pretty clear to me that I would have to eject and my only problem was either to eject over Sinai, still in Egyptian hands, or hope I would make it past the border. From Cairo we flew north and then northeast toward the Mediterranean coast of Sinai, and then east over the coast. It was

clear that my only chance was to reach Hatzerim (air base). I arrived at Hatzerim in a straight-in approach to an emergency landing with no engine (which flamed out due to fuel starvation over El-Arish), my only decision was when to lower the undercarriage. It was 60 per cent luck and 40 per cent skill."

Captain Itshak Barzilai led the other three Shahaks back to Hatzor but they also suffered a fuel problem: for both Captain Barzilai and Captain Richter, the powerplant flamed out immediately after landing, and only 70 litres (15 Imp gal) of fuel remained in the tanks of Captain (reserve) Poraz's Shahak when he switched off the Atar turbojet engine.

With TOT of 08.25, the third 101 Squadron Shahak formation to attack Cairo West was led by Major Oded Marom in Shahak 09, the other pilots being Captain Yair Nueman and Captain Iftach Spector. Their target for the bombing was runway 16/34 but the pillars of black smoke and the fires meant that the hits could not be observed. In the ensuing strafing passes, the formation claimed five Tu-16s as destroyed with another one as a probable.

The last 101 Squadron formation to attack on the first wave had a TOT at 08.40 and its target was Beni Suef, the other EAF Tu-16 air base. This air base was the target of the IDF/AF Sud Aviation Vautour fighter-bombers, which made navigation easy since the smoky air base could be seen from a distance. The formation was led by Major Ezra Aharon in Shahak 04 and the other pilots were Captain Amnon Shamir and Captain Uri Shachar. Captain Avner Slapak was also planned to fly with this formation but he had to abort. Following the bombing of the runway, the pilots discovered that the Vautours had done a great job and no intact targets were left for the Shahaks, as Ezra Aharon recalls.

"It was the most distant target and we were preceded by the Vautours, which was really lucky for us. The navigation in the Mirage was very primitive, just a gyro compass. We crossed Sinai at high altitude and dropped to low altitude when we crossed the Egyptian Red Sea coast. This was the last point which we recognised. We then flew over a featureless terrain and we arrived over the town of Beni Suef, about 2-3 miles

Above: The Shahaks of 101 Sqn attacked Mil Mi-6 'Hook-As' at both Bir Tmada and Ardaka. This example displays a prominent marking on the nose. Twelve of the type are believed to have been supplied to Egypt.

Above: With the cover still on the MiG-21 'Fishbed' in the foreground, a 101 squadron pilots lines his sights on an Egyptian MiG-17 'Fresco'. These pictures say a lot about the level of surprise achieved by the Israelis.

Above: These two stills from a camera-gun sequence show the bullets falling just over the burning hulk of what appears to be a Hunter. Another (more complete) example resides to the left of the target aircraft.

An intact looking Tupolev Tu-16 sits in its revetment while another example burns fiercely. The 'Badger-Bs' were a top priority target during the Six Day War; by 1973 they had been had been replaced by Tu-16K 'Badger-Gs'.

Left: Shahak 12 at the point of rotation carrying the standard pair of fuel tanks. The auxiliary intakes just in front of the Star of David roundel are in the open position.

Below: 101 Squadron Shahaks 09 and 57 taxi out during the Six Day War with the 'captured' 119 Squadron Shahak 84 – the central aircraft in this portrait. Shahak 84 displays the flash and badge of its (late) squadron on its tail.

south of the air base. When we crossed the Nile I recognised where we were by the shape of the river, and then we saw the smoke to the north. We turned right, the Vautours completed their attack and we followed them. The truth is that they did not leave us a lot. They destroyed everything. All the Tupolevs were burning or smoking. We bombed the runway and then strafed. When you enter a strafing pass you can not tell the state of the [target] aircraft, it is a range of 2-3 km. Only when you pass over it can you see if it was destroyed or if the fuel had just leaked and burned.

"Shachar was left with his bombs, his bombs did not release and he did not know. One of the problems in the Mirage was that its armament system was very simple, just two switches: detonators and bombs, single or pair. There were two 500-kg bombs under the belly and there were no indicators. All the way back he trailed behind us and could not close the distance. When he finally closed the distance we were over Beer Sheva and he was very low on fuel. Then we saw the bombs and it was clear why he could not catch up."

While the five bomb-carrying 101 Squadron formations were taking off, the pilots of the two 101 Squadron QRA (Quick Reaction Alert) pairs were waiting in their aircraft for an alert which never came. Finally, after waiting

45 minutes in the cockpits of their Shahaks with engines running, the first pair was launched on a CAP over Sinai. The leader was Lieutenant Colonel David Ivry in Shahak 12 and his wingman was Lieutenant Ilan Gonen in Shahak 59. The leader was one of the most experienced IDF/AF Shahak pilots, and his wingman one of the youngest.

Ilan Gonen recalls: "We patrolled for a long time and there were no MiGs over Sinai. Then Ivry had a communication problem so the procedure was that I communicated with the controller and I took the lead. We then discovered an Il-14, so it turned out that I was the first to shoot at him. The Egyptian pilot acted properly. I shot at him, I hit his engine and it caught fire. He was flying so low that its pilot immediately lowered the landing gear and landed straight ahead in the desert while it was burning. Ivry then hit him while he was already on the ground. It did not crash, he simply made an emergency landing while he was burning since he was so low that he immediately reached the ground."

Weizmann vindicated

When the first wave was over, at about 09.00, it was clear that former IDF/AF CO Major General Ezer Weizman's concept of the Shahak as a multi-role combat aircraft was correct. The

Mirage, which had been developed as a defensive weapon, emerged as an excellent offensive one. Not only did it crater the runways of the enemy and strafe aircraft on the ground, it also achieved air superiority over the enemy's air bases, allowing the less modern IDF/AF fighters to operate relatively safely over enemy territory. The IDF/AF claimed the destruction of 186 aircraft during that first wave, many destroyed by the sleek silver delta fighters. 101 Squadron did not lose a single aircraft during the first wave, while it claimed a single Il-14 and a single MiG-21 in the air-to-air arena. By the time the first wave was over, 101 Squadron also had an additional Shahak on its strength. This is recalled by Reuven Rozen, then a 119 Squadron captain who had to land at Hatzor in Shahak 83 due to a fuel problem after returning from a mission to Cairo West.

"I phoned my squadron commander, Major Ran Ronen, and

he asked me what happened to my aircraft. He did not say well done [for a successful emergency landing] but he asked, 'What was the problem?', so I answered, 'It has a hole in the rear fuel tank'. He said, 'So tell 101 to patch it and bring back the aircraft, it's a war and we have missions.'

"[Captain Iftach] Spector was the [101 Squadron] fighting manager so I told him, 'Ran said that you will patch the aircraft and refuel it.'

"'Forget it.'

"'What do you mean?'

"'Whatever lands here its our aircraft.'

"'But Ran said ...'

"'Ran is your commander, not mine. The aircraft remains here but we do not need you, so if you behave yourself we will give you a [Citröen] Deux Chevaux to return you to Tel-Nof.'

"I tried to be wise but he was very serious, so I was the only pilot to take off in a Mirage and return to his base in a Deux Chevaux!"

0900 hours: The second wave

The three Shahak squadrons each had one two-seat Mirage IIIBJ for conversion training. During the 1967 war 101 Sqn's IIIBJ was 86. A fourth was delivered after the war.

After 09.00 it became apparent that the success of the first wave was overwhelming, while losses were very light when compared

with the anticipated 25 per cent loss rate. The first wave was pre-planned, but the second wave demonstrated the flexibility of the plan. During the second wave the IDF/AF attacked EAF air bases of lesser importance, which had not been attacked during the first wave since it was thought that the EAF might disperse its combat aircraft from the main air bases. Those bases which had been attacked during the first wave were also re-attacked, if necessary. The third type of targets to be attacked during the second wave were distant air bases to which a low-altitude

ingress was not possible; they were attacked by the Mirages and Vautours only during the second wave, when the element of surprise no longer existed.

The second wave lasted between 09.00 and 12.00 and comprised a total of 164 sorties, about 15 per cent less than the 191 sorties of the first wave. Some 107 additional EAF aircraft were claimed as destroyed on the ground during the second wave but there were no air-to-air kills by Shahaks.

During the second wave, 101 Squadron attacked four EAF air

Shahak – Israel's Mirage IIICJ

Israel purchased a total of 76 Dassault Mirage III combat aircraft, which were delivered between 1962 and 1968. Seventy Mirage IIICJs were delivered between 1962 and 1964, two Mirage IIICJ(R) reconnaissance aircraft were delivered in 1964, three two-seat Mirage IIIBJ combat-capable conversion trainers were delivered in 1966, and an additional Mirage IIIBJ arrived in 1968. The Mirage became the first IDF/AF combat aircraft to receive an official Hebrew name, Shahak.

The Israeli purchase of the Mirage in large numbers as a multi-role combat aircraft, rather than the purchase of a small number as an interceptor, was the highlight of Major General Ezer Weizman's period as the IDF/AF CO (1958-1966). Weizman had to overcome the IDF General Staff view that only 24 Mirages should be purchased to equip a single air-to-air squadron in addition to other less capable, and less expensive, aircraft for the air-to-ground mission.

The first Israeli pilot to fly the Mirage III, actually the Mirage IIIA03, was the IDF/AF test pilot Major Daniel Shapira who made his first flight on 23 June 1959 and three days later demonstrated the new fighter to Major General Weizman, becoming on that date the 12th pilot to fly over Mach 2 in the Mirage. Weizman was convinced that the Mirage should become the backbone of the IDF/AF during the 1960s and should be purchased in large numbers; as many as 100 was his target. However, at this stage the Mirage was still a limited point defence interceptor with an additional SEPR 841 rocket motor, a single MATRA R.530 SARH AAM under the fuselage and two external fuel tanks under its wings. Under Israeli pressure, two internal DEFA 552 30-mm cannon were installed, two additional outboard wing hardpoints were added for IR AAMs (Israel was then developing the indigenous Rafael Shafrir) and the available three hardpoints were stressed to carry two 500-kg bombs on the central underfuselage hardpoint or a single 500-kg bomb under each of the inboard wing stations. Israel also rejected the SEPR rocket motor following a series of test flights in May 1960. The Mirage eventually became a multi-role combat aircraft as envisaged by Weizman.

Persuading the IDF General Staff to accept his view was not easy and Weizman never got his 100 Mirages, but finally he got enough that his successor as the IDF/AF CO, Major General Mordechai Moti Hod, would prove his idea during the Six Day War. The initial 1960 Israeli order covered only 24 aircraft but also included an option on a further 36. The option was not fully exercised and the second Israeli contract, signed on 28 April 1961, covered 24 aircraft with an option on a further 12. Finally, a third contract which covered an additional 24 aircraft was signed in late 1961. Two more contracts, which covered the purchase of the four two-seat Mirage IIIBJ combat-capable conversion trainers, were signed in 1964 and 1966.

The first two Shahaks arrived in Israel on 7 April 1962. Initial deliveries were streamed to 101 Squadron at Hatzor air base, previously a Dassault Mystère IVA unit. The second squadron, 117 Squadron at Ramat-David air base which had previously flown the Gloster Meteor, received its first four Shahaks on 7 July 1962. The Shahaks assumed the 5-minute daytime QRA mission in December 1962 and 24-hour QRA responsibility in July 1963. The QRA aircraft were armed with a single MATRA R.530 Yahalom SARH AAM (of which 15 live missiles and eight launchers were purchased) and two Rafael Shafrir IR AAMs (of which 200 missiles were ordered).

A third Shahak squadron was formed in March 1964: 119 Squadron at Tel-Nof air base, which until the summer of 1963 had been the IDF/AF night-fighter unit with Sud Aviation Vautour IINs and Gloster Meteor NF.Mk 13s. This third squadron did not operate the Yahalom AAM and introduced the Shafrir AAM in February 1965, though it accepted the QRA mission in November 1964. The two Mirage IIICJ(R) reconnaissance aircraft arrived in Israel on 10 March 1964 and were operated by 119 Squadron. When the first three Mirage IIIBJs arrived in 1966 each Shahak squadron received a single example.

By June 1967 the three IDF/AF Shahak squadrons were all combat-capable and in full readiness. All flew in bare metal finish, 101 Squadron's aircraft being identified by a red and white striped rudder, 117 Squadron's by a red line along their fuselages and 119 Squadron's by a distinctive red flash on their vertical stabilisers. The growing number of kill markings were painted just below the cockpit on the port side of the nose section.

Following the Six Day War diplomatic relations between France and Israel deteriorated, culminating in an arms embargo which included an April 1966 Israeli order for 50 Mirage 5MJ multi-role combat aircraft. Israel, with the clandestine aid

Above: The IDF/AF purchased only fifteen operational Matra R.530 Yahalom AAMs plus three training rounds and eight launchers for its Shahaks. 101 had four launchers and used two live missiles during air combat on 29 November 1966.

Left: The IDF/AF Chief Test Pilot Maj Daniel 'Danny' Shapira (wearing the flight suit) and the IDF/AF Commander, Maj Gen Ezer Weizman, stand in front of Mirage IIIA 03 on 26 June 1959. Weizman was instrumental in the Israeli Mirage purchase.

Below: Maj Shapira, the first Israeli Mirage III pilot, also became the first member of the IDF/AF to exceed Mach 2, during his evaluation of the design in France during June 1959.

Below: The Cyrano Ibis radar earned a reputation for being highly unreliable and prone to overheating in service with the IDF/AF. Later in the Shahak's career with the air force the radar was replaced by ballast. In all, the IDF/AF's combined Mirage III/Nesher fleet claimed a total of 282.5 kills.

of Dassault, fabricated a local version of the Mirage 5 as the IAI Nesher, of which 51 single-seat and 10 two-seat examples were produced. The last Shahaks were withdrawn in 1982.

---

bases which fell into these three categories: Bilbeis and Helwan were air bases of lesser operational importance, El-Minya was a distant air base, and Cairo West was re-attacked. It was during the attack on Cairo West that 101 Squadron suffered its first casualty: Captain Yair Nueman was shot

down, most likely the victim of an EAF MiG-21.

The formation which attacked Cairo West was led by Captain Avner Slapak and the other pilots were Captains Yair Nueman, Avshalom Ran and Yosef Arazi. Only Captain Nueman had taken part in the first wave attacks on

Cairo West, and to all but him this was their first Operation Moked mission. Avner Slapak recalls this mission.

"We bombed and then strafed. When we entered the first strafing pass No. 3 told me that a MiG-21 was behind me but he could handle him, and that we could

continue to strafe, so we did. We were flying in pairs in line astern and the MiG-21 was between us, so Nos 3 and 4 mixed with him and we continued to strafe. We destroyed several aircraft and had turned for home at very low altitude when we entered terrifying AA fire and SAMs. We were at

145

Israel's second highest scoring pilot is Iftach Spector, who eventually scored 15 kills. Spector achieved ace status in both the Shahak and the Kurnass (F-4 Phantom). This picture dates from around late 1969/early 1970.

Oded Marom (at the rank of Lieutenant Colonel) poses by his Shahak, adorned with seven Egyptian air force kill markings, probably in the early 1970s. As a Hatzach he flew 11 missions in the Six Day War.

low altitude so I was only bothered by the AA fire.

"Then Nueman told me, 'I got hit, I am pulling up.'

"I said, 'Do not pull up.' He was on my right so I turned to the right to see him. I turned 360° but I did not see him. I called, 'Two, two,' but he did not answer. I thought he had pulled up and been hit by an SA-2, but apparently he pulled up to eject."

Mixed feelings

The formation claimed the destruction of two MiG-21s on the ground but the pilots returned with mixed feelings, as Yossi Arazi recalls.

"I missed the first wave because of Yochai Richter. Each one of us had his own aircraft in his particular formation. I was planned to fly with Amos Lapidot to Cairo West but just before the war Yochai Richter took off in my aircraft and retracted the undercarriage too late, at high speed, and he damaged the undercarriage doors so

my aircraft was grounded and I could not fly in the first wave.

"We took off at about 11.00 and the flight over Sinai was fascinating. We flew very low and suddenly, in the middle of the desert, I saw a ship. I thought I was either sick or drunk as we flew toward it. The ship was in the Suez Canal and we were flying so low we could not see the canal, but we saw the ship; it was an amazing sight.

"At that stage there were quite a number of fires in Egypt, a lot of fires and smoke, but we missed the navigation and actually overflew the air base before we identified it. We bombed the runway and there were several MiGs in the air. I did not see the MiGs, I heard that there were MiGs in the air, and Avshalom Ran announced that he was going after a MiG. When I bombed I saw a MiG behind a hangar, only its nose section could be seen, so in a strafing pass I cut off its nose section and set it on fire. I then saw a tractor towing another MiG, coming out of a

grove. I entered another strafing pass to attack it but it returned to the grove and disappeared.

"That was when I heard Yair Nueman reporting, 'I think I was hit, afterburner light is on,' and a few seconds later he said, 'I am ejecting.' We did not see or hear anything else. We returned as singles, I am not even sure that we regrouped together to return as a formation. It was traumatic, because on the one hand you could see the AA fire and think that it was not serious, but suddenly Yair got hit and was killed. It was a flight that was certainly traumatic, but in the overall excitement it simply faded.

First Shahak loss

"[When Nueman was hit] I looked for him but I could see nothing. We became separated very quickly and we did not see each other. Nueman got hit, Avshalom Ran chased a MiG and I do not even remember what Avner Slapak did. I returned from that flight with a lousy feeling that there was no control. I am not proud about that flight, we made a couple of holes in the runway and I destroyed a MiG, but to lose Nueman for that was just not worth it."

(Captain Yair Nueman ejected near Zagazig in the Nile Delta but was killed on the ground by hostile civilians. Years later, after the Egyptian President Anwar Sadat came to Israel to talk peace with Israel, an ex-EAF pilot who was a member of an Egyptian delegation to Israel told his host Ezer Weizman, who was by then the Israeli Minister of Defence, that he shot down an Israeli Mirage. The date and area which the Egyptian pilot mentioned fitted with Captain Yair Nueman's loss. Weizman asked Giora Rom, the first IDF/AF ace and by then a

senior IDF/AF officer, to meet the Egyptian pilot and verify his story. Rom first met Avner Slapak to learn about the mission and then he met the Egyptian pilot. Rom was amazed by the Egyptian pilot's story and he is convinced to this day that he met the Egyptian pilot who shot down Captain Nueman with an AAM.)

Bilbeis was the home of the EAF Air Academy and not an operational air base, but it could have accepted combat aircraft from the damaged operational air bases so it was attacked by a 101 Squadron formation, which claimed the destruction of between six and 10 Il-14 transports. The leader was Major Marom in Shahak 56 and the other pilots were Captain Iftach Spector and Lieutenant Eldad Palter in Shahak 82, the younger brother of Guri. (The third Palter brother, Rafael, was a transport pilot. The Palters were the first set of three brothers to fly with the IDF/AF. The IDF/AF 1967 Shahak community had two more sets of brothers: Yosef Yossi and Ehud Henkin flew with 117 Squadron while Yochai and Ya'acov Kobi Richter flew with 101 Squadron and 117 Squadron, respectively. Lieutenant Meir Shachar, a 117 Squadron pilot, was the younger brother of Major Yonatan Shachar, a Mystère squadron commander.)

Another Il-14 air base attacked during the second wave was El-Minya at Upper Egypt. Two Shahak formations were dispatched at high altitude, the 119 Squadron formation led by Major Oded Sagi being just minutes ahead of the 101 Squadron formation led by Lieutenant Colonel Arlozor Zorik Lev.

The other pilots in the formation were Captain David Baruch and Captain Yoram Agmon, who recalls: "We were a three-ship

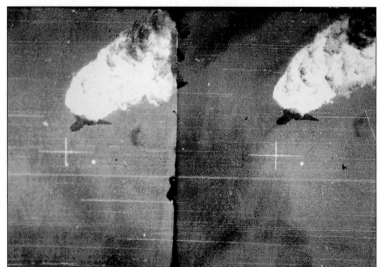

An Egyptian air force MiG-21 'Fishbed' kill by 101 Squadron. Due to the high-octane starter fuel tank being located close to the pilot's oxygen bottle, MiG-21s could not absorb as much damage as the MiG-17 or Su-7.

A rare colour photograph of a 101 Squadron Shahak in flight. This unidentified example (the censor has removed the aircraft's 'serial' from the tail) displays two kill marks. The aircraft behind belongs to 119 Squadron.

formation, No. 4 aborted due to a technical malfunction. We flew at high altitude because we had to save fuel to get there and we flew all the way with another formation from 119 Squadron which Oded Sagi led. They were ahead of us and Zorik tried all the way to catch up and arrive first, but we attacked after them. It was a relatively quiet and uncomplicated strike apart from the long flight."

The 119 Squadron formation actually destroyed all the targets but the following 101 Squadron formation also attacked El-Minya.

The third 'new' air base attacked by the 101 Squadron Shahaks on the second wave was Helwan, where the Egyptian aeronautical industry was located. Like Bilbeis, it was not an operational air base but was attacked to prevent its use by surviving combat aircraft from

the operational air bases. Helwan was attacked by a 101 Squadron formation led by Major Dan Sever in Shahak 08, including Lieutenant Itshak Peer, Captain Amnon Shamir and Captain Guri Palter who flew in Mirage IIIB s/n 86. During the war the Mirage IIIBs were used just like the Mirage IIICs. The two-seaters were a bit less manoeuvrable, they had no radar and less fuel, but with two external fuel tanks they could reach most of the targets which were attacked by their single-seat counterparts.

The attack on Helwan was a testimony to the skill and ability of the Shahak's pilots. An Indian test pilot who was an eyewitness to the

attack reported that following a bombing run on the runway, the Shahaks came in to strafe the small number of Egyptian aircraft. In two strafing passes, three MiG-17s which had just arrived from Cairo West to seek sanctuary at Helwan were destroyed, as were a single resident MiG-19 and two resident HA-200 jet trainers, while an An-12 engine testbed was damaged. In their third strafing pass the Shahaks could not find any other worthwhile targets and simply overflew the EAF air base at low altitude. The only Egyptian casualty was a young mechanic who looked for cover under the wing of the MiG-19.

1200 hours: Egypt's allies hit back

The expected enemy action against the IDF/AF commenced just before noon when Jordanian artillery shelled Ramat David air base, Tel-Nof air base, Lod International Airport and the former IDF/AF air base at Kfar Sirkin. This was followed by air strikes by both the SAF and Royal Jordanian Air Force (RJAF). Israel's hopes that Egypt would not be joined by its Arab allies were shattered, and the third and fourth waves of Operation Moked included attacks on the air bases of four air forces. Several EAF air bases were attacked, the Jordanian and Syrian air forces were wiped out and the Iraqi Air Force (IrAF) H-3 air base was also attacked. During the third wave 101 Squadron attacked just one air base, and another two air bases

were attacked in the fourth and finale wave.

The third wave attack on Cairo IAP was led by Lieutenant Colonel David Ivry in Shahak 57 with Lieutenant Giora Epstein in Shahak 06, Captain Binyamin Romach and Captain (reserve) Maoz Poraz. It was a relatively uneventful mission. The two air bases attacked by 101 Squadron on the fourth wave were Cairo West and Dmeir. The first target was attacked by Lieutenant Colonel Zorik Lev, Lieutenant Eldad Ran and Lieutenant Colonel Danny Shapira. Their mission was to drop six 250-kg delay-fused bombs on the runways and the mission was particularly notable for the three SA-2s which were launched at the Shahaks on their egress. One of the missiles homed on the Shahak

of Lieutenant Colonel Shapira but he managed to evade it with a violent break. The only SAF air base to be attacked by 101 Squadron was Dmeir, which Major Amos Lapidot, Captain David Baruch and Lieutenant Eldad Palter in Shahak 52 attacked on the fourth wave.

Magister attack

Late in the day, at 17.31, a formation of four Fouga Magister armed trainers took off for a BAI mission on the Jerico-Jerusalem road near Ma'aleh Adomim. The formation encountered heavy AA fire and lost a Magister out of which pilot Captain (reserve) Shabtai Ben-Aharon bailed successfully. Captain Avner Slapak had just taken off from Hatzor for a CAP mission when he saw the parachute in the air, as he recalls.

"I was scrambled to somewhere and I immediately saw the parachute. I told the controller, 'I am staying here to protect him.' I flew around him and I did not let anyone get near him. I saw him land on the ground and I saw two Jordanian Jeeps driving down the road toward him. I attacked and nailed them. I waited for the helicopter and did not let anyone get near him. It took a very short time and the helicopter arrived and

landed, but the pilot told me, 'I have his parachute but he is gone, he escaped.' He did not know that if he had stayed in that spot for several more minutes he would have been rescued, but he escaped to hide and was caught by the Jordanians [who killed him]."

By the end of the day 101 Squadron had flown 84 sorties, an average of 2.8 sorties per pilot. Forty of the sorties consisted of 11 missions to attack eight air bases: Beni Suef, Bilbeis, Bir Tmada, Cairo IAP, Cairo West, Dmeir, El-Minya and Helwan. Two sorties were a single mission to attack Egyptian ground forces at Bir Hassaneh, Sinai, and the other 42 sorties were all CAPs. During the day the squadron claimed 35 aircraft (11 Tu-16s, three Il-28s, seven MiG-21s, a single MiG-19, three MiG-17, a single Antonov, six Il-14s and three unidentified aircraft) as destroyed on the ground plus nine additional aircraft as probably destroyed on the ground, including four Tu-16s and a single MiG-21. Additionally, a single EAF MiG-21 and a single EAF Il-14 were claimed in air-to-air engagements. All this was achieved at the cost of just one Shahak and its pilot, Captain Yair Nueman.

Shlomo Aloni

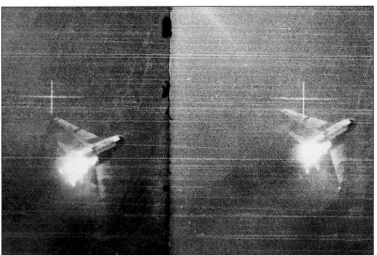

Above: Flames streaming from its upper mid-fuselage, this MiG-19 'Farmer' is seen plunging towards the ground, while the Mirage remains locked on its tail. Egypt still operates MiG-19s, albeit Chinese-built Shenyang F-6s.

An Egyptian air force MiG-21D, with what appears to be rocket pods under the wings, sits forlorn following an Israeli attack. The forward-pivoting cockpit canopy is open, possibly indicating a quick exit by the pilot.

Luftwaffe Markings: Part 1

Tactical Symbols, Markings and Identification Codes of German Military Aircraft 1918-1945

German markings of World War II were governed by a complicated set of rules, but with many exceptions to confuse the student. But before this system could evolve, Germany had to overcome the stringent conditions set by the victorious Allies in 1918.

Military aviation came of age during World War I. In just four short years, from 1914 to 1918, the warplane evolved from stick-and-string novelty, largely frowned upon for frightening the cavalry horses, into a weapon of destruction so feared that the vanquished foe – while allowed to retain a token ground army of 100,000 men – was expressly forbidden by the terms of the post-Armistice Treaty of Versailles to keep a single one of the nearly 20,000 military aircraft which had been on charge at the war's end. So all-encompassing was the aerial ban imposed by the Allies that the 75,000-word Treaty, comprising a staggering 440 separate articles, required just five sweeping clauses to effectively expunge German military aviation from the post-war European scene. Article 198 of the Treaty prohibited Germany from maintaining "either land-based or naval air forces". Article 202 decreed that all existing military aircraft were to be surrendered to the Allies.

Signed in the Palace of Versailles' great Hall of Mirrors on 28 June 1919, the Treaty came into effect on 10 January 1920. It was Article 198 which sounded the final knell for the miscellany of *ad hoc* aerial border defence units which had sprung up in the months following Germany's surrender in November 1918, and which had seen action against the Bolsheviks in the Baltic states and in the eastern provinces during 1919. The aircraft

Until September 1935 German aircraft carried the old Imperial red/white/black fin stripes on at least the starboard side of the fin. The carrier here is a Heinkel He 45, the company's first design for the new military force.

flown by these units, the Fokker D VIIs and D VIIIs and the Junkers D Is of the Geschwader Sachsenberg operating in the Courland peninsula, and the Halberstadts of the Air Detachments (Flieger-Abteilungen) in Upper Silesia – in full camouflage and bearing straight-edged crosses on fuselages, wings and tails – were virtually indistinguishable from their wartime counterparts of some 12 to 18 months earlier.

Withdrawn from the fighting zones in the east, these machines were either destroyed or handed over to the Allies in accordance with Article 202. A similar fate befell the seven internal security squadrons

Left: A Heinkel He 46 (with photographer at work in the rear cockpit) demonstrates the alphanumeric system which constituted Germany's first military markings.

Above: Germany's first (and internationally unofficial) markings consisted of the national designator ('D') followed by numbers, as seen here on a Dornier Do 11C.

German phonetic alphabet	
A = Anton	**N** = Nordpol
B = Berta	**O** = Otto
C = Cäsar	**P** = Paula
D = Dora	**Q** = Quelle
E = Emil	**R** = Richard
F = Friedrich	**S** = Siegfried
G = Gustav	**T** = Theodor
H = Heinrich	**U** = Ulrich
I = Ida	**V** = Viktor
J = Julius	**W** = Wilhelm
K = Konrad	**X** = Xanthippe
L = Ludwig	**Y** = Ypsilon
M = Martha	**Z** = Zeppelin

(Polizeistaffeln) which had been set up by the individual provincial states to provide an aerial police presence within Germany's own troubled borders. Nothing of a military nature was spared. By the autumn of 1921 a detailed report on the Allied Control Commission's activities recorded some 15,000 aircraft surrendered or destroyed, together with close to twice that number of aircraft engines, plus 17 airships, and over 300 hangars (including 37 airship sheds) either seized or demolished; the latter figures alone represent an estimated loss of over 1 million m² (over 10.7 million sq ft) of hangar space.

In comparison to the swingeing military terms of the Treaty, the eight clauses relating to Germany's civil aviation industry could be regarded as almost munificent. The country was allowed to keep a grand total of 140 aircraft and 169 engines for purely commercial use. These would have to be adapted from existing military machines, however, for Article 201 stated that, for the six months following the Treaty's coming into effect, "the manufacture and importation of aircraft, parts of aircraft, engines for aircraft and parts of engines for aircraft shall be forbidden in all German territory."

The Allies themselves lost no time in switching their own considerable manufacturing capacity to the more lucrative commercial sector within weeks of the war's end, the 19-month brake on German development and production (later extended by another three months) ensuring that they had a clear field. By the time Germany was officially permitted to resurrect its own aircraft industry, this lead would be well-nigh unassailable. So convinced were the Allies of this fact that, when the Paris Convention (set up by the League of Nations to frame regulations for post-war international air services) signed the Treaty on Aerial Traffic of 13 October 1919 – which, among other items, determined the system, style and application of international aircraft registrations – Germany was not even consulted, let alone included.

Stung by this slight – they had, after all, on 5 February 1919 inaugurated the world's first commercial scheduled daily passenger service (the 330-km/205-mile Berlin-Leipzig-Weimar route), albeit flown by three-seater civil conversions of the wartime L.V.G. C VI long-range reconnaissance aircraft – the German authorities decided to go their own way. When allocating international registration codes at the Paris Convention, CINA (the Commission Internationale de Navigation Aérienne) had not seen fit to issue the letter 'D'. Germany took advantage of this by appropriating the initial, fortuitously indicating 'Deutschland', as its own. Whereas CINA had stipulated that individual aircraft of the world's civil fleets were to be identified by letter groups, it was decided that German machines would be registered in numbered sequence commencing 'D 1'.

In fact, a temporary aircraft register (Luftfahrzeugrolle) using exactly this system was already in operation. It had been introduced shortly after the Armistice of November 1918 both by certain of the Polizeistaffeln and as a means of identifying those converted warplanes pressed into early commercial service. The L.V.G.s of the Deutsche Luftreederei (German Aerial Shipping Line) plying the Berlin-Weimar route, for example, could be seen wearing an odd mix of markings consisting of lozenge-camouflaged wings complete with crosses, the company initials and emblem on the fuselage, and a low 'D'-number.

With the coming into force of the Treaty of Versailles, however, and the introduction of the definitive register (the Luftfahrzeugrolle 'B'), a fresh start was made. Some of the old registrations disappeared, along with the makeshift aircraft which they had adorned; others were incorporated into the new system. This would remain in use for the next 14 years and eventually reach the 3,500 mark. Although nominally for purely civil purposes only, military machines – under one guise or another – had

begun to appear on the Luftfahrzeugrolle almost from the outset.

The Treaty of Versailles ban had not been as watertight as had at first appeared, and many ploys were used to successfully outwit the Allied Control Commission officers. It is estimated that some 1,000 aircraft were smuggled abroad and sold, others were registered in the Free City of Danzig, and many were simply hidden. Upon instructions given by Anthony Fokker before he himself departed for Holland, about half the completed aircraft and engines held in stock at his Schwerin factory were dispersed about the surrounding Mecklenburg countryside. Over 200 machines and 400 engines were secreted away in this manner; the remainder were left in full view for the Control Officers to discover and duly seize.

Despite the straightforward nature of the regulations governing these early markings (and ignoring the allowances made on undersurfaces for civil aerial advertising purposes), anomalies soon began to arise. These early deviations from such basic, and relatively simple, official guidelines were a portent of things to come over the next 12 years. As military markings grew more complex, and the exigencies of wartime operations intervened, the scope for personal interpretation – or, more accurately, misinterpretation – grew even wider. For every regulation assiduously committed to paper by a hard-working staff officer, an exception was sure to be found in practice. For this reason it is almost impossible to be dogmatic on the subject of Luftwaffe markings. Even surviving documents showing the position and size of specific markings down to the last millimetre are now more of historical interest than practical use; they simply serve to illustrate just how wide had become the gap between the pedantry of officialdom and the priorities of the man wielding the paint brush or spray gun.

Enter the Third Reich

On 30 January 1933 Adolf Hitler became the Chancellor of Germany. Contrary to long-held belief, the Nazi Party did not then immediately lay the foundations for a new military air arm which was suddenly to arise, phoenix-like, just two years later. That process dated back to the early 1920s when the 100,000-man army permitted by Versailles managed surreptitiously to include among its 4,000-strong officer corps some 120 ex-World War I pilots. And since that date men had been secretly trained, and machines had been secretly developed, in ever-increasing

An early example of a post-war registration is carried by this Heinkel HE 5b three-seat floatplane. Later, a hyphen was added. The type took top honours at the 1926 German seaplane event at Warnemünde.

The first post-war system (the Luftfahrzeugrolle "B")

Germany's first official post-World War I marking system consisted of the initial 'D' followed by a simple numerical sequence commencing at '1'. It stipulated that this registration combination was to be carried on all six stations: on either side of the fuselage, and on the upper and lower surfaces of both wings. On biplanes it would be applied to the top surfaces of the upper wings, and bottom surfaces of the lower wings. It was to be as large as possible commensurate with the space available, and presented in a clear manner; dark on light surfaces, and light on dark. All four wing registrations – top and bottom, port and starboard – were to be read in the direction of flight.

But even such an apparently straightforward system as this soon began to throw up the sort of anomalies and inconsistencies which were to plague the whole development of German military aircraft markings over the next two decades and more. Some Heinkel designs made a practice of displaying the wing registrations in the direction of flight on the port wing, and against on the starboard. Other owners simply got confused and had the codes put on the wrong way round completely. When the number sequence reached four figures in the late 1920s, it was decreed that the 'D' should be separated from the number group by a hyphen. An official ruling to this effect was introduced in July 1930; only to lead to further discrepancies. Hyphens were subsequently added to some very low numbers, while other – higher – registrations remained obstinately without. Other operators interpreted the separation ruling by painting a chord-wise stripe across the wing between the 'D' and the number group. On some Junkers monoplanes this became a wrap-around band, black on the natural metal upper surface of the wing, changing to white on the black undersides.

D.98   D.98   D-749   D-749

D.98   D 749

RUMPLER C I, FL.ABT. BAYERN c.1920   JUNKERS A 20, DVS STAAKEN 1927

D 1160   D 1160   D-3252   D-3252

D 1160   D-3252

HEINKEL HD 24, DVS GmbH c.1929   HEINKEL He 72A, DLV BERLIN 1933

numbers. Just how unaware even the highest of the new régime were of the strides that had been made was demonstrated by the reaction of the newly-appointed Reich Commissar for Aviation, Hermann Göring who, when first shown round the secret Rechlin test centre in March 1933, remarked, "I had no idea you had progressed so far. All the better!"

On 6 July the Nazi government stamped their presence on German aviation by decreeing that henceforth all aircraft would carry the swastika, in a white circle on a red field, on the port side of their vertical tail surfaces. Perhaps not yet fully secure in their position, it was decided that the corresponding area on the starboard side should be painted in horizontal black, white and red stripes, the colours of old Imperial Germany. By this time it was clear that the numbered sequence system of aircraft registration was becoming impracticable, and in the spring of 1934 Germany fell into line with international practice by adopting a standard four-letter block in place of the previous numbers.

All aircraft carrying numbered registrations were, over a period, repainted in accordance with the new ruling ... with one notable exception. The Führer, already a prey to the superstition which would take an ever-greater hold over the years, decided he would keep the 'lucky' D-2600 registration of his personal Junkers Ju 52 transport, which was named *Immelmann* in honour of the famous fighter pilot of World War I.

In fact, Hitler retained the same number on both *Immelmann II*, a second Ju 52, and on *Immelmann III*, a four-engined Focke-Wulf Fw 200. After the outbreak of war in 1939 the 'D' and the hyphen were dropped, and *Immelmann III* carried just the four 'lucky' figures divided by the fuselage cross: 26+00.

In March 1935 Hitler felt strong enough to renounce the military restrictions imposed on Germany by the hated 'Versailler Diktat'. Article 198 was swept away, and the Luftwaffe – no longer a weakling force requiring secrecy and subterfuge to survive, but now representing a powerful psychological addition to the Führer's armoury – was revealed to the world.

For the first 16 months of their overt existence, the Luftwaffe's early units (by October 1935 numbering some 10 individual Fliegergruppen) continued to sport the standard letter registration system introduced early the previous year. On 15 September 1935 the old Imperial colours had been quietly dispensed with, and the swastika banner now adorned both sides of every aircraft's vertical tail surface. It was not until 1 June 1936, however, that a distinction was finally drawn between civil and military machines. While the ever-diminishing civil fleet retained its combination of 'D' and four-letter codes right up until the final collapse of May 1945, the operational units of the Luftwaffe were now, for the first time, to wear Balkenkreuze (straight-edged crosses) on fuselage and wings, and be allocated their own system of unit markings.

The first military markings

By mid-1936 the initial generic – and deliberately anonymous – title of 'Fliegergruppe', which had been applied to all early military units, had been largely replaced by a much more specific three-figure designation. This latter referred to the new basic unit, which was to be the Geschwader; the three figures indicated respectively (a) the Geschwader's seniority by role (e.g. fighter, bomber), (b) the actual role itself, and (c) the Geschwader's location within the five territorial commands (Luftkreiskommandos I to V) into which Germany had been divided. Thus, for example, Geschwader No. 132's designation would show it to be the first fighter unit to be established in the Berlin-Brandenburg region: '1' indicated seniormost unit of its type, '3' was the code for a fighter unit, and '2' referred to Luftkreiskommando II, i.e. the Berlin area.

Organisationally, each Geschwader (group) would comprise three Gruppen (wings), indicated by Roman numeral prefixes I to III. In turn, each Gruppe consisted of three Staffeln (squadrons), i.e. a total of nine Staffeln, indicated by Arabic numeral prefixes 1. – 3. (I. Gruppe), 4. – 6. (II. Gruppe) and 7. – 9. (III. Gruppe). Although later changes occurred, this was the framework upon which all four major Luftwaffe marking systems were based. The first of these, introduced on 1 June 1936 and intended to apply to all operational units, was an ambitious and complicated

Despite the introduction of later systems, the Führer's personal aircraft retained the original post-war letter/number combination first worn by a Junkers Ju 52/3m, on the basis of Hitler's superstitious nature. Here the registration is carried by Focke-Wulf Fw 200A-0 D-2600 (named Immelmann III*), the third prototype Condor.*

five-part alphanumeric grouping designed to include all the information contained in the two paragraphs above, with the exception of the unit's role – e.g. fighter, bomber or dive-bomber – this presumably being considered self-evident from the type of aircraft bearing the markings.

At the time of the introduction of this system, there were nine Geschwaderstäbe in existence. This number quadrupled over the next three years; there being some 36 Geschwadern (many still incomplete) on the Luftwaffe's order of battle upon the outbreak of World War II. The intervening period was one of frantic expansion, with individual Gruppen splitting from one Geschwader to form the nucleus of another, being redesignated, reorganised under new Stäbe (staffs) or even being assigned different roles. The complexity of these processes, coupled with the 1938 reorganisation of the overall Luftwaffe command structure – which saw the Luftkreise replaced by Luftwaffengruppenkommandos and resulted in wholesale redesignations within their subordinate units (the long-standing and well-known Jagdgeschwader No. 132 'Richthofen', for example, spending the last six months of its 'three-figure' existence as JG 131) – played havoc with the already somewhat cumbersome system of unit markings. A representative list of Geschwader codes as carried at specific times throughout this period (with the units' later wartime identities also included to provide some semblance of continuity) is given below:

Year of formation	Contemporary designation	Wartime designation	Code
1936:	JG 132	(JG 2)	21
	JG 135	(JG 51)	51
	KG 152	(KG 1)	27
	KG 253	(KG 4)	33
1937:	KG 153	(KG 2)	32
	KG 155	(KG 76)	53
	KG 157	(KG 27)	71
	St.G 165	(St.G 77)	52
1938/39:	KG 155	(KG 55)	56
	KG 255	(KG 51)	54
	KG 355	(KG 53)	55
	St.G 163	(St.G 2)	35

As may be deduced from the inclusion of KG 157 above, a Luftkreis VII had subsequently (October 1936) been added to the five original territorial Luftkreiskommandos. And when, in 1937, three of the Kampfgeschwader had each been allocated a IV. Gruppe (Staffeln 10. - 12.), the existing system was simply extended to cope with the increase. Thus, for example, Liegnitz-based Ju 86 'C'-Cäsar of 12. Staffel, IV./KG 153 could be seen sporting the code 32+C412. It was not just the fighter, bomber and dive-bomber units which carried early alphanumeric

The Arado Ar 65 was the nascent Luftwaffe's first single-seat fighter, entering service in April 1934 with the DVL Reklame-Staffel Mitteldeutschland. The Reklamefliegerabteilung was the 'Publicity Flying Department', ostensibly used for sky-writing but in reality a thinly-veiled military fighter organisation. This is an Ar 65F, the main production version

markings. Four other types of unit were similarly encumbered, these being the one Lehrgeschwader then in existence, all reconnaissance and coastal Gruppen, and some advanced weapons training schools.

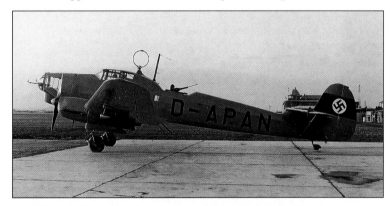

Despite its 'civil' registration, there is no mistaking the military purpose of this Focke-Wulf Fw 58B-2 Weihe. The guns and underwing bomb racks were used to train bomber crews.

The all-letter code

In April 1934 Germany replaced the numerical sequence system with an individual four-letter aircraft identity marking more in line with common international practice. They added a refinement, however, by using the first letter of the four to classify the aircraft in terms of all-up weight and carrying capacity (or number of engines). The six letters selected for the purpose (the five vowels, plus 'Y') were assigned as follows:

Code	All-up weight (seaplanes in brackets)	No. of personnel (or engines)	Class
D-Axxx	above 5,000 (5,500) kg	(multi-engined)	C
D-Exxx	max. 1,000 (2,200) kg	1-3	A2
D-Ixxx	1,000 - 2,500 kg (max. 5,000 kg)	1-4	B1
D-Oxxx	2,500 - 5,000 kg	1-8	B2
D-Uxxx	above 5,000 kg	(single-engined)	C
D-Yxxx	max. 500 (600) kg	1	A1

D-I LYU
D-ILYU

HEINKEL He 51, FL.GR. DÖBERITZ 1935

The new fuselage codes were applied in the same manner as before. On the wings, however, the new registration appeared in enlarged presentation across the whole span; the 'D', hyphen, and classification letter on one wing; the aircraft's individual 'last three' on the other. The codes were to be read in direction of flight on both upper and lower surfaces.

A trio of pre-production Heinkel He 51 fighters fly formation in the early summer of 1934, marked in the recently introduced all-letter system. The nearest aircraft is the He 51A-05 (D-IDIE) with He 51A-04 (D-IJAY) and A-01 (D-IQEE) behind. At this time, between July 1933 and September 1935, the aircraft wore a swastika on the port side of the fin and Imperial colours on the starboard. The first He 51As were delivered to the Luftwaffe in July 1934 for evaluation by the Reklame-Staffel Mitteldeutschland at Döberitz.

The alphanumeric system

The first purely military markings were introduced on 1 June 1936. Comprising a basic five-part alphanumeric combination, an aircraft's markings – while not revealing its parent unit (indicated in code by the first two numbers; see text) – now contained a wealth of other information.

On the fuselage sides the new military code consisted of two numbers to the left of the Balkenkreuz, plus a letter followed by two further numbers to the right of it. These five component parts, when taken separately, indicated respectively: (a) the Luftkreis within which the unit was stationed, (b) the seniority of the Geschwader within the Luftkreis (although, unlike the composition of the three-figure unit designation system (see text), this was now simply in sequence of activation irrespective of the unit's role), (c) the aircraft's individual identity letter, (d) the Gruppe within the Geschwader, and (e) the Staffel within the Geschwader. To take Jagdgeschwader Nr. 132 as an example: one of this unit's He 51s bearing the code '21+G25' thus proclaimed itself to be (a) from the Luftkreis II area; (b) part of the first Geschwader (of any type) to be established within that area; (c) individual aircraft 'G'-Gustav of (d) the II. Gruppe within the Geschwader and, more specifically, (e) of the 5. Staffel.

Strictly speaking, given that the nine Staffeln were always allocated to the three Gruppen in strict numerical sequence, the fourth digit of the above system (i.e. that indicating the Gruppe) was, in fact, redundant. Every member of the Geschwader (theoretically, every serving member of the Luftwaffe) would know that a 5. Staffel machine was automatically part and parcel of a II. Gruppe. But this piece of administrative tautology at least served to balance the upper plan-view presentation of the code, wherein the first two numbers were carried inboard of the port wing Balkenkreuz, and the last two inboard of the starboard wing Balkenkreuz; the individual aircraft letter's being midway between the two on the centre line (either of

the upper wing, in the case of biplanes, or on the fuselage spine). The same arrangement was used for both upper and lower surfaces. If, however, in the latter case the undercarriage assembly, or some other obstruction (such as the Ju 52's retractable ventral gun position) obscured the centre line, then the aircraft's individual letter would appear immediately before the 'last two' on the lower port wing (as before, both upper and lower markings were read in the direction of flight).

In addition to the fighter, bomber and dive-bomber Geschwadern, a number of other types of units used this system; some introducing slight variations of their own. The first of these, one of the original nine Geschwaderstäbe established by the Luftwaffe, was a one-off. The Lehrgeschwader, based at Greifswald, was an experimental unit charged with developing combat techniques for the various types of aircraft currently being introduced into Luftwaffe service. For this task, each of its four component Gruppen operated as a separate entity: I. (light fighter), II. (heavy fighter, later Zerstörer), III. (bomber) and IV. (dive-bomber). The Lehrgeschwader used the same system as described above aft of the fuselage cross, but replaced the 'first two' in front of it by the letters 'LG'. When a second Lehrgeschwader was activated in 1938, these two letters gave way to 'L1' and 'L2' respectively.

Two other types of unit using five-part codes – reconnaissance and coastal – differed in that they were still organized on an autonomous Gruppe, rather than a Geschwader, basis. For this reason the second digit (referring to the Geschwader's seniority within the Luftkreis) was inapplicable, and was replaced by a zero; the indication of seniority being transferred instead to the fourth digit, which now no longer signified the position of the Gruppe within the Geschwader, but rather the autonomous Gruppe's own seniority within the Luftkreis as a whole. A number of reconnaissance Gruppen also comprised more than three Staffeln. Markings on reconnaissance aircraft, both short- and long-range, therefore gave no clue as to their identity, other than their being based within a particular Luftkreis. In the early days of the system, when there was only one such unit in each Luftkreis, this did not pose a problem. In 1937 Heinkel He 46, coded '50+B24', had to be 'B'-Berta of the 4. Staffel of the

3./Küstenfliegergruppe 106 was one of the first two units to receive the Heinkel He 59B-2. This example is seen at List in 1936.

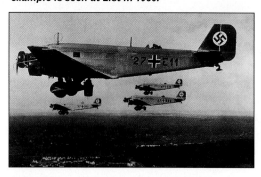

In 1936 the Ju 52/3m g3e makeshift bomber equipped over half of the Luftwaffe's bomber units. This quartet flew with I./KG 152, including one aircraft from 1. Staffel and two from 3. Staffel.

Göppingen-based Aufklärungsgruppe 15; the only short-range reconnaissance unit in Luftkreis V at the time. But as the expansion programmes added to the numbers of such units, and redesignations began to occur, the picture becomes more complex.

By contrast, the coastal Gruppen – while using the self-same system – actually carried their unit designations (albeit unwittingly and in reverse!) for all to see. They too replaced the second, redundant, Geschwader digit with a zero. But as all coastal formations came under the control of the maritime Luftkreis VI (See), every Gruppe's 'first two' read the same, i.e. '60'. And with the seven pre-war Küstenfliegergruppen simply being numbered in sequence, the fourth (gruppe) digit automatically revealed the unit's identity. In fact, every coastal Gruppe aircraft displayed its full unit designation in its markings (simply read the four numbers backwards, and add a mental oblique). Thus, Dornier Do 18 flying-boat '60+A52' reveals itself to be 'A'-Anton of Küstenfliegergruppe 2./506.

The last type of unit to employ the early alphanumeric system were the advanced flying and weapons training schools. But theirs was made up somewhat differently. With no Geschwader organization to be identified, they too included a zero; but as the first digit. The Luftkreis number was placed second (i.e. '01' to '07'; with '06' used for maritime training establishments). Behind the fuselage cross, the letter no longer indicated the individual aircraft, but rather signified the flight within the particular school. And it was the 'last two' (in some cases the 'last three') which now provided the aircraft's own identity. An early example of this system is afforded by Junkers Ju 52,

Left: The Dornier Do 17E-1 bomber was the first production version of the 'Flying Pencil', entering service in early 1937 and equipping four Geschwadern. The Do 17F-1 was an equivalent reconnaissance version.

Below: In late 1935 the Dornier Do 23G was introduced, allowing the unpopular Do 11 to be retired to the training units. These aircraft are from 4./KampfGeschwader 253, based at Erfurt. Under the alphanumeric system, aircraft carried their individual code letter on either the right wing (as here), or on the centreline.

The BMW 132F-powered Ju 86E-1 was introduced to Luftwaffe service in the late summer of 1937. This example served with 8./KG 253.

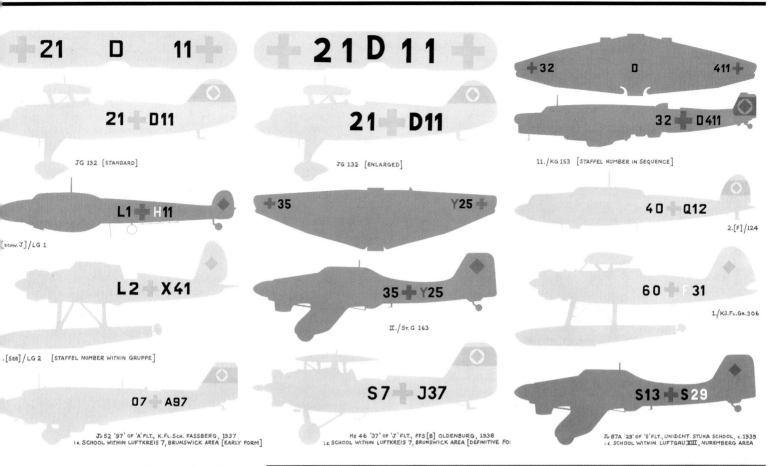

21 D 11

21+D11

JG 132 [STANDARD]

L1+H11

[SCHW.J]/LG 1

L2+X41

.[SEE]/LG 2 [STAFFEL NUMBER WITHIN GRUPPE]

07+A97

Ju 52 '97' OF 'A' FLT., K.FL.SCH. FASSBERG, 1937
i.e. SCHOOL WITHIN LUFTKREIS 7, BRUNSWICK AREA [EARLY FORM]

21 D 11

21+D11

JG 132 [ENLARGED]

35+Y25

35+Y25

II./St.G 163

S7+J37

He 46 '37' OF 'J' FLT., FFS [B] OLDENBURG, 1938
i.e. SCHOOL WITHIN LUFTKREIS 7, BRUNSWICK AREA [DEFINITIVE FO]

32 D 411

32+D411

11./KG 153 [STAFFEL NUMBER IN SEQUENCE]

40+Q12

2.[F]/124

60+F31

1./KÜ.FL.GR.306

S13+S29

Ju 87A '29' OF 'S' FLT., UNIDENT. STUKA SCHOOL, c.1939
i.e. SCHOOL WITHIN LUFTGAU XIII, NUREMBERG AREA

Two more examples of coastal aircraft markings are worn by a Heinkel He 60C of 1./KüFlGr 106 (right) and a Heinkel He 114A-2 of 1./KüFlGr 506. The latter was the only user of the unpopular He 114A, and switched back to its He 60s after a short period of service with the He 114.

coded '07+B38', or in other words, aircraft '38' of 'B' flight of a training establishment within Luftkreis VII; in this instance, the Blindflugschule (Blind-Flying School) at Celle. Within a year of its introduction, however, the initial zero was replaced by the letter 'S' to indicate Schule (school).

Within each Luftkreis, flight code letters were allocated alphabetically to the various training establishments – in groups of two or more – depending upon the number of flights operated by the individual school. The division of these groups throughout the alphabet was therefore purely arbitrary, and consecutive letters did not necessarily indicate their being part of the same establishment. In Luftkreis II, for example, Messerschmitt Bf 109B 'S2+M53' belonged to the Jagdfliegerschule (Fighter School) at Werneuchen; whereas Junkers Ju 52 'S2+N91' was on the strength of the Kampffliegerschule (Bomber School) at Tutow. On the other hand, in Luftkreis VII, Heinkel He 45 'S7+B155' and Junkers Ju 52 'S7+C212' did both belong to the Kampffliegerschule at Lechfeld.

It is also believed, though not yet confirmed, that some training establishments later adopted the practice of indicating the particular Luftgau in which they were situated, rather than the Luftkreis (Luftgaue were further sub-divisions of the larger Luftkreise). This would explain the higher numbers displayed ahead of the fuselage cross on some obsolescent, ex-operational aircraft in the late 1930s, e.g. Dornier Do 23 'S13+C92' and Junkers Ju 87A 'S13+S29'; the latter, in addition, having its 'last two' painted white instead of the more usual black.

By the end of the 1930s the advanced schools were already becoming the depositories for the first waves of operational aircraft being retired from first-line service. Many of these machines retained their previous unit's markings. And because the pilot and weapons training schools – being, by their very nature, a heterogeneous collection of various aircraft types and classes – already operated advanced aircraft alongside other machines bearing one or other of the current basic training marking systems (of which more later), it was the rule – rather than the exception – for three or more completely different styles of markings to be found in the one establishment.

If the all-embracing five- (or six-) part alphanumeric system was the administrative officer's dream, for others it was proving a nightmare. Fighter pilots were particularly loud in their condemnation. It might be perfectly feasible, they argued, for bomber crews to read another machine's codes when perambulating slowly about the sky in rigid formation; but it was another matter entirely in the split-second reaction times demanded during the simulated dogfights which formed such an essential part of their training programme. A short-lived attempt at using oversized markings on fuselage and wings did little to remedy the situation.

The powers-that-be were remarkebly prompt in conceding the validity of their argument. Just one month and one day after the introduction of the complicated five-part code system, a Luftwaffe directive laid down a whole new set of high-visibility, instant-recognition white marking symbols and numerals to be applied to single-seat fighter aircraft from 1 September 1936. At the time, the combination of these markings and colourful individual Geschwader trim no doubt served their purpose

admirably. (Unfortunately, the latter has not translated well into black-and-white photography. It is difficult now to interpret and identify pictures of these machines without additional knowledge of exact individual unit colour trim pattern, dates, locations, etc.). This new system of chevrons and bars, in particular, was to prove extremely successful. So much so that, with some revisions and additions to cope with wartime developments and expansion, it formed the basis for all fighter markings for the remaining nine years of the Luftwaffe's existence.

Towards and into World War II

Hardly was the paint dry on the colourful biplanes, however, before the advent of the Messerschmitt Bf 109 forced the first of these changes. The conspicuous absence of an upper wing on the sleek new monoplane fighter meant the disappearance of all wing markings other than the Balkenkreuze. At the same time, the Staffel symbols – the vertical bar and disc – were done away with.

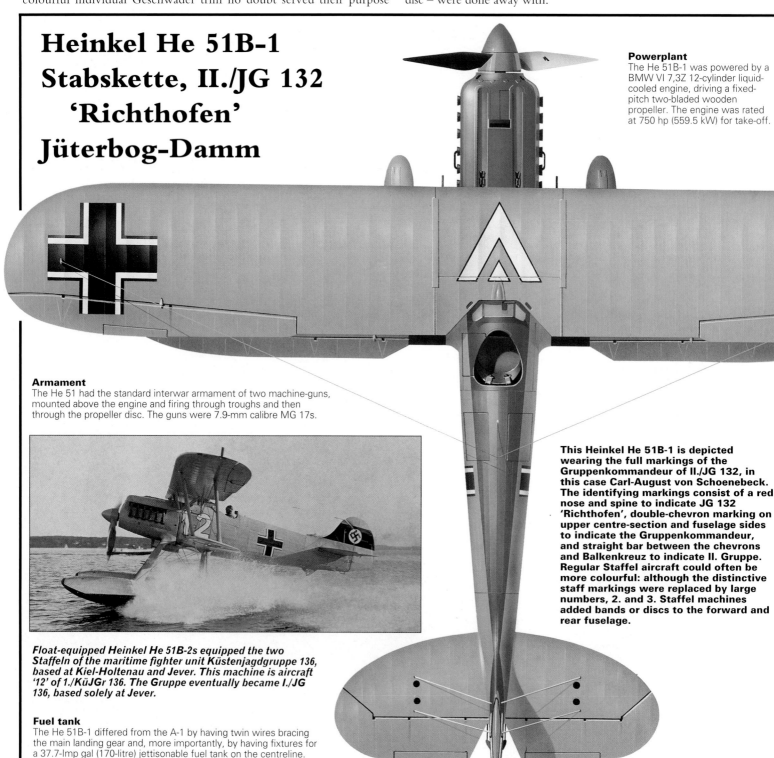

Heinkel He 51B-1 Stabskette, II./JG 132 'Richthofen' Jüterbog-Damm

Powerplant
The He 51B-1 was powered by a BMW VI 7,3Z 12-cylinder liquid-cooled engine, driving a fixed-pitch two-bladed wooden propeller. The engine was rated at 750 hp (559.5 kW) for take-off.

Armament
The He 51 had the standard interwar armament of two machine-guns, mounted above the engine and firing through troughs and then through the propeller disc. The guns were 7.9-mm calibre MG 17s.

Float-equipped Heinkel He 51B-2s equipped the two Staffeln of the maritime fighter unit Küstenjagdgruppe 136, based at Kiel-Holtenau and Jever. This machine is aircraft '12' of 1./KüJGr 136. The Gruppe eventually became I./JG 136, based solely at Jever.

Fuel tank
The He 51B-1 differed from the A-1 by having twin wires bracing the main landing gear and, more importantly, by having fixtures for a 37.7-Imp gal (170-litre) jettisonable fuel tank on the centreline.

This Heinkel He 51B-1 is depicted wearing the full markings of the Gruppenkommandeur of II./JG 132, in this case Carl-August von Schoenebeck. The identifying markings consist of a red nose and spine to indicate JG 132 'Richthofen', double-chevron marking on upper centre-section and fuselage sides to indicate the Gruppenkommandeur, and straight bar between the chevrons and Balkenkreuz to indicate II. Gruppe. Regular Staffel aircraft could often be more colourful: although the distinctive staff markings were replaced by large numbers, 2. and 3. Staffel machines added bands or discs to the forward and rear fuselage.

The first fighter markings

Based on the standard organization of three Gruppen/nine Staffeln to a Geschwader, the new system of fighter markings introduced, for the first time, tactical symbols for formation leaders. Every Jagdgeschwader, and each of its three component Gruppen (if it were fortunate enough yet to possess such), operated a Stabskette (staff flight) of three machines. Each of these aircraft was individually identified by a set combination of chevrons and bars carried on the fuselage and wing upper surfaces. The Geschwaderstab's markings extended the length of the fuselage and for much of the span of the upper wing between the Balkenkreuze. The Gruppenstab's markings, in contrast, were restricted to the forward fuselage (approximately in the area between the mainplanes of the then-current biplane fighters) and to the centre-section of the upper wing. These latter locations, plus the underside of the fuselage between the lower wing roots, were also used to display the large white numerals carried by each ordinary Staffel member. These individual numbers were normally 1-12; a Staffel at this time consisting of three Ketten of three aircraft each, plus three spare machines.

The three component Gruppen of a Jagdgeschwader utilized the mid-fuselage space, between the individual aircraft number (or tactical symbol in the case of a Stabskette machine) and the fuselage cross, to establish their identity: I. Gruppe left this space blank; II. Gruppe carried a horizontal straight bar; and III. Gruppe a horizontal wavy bar.

Likewise, within each Gruppe, the three Staffeln were identified by symbols: none for 1. Staffel; a vertical band around the nose and rear fuselage for 2. Staffel; and a disc on either side of the nose and rear fuselage, repeated on dorsal and ventral surfaces, for 3. Staffel. The 2. and 3. Staffeln's bands and discs were sometimes applied to the basic pale grey finish of the fighter, but were more commonly superimposed on background bands of the respective Geschwader colour (see below).

From the above, two facts emerge: one, although the Gruppe identity was often masked by the wings in anything but straight and level flight, the Staffel identity was visible from all quarters, other than directly ahead or astern, and from both above and below. Secondly, it required visual sighting of both Gruppe and Staffel

The white discs and lack of Gruppe markings identify these He 51B-1s as being from a 3. Staffel. The Geschwader was JG 134 'Horst Wessel'.

markings positively to identify a particular Staffel within the Geschwader. A machine bearing white disc markings could belong to any one of the three third Staffeln. Only if the mid-fuselage wavy bar, for example, was visible would it be possible to ascertain the aircraft's actually being part of the third Staffel of the third Gruppe, i.e. 9. Staffel.

None of these markings identified the actual

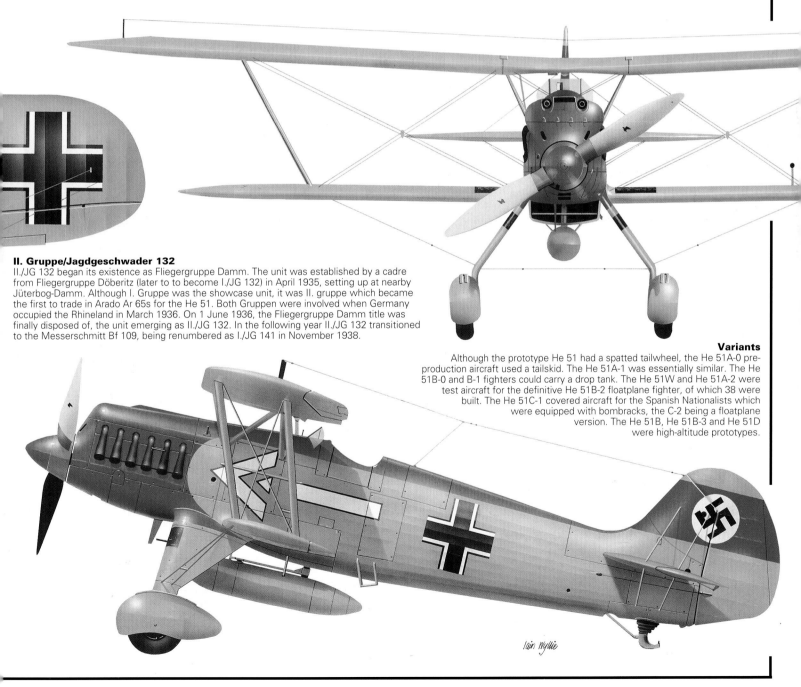

II. Gruppe/Jagdgeschwader 132

II./JG 132 began its existence as Fliegergruppe Damm. The unit was established by a cadre from Fliegergruppe Döberitz (later to to become I./JG 132) in April 1935, setting up at nearby Jüterbog-Damm. Although I. Gruppe was the showcase unit, it was II. gruppe which became the first to trade in Arado Ar 65s for the He 51. Both Gruppen were involved when Germany occupied the Rhineland in March 1936. On 1 June 1936, the Fliegergruppe Damm title was finally disposed of, the unit emerging as II./JG 132. In the following year II./JG 132 transitioned to the Messerschmitt Bf 109, being renumbered as I./JG 141 in November 1938.

Variants

Although the prototype He 51 had a spatted tailwheel, the He 51A-0 pre-production aircraft used a tailskid. The He 51A-1 was essentially similar. The He 51B-0 and B-1 fighters could carry a drop tank. The He 51W and He 51A-2 were test aircraft for the definitive He 51B-2 floatplane fighter, of which 38 were built. The He 51C-1 covered aircraft for the Spanish Nationalists which were equipped with bombracks, the C-2 being a floatplane version. The He 51B, He 51B-3 and He 51D were high-altitude prototypes.

Luftwaffe Markings: Part 1

The first fighter markings (continued)

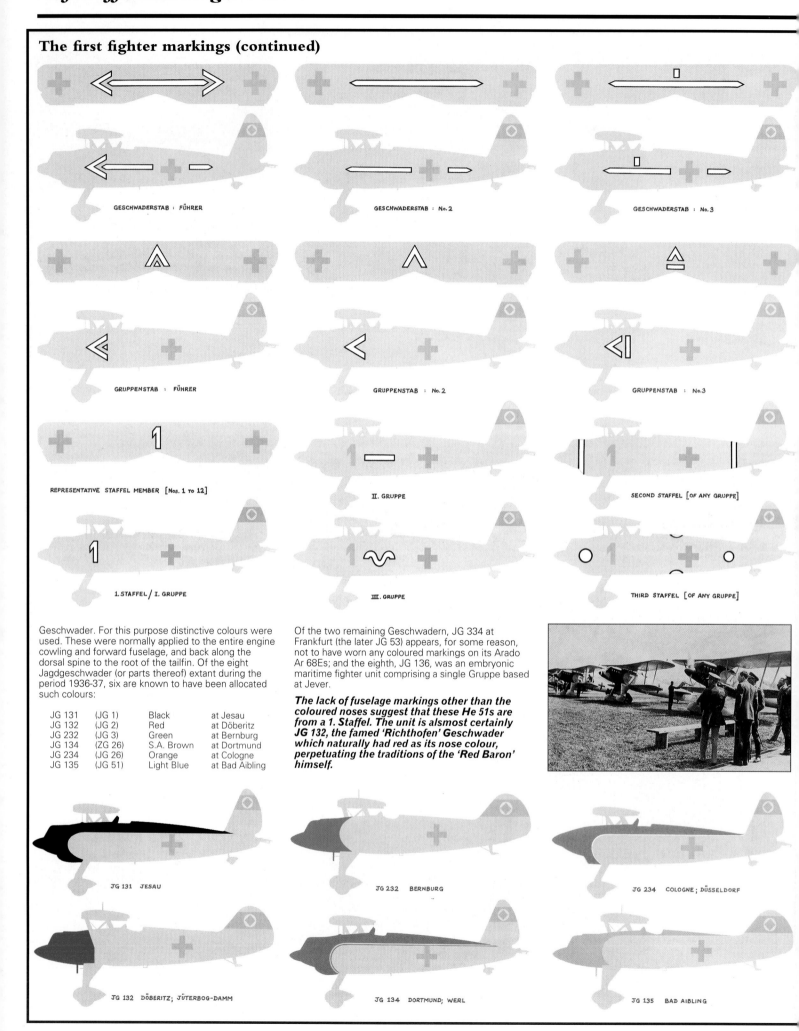

GESCHWADERSTAB : FÜHRER

GESCHWADERSTAB : No. 2

GESCHWADERSTAB : No. 3

GRUPPENSTAB : FÜHRER

GRUPPENSTAB : No. 2

GRUPPENSTAB : No. 3

REPRESENTATIVE STAFFEL MEMBER [Nos. 1 to 12]

II. GRUPPE

SECOND STAFFEL [OF ANY GRUPPE]

1. STAFFEL / I. GRUPPE

III. GRUPPE

THIRD STAFFEL [OF ANY GRUPPE]

Geschwader. For this purpose distinctive colours were used. These were normally applied to the entire engine cowling and forward fuselage, and back along the dorsal spine to the root of the tailfin. Of the eight Jagdgeschwader (or parts thereof) extant during the period 1936-37, six are known to have been allocated such colours:

JG 131	(JG 1)	Black	at Jesau
JG 132	(JG 2)	Red	at Döberitz
JG 232	(JG 3)	Green	at Bernburg
JG 134	(ZG 26)	S.A. Brown	at Dortmund
JG 234	(JG 26)	Orange	at Cologne
JG 135	(JG 51)	Light Blue	at Bad Aibling

Of the two remaining Geschwadern, JG 334 at Frankfurt (the later JG 53) appears, for some reason, not to have worn any coloured markings on its Arado Ar 68Es; and the eighth, JG 136, was an embryonic maritime fighter unit comprising a single Gruppe based at Jever.

The lack of fuselage markings other than the coloured noses suggest that these He 51s are from a 1. Staffel. The unit is alsmost certainly JG 132, the famed 'Richthofen' Geschwader which naturally had red as its nose colour, perpetuating the traditions of the 'Red Baron' himself.

JG 131   JESAU

JG 232   BERNBURG

JG 234   COLOGNE ; DÜSSELDORF

JG 132   DÖBERITZ ; JÜTERBOG-DAMM

JG 134   DORTMUND ; WERL

JG 135   BAD AIBLING

The early Bf 109s

When the first Bf 109s entered service they replaced the biplanes' earlier Staffel symbols by colour coding the aircraft's individual numbers: white for the first Staffel within a Gruppe, red for the second, and yellow for the third.

The first recipients of the Bf 109 initially placed their individual aircraft numbers on the rear fuselage aft – and at approximately half the height – of the fuselage cross. II. Gruppen aircraft (there were no III. Gruppen flying Bf 109s at this period) also positioned their horizontal bar Gruppe symbol to the rear of the cross; usually atop the small numeral. This again began to give rise to problems of rapid air-to-air identification. And in December 1937 the Luftwaffe General Staff laid down a new set of marking rules relating specifically to the Messerschmitt Bf 109 (but which were also adopted by some of the last biplanes to remain in first-line service).

The three Stabskette machines of each Geschwader and Gruppe were given symbols very similar to those displayed by the current majority biplane units. But for ordinary Staffel members it was now stipulated that individual numbers were to be enlarged and situated forward of the fuselage cross. The rear fuselage area was to be utilized solely for Gruppe identification: no markings aft of the cross indicating I. Gruppe; the same horizontal bar as before for II. Gruppe; and a new vertical bar symbol (akin to the biplanes' 2. Staffel band; and in some later cases, in fact, actually encircling the rear fuselage) to indicate III. Gruppe. When, in the summer of 1938, the first IV. Gruppen (of JGs 132 and 134) were established, they were to adopt the biplanes' other Staffel symbol – the third Staffel disc – as a Gruppe marking on their rear fuselages.

Both individual numbers and Gruppe symbols were to be in the respective Staffel colours of white, red and yellow. Given the dark background tone of the early Bf 109s it was decided, for the sake of clarity, that whereas 1., 4. and 7. Staffeln's numerals would be plain white, 2., 5. and 8. Staffeln's red numerals should be given a thin white outline, and that 3., 6. and 9. Staffeln's yellow numerals should be edged in black. This practice continued long after the dark green camouflage of the first Bf 109s had given way to lighter mottled finishes (by which time some white numerals were also being outlined in black), and provides a handy – though by no means infallible – rule of thumb when studying black and white photographs. Some types of film used during the war years made yellows appear very dark; almost black. But if an apparently dark numeral (at first glance perhaps taken for red) has an even darker outline edging, it is, in fact, almost certain to have been yellow. (Of course, there were the inevitable exceptions to the above. Some second Staffel aircraft were using black numerals in place of the 'official' red as early as the first winter of the war. This general rule can no longer be applied after the 1944 restructuring of the Luftwaffe's fighter forces, when the addition of a fourth Staffel per Gruppe led to the introduction of other colours, such as blue, brown and green, for individual numbering.)

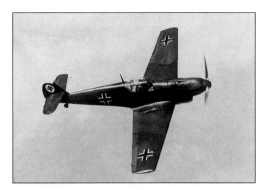

Above: The drab colours and monoplane layout of the Messerschmitt Bf 109 required a new system of markings to be introduced, although based on those worn by the biplane-operating units. Shown here is a Bf 109B-1, the first service variant. Early Bf 109s all wore the swastika marking on a white circle and red band.

Below: With the introduction of the Bf 109, badges became the only way to tell which unit the aircraft belonged to, although its place within the unit could be gleaned from markings. This Bf 109D served with 1./JG 137.

Below: This is a Bf 109B-2 seen prior to delivery to the Luftwaffe. The standard camouflage consisted of 70 Schwarzgrün and 71 Dunkelgrün worn in a splinter scheme on the top and sides, while the undersurfaces were in 65 Hellblau. The red fin band dispeared during 1938.

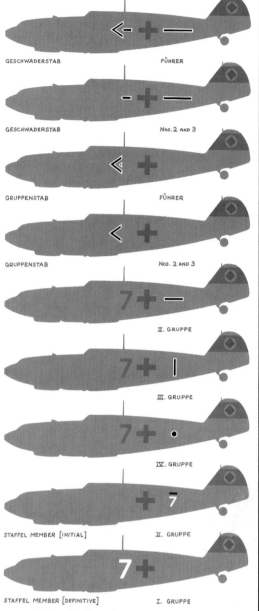

GESCHWADERSTAB — FÜHRER

GESCHWADERSTAB — Nos. 2 and 3

GRUPPENSTAB — FÜHRER

GRUPPENSTAB — Nos. 2 and 3

II. GRUPPE

III. GRUPPE

IV. GRUPPE

STAFFEL MEMBER [INITIAL] — II. GRUPPE

STAFFEL MEMBER [DEFINITIVE] — I. GRUPPE

This Bf 109E-3 displays four-letter codes, used by manufacturers for flight tests prior to delivery to the Luftwaffe.

The appearance of the drably-camouflaged Bf 109 also perforce saw the end of the colourful Geschwader identification trim worn by their biplane predecessors. Henceforth, the only clue as to a fighter's actual identity (i.e. its parent unit) would be that provided by a Geschwader, Gruppe or Staffel badge. And although such emblems proliferated during the early months of the war, their use became gradually less common as the tide of battle turned, until – by the closing months of hostilities – most Luftwaffe fighter units had, by choice, reverted to the same state of anonymity which had officially surrounded their creation some ten years earlier. **John Weal**

INDEX

INDEX

Picture acknowledgments

Front cover: Charles E. Brown/RAF Museum. **4:** Aerospace. **5:** Aerospace, NACA (two), Lockheed. **6:** Associated Press, Convair (two). **7:** Convair, via Bill Yenne, Aerospace (three). **8:** Aerospace (two), Convair (two), Lockheed. **9:** Aerospace (three). **10:** Convair (four), Associated Press. **11:** Aerospace (two). **12:** Robert Wollitz via Warren Thompson (WT), James Edmundson via WT. **13:** Harry Wolfe via WT, USAF via WT. **14:** Robert Wollitz via WT, Leo Goff via WT, NASM. **15:** Lyle Patterson via WT, Ercel Dye via WT, Harry Wolfe via WT. **16:** USAF, Jim Lynch via WT, Bernard Stein via WT. **17:** Jim Lynch via WT, USAF, Vern van Nappen via WT. **18:** Ralph Walt via WT, USAF, Don Miller via WT. **19:** Ralph Walt via WT, John Johnson via WT, J. B. Stark via WT. **20:** Charles Higgins via WT, USAF, Jim Lynch via WT, Don Seesenguth via WT. **21:** James V. Edmundson via WT (two), Charles Higgins via WT. **22:** Chuck Baisden via WT, Frank Sylvester via WT, Bernie Stein via WT, Harry Ruch via WT. **23:** Harry Wolfe via WT, Wante Bartol via WT. **24:** Richard Oakley via WT (two), USAF, Bob Maier via WT (two). **25:** USAF (three), Louis Braich via WT. **26:** Harrt Wolfe via WT (two), Earl Presia via WT, Royal Veatch via WT. **27:** Don Seesenguth via WT, Vern van Nappen via WT, Robert Wollitz via WT, Griff Jones via WT, J. Edmundson via WT, John Johnson via WT (two), C. E. Atkinson via WT. **28:** Frank Sylvester via WT (two), Harry Wolfe via WT. **29:** Harry Wolfe via WT, Louis Branch via WT. **30-31:** Charles E. Brown/RAF Museum. **31 (inset):** Aerospace. **32:** Ministry of Defence (MOD), via Dr Alfred Price (three), Aerospace. **33:** RAF Museum, via Dr Alfred Price (two), Aerospace, MOD. **34:** RAF Museum, via V. Flintham, Aerospace. **35:** RAF Museum (two), Aerospace (two). **36:** Aerospace (two), Imperial War Museum (IWM). **37:** RAF Museum, Aerospace (three). **38:** Aerospace, MOD (two), via Dr Alfred Price (four). **39:** RAF Museum, via Dr Alfred Price, Peter R. Arnold collection (two), via Andrew Thomas. **40:** IWM, via Dr Alfred Price (three). **42:** via Dr Alfred Price (three), **43:** Aerospace (two), via Dr Alfred Price (two), MOD. **44:** RAF Museum, via Dr Alfred Price (two). **45:** via Dr Alfred Price (two), MOD, Aerospace (two). **46:** Public Archives of Canada via Dr Alfred Price, Arthur Houston via Dr Alfred Price, IWM. **47:** IWM (three), Aerospace, via Dr Alfred Price. **48:** via Dr Alfred Price (two). **49:** via Dr Alfred Price (two), via Andrew Thomas. **50:** MOD (four), via Dr Alfred Price (five), MOD. **52:** via Dr Alfred Price (two). **54:** RAF Museum, Aerospace, via Dr Alfred Price, Vickers. **55:** Aerospace (two), MOD. **56:** via Dr Alfred Price (three). **57:** via Dr Alfred Price. **58:** MOD, via Dr Alfred Price (three). **59:** via Dr Alfred Price (four), Aerospace. **60:** John Kenyon via Peter R. Arnold, Peter R. Arnold collection, via Dr Alfred Price (three), MOD. **61:** Public Archives of Canada via Dr Alfred Price. **62:** MOD, via Dr Alfred Price, Aerospace. **63:** via Dr Alfred Price (two), Aerospace, via V. Flintham, Charles E. Brown. **64:** Aerospace, via V. Flintham (two), via Andrew Thomas, Aerospace. **65:** Charles E. Brown, Vickers (two), Aerospace, Peter R. Arnold collection. **66:** via Dr Alfred Price (three), via Grant Race. **75:** Aerospace (three). **76:** Rolls-Royce, via Dr Alfred Price (three), RAF Museum. **77:** via Dr Alfred Price (five), Aerospace,

Westland (two). **78:** MOD (two), Aerospace (two), via Dr Alfred Price. **79:** Peter R. Arnold (11), Peter R. Arnold collection, Peter R. March. **80:** via Andrew Thomas (three), via Dr Alfred Price. **81:** Aerospace, Brit, Aerospace, MOD, via Andrew Thomas, Ian Peak via Peter R. Arnold. **82:** via Dr Alfred Price, Peter R. Arno, collection (two), via Andrew Thomas. **83:** via Andrew Thomas, via Peter R. Arnold (four). **84:** via Grant Ra MOD, Aerospace, via Dr Alfred Price (two), Peter R. Arnold collection, Ian Pedder via Peter R. Arnold. **85:** Dr Alfred Price (three), via V. Flintham, Irish Air Corps via Robert Hewson. **86:** Aerospace, via Carlos Lorch **87-88:** via Carlos Lorch. **89:** via Carlos Lorch (four), Aerospace. **90-95:** via Carlos Lorch. **96:** Rudnei Dias da Cunha (three), via Carlos Lorch (two). **97:** via Carlos Lorch, Aerospace. **98-100:** via Carlos Lorch. **101:** via Carlos Lorch (three), Rudnei Dias da Cunha (two). **102:** Mike Reyno, Randy Jolly. **103:** Aerospace (two **104:** Aerospace (seven). **105:** Aerospace (four), Patrick Laureau, via Simon Watson. **106:** Aerospace (three), AMI via Enzo Maio, Julio A. Montes, Paul van Oers. **107:** Aerospace (four), Randy Jolly, via Simon Watson, Koninklijke Luchtmacht, Peter Steinemann. **108:** NASA via Terry Panopalis, Chris Ryan, via Mike Hooks, Aerospace (three), Peter R. Foster, J. Sjoersdma, via Dave Menard (two). **109:** Aerospace (five), via Terry Panopalis, Peter Steinemann, Patrick Laureau. **110:** Aerospace, USAF via Dave Menard, via Dave Menard (two), Ministry of Supply. **111:** USAF, Lockheed, via Dave Menard. **112:** via Warren Bodie, Aerospace, Godfrey Mangion, via Carlos Lorch. **113:** Calspan, via Dave Menard (two), via Wayne Mutza, USAF, Calspan via Terry Panopalis. **114:** Aerospace (two), Harry Gann. **115:** Lockheed (two), Aerospace (two), Daniel Soulaine. **116:** Aerospace (three), US Navy, Chance Vought. **118:** Aerospace (fou Lockheed, McDonnell Douglas. **119:** Aerospace (five), NRC via Bill Upton. **120:** Canadair via Bill Upton, Aerospace (two), Canadair via Terry Panopalis, NRC via Bill Upton. **121:** Canadian Armed Forces via Terry Panopalis, Andrew H. Cline (two), Peter R. Foster (two), D. Sorochan. **122:** Aerospace (two), Jeff Rankin-Lowe, NRC via Bill Upton (two). **123:** Peter R. Foster, Aerospace (four), Patrick Laureau (two). **124:** Aerospace (two), Peter Steinemann (two), Boeing. **125:** Skyfox Corporation, Aerospace (two), Rob Portengen, Frits Widdeshoven, M. D. Tabak (two). **126:** Aerospace (two), Bristol. **127:** Peter R. Foster (two), RAF Museum, MOD. **128:** MOD, Aerospace. **129:** Aerospace (two), RAF Museum (two). **13 MOD, Aerospace (three), Charles E. Brown. **131:** Aerospace (three), Charles E. Brown. **132:** MOD, RAF Museum, Aerospace. **133:** Bristol (two), Blackburn, Westland, RAF Museum, Aerospace (two), via Peter I March. **134:** MOD. **135:** Aerospace. **136:** Westland (two), Aerospace. **137:** Gloster, RAF Museum, Mar Baker, Aerospace. **138:** Shlomo Shapira collection via Shlomo Aloni (SA), Giora Epstein via SA. **139:** GPO via SA, via Peter Mersky, Shlomo Shapira collection via SA, Dan Sever collection via SA. **140:** Dan Sever collection via SA, Giora Epstein via SA, IDF/AF via SA. **141:** Shlomo Shapira collection via SA, Avner Slapak via SA, Peter Mersky. **142:** Amos Amir via SA, IDF/AF via SA, Giora Epstein via SA. **143:** Giora Epstein via SA (fo **144:** IDF/AF via SA, Shlomo Shapira collection via SA, Dan Sever collection via SA. **145:** GPO via SA, IDF via SA, Daniel Shapira collection via SA. **146:** Peter Mersky collection (two), Giora Epstein via SA. **147:** Israel Baharav collection via SA, Giora Epstein via SA, Peter Mersky collection. **148:** Aerospace (two). **14** Aerospace, Heinkel. **150-157:** Aerospace.